# CONTEMPLATING MATERNITY IN AN ERA OF CHOICE

# CONTEMPLATING MATERNITY IN AN ERA OF CHOICE

## Explorations into Discourses of Reproduction

Edited by Sara Hayden
and D. Lynn O'Brien Hallstein

LEXINGTON BOOKS
A division of
ROWMAN & LITTLEFIELD PUBLISHERS, INC.
Lanham • Boulder • New York • Toronto • Plymouth, UK

Published by Lexington Books
A division of Rowman & Littlefield Publishers, Inc.
A wholly owned subsidiary of The Rowman & Littlefield Publishing Group, Inc.
4501 Forbes Boulevard, Suite 200, Lanham, Maryland 20706
www.lexingtonbooks.com

Estover Road, Plymouth PL6 7PY, United Kingdom



British Library Cataloguing in Publication Information Available

**Library of Congress Cataloging-in-Publication Data**
Contemplating maternity in an era of choice : explorations into discourses of reproduction / edited by Sara Hayden and D. Lynn O'Brien Hallstein.
p. cm.
Includes bibliographical references and index.
ISBN 978-0-7391-3890-8 (cloth : alk. paper) — ISBN 978-0-7391-3892-2 (electronic)
1. Motherhood. 2. Reproductive rights. 3. Maternity leave—Law and legislation. I. Hayden, Sara, 1963- II. Hallstein, D. Lynn O'Brien.
HQ759.C7257 2010
306.874'301—dc22 2010006397

∞ ™ The paper used in this publication meets the minimum requirements of American National Standard for Information Sciences—Permanence of Paper for Printed Library Materials, ANSI/NISO Z39.48-1992.

Printed in the United States of America

# CONTENTS

# DEDICATION

To our own mothers, Geraldine Hayden and Nancy May O'Brien, and to our feminist foremothers who have consistently, if imperfectly, advocated for women's reproductive rights. Our ability to contemplate maternity in an era of choice, no doubt also imperfectly, is a direct result of their work and their sacrifices.

**Sara's:** To my partner, Scott Manning, who accepts my obsessive work patterns with good cheer and minimal teasing; to my stepson Jesse, with whom I share a close but decidedly nonmaternal relationship; to my father, John Hayden, who along with my mother has taught me the importance of play; and to my siblings Mary Hayden, Michael Hayden, and Elizabeth Wagner, each of whom, in their own way, is a supportive and loving presence in my life.

**Lynn's:** Lynn also dedicates this book to her family—her twin sister, Denice Hallstein (for helping her carry feminist placards when they were too little to do so on their own and for continuing to be politically active), her father, Richard Hallstein (for his willingness to initiate a before-it-went-to-court Title IX lawsuit so his young daughters could play on the boys soccer team before there were girls soccer teams and for his ongoing commitment to women's rights), her brother, Jon O'Brien Hallstein (for his own political activism and encouragement), Jean-Philipp and Joshua Bruehwiler (for not complaining too much when Lynn said, yet again, "I can't do that because I have to do something for the book"), and most of all, to the best index-helping partner, Michel Bruehwiler.

# ACKNOWLEDGMENTS

Initially this book was a collaboration among four authors: Suzanne Daughton, Elissa Foster, Sara Hayden, and Lynn O'Brien Hallstein, a group that Elissa named "the motherhood quartet." Our basic goals for this book were the same as are noted in the "Introduction"—to tease out some of the implications of living in an era of choice across the arc of maternity: becoming pregnant, pregnancy, giving birth, and (non)mothering. As the book developed and as the four original collaborators lived our lives, we began to consider the possibility that the addition of other voices, perspectives, and experiences would enable us to explore choice more fully. Hence, that original collaboration turned into this edited volume. We would like to acknowledge that the "motherhood quartet" initiated the idea for this book, and we are grateful for the inspiration and preliminary work done by both Suzanne and Elissa. We also want to thank the Organization for the Study of Women and Communication and the College of Arts and Sciences at the University of Montana for their financial support of this project.

# INTRODUCTION

*Sara Hayden*[1] *and D. Lynn O'Brien Hallstein*

> With the mass-marketing of birth-control pills starting in 1960, the founders of women's liberation became the first generation to enter adulthood with the possibility of reliably separating sex from reproduction. This group of women would not tolerate lack of control over their destinies.
>
> —Baxandall and Gordon (2000), p. 134

> No social movement, no matter how liberating, can bring permanent happiness to the people it touches. . . . When history opened up to American women in the late twentieth century, it did not offer them perfect bliss. It gave them the opportunity to face the dark moments on their own terms and to exalt in the spaces between.
>
> —Collins (2009), p. 395

## GERI'S STORY

As a child Geraldine Fontecchio dreamed of becoming a lawyer. Born in 1936 and raised in a small Wisconsin town, Geri was smart and driven—the kind of person who would have excelled in the field of law. However when she shared her dream with teachers and friends, they laughed. "Women," she was told, "do not go to law school." And so when Geri graduated from high school, she applied to a nursing program offered through a nearby Catholic women's college. Geri didn't really want to become a nurse, but she did want an education and nursing was one of the few fields of study considered appropriate for women in the 1950s.

Geri filled out the college's application with a keen understanding of the gender norms that defined the era not to mention the religious sentiments that undergirded a Catholic women's school. In response to the question "How do you plan to use your education?" she wrote "I will use my nursing skills to serve God and care for my husband and children." Of the 200 applicants who applied that year she was one of 40 women chosen to participate in the program. She believes her answer to this question was key to her acceptance.

Geri completed her training in September 1956; the day after graduation she started working as a registered nurse. Three months later, she married and ten months after that her first child was born. The first seven years of Geri's marriage were marked by seven pregnancies; five came to term, one of the five children died within hours of birth. The birth of her fifth child was particularly difficult and at that point Geri and her husband John decided they would have no more. In spite of their Catholic faith, which prohibited any form of contraception, John had a vasectomy.

Geri worked part-time throughout most of her reproductive years. Nurses were in short supply so she could dictate her own schedule, taking off eight to nine months after the birth of each child and returning to work two to three days a week. Her part-time schedule notwithstanding, during this period being a mother and a wife were her defining and most time-consuming roles.

As Geri's children grew, she transitioned to full-time work. Although she still sometimes wishes she had had the opportunity to become a lawyer, she was able to turn nursing into a career she found fulfilling, eventually becoming a nursing instructor at a vocational college. Today Geri and John remain married and they enjoy close relations with their ten grandchildren and four children, one of whom is Sara, a coeditor of this book.

## NANCY'S STORY

Born in 1943, Nancy O'Brien was the child of working-class parents, neither of whom finished high school. Nancy did though; indeed, she even went to college. Her dream was to become a physical therapist, but financial constraints precluded her from going to a school that offered a program in physical therapy and so she became a physical education major instead. During her sophomore year, Nancy met Richard. They were married within a year. Three months after they were married, Nancy became pregnant. Even though she gained eighty pounds in her pregnancy, Nancy continued to play on the field hockey team. When she finished her junior year in April, she was seven months pregnant. Two months later, having just turned twenty-one, Nancy delivered identical twin girls. With twins to care for, Nancy dropped out of college while Richard finished his senior year and worked two part-time jobs. Nancy and Richard never discussed what should happen after Nancy delivered. It was 1963 and the gender roles were crystal clear: Nancy would care for the twins while Richard would finish his degree so that he could be the "provider" of the family. Four years later, Nancy and Richard's son was born.

While she was at home with her three children, Nancy was introduced to the growing feminist movement of the mid- and late 1960s. Inspired by feminism, Nancy became a regular at consciousness raising groups, joined both the League of Women Voters and the National Organization for Women, and became an activist in white second wave feminism's fight to pass the Equal Rights Amendment. Indeed, Nancy included her twin daughters in her activism to such an extent that they both consider themselves pass-the-ERA-now-envelope-licking-NOW children of the late 1960s and early 1970s. Nancy's participation in feminism allowed her to name the anger that she felt about having to drop out of college as well as her resentment over the fact that she and Richard had not even considered alternative caretaking arrangements when their twins were born.

Her activism in white second wave feminism also inspired Nancy to return to school to complete her education, which Richard fully supported. When her youngest child was in elementary school full-time, Nancy returned to school to become a physical therapist. Nancy took classes part-time so that she could be home when her children returned from school. After a few courses, however, she realized that becoming a physical therapist was no longer what she wanted to do. Unsure about her goals, Nancy stopped going to college and decided to work. Rather than working full-time, she worked part-time so that she could, again, be home when her children returned from school. Nancy decided to return to college in the late 1970s and she finally graduated in 1981.

While she was completing her degree, Nancy and Richard divorced. Shortly after the divorce, Nancy decided to attend graduate school for two reasons. As an undergraduate student, Nancy became engaged with the possibility of becoming a professor. Second, at the time—the early 1980s—many women in her circle of friends who had been out of the workforce due to childrearing began to believe that reentering the workforce with graduate degrees might help them "make up" for their long unemployment outside of the home. For both reasons, Nancy decided to apply to a Ph.D. program. She was very clear, however, that she was unwilling to relocate her children and applied only to programs in the area. She was accepted to a local university and spent the next five years earning a Master's in Communication and completing the course work for a Ph.D.

Because she was only twenty-one when she became a mother in 1963, and due to her activism in 1960s and 1970s white second wave feminism, Nancy had a complex relationship to her life as a mother and the continual sacrifices she made in terms of her own goals as a woman. All of her children, but especially her daughters, believe that their lives were profoundly shaped by both Nancy's anger as a young mother and the deep joy she found via her involvement in the second wave. While Nancy found great pleasure in her second marriage later in her life at fifty-six and was thrilled when she became a grandmother, her life was profoundly shaped by being caught between the roles she was raised to fulfill and her feminist awakening in the 1960s. Nancy was Lynn's mother.

## EXPLORING DISCOURSES OF CHOICE

We begin with our mothers' stories not because they are unusual. To the contrary, these stories are representative of the opportunities and constraints faced by many (white) women coming of age in the mid-twentieth century. Unlike their daughters, neither Geri nor Nancy was in a position to "choose" whether to become a mother, and the centrality of maternity in their lives was paired with limited opportunities in the public sphere. In contrast, the editors of this volume were raised in an era of choice. We grew up believing that reproductive decision-making was our political right, our responsibility as women living the successes of second wave feminism, and under our control. Hand-in-hand with reproductive control, we grew up thinking that our options in the public sphere were unlimited. We could be doctors, lawyers, professors, maybe even the president of the United States; we were "free to be" whatever our hearts desired and our abilities warranted.

Unquestionably, the ability to make decisions about reproduction has been a defining and empowering factor in our lives; for this we are indebted to our feminist (fore)mothers. Nonetheless, as we have made reproductive decisions, enacted contemporary maternity (or not), watched friends and family members struggle with issues around reproduction, and studied discourses of choice and contemporary motherhood, we have found that living in an era of choice is more complex and challenging than the term *choice* might imply. Choice suggests rational deliberation—as if women consider all of the options in informed ways, choose the option they prefer, take appropriate action, and achieve their goals. It's true, of course, that some women's reproductive lives unfold this way. Some women decide early and easily that they do not want children, they use birth control effectively, and they go about their lives childfree. At the other end of the spectrum, some women have "always known" that they wanted to be mothers, they achieve their reproductive goals, and they embrace their maternal roles with or without accompanying professional and civic identities. Yet we argue that most contemporary women exist somewhere between these polar ends: that in questions of reproduction and maternity, many women do not "get what they want." Moreover, we maintain that women's reproductive desires are often ambivalent, vague, and subject to change.

In the United States and many other industrialized countries, women can and do exercise choice. However those choices are shaped by various factors including relationships with others, mental and physical health, race, sexual orientation, and economic status, public and workplace policies, developments in reproductive technology, and the social norms and messages communicated to women about the appropriateness of becoming mothers (or not). Additionally, making a "choice" about reproduction is not a singular event; rather, women are faced with a series of choices over the course of their reproductive lives. Moreover, for those women who become mothers, the choices are ongoing as they make decisions about how to parent. In this edited volume, then, the contributors investigate how women (and men) shape, are shaped, and "exalt in the spaces between" discourses of choice as they move through the many stages of reproductive decision-making and (non)motherhood.

We are not alone in our efforts to turn a scholarly eye to issues of maternity and reproduction. Indeed, reproduction and contemporary motherhood are topics that scholars and intellectuals from a wide range of disciplines have begun to explore. For example, Joan Williams (2000) investigates the ways that legal and professional institutions penalize women as mothers in *Unbending Gender: Why Family and Work Conflict and What to Do about It;* contributors to *Mother Outlaws: Theories and Practices of Empowered Mothering* (2004) explore how mothering can be empowering if women are allowed to define it for themselves; Susan Douglas and Meredith Michaels (2004) probe the role media play in supporting intensive mothering practices in *The Mommy Myth: The Idealization of Motherhood and How It Has Undermined Women;* Daphne de Marneffe (2004) addresses the desire to mother within the context of second wave feminist gains in public and professional realms in *Maternal Desire: On Children, Love, and the Inner Life*; Sylvia Hewlett (2003) focuses on how women can succeed with both family and career given the ongoing masculine structure of professional institutions in *Creating a Life: What Every Woman Needs to Know about Having a Baby and a Career;* and Anne Crittenden (2001) in *The Price of Motherhood: Why the Most Important Job in the World Is Still the Least Valued* documents the economic costs women pay as a result of being the primary parent in most families. In short, these authors are attempting to articulate reproduction and contemporary motherhood as both public and private issues with implications across legal, professional, psychological, medical, mediated, and economic realms.

*Contemplating Maternity* contributes to this body of scholarly work by bringing the lens of Communication Studies to these ongoing discussions. To date, with the exceptions of *The Mommy Myth*, which limits its focus to representations of maternity in the media, and Della Pollock's (1999) *Telling Bodies, Performing Birth*, which focuses on birth stories as performance of and by maternal subjects, there has been no text that explores reproductive decision-making and maternity as practices and roles that are constituted through and within communication. *Contemplating Maternity* helps fill this void by exploring how discourses of choice shape and are shaped by women's identities and experiences as (non)mothers and how those same discourses affect and reflect private practices and public policies related to reproduction and motherhood. The authors of the collected chapters employ a variety of ways of conducting feminist thinking, research, and practices within the communication discipline. Indeed, major subdisciplines within Communication Studies are represented here: feminist organizational, interpersonal, rhetorical, critical/cultural, and social movement studies. The book is enriched by its diversity in terms of communication approaches and also enriches communication studies' understanding of choice. Finally, whereas much of the extant literature highlights only one aspect or phase of motherhood, this book is unique in investigating discourses of choice across the arc of maternity and as enacted through various (non)maternal subject positions.

To situate our understanding of contemporary discourses of choice, next we offer a brief history of the concept and reality of "choice," tracing some of the cultural, legal, and discursive shifts that created such profound differences between the generation of women who came of age in the 1950s and those of us who came of age in the 1970s and beyond. Following this, we offer an overview of the collected chapters.

## A BRIEF HISTORY OF CHOICE

### Educational and Occupational Choices

Emerging on the heels of the Great Depression and the Second World War, the 1950s was a decade of conformity and consumerism. The primary locus for both activities was the myth of the happy nuclear family, and the heart of that family was the "mom." Created in part by government propaganda aimed at moving women out of wartime jobs and into their homes, the myth was reinforced by media images of (white, middle-class) families with dads who went to work wearing suits and ties, briefcases swinging, and moms adorned in shirtwaist dresses and pearls who nourished their children with homemade cookies. In the 1950s *that* women would become mothers was unquestioned; any other aspiration a woman might have was deemed secondary and circumscribed by her primary maternal role (Rosen, 2000).

Importantly, however, to say that the nuclear family was a myth created by government propaganda and media images is not to say that women uniformly resisted these images. To the contrary, responding to the devastation and disruption caused by depression and wars, many young women and men eagerly sought to embody the myth of the nuclear family in their own lives. During the postwar period, college education became more accessible, and the numbers of both male and female students rose, yet women rarely viewed college as a path to a career. Two out of every three women attending colleges or universities dropped out before graduating, prioritizing a "Mrs." over an academic degree. From 1946 until 1964, the average marriage age plummeted and the birthrate soared, leading to the biggest baby boom in U.S. history. Many white families moved to the newly constructed suburbs where women's main job, they were told, was to ensure the cleanliness of their homes and the health and well-being of their families. Advertisers, journalists, and various "experts" urged newly "professionalized" homemakers to spend their time cooking, cleaning, and caring for their children and husbands; many women followed this advice (Rosen, 2000; Rosenberg, 1992; Roth, 2004).

Women's newly heightened emphasis on domestic chores notwithstanding,[2] the years following World War II also saw an increase in the number of working women, many of whom were married with children. By 1960, 48 percent of black women, 29 percent of Chicanas, and 36 percent of white women were in the labor force; 52 percent of those women were married and a third had children under the age of eighteen (Roth, 2004, p. 34; Rosen, 2000, p. 20). Women's greater involvement in paid employment reflected the public sector's need for women's labor. There were many more jobs than men could fill, so women and men had to be convinced (again) that it was appropriate and even desirable for women to work. Marketers thus began promoting the "two-income" family lifestyle (Collins, 2009, p. 100). Of course, for many women, working was a financial necessity; for others, however, it provided the "little bit extra" that enabled their families to purchase the consumer goods that were readily available. Consequently, as Collins (2009) argues, "An entire middle-class generation grew up in the postwar era taking for granted a lifestyle of three-bedroom homes, washer/dryer combos, annual family vacations, and college education for their children" (pp. 100–1). Yet, like their stay-at-home counterparts, mothers who worked outside of the home understood that they were responsible for the well-being of their families. In order to avoid a "disruption in their services," many women took on part-time "pink-collar" jobs for low pay and few benefits, leaving them time to tend to their domestic responsibilities (Rosen, 2000; Roth, 2004).

By all outward appearances, the women who enacted suburban motherhood were living the American dream, yet as the years wore on, many of these women discovered that a life focused wholly or even mostly on husbands and children was not all that the media images made it out to be. In 1963 Betty Friedan gave voice to the lingering dissatisfaction of the suburban housewife in *The Feminine Mystique.* Based on interviews with women who had graduated from her alma mater, Smith College, Friedan (1963) wrote eloquently about the ennui that many of her former classmates were experiencing. "It was a strange stirring," she wrote, "a sense of dissatisfaction, a yearning that women suffered in the middle of the twentieth century in the United States" (p. 6). Friedan's solution to this ennui was for women to "break out of the housewife trap" so that they might fulfill "their own unique possibilities as separate human beings" (p. 325). An instant best-seller, *The Feminine Mystique* served as a wake-up call and a rallying cry for thousands of women–many of whom had little in common with the college-educated women Friedan interviewed—who saw in the book an explanation for their distress (Rosen, 2000).

Of course, Friedan's analysis was not without problems. Her focus was largely psychological, eschewing a deeper inquiry into the structural issues that precluded women from branching out of the home. In particular, she failed to acknowledge the unique problems faced by minority and poor women; indeed, she discussed the situation of white, middle-class women as if it was representative of *all* women.[3] Another limitation of Friedan's analysis is that it did not address who would assume white women's domestic responsibilities if they redirected their energies toward developing themselves in the public sphere (hooks, 1984). Yet for all its shortcomings, *The Feminine Mystique* had a profound impact on its readers, "mobiliz[ing] one potential constituency of the modern women's movement" (Rosen, 2000, p. 6) around the idea that women could and should be something beyond wives and mothers. Although Friedan did not specifically use the language of "choice," her book was one of the first to introduce the idea that women must have *educational* and *occupational* choices to the broad reading public.

## Reproductive Choice

White, middle-class women's desire for expanded educational and occupational choices in the early 1960s was a catalyst for white second wave feminisms, yet women's ability to exercise educational and occupational choices could not be enacted until and unless they also had *reproductive* choice, an ability that was profoundly circumscribed throughout the early part of the twentieth century. Prior to 1960, abortion was illegal in almost all cases; contraceptives were largely unreliable; and in many states, contraception, like abortion, was prohibited by law (Gordon, 1990; Rosen, 2000; Solinger, 1998).

This dearth of control over reproduction did not reflect a lack of feminist effort. To the contrary, feminists had been lobbying for access to reliable contraception since the early 1900s. Margaret Sanger was a key figure in these efforts; indeed, it was Sanger who coined the phrase "birth control" and an organization she founded, the American Birth Control League, eventually morphed into Planned Parenthood. From early in her career, Sanger dreamed of a contraceptive pill that would be "as easy to take as aspirin" and in women's control (Public Broadcasting System, n.d.; also see Chesler, 1992).[4] Her dream was realized in 1960 when the FDA approved Enovid for the use of the prevention of conception. Marketed as more than 99 percent effective, "the Pill" held out the promise of an almost perfect contraceptive form. As Condit (1990) argues, "although in practice the birth control pill did not deliver that level of effectiveness, the *promise* of that kind of control was enough to revolutionize the expectations regarding female fertility" (p. 69, emphasis in the original). In the twelve years that followed, two decisions by the U.S. Supreme Court expanded the promise of reproductive control. In *Griswold v. Connecticut* (1965) the Court ruled that married persons have the right to use contraceptives and in *Eisenstadt v. Baird* (1972) the Court extended this ruling to unmarried adults (see Bone & Meyers-Bass, this volume).

The potential to control reproduction through reliable contraception was a key factor in the development of the era of choice. However, feminists were keenly aware that women's control over their reproductive lives would not be assured until abortion was made legal. Second wave feminism was not a singular movement; to the contrary, it was composed of numerous organizations and groups divided along ideological, racial, and generational lines. White second wave feminists were composed of two main branches. The older and more conservative branch included groups such as the National Organization for Women, an organization in which Betty Friedan played a central role. Another, more radical and amorphous branch, often referred to as "women's liberation," grew out of student, Civil Rights, and New Left movements. Some women of color participated in these feminist efforts, however they also engaged in feminist advocacy within their specific communities. Sometimes their advocacy took place within extant civil rights organizations such as the NAACP, the Young Lords, the American Indian Movement, and El Partido de la Raza Unida. At other times, women of color organized in separate groups, such as the National Black Feminist Organization and the Mount Vernon/New Rochelle Group (Silliman, Gerber Fried, Ross, & Gutiérrez, 2004; also see Baxandall & Gordon, 2000; Rosen, 2000; Roth, 2004).

The demand for abortion rights tends to be linked to the younger, white branch of the movement, and indeed, abortion was an important issue for many women's liberation groups. For example, the first public action by a group that dubbed itself "The Feminists" involved a demonstration demanding the repeal of all abortion laws and one of The Redstockings' most important contributions to the movement was the introduction of abortion "speak-outs," public events during which women testified about their abortion experiences (Echols, 1989; Dubriwny, 2005). Advocacy for abortion was not limited to women's liberation groups, however. The more conservative National Organization for Women included legal abortion in its Bill of Rights, and the right to abortion was one of three demands articulated during the "Women's Strike for Equality," a 1970 demonstration Friedan organized to commemorate the fiftieth anniversary of the ratification of the woman's suffrage amendment (Rosen, 2000).

Women of color also supported abortion rights; indeed, according to Benita Roth (2004) "abortion rights and reproductive choice . . . [were] items of a general feminist agenda in the second wave" (p. 179). Thus the 1971 Conferencia de Mujeres por las Raza, the first National Chicana Conference, produced "calls for free, legal abortion and birth control by Chicana-controlled community clinics" (Roth, 2004, p. 146), and in a speech titled "An African American Woman Speaks Out for Abortion Rights," Mary Treadwell (2000) rebutted the contention that "legalized abortion is simply another white man's trick to foster racial genocide" insisting that "Black women in particular need this personal freedom to be able to fulfill themselves sexually without fear of conception" (Baxandall & Gordon, 2000, p. 149). Importantly, however, although women of color supported the call for reproductive rights and legal abortion, they were also critical of the narrow lens through which white feminists often framed these issues. According to Roth (2004), women of color "criticized the (white) women's liberation program of abortion on demand, divorced from other issues of reproductive rights that were directly tied to class and racial status" (p. 102). Indeed, reflecting a history of racist population control policies such as forced sterilization and welfare reform designed to limit the fertility of racial minorities, for women of color, reproductive rights involved not only the right to birth control and abortion but also the right to *have* and *support* their children (Silliman et al., 2004; Solinger, 2001; also see Fixmer-Oraiz, this volume and Palczewski, this volume).

Feminist advocacy was central to the debate over abortion rights; however, feminists were neither the first nor the only people to call for changes in abortion laws. In fact, social workers, physicians, and members of the clergy were active in efforts to reform abortion laws before feminists took up the call, and, as a result of these early efforts, support for reform gained momentum throughout the 1960s. Yet feminists' demands were unique in that they sought more than the partial legalization of abortion; they demanded repeal. Women, they argued, had the right to control what happened to and in their bodies; to limit that control was to deny women autonomy and full citizenship (Cisler, 2000; Chisholm, 1995). White second wave feminists framed the issue as a matter of *choice*. Indeed, it was through white feminists' efforts to legalize abortion that the term *choice* gained currency, raising a key challenge to the dominant ideology that positioned motherhood as a woman's central role (Condit, 1984).[5]

## The Institutionalization of Choice

By the early 1970s the (white) feminist movement had assumed a visible and legitimate place in U.S. culture, and the demand for choice began to resonate with a significant portion of the population (Condit, 1984). This is not to suggest, however, that the public accepted feminists' demand for the repeal of abortion laws in toto. Opponents of abortion relied on scientific arguments and powerful visual imagery in an effort to convince the public that a fetus was a full human *life*. These efforts were persuasive, seeming "to make great headway in undermining the 'choice' ideology" (Condit, 1984, pp. 415–16) and positioning pro-choice and pro-life[6] factions to engage in a vigorous debate over abortion. The tone and tenor of that debate was fundamentally altered, however, when the Supreme Court issued its 1973 ruling in *Roe v. Wade,* which guaranteed women the right to choose abortion during the first six months of pregnancy (Rosen, 2000).

Of course, pro-choice and pro-life advocates had profoundly different responses to *Roe*. For pro-life advocates, the decision served as a catalyst for more intense and focused organizing efforts. Almost immediately, members of Congress were inundated with calls from constituents demanding that something be done and eight days after the *Roe* ruling was issued, Representative Lawrence Hogan introduced an amendment to the U.S. Constitution that would have banned abortion nationwide. That same year, the National Right to Life Committee was formed; a key plank of its platform was the repeal of *Roe* (Hayden, 2009).

The responses of feminists and other advocates for abortion rights, on the other hand, were mixed. Some, especially women of color and advocates for the poor, were skeptical, raising specific concerns about the language of *choice* that had come to frame the demand for reproductive rights. For example, in a 1973 editorial that was supportive of *Roe*, the National Council of Negro Women offered this warning:

> The key words are "if she chooses." Bitter experience has taught the black woman that the administration of justice in this country is not color blind. . . . We must be ever vigilant that what appears on the surface to be a step forward, does not in fact become yet another fetter or method of enslavement. (Silliman, Gerber Fried, Ross, & Guitiérrez, 2004, p. 5; also see Fixmer-Oraiz, this volume and Palczewski, this volume)

Other advocates for abortion rights, however, assumed the battle was over; they believed that with *Roe*, women's right to abortion was guaranteed. And indeed, for some women it was. Silliman, Gerber Fried, Ross, and Gutiérrez (2004) argue that *Roe* initiated a class- and race-based schism in the movement: "Because the ability to find and finance abortion services was not a problem for middle-class white feminists, it appeared to them that the battle for abortion rights had been won" (p. 30). This was not the case for poor women, many of whom were women of color. The challenges faced by poor women seeking abortion services became even more acute in 1977 when Congress passed the Hyde Amendment prohibiting federal funding for abortions. Again, according to Silliman et al.:

> the leading women's organizations that had rallied for *Roe* did not marshal a large-scale response. . . . [The pro-choice movement] could have confronted the overt white supremacy of the Right's agenda and its own internal racism, had it made overturning Hyde and fighting for public funding a priority. By not doing so, it seemed to women of color that the pro-choice movement was not concerned with their rights. (p. 30)

By the end of the 1970s, then, feminist solidarity around abortion rights, fragile from the outset, had fractured. Responding to an invigorated opposition, white, mainstream feminist groups continued to employ the term *choice* to reference the demand for abortion rights. Moreover, as the electorate became more conservative, mainstream groups shifted their arguments to reflect this conservative turn. Rather than focusing on *choice* as an issue of woman's rights or woman's autonomy, pro-choice organizations such as NARAL crafted their arguments in terms of privacy, the sovereignty of families, and an opposition to intrusive government. This, in turn, led to a discursive and political landscape that exacerbated the marginalization of poor women and women of color (Hayden, 2009; Saletan, 2003). In response, some women of color continued to work with these mainstream groups, seeking to broaden their agendas. Others began working with organizations that placed reproductive rights advocacy within a broader set of goals, and still others formed reproductive rights organizations focused on the needs of poor women and women of color, seeking to shift the focus of the debate from "choice" to "reproductive rights," "reproductive freedom," and "reproductive health" (Silliman et al., 2004, p. 4; also see Palcezski, this volume).

The fragmentation that marked the women's movement notwithstanding, Condit (1984) argues that by the end of the 1970s, the terms *choice* and *life* had assumed a central and mutually moderating place in U.S. culture. "*Fragmentation*," she writes,

> signalled [*sic*] that elements of a new ideological structure had become widely accepted by the public—abortion was legal, a majority favored a "woman's choice," and millions of women were exercising the option of legal abortion.

However, this structure was tightly hedged by other values, and "choice" was thus limited by "life" and "family." (p. 419, emphasis in the original)[7]

## Life in an Era of Choice

As this brief history suggests, in the tumultuous decades that followed World War II, a profound ideological shift took place relevant to women's lives, in general, and women's reproductive rights and choices, in particular. Whereas in the 1950s women's lives were inextricably linked to maternity, by 1980 it was assumed that motherhood (for white, middle-class women, anyway) was a matter of *choice*. The concept of choice has also seeped into cultural assumptions about women's participation in the public sphere. No longer is it considered unusual for women to seek out higher education and full-time, professional careers; to the contrary, as Rosen (2000) suggests, the 1980s was the decade of "the new superwoman" as the public was inundated with media images of physically fit, attractive women who successfully managed high-powered careers and happy families, images that continue to be built upon today (Douglas & Michels, 2004; O'Brien Hallstein, this volume; Vavrus, 2000).

Of course, media images of superwomen confidently balancing family and careers belie the reality of most women's lives. Although assumptions about women's participation in the public sphere have shifted, institutions and family structures have not, meaning that women largely are on their own as they seek to meet their responsibilities in both the public and the private spheres (Douglas & Michaels, 2004; Rosen, 2000). Moreover, to refer to this period as an "era of choice" is not to suggest that struggles over reproductive rights are over. To the contrary, the past three decades have seen numerous battles over reproductive rights in both the political and the legal arenas. Many of these struggles have led to increased restrictions on women's right to choose; most recently, in April 2007, the Supreme Court upheld a federal ban on late-term abortion in *Gonzales v. Carhart* (Bone & Meyers-Bass, this volume; Hayden, 2009).

At the same time, feminists and other activists continue to debate the appropriateness and the political value of the term *choice*. Reflecting arguments they first articulated immediately following the passage of *Roe*, advocates for the poor and women of color continue to point to the ways in which the legal and political systems circumscribe some women's abilities to exercise *choice*, suggesting that the term itself limits discussion to abortion rights and obscures the realities of many women's lives (Silliman et al., 2004; Gerber Fried, 1990; Palczweski, this volume). Silliman et al., for example, argue that

> choice is rooted in the neoliberal tradition that locates individual rights at its core . . . [thus obscuring] the social context in which individuals make choices, and discount[ing] the ways in which the state regulates populations, disciplines individual bodies, and exercises control over sexuality, gender, and reproduction. (p. 5; also see Solinger, 2001)

In 2004, mainstream pro-choice organizations joined forces with advocates for reproductive rights in the March for Women's Lives. Held on the Mall in Washington, D.C., the March was the largest demonstration the United States had ever witnessed. The messages offered were multiple and complex, reflecting the backgrounds and arguments of the various groups involved. As a whole, the March highlighted both the importance of and ongoing conflict over "choice" (Hayden, 2009; also see Palczewski, this volume).

Finally, technological developments have complicated the reproductive process, thus expanding understandings of and demands for reproductive choice. In 1978, Louise Brown, the first child conceived through in vitro fertilization was born in Great Britain; by the year 2000, over 100,000 children had been born using Assisted Reproductive Technologies (ART) (Shaykh, 2000) offering an option for (some) people struggling with infertility. Additionally, today ART is used to extend women's ability to reproduce beyond the boundaries that biological processes typically impose. Thus the past few years have witnessed births by women in their fifties and beyond as well as an increase in the number of multiple births, with some women bearing six, seven, even eight children through a single pregnancy (Cruz, 2009; Salihu, Shumpert, Slay, Kirby, & Alexander, 2003). In 1980, the United States legalized surrogacy, the process through which a woman agrees to gestate a fetus in her body with the understanding that another woman will assume the role of the child's mother. Children born of surrogate mothers are often conceived via in vitro fertilization; they might be the product of the "contract" mother's or the gestational mother's egg, or, a donor egg may be used (Surrogacy, 2008). On another front, advances in prenatal imaging and diagnosis have led to the potential for "selective abortion." Although women may choose abortion for any reason, the fact that some women make abortion decisions based on a child's sex or potential disabilities has led to impassioned public debate (Landsman, 2004). These are just some of the developments in reproductive science; each is fraught with difficult ethical, personal, and political questions. As reproductive technologies continue to develop, undoubtedly, such questions will multiply, contributing greater complexity to what is already a multifaceted and vexing set of issues.

Thus, we may live in an era of "choice," but clearly, choice is a far more complicated concept than at first glance or historically, the term suggests. The purpose of this volume is not to resolve the questions and disputes we have identified nor do we seek to offer clarity to replace complexity. Instead, we begin with a recognition that *choice* is part of the contemporary lexicon, a term that, to greater or lesser extent, shapes and is shaped by women's and men's (reproductive) lives. In the chapters that follow, our and our contributors' collective goal is to tease out some of the implications of *choice* as it is articulated in a variety of different discursive forms and as it is experienced by individual women and men.

## OVERVIEW OF CHAPTERS

The book is organized by two main areas of foci: Discourses of Choice and Experiences of Choice. This organizational structure emerges from the long-standing feminist notion that the personal is political. Inspired by this second wave principle, in *Of Woman Born,* Adrienne Rich (1976) proposed that understanding maternity[8] required exploring both institutionalized motherhood—institutionalized ideologies of good mothering—and the potential for mothering to be a site of agency for women—women's lived experiences of mothering. At the core of Rich's insight was the realization that institutionalized motherhood is shaped by legal, political, and ideological beliefs and practices and these are symbiotically linked with women's actual experiences of mothering. But, for Rich, this did not mean that the institution of motherhood and the potential of mothering practices were one in the same; rather, Rich argued that mothering could be a site of agency for women if women were able to define mothering themselves and on their own terms. In short, Rich understood that maternity is a complex site of agency and constraint, a negotiation between larger shaping forces and women's abilities to resist, reshape, and rework maternity.

We believe that Rich's argument remains relevant to contemporary maternity in an era of choice. Thus, in this book, we explore the large-scale institutionalized discourses of choice juxtaposed with experiences of living with and making choices across the arc of maternity

## Discourses of Choice

The chapters in Discourses of Choice explore how choice works ideologically, rhetorically, and/or politically to reinforce particular understandings of choice or to reshape understandings of choice in relation to changes in culture. Chapters fall into two main subsections: Mediated Images of Choice and Choice in the Public Sphere.

***Mediated Images of Choice*** The three chapters in this section explore how various aspects of choice are both discussed and represented via media texts.

Utilizing ideological rhetorical criticism to analyze mediated images of "mom labels"—supermom, soccer mom, the mommy wars, and the now-current alpha mom—Lynn O'Brien Hallstein traces the development of these labels in "Public Choices, Private Control: How Mediated Mom Labels Work Rhetorically to Dismantle the Politics of Choice and White Second Wave Feminist Successes." O'Brien Hallstein explores how the mom labels have played and continue to play a key role in systematically stripping white second wave feminists' politics of choice in the service of reinscribing mothering as the most important part of femininity, while re-entrenching mothering and family life as only a private sphere and not an important public-sphere concern. O'Brien Hallstein concludes that feminist communication scholars must both retool our understanding of how choice is working rhetorically in the context of intensive mothering and retool feminist employment of the rhetoric of choice, if we hope to make choice meaningful and politically important, again, for more women and contemporary feminism.

In "No Exception Postprevention: 'Differential Biopolitics' on the Morning After," Natalie Fixmer-Oraiz analyzes emergency contraception's (EC) discursive figuration, specifically how EC is imagined to shape sexuality, reproduction, social relationships and even identities. Using critical discourse analysis as a theoretical framework, Fixmer-Oraiz explores the "the politics of *doxa,*" the myriad ways in which dominant (popular) discourses—prominent newspaper and magazine articles about EC—operate alongside one another to constrain, discipline, or otherwise function ideologically and materially. Ultimately, she argues that the EC debates illustrate the discursive limits of choice because some women are accorded rights, others responsibilities—distinctions that continue to deepen, rather than redress, race and class divisions within the context of reproductive politics. At best, Fixmer-Oraiz maintains, this is inadequate in securing reproductive rights for all women and, at worst, it works to reinscribe the very inequities and disparities it ought to dismantle, all under the banner of feminism.

In "Politicizing Personal Choices? The Storying of Age-Related Infertility in Public Discourses," Jennifer J. Bute, Lynn M. Harter, Erika L. Kirby, and Marie Thompson utilize a poststructural feminist approach to investigate the discursive moves through which age-related infertility (ARI) and associated reproductive choices have been storied in public discourses, primarily via the discussion of Sylvia Hewlett's (2002) groundbreaking and controversial book, *Creating a Life: Professional Women and the Quest for Children.* Focusing specifically on women's choice to delay childbearing and the concomitant consequences of that choice, Bute et al. explore the ARI discussion in relation to two kinds of choice: creeping non-choice versus smart choices (planning childbearing strategically). They conclude that the ARI discussion was almost entirely framed as a personal choice, focused only on the choices of a narrow group of elite women (white, well educated, middle class) and with a pervasive notion that the responsibility for making difficult life decisions regarding career and family belongs solely with women, while almost universally failing to address the organizational and structural forces that shape and constrain reproductive decisions.

***Choice in the Public Sphere*** In this section of Discourses of Choice, the authors explore how choice is and has been understood within feminist social movements, both past and present, transnationally in surrogacy websites, and in major U.S. Court reproductive rights decisions, also past and present.

In "Reproductive Freedom Transforming Discourses of Choice," Catherine H. Palczewski offers a rhetorical analysis of feminist social movements as a counterpublic to explore the implications of the call for a shift from choice to reproductive freedom on the topography of the abortion argument and on social protest theory. After explaining why counterpublic sphere theory can explain better the significance of the reproductive freedom movement than traditional movement studies, Palczewski explores the implications of women of color and poor women's insistence on focusing on "reproductive freedom" rather than "choice" to secure rights for all women. As did Fixmer-Oraiz, Palczewski concludes that a focus on choice is problematic because it frames the debate in ways that marginalize the concerns of women of color and poor women, a framing that has proven irresolvable. As a result, Palczewski maintains that a successful framing requires broadening the scope of the debate to tap into the argument for reproductive freedom for all women.

The second chapter in this subsection, "The Commodification of Motherhood: Surrogacy as a Matter of Choice," by Charlotte Kroløkke, Karen A. Foss, and Jennifer Sandoval, examines the choices that are constructed around and play out in four surrogacy websites directed toward Western couples and individuals: Circle Surrogacy, Surrogacy India, International Surrogacy Partners, and Surrogate Mothers Online. After detailing the two dominant framings typically offered for choice and surrogacy—gift-giving choice and commercial choice—the authors analyze the body as a rhetorical situation to investigate whether and how choice plays out in the marketing of surrogacy. They conclude that considering the body as a rhetorical situation—whether the bodies, in this case, are literally those of the surrogates, the intended parents, the unborn child, or even the "body" that is the agency—demonstrates that choices and constraints shift and change, creating hybrid in-between zones of partial agency and constraint for those involved in the surrogacy process.

Jennifer Emerling Bone and Beth Meyers-Bass, in "Law, Politics, and Reproductive Choices," explore how seven U.S. court decisions from the twentieth and twenty-first centuries have affected women's reproduction and family planning. Beginning with the 1918 New York court decision that gave physicians the right to provide information about contraception to married patients whose health required it and continuing through the United States Supreme Court's ruling to uphold the ban on late-term abortions in *Gonzales v. Carhart* (2007), Bone and Meyers-Bass explore how laws have impacted some women's choices and experiences with family planning. Including personal stories from birth control advocates, doctors, and women themselves throughout the chapter, the authors maintain that juxtaposing personal narratives with legal and political developments provides insight into the difficult, and often painful, choices and experiences women have in making reproductive decisions.

## Experiences of Choice

While Discourses of Choice explores institutional, legal, and/or ideological discourses of choice, section two of the book explores women's experiences living with choice in a variety of contexts and settings: pregnancy, work, and postreproductive decision-making. In other words, part two details the complex and myriad ways that women live with and make choices within their lives, while also reshaping what choice should or can mean.

***Pregnancy and Choice*** In this first subsection of Experiences of Choice, two chapters document the struggles of women seeking pregnancy in the face of infertility, and one chapter addresses the situation of two women making decisions in light of unintended pregnancies.

In, "My Eyes Cry without Me: Illusions of Choice in the Transition to Motherhood," Elissa Foster combines autoethnographic narrative and critical analysis to articulate the lived experience of seeking to become a mother. Addressing the medicalization of fertility and miscarriage, Foster critiques the assumption of choice in the transition to motherhood, noting that the concept of choice is only appropriate to describe actions in the context of *recognizing* and having *material access* to one's options. Foster concludes by acknowledging the complex social, relational, and biological factors that must converge for successful reproduction. "Choice" is revealed as an oversimplification that obscures the real challenges and heartbreaks that accompany some women's experiences with motherhood.

In "Two Women, Two Stories: Complicating Our 'Right to Choose,'" Summer R. Cunningham and Amy R. Pearson apply their backgrounds in feminist organizational thinking and autoethnography to tell their personal stories about the different decisions they made when faced with unintended pregnancies. By locating points of commonality among their differences, Cunningham and Pearson explore how their individual choices were shaped amidst discourses of family, religion, feminism, academia, and motherhood, amongst others. As feminists they conclude that the legal "right to choose" continues to be a critical component of women's liberty; however, they also believe that discourses—above and beyond those of a legal origin and including feminists' own—can both empower and disenfranchise, liberate and alienate, enable and constrain women's lives as they make pregnancy choices.

In "The In/Fertile, Un/Natural Body: Ecofeminism, Dis/Embodiment, Technology, and (the Loss of) Choice," Tracy Marafiote, informed by her commitment to ecofeminism and employing an autoethnographic method, details her experience with infertility. In doing so, she intersperses ecofeminist theorizing with excerpts from her journaling of her experiences with the inability to conceive, the discovery and denial of infertility, the labor (pun intended) to resist and overcome that pronouncement, and her loss of reproductive choice. She concludes that her lack of choice is not limited to the unforeseen realization of constraints on her maternal options and the ability to choose from among them, but also entails the shocking realization that she cannot expect to attain a goal that she chose to pursue.

***Working with Choice*** The second subsection of Experiences of Choice addresses mothering/parenting as it interfaces with work. One chapter details the "informal parenting support system" in professional contexts, a second explores a woman's conflicting narrative choices in relation to her maternity leave, and the third explores women police officers' perceptions of their choices within a male-dominated profession.

In "The Invisible Politics of 'Choice' in the Workplace: Naming the Informal Parenting Support System," Julia T. Wood and Bonnie J. Dow, employ grounded theory to explore their professional experiences as academics and analyze the ways that some working parents' childrearing choices impact their colleagues in the workplace. Troubled by the neoliberal framing of reproduction and childrearing as "personal choice," Wood and Dow argue that a primary emphasis on choices made by parents in the paid labor workforce functions to erase the involvement of colleagues in what they term the "informal parenting support system." They conclude that clear and effective criteria for informal support that are understood by all members of a given workplace coupled with candid discussions that respect the perspectives of both workers who are parenting and their colleagues are the first critical steps in generating systems that permit all workers to understand and plan for what is expected and create better choices and options for all in the workplace.

In, "Cutting the Meeting Short: Conflicting Narrative Choices in One Woman's Maternity Leave," Lori West Peterson employs feminist standpoint theory to explore the concept of choice through an examination of the discursive choices one woman—Patricia—uses to narrate her maternity leave story. By focusing on choices that reflect the language our culture provides for talking about maternity and maternity leave, Peterson examines how Patricia's choices reveal the complexity of such issues as selfhood, gender, and identity(ties) surrounding this female-centered experience. Peterson concludes that Patricia's story reveals her shifting identity and the conflicts that emerge between being an empowered professional woman and a mother disjointed from the ideal worker norms. As a result, Peterson suggests contemporary maternity demands that women make choices among these identities that are not really "choices" at all.

Jaime E. Bochantin and Renee L. Cowan, in "Total Motherhood and Having It All: Reproduction, Maternity, and Discourses of Choice among Female Police Officers," employ dialectical theory within organizational studies to explore fifteen female police officers' perceptions of pregnancy, choice, and the repercussions and trajectories of those choices within the male-dominated police profession. In doing so, they explore three tensions concerning motherhood—(1) Supportive-unsupportive workplaces; (2) Work-family; and (3) Mothering as valued-devalued. They conclude that their participants' perceptions and experiences call into question the notion that women "get what they want" when it comes to pregnancy and motherhood and instead reveal women struggling with choices they felt would inevitably have negative consequences for either their families or their careers.

***Ongoing Choices*** A third set of chapters in Experiences of Choice details the ongoing choices women (and men) confront once initial decisions about reproduction have been made. One chapter explores childless women's efforts to construct positive identities in a pronatalist culture; a second chapter explores what fathers say about their female partners' choices, and a third chapter details two women's choice-making within mother-son relationships.

In "Purposefully Childless Good Women," Sara Hayden examines how twenty-four women who define themselves as childless by choice navigate assumptions about femininity, selfishness, and selflessness as they craft their identities. Employing a poststructural approach to interview data, Hayden explores how some of the women internalize and reinforce the negative attributes associated with purposeful childlessness while others resist such judgments by reversing charges, referencing alternative discourses, or negotiating the borders between dominant and alternative discourses. Hayden concludes by suggesting that childless women's efforts to craft positive identities participate in the process of broadening the meaning of good womanhood and good mothering in contemporary culture.

Patrice Buzzanell, Suzy D'Enbeau, and John Duckworth, in "What Men Say about Women: Fathers Contemplate Work Family Choices and Motherhood," present five minicases of men from different occupations, socioeconomic statuses, race/ethnicities, and life stages who discuss choices in their partners' lives. Based on in-depth interviews with the men, the authors explore unexamined choice in taken-for-granted gender relations; partial awareness and choice about *when* to have children but not about caregiving arrangements; choice both dictated by gender, class, and fatherhood ideologies and by the challenges that having children represent; to constrained choices and choices reflecting, and resisting divergent and sometimes unconventional gender priorities. They conclude that the work of the unfinished second wave and much needed third wave feminism includes enlarging the discursive space surrounding choice and encouraging men and women to realize that there is choice and agency in situations currently perceived as taken-for-granted through gender normative lenses.

In, "Outlaw Mothers Raising Gentle-men: Choosing to Disrupt Hegemonic Tensions between Masculinity and Feminism," Cindy Griffin and Kirsten J. Broadfoot explore aspects of their own mother-son relationships in an attempt to close what they see as a theoretical gap between hybridizing masculinity, feminism, and maternal choices. Utilizing their own narratives within a gender theoretical framework, they explore how mothers can reject, reframe, and re-create historical, societal, and familial pressures and codes as they navigate away from what often feel like unnecessary and unnecessarily limiting norms for their sons, while simultaneously embracing aspects of masculinity that will allow their sons to exist, survive, and even thrive in the worlds they, as boys and men, occupy. They conclude choice is fleeting and fluid, contentious, contextualized, an ongoing process of choice-making and taking up, and is far from being infused with freedom to act as is commonly implied.

## (NO) CONCLUSION

We began with our mother's stories; in closing, we want to acknowledge our privileged positions as women who came of age in an era of choice. For Sara, this meant choosing to remain childless while also being a stepmother to her partner's son. Lynn's choices, in contrast, involved bearing and raising two sons with her partner. For us, then, reproductive decision-making was indeed a political right, a responsibility, and (mostly) under our control. We are both happy with the choices we made and deeply grateful that they were, in fact, *choices*. Nonetheless, for neither of us were or are reproductive choices straightforward or simple. Instead, they were and are wrapped up in a variety of other issues, not the least of which are our professional identities and goals.

As the chapters in this book demonstrate, we are far from alone; indeed, as white, middle-class women, in many ways our choices were and are far less fettered than many other women's (and men's) choices are and have been. Read in total, the fifteen chapters in this book begin to reveal just how complex and multifaceted choice is in the so-called post–second wave context.[9] As noted above, the purpose of this volume is not to resolve the questions, disputes, and complexities the contributors have raised. We offer no final conclusions. Rather, forty years into the era of choice, we maintain that it is past time to acknowledge the complexities that the term "choice" tends to obscure; it is to this end that we offer this book. As the second decade of the twenty-first century unfolds, we hope that this acknowledgement and the various explorations into discourses of choice presented here will prove valuable to contemporary women and men as they and we continue to help shape public policy around issues related to reproduction and parenting and as we all make and live out reproductive decisions.

## REFERENCES

Baxandall, R., & Gordon, L. (Eds.). (2000). *Dear sisters: Dispatches from the women's liberation movement.* New York: Basic Books.

Chesler, E. (1992). *Woman of valor: Margaret Sanger and the birth control movement in America.* New York: Simon & Schuster.

Chisholm, S. (1995). Facing the abortion question. In B. Guy-Sheftall (Ed.). *Words of fire: An anthology of African-American feminist thought* (pp. 390–95). New York: New Press.

Cisler, L. (2000). On abortion and abortion law. In R. Baxandall & L. Gordon (Eds.). *Dear sisters: Dispatches from the women's liberation movement* (pp. 140–43). New York: Basic Books.

Collins, G. (2009). *When everything changed: The amazing journey of American women from 1960 to the present.* New York: Little, Brown and Company.

Collins, P. H. (1991). *Black feminist thought: Knowledge, consciousness, and the politics of empowerment.* New York: Routledge.

Condit, C. M. (1990). *Decoding abortion rhetoric: Communicating social change.* Urbana: University of Illinois Press.

Condit (Railsback), C. M. (1984). The contemporary American abortion controversy: Stages in the argument. *Quarterly Journal of Speech, 84*, 410–24.

Crittenden, A. (2001). *The price of motherhood: Why the most important job in the world is still the least valued.* New York: Henry Holt.

Cruz, G. (2009, Janurary 28). Multiple births. *Time.* Retrieved from http://www.time.com/time/printout/0,8816,1874637,00.html.

de Marneffe, D. (2004). *Maternal desire: On children, love, and the inner life.* New York: Little, Brown.

Douglas, S. J. & Michaels, M. W. (2004). *The mommy myth: The idealization of motherhood and how it has undermined women.* New York: Free Press.

Dubriwny, T. (2005). Consciousness-raising as collective rhetoric: The articulation of experience in the Redstockings' abortion speak-out of 1969. *Quarterly Journal of Speech, 91*, 395–422.

Echols, A. (1989). *Daring to be bad: Radical feminism in America, 1967–1975.* Minneapolis: University of Minnesota Press.

Friedan, B. (1963). *The feminine mystique.* New York: Dell.

Gerber Fried, M. (Ed.) (1990). *From abortion to reproductive freedom: Transforming a movement.* Boston: South End Press.

Gordon, L. (1990). *Woman's body, woman's right: Birth control in America, revised and updated.* New York: Penguin (original work published in 1976).

Hayden, S. (2009). Revitalizing the debate between <life> and <choice>: The 2004 March for Women's Lives. *Communication and Critical/Cultural Studies, 6,* 111–31.

Hewlett, S. A. (2002). *Creating a life: What every woman needs to know about having a baby and a career.* New York: Miramax Books.

hooks, b. (1984). *Feminist theory: From margin to center.* Boston: South End Press.

Landsman, G. (2004). "Too bad you got a lemon": Peter Singer, mothers of children with disabilities, and the critique of consumer culture. In Janelle S. Taylor, Linda L. Layne, and Danielle F. Wozniak (Eds.). *Consuming motherhood* (pp. 100–21). New Brunswick: Rutgers University Press.

O'Brien Hallstein, L. D. (2010). *Contemporary white feminisms and maternity,* New York: Palgrave Macmillan.

O'Reilly, A. (Ed.). (2004). *Mother outlaws: Theories and practices of empowered mothering.* Toronto, Canada: Women's Press

Pollock, D. (1999). *Telling bodies, performing birth.* New York: Columbia University Press.

Public Broadcasting System (n.d.). *The American experience: The pill.* Retrieved from http://www.pbs.org/ wgbh/amex/pill/peopleevents/p_Sanger.html.

Rich, A. (1976). *Of woman born: Motherhood as experience and institution.* New York: Bantam.

Rosen, R. (2000). *The world split open: How the modern women's movement changed America.* New York: Penguin.

Rosenberg, R. (1992). *Divided lives: American women in the twentieth century.* New York: Hill and Wang.

Roth, B. (2004). *Separate roads to feminism: Black, Chicana, and white feminist movements in America's second wave.* New York: Cambridge University Press.

Saletan, W. (2003). *Bearing right: How conservatives won the abortion war.* Berkeley: University of California Press.

Salihu, H. M., Shumpert, M. N., Slay, M., & Alexander, G. R. (2003). Childbearing beyond maternal age 50 and fetal outcomes in the United States. *Obstetrics & Gynecology, 102,* 1006–14.

Shaykh, M. M. (2000). Assisted reproductive technologies. Retrieved from http://www.dcmsoonline.org/jax-medicine/2000journals/may2000/art.htm.

Silliman, J., Fried, M. G., Ross, L., & Gutiérrez, E. R. (Eds). (2004). *Undivided rights: Women of color organize for reproductive justice.* Cambridge: South End Press.

Solinger, R. (Ed.). (1998). *Abortion wars: A half century of struggle, 1950–2000.* Berkeley: University of California Press.

Solinger, R. (2001). *Beggars and choosers: How the politics of choice shapes adoption, abortion, and welfare in the United States.* New York: Hill and Wang.

Surrogacy. (2008). In *Encyclopedia of children and childhood in history and society.* Retrieved from www.faqs.org/childhood/So-Th/Surrogacy.html.

Treadwell, M. (2000). An African-American woman speaks out for abortion rights. In R. Baxandall & L. Gordon (Eds.). *Dear sisters: Dispatches from the women's liberation movement* (pp. 149–50). New York: Basic Books.
Vavrus, M. D. (2000). From women of the year to "soccer moms": The case of the incredible shrinking woman. *Political Communication*, *17*, 193–213.
Williams, J. (2000). *Unbending gender: Why family and work conflict and what to do about it*. Oxford: Oxford University Press.

## NOTES

1. The authors contributed equally to this chapter; our names are listed alphabetically.

2. Of course, women had been doing domestic chores long before this time. What was different was that—at least for middle-class women—doing them had been professionalized and elevated, as well as made "easier" with labor saving inventions such as washing machines and dishswashers. Thanks to Julia T. Wood for this insight.

3. In fact, the experiences of white, middle-class women and those of women of color around education, employment, and family were profoundly different. As Roth (2004) notes, black women "had never been excluded from the privilege of working to support their families" (p. 102). Moreover, black urban women frequently practiced a communal form of mothering referred to as other mothering, enabling them to avoid the isolation that marked suburban motherhood (Collins, 1991; Roth, 2004). For black women, then, the family was often a supportive oasis from an otherwise hostile and racist world. Chicanas, on the other hand, were less likely to participate in the paid labor force and they often experienced real discrimination within their families. Nonetheless, unlike white second wave feminists, their solution did not involve moving from the private to the public sphere. Instead they advocated a restructuring of the family so that it could serve as a base of support and culture in the face of Anglo culture and oppression (Roth, 2004).

4. Sanger's roots were in the working class and her goals were consistently feminist. She believed birth control was central to women's emancipation. This did not, however, keep her from embracing eugenic arguments that were at times both racist and classist (see Chesler, 1992; Gordon, 1990).

5. As suggested in the 1973 National Council of Negro Women editorial cited in the following section, although supportive of legal abortion and reproductive rights, women of color did not frame their advocacy around "choice," accurately anticipating that the term would be used in limited, racist, and classist ways. That "choice" was taken up in the public sphere in spite of the warnings of women of color speaks to the greater power and visibility of white women's organizations as well as the racism and classism within those organizations. For a discussion of women of color's

participation in reproductive rights activism see Gerber Fried, 1990; Silliman, Fried, Ross, and Gutiérrez, 2004; and Palczewski, this volume.

6. We recognize that advocates continue to debate the implications and uses of these labels. In this chapter, our goal is not to take sides in that debate; rather, we employ the terms "pro-choice" and "pro-life" to reflect the labels advocates use to refer to their efforts.

7. Condit discusses the fragmentation that occurred in both the pro-life and the pro-choice camps; given our concern with choice, we focus our attention on the latter.

8. While Rich did not use the word *maternity*, as O'Brien Hallstein (2010) has argued elsewhere, Rich's approach is best understood and employed when her focus on both the institution of motherhood and the potential in mothering is described under the rubric of maternity.

9. We are not employing the term "post–second wave feminist context" as synonymous with "postfeminism," a colloquial term for the idea that feminism is "dead" or no longer necessary. Rather, following O'Brien Hallstein's (2010) understanding of "post–second wave feminism," we mean "as a result of second wave feminism." In terms of maternity specifically, then, we employ the term to indicate a maternal context that is shaped by the new complexities of living with and in the successes of second wave feminism.

# PART I

# DISCOURSES OF CHOICE

# Section I

# Mediated Images of Choice

# 1

# PUBLIC CHOICES, PRIVATE CONTROL

## How Mediated Mom Labels Work Rhetorically to Dismantle the Politics of Choice and White Second Wave Feminist Successes

*D. Lynn O'Brien Hallstein*

> After all, many residents of the United States have perceived themselves since 1973 as living in a country that is governed, regarding matters of pregnancy and motherhood, by 'choice,' that is by a public policy that empowers every woman to do as she wishes in this arena—a public policy that seems to encompass *rights,* but does not.
>
> —Solinger, 1997, p. 383

Feminist scholars (Douglas & Michaels, 2004; Hays, 1996; O'Brien Hallstein 2010; O'Reilly, 2004) have decisively shown that domesticated[1] intensive mothering is the contemporary ideology of "good" mothering. Indeed, as Hays (1996) first argued, even though not all women practice intensive mothering, it is the *proper* ideology of contemporary mothering that all women are disciplined into and judged against, across race and class lines. As feminist academics (Douglas & Michaels, 2004; Hays, 1996; O'Reilly, 2004) argue, intensive mothering has three core beliefs: 1) children need and require constant and ongoing nurturing by their biological mothers who are single-handedly responsible for meeting these needs; 2) in meeting those needs, mothers must rely on experts to guide them, and 3) mothers must lavish enormous amounts of time and energy on their children. In short, intensive mothering requires mothers to put their family's and children's needs first, always, before their own to be a "good" mother. As a result, as feminist scholars (Douglas & Michaels, 2004; Hays, 1994; O'Brien

Hallstein, 2008; O'Reilly, 2004) have already established, intensive mothering is a hegemonic ideology that functions as a form of patriarchal social control of women.

The relationship between white feminism and intensive mothering is and has been complex, especially as we live within the successes of white second wave feminism. In fact, in their focus on mediated images of intensive mothering, Douglas and Michaels (2004) argue feminism and intensive mothering were *competing* discourses during white 1970s feminism. Indeed, Douglas and Michaels (2004) suggest, as 1970s feminism gave "women permission to say that the rosy myths of marriage and motherhood weren't what they were cracked up to be, we began to see the rise of the mouthy mother [in media representations of mothers], sometimes deadly serious, most often making a joke of her predicament" (p. 74). In other words, mouthy mothers were mothers who "mouthed off" to and challenged the domesticated intensive ideology. As a result, Douglas and Michaels also argue there was a conflict between domesticated intensive mothering and the women's movement, such that a "new 'common sense' about motherhood began to emerge, although it too was not without major contradictions" (p. 80). Consequently, the women's movement suggested that it was acceptable, often necessary, for women to work and to even let housework go, to let go of domesticity and women's primary job as caretakers in the domesticated private sphere. In short, the conflicting discourse that feminism provided in relation to mediated images of intensive mothering allowed the possibility of seeing the images of the domesticated intensive mother as problematic, as creating conflict with the goal of gender equality for women that drove white 1970s second wave feminisms.

Feminism's relationship as counterdiscourse, however, began to change with the rise of the new momism in the 1980s. Although Douglas and Michaels (2004) argue the new momism continues to support the core beliefs of domesticated intensive mothering, they also suggest it is different from domesticated intensive mothering in its incorporation of the feminist idea and rhetoric of choice. As Douglas and Michaels (2004) argue, the new momism is a direct descendant of what Friedan called the "feminine mystique," although the new momism appears to be more progressive and hip because women now have choices that were previously unavailable to them. Douglas and Michaels (2004), in fact, suggest, embedded in the new momism is the idea that women:

> have their own ambitions and money, raise kids on their own, or freely choose to stay at home with kids rather than being forced to. . . . Central to the new momism, in fact, is the feminist insistence that woman [sic] have *choices*,

that they are active agents in control of their own destiny, that they have autonomy. (italics added, p. 5)[2]

Thus, as the new momism arose in the 1980s, rather than *compete* with feminism, the new momism began to *integrate* feminist ideas and the rhetoric of choice explicitly.

Douglas and Michaels conclude that this integration of the ideology and rhetoric of choice are no more apparent than in the emergence of the supermom ideal that emerged as white second wave feminism gained prominence in culture. In fact, Douglas and Michaels, along with Parker West (2004), argue the classic example of the supermom is the famous 1970s Enjolie perfume ad of a woman who could do it all and make everyone happy. In the ad, the "new modern mom shimmied onto the screen singing, 'I can bring home the bacon, fry it up in a pan, and never, ever let you forget you're a man'" (Douglas & Michaels, 2004, p. 79). The supermom, then, was a woman and mom who could "do it all": who could do both private mothering work and public, professional work. Thus, the ideological message communicated in the supermom image is that women can choose to be both public professionals and private mothers.

Feminism, then, was fused with the intensive ideology such that feminism was connected or linked to the new momism rather than positioned as a challenge to it. The supermom ideal recognizes the fact that women *did* gain access to educational and professional arenas, and as such, the label does integrate second wave feminist gains. While the supermom label appears to embrace feminist ideas, even support the changes in women's lives, from the beginning, the label worked rhetorically to entrench the feminist notion and rhetoric of choice while simultaneously making it clear that women would be responsible for managing any difficulty or struggle brought about by women's newly gained choices As Douglas and Michaels (2004) put it: "If women wanted to work, they were just going to have to add it on to their other endless responsibilities. If they couldn't hack it, well, too bad for them" (p. 81). Thus, as Douglas and Michaels's analysis also reveals: whether to mother or not went hand-and-hand with depoliticizing choice to mean a *personal choice* and, as a result, mothers were made responsible for working out how to manage that access in the private realm.

Sadly, as I show in this chapter, as subsequent "mom" labels—soccer mom, the mommy wars, and the now-current alpha mom—have developed, each new label dismantles choice, one brick at a time.[3] In fact, by tracing the labels as they have developed, I reveal that the mom labels have played and continue to play a key role in systematically stripping the politics of choice in the service of reinscribing mothering as the most important part of femininity, while reentrenching mothering and family life as only a private sphere and not an important public-sphere concern. Thus, a rhetorical analysis of the labels that have and continue to emerge within the new momism can reveal much about how the rhetoric of choice is systematically being dismantled and, equally important, how the relationship between intensive mothering and contemporary feminism continues to evolve in problematic and deeply troubling ways.

To substantiate these arguments, this chapter unfolds in three parts. First, I begin the analysis by detailing the shared agreements that already exist among scholars about the labels. Second, I read the mom labels rhetorically as a feminist ideological critic. Drawing on Foss's (2009) understanding of ideological criticism, I understand an ideological analysis as discovering "the beliefs, values, and assumptions" suggested in artifacts (p. 209). As such, I explore how the rhetoric of choice works via the mom labels to communicate and shape a particular set of values, beliefs, and assumptions about the new momism as it has continued to develop as our contemporary "good-mothering" ideology. By doing so, I also explore how intensive mothering works as a hegemonic ideology. My analysis of intensive mothering as a hegemonic ideology draws on the work of communication scholars. Specifically, I follow Condit (1994) and Grossberg (1993) who argue hegemonic ideologies function as a form of social control when they shape what counts as "normal" or "good" in culture. Communication scholars (Cloud, 1996; Condit, 1994; Grossberg, 1993) also argue media can be a primary tool for entrenching rather than challenging hegemonic ideologies. Thus, in my rhetorical analysis of the mom labels, I explore how choice now works within each mom label as a means of contemporary patriarchal social control or symbolic coercion of women, while also driving a larger wedge between the public and private spheres. Third, I conclude the chapter by arguing feminist communication scholars must retool both our understanding of how choice is working rhetorically in the context of intensive mothering and retool feminist employment of the rhetoric of choice, if we hope to make choice meaningful and politically important, again, for both women and contemporary feminism.

## ANALYZING THE MOM LABELS RHETORICALLY

### Scholars' Agreements about the Mom Labels

In addition to Douglas and Michaels (2004), a limited number of feminist scholars (Vavrus, 2000; Parker West, 2004) have begun to explore the new-momism labels. The work done to date suggests two key components. First, the mom labels are mediated images of contemporary mothering, developed for and by advertisers to sell products and, as such, these labels are being *applied* to women rather than created by women. Consequently, the labels are deeply entrenched in an ideology of consumerism that equates mothering with consumption and conflates personal choices with "product consumption and 'lifestyle'" (Vavrus, 2000, p. 194). Thus, the moment that white second wave feminism and intensive mothering were linked, the political component of choice began to be stripped from it and replaced with the rhetoric of consumerism such that good mothering began to be linked to making good consumer choices.

Equally important, Douglas and Michaels (2004) reveal the shift to using the term "mom" is a rhetorical move that is ideologically laden and problematic. Unlike the term *mother, mom* suggests a familiarity and a devaluation of the woman who is mothering. As they suggest:

> "Mom"—a term previously used only by children—doesn't have the authority of "mother," because it addresses us from a child's-eye view. It assumes a familiarity, an approachability, to mothers that is, frankly, patronizing; reminiscent, in fact, of the difference between woman and girl. At the same time, "mom" means you're good and nurturing while "mother" means you're not. (pp. 19–20)

Thus, in addition to being defined first and foremost by their filial relations, once defined in this way, "mom" works to devalue women's subjectivity or "personhood" outside of mothering. In other words, in addition to positioning women from children's perspective rather than an adult perspective, "mom" reinscribes mothering as the most important part of femininity regardless of any other role or position a woman might occupy. Consequently, the second layer of dismantling is revealed, then, in the word *mom* because women are stripped of their subjectivity and, equally important, autonomy from mothering. This also suggests in a complicated ideological move, the battles that white second wave feminists undertook to challenge the position of women as capable *only of mothering*—as having neither legitimate subjectivity nor autonomy outside of mothering—is being reinscribed via the new momism. Both the dismantling of choice by linking it to personal consumer choice and women's subjectivity began first with the supermom label.

## Supermom: The First Post–Second Wave Backlash Label

As noted already, the supermom label was the first mom label to address women's newfound ability to "have it all." As such, the label was the first to acknowledge women's double shift responsibilities: being responsible for both full-time work and primary parenting. "Do it all," the double shift, and the more-contemporary understanding of the work/life balance, then, all are important symbols of second wave feminist gains in that they represent the struggle women face managing their position as second wave beneficiaries in the public sphere and as mothers in the private sphere. As such, the solutions offered in public messages—the mom label—to manage doing it all—manage the work/life balance—reveal much about how feminism and intensive mothering and the relationship between the public and private spheres are being worked out via the new momism labels.

In terms of feminism specifically, it is important to understand the rhetorical effect of the new momism labels integrating feminism within intensive mothering. In other words, even though Douglas and Michaels (2004) reveal how the relationship between feminism and intensive mothering has begun to change as a result of the emergence of the new momism, it is also important to extend Douglas and Michaels's work in light of the rhetorical effect or consequences of the changed relationship. In fact, it is imperative to recognize, while the label appears to embrace feminist ideas, even support the changes in women's lives, from the beginning, the label worked rhetorically to entrench the language of choice while, simultaneously, making it clear that women would be responsible for managing any difficulty or struggle brought about by choice in the private sphere. Importantly, this also suggests that the supermom label was also the first post–second wave backlash label ala Susan Faludi's (1991) more complex understanding of backlash.

Faludi (1991) provided one of the first detailed analyses of this 1980s backlash and, in fact, popularized the term *backlash* in her book *Backlash: The Undeclared War against American Women.* In the book, Faludi (1991) argues that a "backlash" against second wave feminist successes has been evident throughout culture, but especially in popular culture and media venues like film, advertising, and television shows since the early 1980s. Braithwaite (2004) argues many feminist scholars, but especially North American feminist scholars,[4] understood Faludi's idea of backlash as the attempt to roll back or forestall the gains made by second wave feminists in terms of women's social, professional, educational, and political access. As such, as Braithwaite also argues, both feminists and nonfeminists alike have subsequently employed the term *backlash* to mean an "antifeminism" or "antiwoman" reaction, as do Douglas and Michaels (2004) in their work on the new momism.

Braithwaite, however, contends Faludi's initial description of backlash was more nuanced and sophisticated. In substantiating this claim, Braithwaite (2004) suggests Faludi recognized that the 1980s and early 1990s backlash was filled with mixed messages that simultaneously celebrated and acknowledged the successes of second wave feminism, while also blaming that feminism for any difficulty women might have in managing those changes to women's lives. Indeed, Faludi (1991) argues: "Behind this celebration of the American woman's victory, behind the news, cheerfully and endlessly repeated, that the struggle for women's rights is won, another message flashes. You may be free and equal now, it says to women, but you have never been more miserable" (p. ix). Central, then, to how the post-second wave backlash works is the rhetorical strategy of blaming feminist successes for creating problems for contemporary women's lives. Faludi, in fact, concludes that women repeatedly got the message in the 1980s that the cause for women's misery is feminism itself. As Faludi (1991) puts it: "The women's movement, as we are told time and again, has proved women's own worst enemy" (p. x). Thus and ironically, contemporary post–second wave backlash simultaneously celebrates second wave feminist successes *and* insists that women are miserable because of those successes. Clearly, then, as Braithwaite argues: "What is so notable for [Faludi] about this most recent backlash, though, is the incorporation[5] of feminism's successes into it, and the series of tensions and paradoxes this inclusion leads to" (p. 21).

Employing Faludi's (1991) more complex understanding of backlash in light of its rhetorical dimensions reveals that the changing relationship between second wave feminism and intensive mothering that Douglas and Michaels (2004) first noted is more complex than they originally theorized. Rather than only integrate feminism within intensive mothering and communicate the message that women were responsible for managing any difficulty they might be experiencing juggling it all, the new momism includes the dual rhetorical strategies of simultaneously acknowledging/integrating feminism while also refuting/blaming feminism for any difficulties women experience as mothers. In other words, the new momism—beginning with the supermom label—employs a more complex backlash strategy of simultaneously identifying with and refuting white second wave feminism in the service of blaming feminism for any difficulties contemporary women experience "having it all." As I have argued (O'Brien Hallstein, 2010) elsewhere, this also means that the new momism has begun to create a specifically post–second wave intensive mothering that is qualitatively different from domesticated intensive mothering in its approach to and incorporation of feminist rhetoric and ideas in ways that, ultimately, erode many of the gains of white second wave feminism, while blaming white second wave feminism for women's contemporary difficulties "having it all." Equally important, as I show next, with each new label, these "twin rhetorical" strategies embedded in the new momism continue to develop in ways that systematically dismantle the rhetoric and idea of choice in the service of reinscribing mothering as the most important part of femininity, while also driving a larger ideological wedge between the public and private spheres. How these processes continued to unfold becomes much clearer in the next label analyzed: the soccer mom.

## Soccer Mom: Trivializing the Work/Life Balance and Encouraging More Consumerism

By the mid-1990s, soccer mom began to be the label of choice to describe contemporary moms. The phrase *soccer mom* generally refers to married, middle-class suburban women with children. Literally, a soccer mom is viewed as driving her children to and from their soccer games in her minivan. Metaphorically, a soccer mom is viewed as a mom who is devoted first and foremost to her family's needs and, as a result, puts her children's desires and activities above her own. Interestingly and unlike the media-created supermom label, however, Peskowitz (2005) argues that the term *soccer mom* originated in Susan Casey's 1995 Democratic campaign for the Denver City Council (p. 24). According to Peskowitz (2005):

> Casey used the term to reassure voters that even though she was an accomplished and well-educated woman, voters could trust her to be just like them. The phrase cut to the heart of anxiety about women's achievements, and it cut against stereotypes about smart and accomplished women—that they can't manage professional success and family love simultaneously. (p. 24)

When Casey was asked about the term after it became introduced a year later in the 1996 presidential campaign between Bill Clinton and Bob Dole, Casey "insisted that she meant no gender stereotype" (Peskowitz, 2005, p. 24). Rather, Casey was simply trying to describe her dual responsibilities as an accomplished woman and mother and to suggest she could manage both. It is notable, then, that Casey was trying to communicate three key messages with the label: that she could be a second wave beneficiary and mother—she could have both a public and private life—she could balance both roles, and, importantly, still be likeable.

By 1996, however, soccer mom became the term Republican strategists[6] used to describe what was believed to be a primary swing vote in the presidential campaign (Parker West, 2004; Peskowitz, 2005; Vavrus, 2000). Republican strategists, in fact, believed that part of the reason soccer moms needed to be reached was that they were just too busy with working and mothering to have time to pay attention to politics. Indeed, Vavrus (2000) notes soccer moms' lives were perceived as "so hectic many barely have time to think about eating, let alone voting" (p. 203). Vavrus's analysis makes it clear that the primary descriptors of soccer moms was as "harried," as stressed women who were attempting to juggle both their domestic and professional responsibilities. As a result, the soccer mom label began to reveal in earnest that the double shift responsibility was a problem for women, that doing it all puts women in untenable binds between the public and private spheres.

Implicitly, then, the soccer mom label continues to acknowledge the work/life struggle: soccer moms were struggling to meet the demands of the ideal, unencumbered worker[7] in the public sphere and their family obligations in the private sphere. Sadly, as Vavrus (2000) concludes, "rather than addressing these strains as indicative of larger structural problems, mainstream television and print accounts of soccer moms suggest that the solutions are individual; the road out of the morass can be constructed on personal choice, much of it commercial in nature" (p. 209). Thus, soccer mom continued to depoliticize choice, encourage consumerism as the solution to the work/life struggle, and place the burden of responsibility for managing that struggle on women.

Vavrus (2000) also notes that soccer mom was a very important political shift from the news discourse of "Year of the Woman" that dominated the 1992 political campaign to "women as mothers" that dominated the 1996 presidential campaign. As she put it, "This period of time represents a dramatic shifting news discourse: from discussing women as political power wielders (Women of the Year) to discussing women as a group of swing voters defined primarily by their filial obligations" (Vavrus, 2000, p. 194). To put it another way, there was an important shift from seeing women as accomplished public women *and* mothers to "just" primarily private moms. Parker West's (2004) analysis also confirms this shift when she argues: "the Soccer Mom is unquestionably a mother first, with all other roles as secondary" (p. 95). Consequently, the soccer mom worked to obscure and diminish women's public success in the service of seeing them most importantly as private women whose primary work was as mothers in the home. Thus, the soccer mom label worked to reinscribe a pre–second wave positioning of women: it worked to communicate the idea that the most important and "essential" component of women's lives were their reproductive capacity and their role as mothers in the private sphere. In doing so, the soccer mom label also worked to return women back to the private realm and to their homes.

Reading this shuttling to domestic life and the soccer mom label in relation to how choice works rhetorically reveals key shifts in terms of how both feminism and choice continued to be dismantled and how the ideological wedge between the public and private grew larger. Indeed, the soccer mom label strips the feminist critique of women's double shift to a personal and trivial problem for individual women to solve in the private sphere. Vavrus (2000) explicitly speaks to the fact that feminism was taken out of the soccer mom label. As Vavrus (2000) notes, actual soccer moms interviewed for media accounts articulated a need for assistance:

> assistance that 15 to 20 years earlier would have been the subject of feminist commentary and political agitation. But rather than engaging a substantive critique of the domestic and professional expectations of soccer moms, the label and the ensuing media discussions tend to diminish them in importance, make them seem trivial or cute, and/or link them with consumer products—as if a minivan or organic rice cakes could address the cultural and structural inequities that conspire to make even middle-class women's lives difficult. (p. 209)

Clearly, the trivialization of the work/life problem along with the suggestion that any remaining difficulties related to this problem could be resolved by making good personal consumer choices added another dismantling of feminism's political, public potential to address the structural inequities that play a key role in creating the "harried" lives of women. As a result, the soccer mom label depoliticized and destructuralized the stress of the work/life balance and communicated the message that it was no longer a political or public sphere issue and instead was easily solved by making good consumer choices in the private sphere.

Equally significant, like the supermom label, the soccer mom label makes additional important "contributions" to entrenching backlash via a post–second wave hegemonic intensive mothering. The soccer mom label implicitly acknowledges women's gains but actively works to strip the feminist critique, while any challenge or refutation of intensive mothering is subsumed and trivialized. This trivialization also works to further link choice with private consumption, while continuing to strip any political component out of choice. Moreover, where the supermom label began the ideological and rhetorical work of placing the onus of responsibility for managing "having it all" on women, the soccer mom takes it one step further by diminishing the importance of the struggle to women's everyday lives and offers trivialized solutions for solving the struggle.

As such, reading the soccer mom label rhetorically reveals that it makes another important "contribution" in terms of driving the ideological wedge between the public and private spheres that first began with the supermom label. Rather than only communicate the message that the public and private must be separate, the soccer mom label suggests that any difficulty moving between the two spheres is easily solved through personal choices in the private sphere. Thus, because the soccer mom label works to trivialize and diminish the work/life balance, it creates a much larger ideological space between the public and private spheres, while reenforcing the notion that any problem women face within both spheres is easily solved by their own personal consumer choices. Finally, soccer mom also expanded the wedge between women's lives as public women and their private lives as mothers by privileging their private lives as moms over their public lives as competent, professional women.

Depoliticizing both choice and feminism, while also driving a larger ideological wedge between the public and private also continued in the next label, the mommy wars: the so-called battle between women who choose to be stay-at-home mothers and women who choose to work and mother.

## The Mommy Wars: Deliberately Choosing to Opt-Out and Second Wave Feminism's Fault

The mommy wars pits two groups of moms against one another: the "traditional" mom who stays at home with her children and devotes herself to the happiness of her family and the working mom, often still described as the *supermom,* who effortlessly juggles home and work and is viewed, as Hays (1994) argues, as pushing a "stroller with one hand and carry[ing] a briefcase in the other" (p. 132). The "war" between them is such that both kinds of mom are viewed as angry and defensive against one another. As Hays (1994) describes it, "Supermoms, according to the portrait, regularly describe stay-at-home mothers as lazy and boring, while traditional moms regularly accuse employed mothers of selfishly neglecting their children" (p. 132).

Although, as Young (2004) argues, the mommy wars have raged periodically since the rise of second wave feminism, the latest version of the mommy wars began to rage again in earnest after Lisa Belkin's October 23,

2006, *New York Times Magazine* cover story "The Opt-Out Revolution." The article featured ivy-league educated women—mostly lawyers and MBAs—who quit their high-powered jobs to stay home full-time with their children. Peskowitz (2005) notes that "'Opt-Out Revolution' was the most emailed *New York Times Magazine* article in *Times* history; friends would send it round with commentary, asking others what they thought" (p. 87). The opt-out language quickly caught on and became common parlance to describe high-powered women choosing to quit jobs to stay at home full-time. This new vocabulary word, however, came with a price in terms of choice as is indicated most clearly in how the article was framed on both the cover and contents pages.

While the article itself did try to convey a more nuanced understanding of why professional women were opting out, even "hinting" that many of the women would not opt out if there were more public support for working and mothering, the framing of the article captured none of this nuance and made it clear how choice was reconceived via the opt-out discussion. On the cover page directly below a white woman sitting cross-legged with a child on her lap, the question of why women are not getting to the top professionally—the classic feminist glass ceiling issue—is asked and answered in the following manner. "Q: 'Why Don't More Women Get to the Top?'" The answer: "A: They Choose Not To." And, next, "Abandoning the Climb and Heading Home." Moreover, on the contents page, the description of the article reads, "Many high-powered women today don't ever hit the glass ceiling, choosing to leave the workplace for motherhood. Is this the failure of one movement, or the beginning of another?" The sidebar continues, "while the absence of women in positions of power was once chiefly a result of sexism, the fact that women still don't rule the world is now increasingly a result of deliberate choice."[8]

Crucially, then, there are at least two issues in relation to the continued dismantling of both choice and feminism suggested by the frame of the article. First, any ambivalence embedded in women's choice was replaced with a deliberate choice. In other words, women's personal choice shifted to becoming a *determined personal choice*. Second, in terms of the classic feminist issue of the glass ceiling, in one fell swoop, the contents page makes it clear that women need to be held responsible for any remaining inequity in professional settings because they deliberately choose to quit work. And, equally important, the question about whether the new glass ceiling is a failure of one movement—clearly a reference to feminism—or the start of another seems to suggest that the glass ceiling might just be feminism's problem for fighting for women's choice in the first place. In other words, women's personal deliberate choices, particularly in terms of opting out, are creating the glass ceiling, not some other issue like gender inequity in the workplace.

The suggestion that the work/life balance negotiation is really a "women's problem" also further pushes the work/life balance into the private sphere. Indeed, as a "women's problem" that is a result of women's own deliberate choice, the mommy wars now communicate the message that any work/life struggle is a private women's issue that no longer needs any public, political action because it is really just a problem among women that they freely choose. Moreover and related, similar to the soccer-mom label, the mommy wars via the opt-out discussion further depoliticize choice to mean a *personal choice* that mothers are now entirely responsible for managing in the private realm. But, it adds another element: it suggests that the work/life balance is no longer a feminist issue because feminism failed women by guaranteeing choice and, anyway, women do not want to be successful because they are deliberately choosing intensive mothering. Clearly, then, the mommy wars reveal a dismantling of choice such that deliberately choosing now also confirms no need for feminism and, equally important, that women want to focus on mothering and define themselves first and foremost as mothers. Thus, the pre–second wave connection between femininity and mothering has been reinscribed as a sort of post–second wave mothering that appears to be informed fully with the second wave feminist notion of choice.

As with the soccer mom label, then, reading the contemporary mommy wars rhetorically reveals how choice is operating and suggests interesting insights. Choice changed significantly: no longer just a reaction to circumstance and making better, personal consumer choices, the opt-out discussion reveals that women are now making deliberate choices that, importantly, are fully under women's control. Moreover, the opt-out discussion also reveals that the primary reason women now have to make these choices is because of feminism's failures; feminism, in fact, is to blame for women's difficulties having it all. As such, the contemporary mommy wars indicate a very important rhetorical and ideological shift to blaming second wave feminism while continuing to pit women against one another. In other words, while the soccer-mom label trivialized, diminished, and depoliticized the struggle to place the burden of responsibility for managing the work/life problem on women, the contemporary mommy wars via the opt-out discussion takes the dismantling one step further to suggest that not only is the struggle a personal problem as a result of women's own deliberate choices, it is really now a problem feminism created.

In short it is a "women's problem" rather than a parent problem; it is neither a problem of importance to men nor a problem outside the private realm/sphere. Of course, this means the mommy wars help create an even larger ideological space between the public and private spheres. Like the supermom label, the opt-out discussion communicates the message that the work/life balance is a private sphere issue, but it adds another layer of separation by suggesting that it is "just women's problem." As such, the mommy wars create an even larger ideological space between the public and private sphere, while continuing to reinforce the hegemonic idea that women are entirely responsible for managing the not-so-important problems they face negotiating the public-private sphere split.

This pattern of systematically stripping feminism of the politics of choice, while appearing to support feminism, continues in the now-contemporary alpha mom label. Moreover, as I reveal next, the alpha mom also adds the latest layer of dismantling to both choice and second wave feminism.

## Alpha Mom: The Negative but Efficient and Control Freak Mom

Graphic designer Constance Van Flandern coined the term *alpha mom* in 2005. She was asked to design a logo for "a new video-on-demand cable TV service that wanted to attract information-hungry, multitasking moms. Names being considered: Mommy TV, Mommy Channel, even Mommy Says" (Horovitz & Newman, 2007, par. 9). None of the names fit for Van Flandern because she "realized that the audience is me: a hip mom who wants to be involved with her children's lives but doesn't want to give up her identity" (Horovitz & Newman, 2007, par. 11). So, she came up with the name *alpha mom*, which was embraced by her client, Isabel Kallman, CEO and founder of Alpha Mom TV, launched in 2005. Interestingly, Kallman was profiled in what was later described as a "biting profile" in *New York Magazine* that portrayed the "Alpha Mom as an ultracontrolling, hyperambitious Robo Mom" (Horovitz & Newman, 2007, par. 15). This description of Kallman will probably "stick" to alpha moms generally because, while it is relatively new, a common understanding of the label is developing that has a negative tone and, importantly, focuses on issues of control and efficiency.

Indeed, descriptions of alpha moms focus on these moms as fundamentally about control and bringing work-related skills to mothering. As one report puts it: Alpha moms have "emerged as the generation of college educated woman [sic] who take their experiences from the workplace and apply them to parenting with the same intensity" (Madison Avenue Discovers Alpha Moms, 2007, par. 3). Or, as Palmer (2007) suggests, alpha moms:

> project independence, balance, and competence at both work and home, in contrast to past images of harried working moms and uber-domestic stay-at-home moms. Alpha moms are women who are in control of their own destiny. She sometimes works and sometimes doesn't. . . . The idea is that you can be good at both [motherhood and career] now. (p.42)

Alpha moms, then, are clearly women who are unlike harried soccer moms and are direct descendents of the mommy wars but, importantly, they add a new element to women's deliberate choosing: alpha moms are now *in control*; they have deliberately chosen their circumstances and, as a result, have control over their lives.

Moreover, in the *New York Magazine* article, alpha moms are described as the latest model of mothers who are "not different from Betty [Crocker] but better, stronger, faster" (Patterson, 2007, p. 2). In short, alpha moms are in control and are both stronger and faster at their mom duties; they have become far more efficient and better than supermom. While in another description of the label, alpha moms were described as believing: "With the right planning, resources, and work ethic, you can, too, be a perfect and fulfilled woman, raising a perfect and happy child" (Patterson, 2005, p. 2). In fact, the profile of Kallman brings the issue of control front and center when Killman is quoted as saying the following: "'I hate that word, *control,* she says, but control is what it means to be an Alpha Mom. You're the leader of the pack, and the pack, says Isabel, is your family'" (Patterson, 2005, p. 5). In addition to being the leader of the family, alpha moms are also leaders among women. As Horwitz and Newman (2007) write in *USA Today,* "An Alpha Mom typically has money to spend, and—key for marketers—she is, as the label implies, a leader of the pack who influences how other moms spend" (par. 4). Or, as Kallman said herself in the *New York Magazine* interview, an alpha mom is "you know, the maven of mommyhood, the leader of the pack" (Patterson, 2005, p. 1).

The alpha mom, then, turns on three core ideas: they are leaders of the pack of moms—which continues to pit women against one another—in control, and making deliberate and efficient choices. In other words, the alpha mom label communicates the message that, because alpha moms make deliberate choices, they are now portrayed as, finally, having complete control in their lives. Moreover, as the "top-dog" mom, the alpha mom completes the process of pitting women against one another by creating a hierarchy between groups of women: alpha moms are at the top, while all other moms are beneath them.

Although alpha mom, then, is similar to supermom because alpha moms "do it all," alpha mom is different because, unlike supermom who was celebrated in the media, alpha mom is viewed negatively by the media. That this negative coverage will continue and probably "stick" to alpha mom is likely because, as Hays (1996) argues, expert advice about intensive mothering insists that good mothering requires mothers to resist any market/work values if mothers want to be good mothers. Indeed, quoting Brazelton, Hays (1996) argues, "Although emotional distance and efficiency are appropriate in the workplace, Brazelton writes 'an efficient woman could be the worst kind of mother to her children'; at home with her child, 'a woman must be warm, flexible, and concerned'" (p. 65). In this view, working mothers must learn to "switch gears" between the work world and home since work values—particularly efficiency—are seen as antithetical and harmful in childrearing and the private sphere. Thus and ironically, alpha moms are also different from supermom because they are no longer "switching gears" between the world of work and the world of home, and the media are penalizing alpha moms for that at the same time that media are popularizing alpha moms.

As with the analysis of the previous three mom labels, then, reading the alpha-mom label rhetorically in relation to understanding how choice is working is illuminating. Like the mommy wars, alpha mom depoliticizes choice to mean that any work/life problem can be managed by a *deliberate personal choice* but it also adds another element: it suggests that the work/life balance is no longer an issue. In other words, whereas the mommy wars take out the need for feminism in solving the work/life balance, alpha mom communicates the message that *there is no longer a problem.* Indeed, alpha mom suggests that, because women are independent, in control, and efficient at both work and home, in contrast to previous harried soccer mom or women who are opting out, alpha moms are women who are in control of their own destiny. And, importantly, as "top dogs" that other mothers follow, as trendsetters, any woman who thinks otherwise simply needs to also become an alpha mom.

In terms of the ideological space between the public and private spheres, alpha mom makes the wedge the largest to date. Indeed, while the soccer mom label trivialized and diminished the importance of the work/life balance and the mommy wars "insisted" that the work/life struggle is really "just" a women's issue, alpha mom communicates the message that there really is no longer a problem if mothers simply become more efficient, in control, and leaders of the pack. In short, the label communicates the idea that, if alpha moms simply "import" the skills they have learned in the public sphere, then, there will be no problems in the private sphere. Consequently, not only has the public-private split become more expansive, any problems for women living within both is now understood to be fully under women's control in the private sphere if they simply use their public sphere skills. In short, the alpha mom label reinscribes and revalues the public sphere over the private sphere. Finally and ironically, by doing so, however, alpha moms are also viewed with much disdain or in a negative light for importing their work skills into the private sphere.

Tracing the labels both rhetorically and in light of how choice has continued to become embedded within the new momism, then, suggests that, as the labels have developed in response to women living within the successes of white second wave feminism, choice has become more and more entrenched in contemporary understandings of mothering, while, simultaneously and ironically, choice is being used not to liberate women but to penalize them for the choices they make in terms of mothering. Moreover, the rhetorical analysis reveals that each new label exposes a new dismantling of the second wave feminist politics of choice that ultimately works to depoliticize feminism, creates a link between feminism and intensive mothering that suggests that intensive mothering is post–second wave feminist or liberated mothering, even though the new momism functions as a complex hegemonic backlash ideology, depublicizes public support for mothering, and reinscribes a pre–second wave view that mothering is the most important part of femininity, while enlarging the ideological space between the public and private spheres. Thus, the analysis has important insights for understanding both feminism and why, at both the ideological and communicative levels, there is so little public policy support for contemporary women's mothering.

## CONCLUSION

### Retooling Both Our Understanding and Use of Choice

The rhetorical analysis of the mom labels suggests important theoretical insights. In terms of feminist understandings of contemporary motherhood, the analysis reveals that the mom labels are neither just a backlash nor a co-optation of second wave feminism, even though both elements are tied up in the mom labels. Rather, the rhetorical analysis reveals that the mom labels are participating in a complex ideological and hegemonic post–second wave backlash form of intensive mothering that appears to be feminist mothering or, at minimum, a deliberatively chosen "liberated from pre–second wave" intensive mothering. This post–second wave mothering is especially dangerous because it integrates a depoliticized, destructrualized feminism and rhetoric of choice in the service of entrenching a "normal" hegemonic mothering ideology that is a form of social control of women once they become mothers. Related, the analysis reveals that contemporary depoliticized and destructuralized choice works to reinforce motherhood as both the most important component of hegemonic femininity and as a private-sphere issue outside the purview of the public sphere. Thus, our post–second wave intensive mothering is more complex and problematic than Douglas and Michaels originally understood, and the new momism is continuing to develop with each new label in ways that entrench dangerous and problematic understandings of the idea and rhetoric of choice. Feminist communication scholars must begin to recognize these complexities in relation to the new momism if we hope to respond fully to contemporary intensive mothering.

Moreover, the rhetorical analysis also reveals that the mom labels suggest choice benefits women when they become mothers—that choice is a public policy that supports women and mothers and changes to traditional gendered family roles—when, in fact, choice is now being used in the service of a sophisticated backlash against both women and second wave feminist gains. Indeed, the analysis reveals that choice is at work in the mom labels such that a new but very old form of gendered family life is emerging. Peskowitz (2005) has described this change as creating *neotraditional families*. Neotraditional families appear to be new because women's lives have changed but the basic foundation of pre–second wave family roles and responsibilities and the private-public split have not changed in ways that support second wave beneficiaries' mothering. Clearly, the analysis reveals that the mom labels are thoroughly ensconced in supporting neotraditional families at the ideological level in ways that make neotraditional families a new hegemonic family configuration that constrain women's lives. This hegemonic family type also reentrenches mothering and caretaking *as only* private sphere concerns outside the purview of the public sphere.

Related, it is important to note that neotraditional families are also especially dangerous for contemporary women because, in terms of femininity, the analysis also reveals that, while the second wave brought women's liberation, there has *not been a mothers' liberation*. Indeed, as Peskowitz (2005) puts it: "the gains for women in the past decades have not meant a similar gain for mothers" (p. 66). In other words, while unencumbered women have benefited in real and important ways from second wave feminism, our post–second wave intensive mothering ideology remains deeply problematic for those very women once they become mothers. As a result, the glass ceiling—the focus of much second wave analysis and activism—is no longer the most pressing barrier to women's professional success. Instead, in new and complex ways, motherhood is the "new/old" hegemonic barrier to women's lives because the new momism continues to position women as primary caregivers of children, while it also systematically dismantles choice one brick at a time. Ironically, then, one point that the opt-out discussion accurately identifies is that the glass ceiling is no longer a primary problem in contemporary women's lives. However, the opt-out discussion inaccurately identifies the work/life struggle as second wave feminism's fault rather than a result of hegemonic neotraditional families. To put it another way: even though the changes brought about by choice were empowering for many women, the analysis here suggests that choice is being dismantled in ways that penalize women once they become mothers and plays a significant role in encouraging neotraditional families and in reinscribing mothering as the most important component of femininity.

As a result, the mommy labels and contemporary depoliticized and destructualized choice are part of a powerful social system that continues to direct "women homeward" (Hirshman, 2006, p. 26). This, then, is why the mom labels are so dangerous ideologically and politically, and why they play a key role in discouraging public policy support for mothering in the public sphere. In fact, as the analysis revealed, because choice has been systematically dismantled, the most contemporary mom label—alpha mom—now suggests the work/life struggle is a "woman's" problem that any given woman is fully able to solve in the private sphere if she makes the correct deliberate and efficient choices. As such, at the ideological level, the mom labels have and continue to work to encourage public policy to distance itself from the work/life struggle, while simultaneously placing the responsibility for managing it on women's deliberate choice-making in the private sphere. In short, as the opening epigraph suggests, "choice" now appears to be "a public policy that empowers every woman to do as she wishes in this arena—a public policy that seems to encompass *rights,* but does not" (Solinger, 1998, p. 383). Thus, it is imperative that feminist communication scholars understand how choice has been co-opted to appear to be granting women rights, while simultaneously working in the service of supporting a new post–second wave hegemonic and sophisticated backlash intensive mothering ideology, a new/old hegemonic femininity, and neotraditional families.

Understanding how choice appears to support women's lives while actually reinscribing hegemonic femininity allows contemporary feminists to begin the process of rethinking and retooling choice. This includes, of course, understanding how choice has been dismantled, co-opted and, equally important, as the analysis suggests, how choice has been destructuralized and depoliticized. At minimum, doing so requires moving from an early second wave rhetoric of choice to retooling choice—repoliticizing and restructuralizing it—in light of our post–second wave context and new hegemonic intensive mothering ideology. Thus, if we do not make this important shift in our own thinking and use of the rhetoric of choice, then, we will be unable to rebuild the idea and rhetoric of choice so that both are meaningful, real, and politically important rights for all women, but especially for mothers.

## REFERENCES

Belkin, L. (2003, October 26). The opt-out revolution. *New York Times Sunday Magazine*, 42–47, 58, 85–86.

Braithwaite, A. (2004, June). "Politics of/and backlash." *Journal of International Women's Studies*, 5, 18–33.

Cloud, D. L. (1996). "Hegemony or concordance?: The rhetoric of tokenism in Oprah Winfrey's rags-to-riches biography." *Critical Studies in Mass Communication*, 13, 115–37.

Condit, C. M. (1994). "Hegemony in a mass-mediated society: Concordance about reproductive technologies." *Critical Studies in Mass Communication, 11*, 205–30.

Douglas, S. J. & Michaels, M. W. (2004). *The mommy myth: The idealization of motherhood and how it has undermined women.* New York: Free Press.

Faludi, S. (1991). *Backlash: The undeclared war against American women.* New York: Crown.

Foss, S. K. (2009). *Rhetorical criticism: Explorations and practices*. 4th. ed. Long Grove, IL: Waveland Press.

Grossberg, L. (1993). Cultural studies and/in new worlds. *Critical Studies in Mass Communication*, *10*, 1–12.

Hays, S. (1996). *The cultural contradictions of motherhood.* New Haven, CT: Yale University Press.

Hirshman, L. R. (2006). Get to work: *A manifesto for women of the world.* New York: Viking.

Horovitz, B & Newman, A. (2007, March 27). Alpha moms leap to the top of trendsetters. *USA Today*. Retrieved from: http://www.usatoday.com/tech/webguide/internetlife/2007-03-26-alpha-mom_n.htm.

Katzenstein, M. F. (1990). Feminism within American institutions: Unobtrusive mobilization in the 1980s. *Signs: Journal of Women in Culture and Society, 16,* 27–54.

Madison avenue discovers alpha moms. (2007, April 9). Retrieved from: http://abc-news.go.com/GMA/AmericanFamily/story?id=3022510&page=1

O'Brien Hallstein, D. L. (2008). Second wave silences and third wave intensive mothering. In A. Kinser (Ed.), *Mothering in the third wave* (pp. 107–18). Toronto: Demeter Press.

O'Brien Hallstein, D. L. (2010). *White feminists and contemporary maternity: Purging matrophobia*. New York: Palgrave Press.

O'Reilly, A. (Ed.) (2004). *Mother outlaws: Theories and practices of empowered mothering*. Toronto, Canada: Women's Press.

Palmer, K. (2007, Sept. 3). The new mommy track: More mothers win flextime at work, and hubbies' help (really!) at home. *U.S. News and World Report, 143,* 40–45.

Parker West, L. (2004). *Welfare queens, soccer moms, and working mothers: The socio-political construction of state child care policy*. Unpublished doctoral dissertation, Emery University, Atlanta Georgia.

Patterson, F. (2005, June 20). Empire of the alpha mom. *New York Magazine*. Retrieved from http://nymag.com/nymetro/news/features/12026/

Peskowitz, M. (2005). *The truth behind the mommy wars: Who decides what makes a good mother?* Emeryville, CA: Seal Press.

Solinger, R. (2001). *Beggars and choosers: How the politics of choice shapes adoption, abortion, and welfare in the United States*. New York: Hill and Wang.

Solinger, R. (1998). "Poisonous choice." In Molly Ladd-Taylor & Lauri Umansky (Eds.), *Bad mothers: The politics of blame in the twentieth century* (pp. 381–402). New York: New York University Press.

Young, C. (2004, June). Opting-out: The press discovers the mommy wars, again. *Reason Magazine*. Retrieved from http://www.reason.com/news/show/29157.html.

Vavrus, M. D. (2000). From women of the year to "soccer moms": The case of the incredible shrinking woman. *Political Communication, 17,* 193–213.

Williams, J. (2000). *Unbending gender: Why family and work conflict and what to do about it*. Oxford: Oxford University Press.

## NOTES

1. Although Hays does not describe intensive mothering as *domesticated intensive mothering*, the distinction between domesticated and contemporary intensive mothering is quite important. As I argue (O'Brien Hallstein, 2010) elsewhere, it is more accurate to view the form of intensive mothering that Hays first described as domesticated intensive mothering in order to understand more fully how the

feminist rhetoric of choice has been incorporated in our new form of contemporary intensive mothering. I refer to this new form as *post–second wave intensive mothering*. I will continue to make the distinction between the two different forms of intensive mothering in this chapter for clarity and precision.

2. O'Reilly (2004) also argues the contemporary form of intensive mothering is different from the form Hays first described. O'Reilly, however, uses the term *custodial intensive mothering* rather than *domesticated intensive mothering* to describe the early version of intensive mothering.

3. I am adopting the "one-brick-at-a-time" metaphor from Douglas and Michaels who also argue the new momism dismantles feminist gains in this way.

4. In fact, Braithwaite (2004) argues that there is a geographical divide in terms of reconceptualizing both postfeminism and backlash. As she puts it in a footnote specifically about postfeminism but which is also consistent with her writing about backlash:

> Interestingly, this redefinition of postfeminism as similar to other current (and complex) theoretical languages so far appears quite geographically divided. Brooks and Gamble, for example, who ultimately argue for this shift in understanding, publish in Australia and England respectively, while the more popular understanding I outlined earlier [in the essay] is almost entirely one found in North American writing about the term. (2004, footnote 20, p. 31)

5. Katzenstein (1990) uses the term *intermixing* to describe this process of incorporating feminism with backlash against it. As Katzenstein (1990) writes, "What is also significant about the spread of gender consciousness is its diffusion across a liberal-conservative axis. This diffusion gives rise to an interesting intermixing of feminism with continued strains of antifeminist thinking" (p. 31).

6. Waitress moms, a Democratic invention to counter the Republican middle-class-time-for-leisure mom, were "working-class, non–college-educated mothers who struggled to make ends meet" (Vavrus, 2004, p. 28). Because I am analyzing the mom labels targeted at the ideal intensive mother—white, middle-to-upper-middle class, and heterosexual women—I am not analyzing waitress mom. However, I recognize that waitress mom offers an important counter to the ideal mom labels. As such, I also recognize the limits of my exploration in that it only represents an analysis of the lives of a limited and privileged group of women.

7. Here, I am drawing on Williams's (2001) work on the unencumbered worker. Williams argues that professional organizing systems continue to be structured on the notion of workers as unencumbered with family responsibility, i.e., continue to assume that professional workers are fully available to employers because they have a "wife" at home managing home life and raising children.

8. In her own critique of the Belkin chapter, Peskowitz (2005) also details this opening frame of the article in a very similar manner. Her primary interest in doing so, however, is different from mine. Peskowitz does so to describe her personal reaction and subsequent Internet follow-up discussions about the article.

2

# NO EXCEPTION POSTPREVENTION

## "Differential Biopolitics" on the Morning After[1]

*Natalie Fixmer-Oraiz*[2]

> *Amy Cappiello was twenty-four years old the night the condom broke. She sat up in a panic, thought about her job on Capitol Hill and her grad school commitments, and cried. Then there was the fact that she and her boyfriend had only been seeing each other for two months. It was just not the time for her to become somebody's mom. With her boyfriend, Cappiello went right to the emergency room at George Washington University Hospital. There, a doctor and nurse introduced her to the concept of emergency contraception. . . . Cappiello took [the pills]. To her relief, she didn't become pregnant. "Not being married, making less than $30,000 a year and going to grad school, having a baby would have been a nightmare," Cappiello says now, a year later. "Not only was I not physically ready in terms of being able to provide a stable environment for a baby, but emotionally I was nowhere near ready to have a baby thrust upon me. We would have handled it, but it would have been devastating."* (Redfearn, 2002, para. 1–5)

Contraception is often coded as empowering women's reproductive choice, and for many women, this is inarguably the case. Stories like Amy's exemplify and bolster this collective imagining. And yet, within the broader scope of contemporary public debates concerning emergency contraception (EC)[3] and its accessibility for American women, a focus on personalized accounts is exceedingly rare. Amy's story is a narrative respite in a sea of politically contentious dispute over scientific evidence, religious beliefs, and social morality. What, then, does her story reveal? She is, in many ways, the embodiment of the contemporary (white, middle-class) American dream for women, made possible by the gains of twentieth century feminisms. Young, full of promise, pursuing higher education and a career in government, Amy is on the road to success. Hers is a narrative that assumes upward economic mobility and hinges on class privilege. As Amy herself is clear to note, however, her circumstances bar her from responsibly bearing children (yet). She is not in a long-term relationship, makes less than $30,000 annually, and is in school. Thus, the emergency identified and addressed here is not simply a broken condom. The emergency is also the potential pregnancy under Amy's current circumstances—a clear threat to American dream-ness, white, middle-class, heteromormative identity and lifestyle. The use of the term "nightmare" is both fitting in its candor and revealing in its broader cultural context.

Cultural assumptions regarding birth control and women's reproductive "choice" suture the two seamlessly together. "Choice" has become a political and colloquial referent for the unencumbered right to determine when, whether, and with whom to have children; as such, it is invariably wed to notions of women's individual autonomy and empowerment. And yet, imagining birth control in this way is deeply troubling. This characterization ignores the long, disquieting, and myriad histories of material practices in which contraception has been utilized to curtail, rather than enhance, women's reproductive autonomy in ways that fracture decisively along lines of race, class, and nationality (see, e.g., Davis, 1983; Gordon, 2007; Roberts, 1997; Solinger, 2005). In an attempt to guard against state sanctioned reproductive coercion, advocates have argued for birth control methods that place the locus of control in the hands of women themselves. EC appears to do just that—most often, the method is administered by the woman herself and, in a significant departure from other contraceptives, is designed to be taken *after* unprotected sex. And yet, a close examination of EC's discursive figuration, of how it is imagined to shape sexuality, reproduction, social relationships, and even identities, calls this facile equation into question. Using critical discourse analysis as a theoretical framework, this study explores the mediated discourses that work to craft and anchor EC within contemporary U.S. cultural imaginaries. In so doing, I ask how these discourses figure in challenging or reinscripting reproductive (bio)politics, and consider the implications for rhetorics of choice specifically, and issues of reproductive justice more broadly. Ultimately, I argue that the EC debates illustrate the discursive limits of choice as a means of securing a reproductive justice for all women.

Contrary to popular belief, EC itself is nothing new. While Plan B was approved in July of 1999, the practice of combining regular birth control pills and taking them after unprotected sex to prevent pregnancy dates back almost to the inception of hormonal birth control itself. This "off-label"[4] use of the pill began to circulate within the medical community in the mid-1960s, when a Dutch physician administered a concentrated dose of estrogen to a thirteen-year-old victim of rape to prevent pregnancy. Over the next decade, physicians began to experiment with and prescribe this method in what they would determine to be exceptional circumstances. The first scientific study of EC was published in a medical journal by Canadian doctor A. Albert Yuzpe; the standard regimen for EC that ensued bore his name and consisted of a combination of regular birth control pills taken twelve hours apart (Johnson & Burrows, 2007). The Yuzpe regimen, however, remained relatively obscure, and it wasn't until 1997 that the FDA officially sanctioned this practice and solicited pill manufacturers for a new drug explicitly designed for emergency use (Johnson & Burrows, 2007). Between the years of 1997 and 2006, ECs were approved by the FDA, but only available by prescription. For five of those nine years, while Plan B awaited approval for over-the-counter status, an increasingly contentious public debate ensued, at its height ensnaring public health officials, advocacy organizations, medical associations, FDA commissioners and committee members, media outlets, members of Congress, the Government Accountability Office, and even the Bush administration.

These debates reside at the center of this study. Drawing from intellectual traditions that include critical rhetoric and discourse analysis, my interest lies primarily in what John Sloop (2000) has referred to as "the politics of *doxa*" (p. 168), the myriad ways in which dominant (popular) discourses operate alongside one another to constrain, discipline, or otherwise function ideologically and materially. A number of sources would provide insight into an exploration of EC's discursive figuration. To the extent that mediated accounts provide access to mainstream public voices and cultural sentiments, my focus here is on media coverage of the EC debates. To analyze how choice is situated within the EC debates, I studied articles from prominent newspapers and periodicals with national circulation, published between the dates of January 1, 1997 and December 31, 2006.[5] These ten years are particularly significant for the EC debates because 1997 marks the original approval of EC for prescription sale in the United States; 2006 marks its final approval by the FDA to go "behind the counter" for women eighteen and older. While not all articles are included in the direct quotations provided in this study, each readily inform my analysis of these discourses and contribute to my overall argument.

A critical discourse perspective explicitly invites an awareness that technologies "occupy sites of struggle over meanings and power . . . [that] can both reinforce and undermine structures of inequality" (Slack & Wise, 2005, p. 2). A rich body of media studies scholarship (see, e.g., Feenberg, 1991, 2003; Hartouni, 1997; Marvin, 1988; Spigel, 2001) helps to rethink technologies along these lines, to understand them not as inevitable or predetermined forces in sociopolitical contexts, but rather as sites of cultural anxiety onto which codified social roles are projected and played out. In the words of Andrew Feenberg (1991), "technology is not destiny but a scene of struggle" (p. 14). I ground my approach to EC accordingly, foregrounding the complex and mutually constitutive relationship between culture and technology. This critical orientation provides a useful lens through which to interrogate the various economic, social, political, and historical forces that help to shape EC's meaning, and helps to understand the kinds of institutions and/or social relationships that are perhaps (re)enforced or undermined in this process of meaning-making. In other words, rather than assume the ontological status of EC—to ask or assert how it acts on the world—I work to interrogate its epistemological function, to ask how EC is imagined to negotiate social relationships and shape cultural and political communities. Certainly, it is true that EC enables a particular physical effect on the reproductive body. That said, I argue that it also engenders another set of material effects—an expansion (and subsequent contraction) of discursive possibilities through which women's reproductive rights and choices—their experiences of sexuality, maternity, indeed of the body itself—are negotiated and constrained.

This chapter proceeds, then, in three sections. First, in the critical reading of these popular discourses, I explore the ways in which EC occupies highly contested and nebulous ontological ground within reproductive politics, negotiating the borders and chasms between birth control and abortion. One of the fundamental questions animating public debate centers on whether this technology is a method of birth control, a form of abortion, or not quite either. This question is raised in both implicit and explicit terms, as EC is regularly posited as occupying an amorphous space *between* contraception and abortion. In this way, the defining characteristics that anchor EC's imagining in social and political culture are unstable, unfixed, and continuously open to interrogation. This instability between birth control and abortion suggests cultural anxieties regarding an excess of choice, sexuality, and reproduction in American women's lives. Second, I argue that in response to this instability, EC is managed through a rhetoric of "exception" and "emergency" that functions to discipline reproductive bodies through a "differential biopolitics." Drawing from Sarah Sharma's (2009) theoretical contributions to the study of contemporary biopolitics, I argue that this differential biopolitics imbues some women with a "right to choice" and reduces others to scripted "responsible choices." Finally, I turn to the significance of these debates for the meaning and function of "choice" as a public claim to empowerment and autonomy. Rather than supporting or extending such claims, I argue that these debates, in working to figure and fix EC, suggest the vulnerabilities and discursive limits of choice itself.

## NEBULOUS CONCEPTIONS FOR EMERGENCY CONTRACEPTION

> I feel very strongly that this shouldn't be about abortion politics. . . . This is a way to prevent unwanted pregnancy and thereby prevent abortion. This should be something that we should all agree on.
>
> —Dr. Susan Wood, quoted in Harris, 2005, para. 2

> The pill acts to prevent a pregnancy by aborting a child . . . the emergency in this case is a baby.
>
> —Judy Brown, quoted in Kolata, 2003b, para. 21

The introduction of EC began with little political fanfare and an emphasis on scientific progress and technological promise. In 1997, even prior to the introduction of Plan B and Preven, *Time* was quick to celebrate the implications of the FDA's initial decision to approve regular birth control for "morning-after" use. "The Good News" section of a regular health update declares: "America wakes up to MORNING-AFTER PILLS" (emphasis original). "The FDA has okayed the use of megadoses of ordinary birth-control pills, taken within seventy-two hours of sex, to prevent pregnancy. The regimen, which is 75 percent effective, is already widely used in Europe" (Adams & Crumley, 1997, para. 1). Much of the public discourse surrounding (and constituting) EC at its official entry onto the U.S. market reflected a similar emphasis on Western innovation and medical progress, and assumed political neutrality. These assertions, however, were relatively short-lived and quickly overwhelmed by moral and scientific dispute regarding the use and function of EC.

Even the earliest iterations of EC's discursive imagining begin to reveal the nebulous and contentious scientific, cultural, and political terrain in which this contraceptive begins to unfold. For example, just as EC is celebrated as a "new and improved" technique for a long-standing medical practice, these descriptors are tempered by discordant explications of its functioning: "Preven's dose of hormones keeps a fertilized egg from implanting in the uterine wall. It's available only by prescription, but it'll stop a pregnancy 72 hours after sex" (Rogers, 1999, para. 2). As this quote suggests, one of the fundamental tensions that marks the discursive entry of EC into American life at the turn of the century is its tenuous and unstable location within reproductive politics. EC is articulated as both, but not quite, abortion or birth control. And yet, it is figured as the defining issue within contemporary abortion politics:

> [T]he abortion pill and the emergency contraception pill—because of their ease of use, the mechanisms by which they work and the fact that they are taken after sex—have blurred the line between contraception and abortion and have added a new wrinkle to the traditional anti-abortion movement. (Shorto, 2006, para. 8)

This fundamental conflation quickly becomes the site for the expression and embodiment of myriad cultural anxieties, a site that ultimately demands discursive negotiation and redress. Thus, I turn now to examine this common conflation of abortion and birth control, and the "exception"(al) means of negotiation that emerge as a result.

## Postprevention Contraception

As a postprevention contraception, EC is simultaneously defined *as* birth control, while disarticulated *from* birth control. It oscillates between the new and the familiar, the exception and the rule, with regularity, but little ease. First, EC is regularly asserted as a method of contraception, but continually marked, and indeed circumscribed, by the extraordinary: "Plan B, as the name implies, is the backup when Plan A fails. It's the second chance to avoid pregnancy after sex. It's what you can do instead of waiting in a high state of anxiety" (Goodman, 2004, para. 5). The notion of exception both permeates and animates this imagining. EC is figured as postprevention contraception—an opportunity to eclipse fear and distress by preempting the possibility of pregnancy or abortion when all other modes of one's regular preventative practice(s) have failed. The use of EC is clearly the exception, as opposed to the rule—or more precisely, an addendum to the rules: "And if the condom breaks? Or a woman forgets to take her pill? There's something for emergencies now, too, a last stop before pregnancy" (Stepp, 2004, para. 3). This is, clearly, *not* your everyday birth control.

And yet, at times EC is precisely that—ordinary, commonplace, and unremarkable. Particularly for advocates in favor of increasing access and loosening restrictions, aligning EC with everyday birth control is used to compel legitimacy. A medical director for Planned Parenthood states that "[EC] is one of the safest medicines we have available, and it can prevent unplanned pregnancies" (Lifford, quoted in Davey & Belluck, 2005, para. 21). EC's hormonal constitution is often cited as evidence of its normalcy: "The pills are essentially birth control pills in higher doses. But as their name suggests, they are not intended as regular birth control. They are for what advocates say they hope are rare instances of unprotected sex, or when, say, a condom breaks" (Zernike, 2003, para. 13–14). This delicate dance tends to eclipse clear definitional categories. Here, and in much of the public discussion regarding the ontological location of EC within reproductive politics, there is a clear conflation of terms. EC is simultaneously figured as not-at-all birth control and just like birth control; it is both unremarkable and everyday, extraordinary and exceptional.

The exception that marks and legitimates EC is, in part, affectively mobilized by the medication's tenuous relationship to abortion itself. At times, the abortion pill, or mifepristone,[6] simply functions as a counterpoint to distinguish EC and clarify its use: "Unlike Mifeprex or mifepristone, previously known as RU-486, which can induce an abortion safely during the first 49 days of pregnancy, morning-after pills do not cause abortion, advocates say" (Rein & Timberg, 2001, para. 17). Citing "advocates" in this way questions the distinction between EC and mifepristone, even as it is asserted. And indeed, the differences between these two medications are not always entirely clear; at times they are thoroughly confused. Summarizing noteworthy medical advances in 2003, *Time* stated that "Plan B, as the two-pill regimen would be called, would enable women to end pregnancies within 72 hours of unprotected intercourse" (Bjerklie, Park, & Song, 2004, para. 12). This clearly suggests EC as a method of terminating pregnancies, and implicitly invokes the abortion pill. While the technical language was corrected in a later issue, the original description merely exemplifies a common conflation of terms that tends to muddle and complicate EC's constitution. Throughout the discourse that attempts to anchor EC, the abortion pill is continually invoked to position and define EC. It is, at once, conflated with EC, and disarticulated from its function and intent. The instability and unfixity of EC within reproductive politics invites a particular logic to help manage cultural fears surrounding excess, a theme to which I now turn.

## Access to Sexual Excess, or the "Morning After" Problematic

Amidst muddled and contentious debates surrounding EC's nebulous location within reproductive politics, cultural anxieties begin to surface regarding women's, particularly young women's, (excess) sexuality. Certainly, these concerns mimic a similar impulse in response to the introduction of the birth control pill in 1960 and, to the extent that EC poses a unique set of circumstances, invite a new logic—namely, that of emergency—to manage female sexuality. As a contraceptive method designed to be taken after unprotected sex (a noteworthy and significant departure from other methods of birth control), EC is sutured to heightened convenience regarding the consumption of sex and sexuality, and thus problematized through a moral discourse that characterizes this technology as contributing to, if not wholly creating, sexual excess. In other words, EC is thought to be easy, convenient; it trivializes sex and encourages promiscuity. The proposal for over-the-counter status, the fact that EC "would not only be sold in drugstores, but could also be as available as aspirin, on supermarket shelves or in convenience stores or gasoline stations" (Kolata, 2003a, para. 3), rapidly accelerates the circulation of these concerns. To the extent that a morning-after pill might "encourage" women's sexual pleasure and independence through a proliferation of reproductive choice(s), it is simultaneously imagined to threaten a myriad of cultural norms, practices, and relationships of power.

The "problem" of women's sexual excess is overwhelmingly wedded to age. Embedded with a cultural climate of abstinence-only education, father-daughter "purity balls" in celebration of teenage girls' commitment to virginity, and pop stars like Jessica Simpson and Brittney Spears publicly discussing their "True Love Waits" pledges, young women's sexual expression quickly becomes a volatile site for debate regarding the moral dimensions of EC:

> If Plan B goes over the counter . . . what stops teenage girls from using these pills as regular birth control? Will we get to the point where 14-year-old girls are feeding quarters into restroom vending machines for something other than tampons? Will we see a rise in sexually transmitted infections? (Stepp, 2004, para. 5).

Over-the-counter EC is figured as access to excess—the impending seduction of too much choice. Indeed, increased availability of EC is thought to rival, perhaps even eclipse, the pill in validating irresponsible sex and rewarding "deviant"—or otherwise undisciplined—sexual behavior by evacuating it of "consequence," and by removing young women from the medical gaze altogether: "How can you make it available OTC [over the counter] for most women and not have it get into the bodies of girls for who it has not been approved without prescription?" (Wright, quoted in Kaufman, 2005, para. 9). Emerging in the midst of heightened neoconservatism, the resurgence of the religious right, and Bush-era family values politics, this explicit reference to young women's (or "girls") bodies positions EC as a direct threat to purity and virtue. Drawing on common representations of American girls in postfeminist culture (Projansky, 2007), girls at the center of the EC debates are figured as "at risk." They are "endangered by the world around them (including the proliferation of choices in part provided by feminism and postfeminism) and their personal choices within this context" (Projansky, 2007, p. 47–48). EC threatens young women in positing the possibility of unplanned sex without material (or, more specifically, maternal) consequence. It offers superfluous choice and warrants sexual excess; in other words, it provides young women the opportunity to make "bad" choices.

And yet, it is not just teens for whom explicit and expressed fears of sexual excess circulate; single women in general are figured to be "at risk." Reporting on the reactions of New Yorkers to the FDA's eventual easing of restrictions on EC access, Vasquez and Hammer (2006) write that one woman "could not decide whether she was glad the morning-after pill would soon be more readily available. Several of her friends have already used the pill multiple times" (para. 13–14). Throughout much of this discourse, there seems to exist a categorical limit that differentiates emergency from assumed carelessness. EC is regularly thought to enable and even encourage frivolous and irresponsible sex: "Knowing a backup is available over the counter, she said, might make her more likely to have unprotected sex. 'Some girls are probably going to get careless. . . . If I didn't get so sick I would use it more often'" (Vasquez & Hammer, 2006, para. 6–7). Women, it seems, are not to be trusted with this kind of decision-making. Indeed, left to their own devices and without the supervision of a medical professional, women will overuse, even abuse, this method of contraception.

And in some ways, how could they not? The name "morning-after pill" itself evokes and substantiates fears surrounding the threat of sexual excess: "No more trauma over 'Am I or am I not?' No more decisions on whether to abort, adopt, or go ahead and raise a child you can't afford. The morning-after pill, known as Plan B, erases the night before" (Stepp, 2004, para. 3). In a rare moment of candor and clarity, this reporter for the *New York Times* underscores a significant and profound source of cultural distress. The "morning after" implies a "night before"—a euphemism for licentious or otherwise amoral deeds. The "morning after" assumes shame, guilt, and regret for behavior in violation of normative codes of conduct. Thus, any "morning-after pill" is always already marked by and constituted through social and moral aberration. Well-behaved women don't have a "morning after" because they never had a night before. Thus, how can a pill, aimed only to alleviate ills brought on by one's own illicit or amoral action, be properly coded as a woman's rightful choice? This is, of course, precisely the problem—it cannot. Choice becomes a problematic, and ultimately ineffectual, public claim within the context of the EC debates, illustrating the discursive limits of choice with profound clarity. If not through a claim to choice, then, how is this tension negotiated; how is EC effectively legitimized? Having explored the tenuous location of EC within reproductive politics and culture more broadly, I turn now to examine the use of science and its mobilization of "emergency" and "exception" as a legitimizing force. These rhetorics work to effectively overwhelm and undermine the morning-after problematic of sexual excess in the wake of "too much" reproductive choice.

## SCIENCE, EMERGENCY, AND DIFFERENTIAL BIOPOLITICS

> [T]he distinction between social technologies and new reproductive ones is formal at best: not only are individuals being reproduced, but so too are the social relations that organize and render them recognizable as such.
>
> —Hartouni, 1997, p. 119

In order to bracket and refute claims regarding the erosion of female morality in the wake of EC, science becomes the broader discursive terrain that works to negotiate and temper questions of sexual purity and moral decay, while simultaneously introducing concerns regarding another kind of "excess" wed to reproduction itself. Through the logic of emergency, science is deployed to harness and manage cultural anxieties, discipline reproductive bodies, and to (re)inscribe a differential biopolitics.

Biopower, originally theorized by Michel Foucault (1990) in *The History of Sexuality* as "numerous and diverse techniques for achieving the subjegation of bodies and the control of populations" (p. 143), has received a fair amount of attention from contemporary theorists attending to the subtle transformations and adaptations of biopower under late capitalism (Roberts, 2009; Rose, 2007; Rose & Miller, 2008; Samerski, 2009; Sharma, 2009). Contemporary biopolitics are marked by a shift from state governance over the health of the population to a sustained attention to and investment in "biological citizenship" (Rose, 2007). This form of citizenship, Nikolas Rose explains, hinges on individual responsibility and risk management: "individuals themselves must exercise biological prudence, for their own sake, that of their families, that of their own lineage, and that of their nation as a whole" (Rose, 2007, p. 24). Furthermore, biological citizenship is both accompanied and extended by new forms of authority: "ethopolitics—the politics of how we should conduct ourselves appropriately in relation to ourselves, and in our responsibilities for the future—forms the milieu within which novel forms of authority are taking shape" (p. 27). This focus on individual responsibility, tied to broader cultural structures and informed by new forms of authority are crucial in understanding the use of science within the EC debates and its biopolitical implications.

Furthermore, Sharma's (2009) theorizing of "differential biopolitics" both extends and deepens understanding and analysis of EC in the realm of contemporary biopolitical formations. Sharma argues that, "[a] differential theory of biopolitics is necessary, not just to point out [complexity and multiplicity] . . . but in order to consider the various technologies of power/self and the affective dimension of these investments and reductions into human life" (p. 139). Her extension of biopolitics as "differential" accounts for complexity, difference, and nuance; it illuminates and interrogates systematic inclusions and exclusions that are both indicated and exacerbated by the form/functioning of biopower. As Sharma explains, "[t]he biopolitical regulation of life reduces *certain* life to bare life. At the same time it also invests in the lives of others, as in the maintenance of lifestyles. In other words *both* reductions and investments cultivate docile and productive bodies" (p. 139). Thus, differential biopolitics explicitly theorizes a means of grappling with difference in these contexts, an important dimension of any serious attempt to theorize power, if largely overlooked in most literature on biopolitics. Drawing on Sharma's work invites a thorough investigation of the (micro)technologies of reproductive self-government that are distributed differentially, or otherwise stratified, and that reinscribe a particular (gendered, racialized, classed) social order. A theory of differential biopolitics aides in understanding how science is affectively (and differentially) mobilized to legitimize EC, an argument to which I now turn.

First, science is posited as a direct challenge to the articulations between EC and promiscuity. In response to the morning-after problematic, repeated scientific accounts of EC's behavioral banality and women's sexual restraint become a common refrain: "Studies indicate that improving access to EC neither encourages sexual activity by adolescents nor causes women to abandon their regular methods of contraception" ("Public Health Victory," 2003, para. 5). Hard data are offered in support of these claims: "studies showed that making [EC] available did not prompt women to use it repeatedly. Of 540 women in one study, Dr. Camp said, 10 used it more than once" (Zernike, 2003, para. 26). Another report in the *Washington Post* draws a parallel between EC-inspired anxieties and those that circulate around other matters of sexual and reproductive health and rights:

> When sex education was introduced in schools, some Americans predicted that young people would start copulating like rabbits. Talking about sex would make kids have sex. Carefully controlled studies showed that hasn't been the case for the current generation. . . . It looks as if young women have learned something about abstinence and sex, and they don't make decisions about either because of what they can buy. (Stepp, 2004, para. 42–44)

In this way, scientific demonstration of women's sexual restraint—their adherence to EC as a method of exception and only in cases of emergency—becomes the logic through which EC is domesticated and proven palatable to broader U.S. publics. Research studies are regularly cited to counter the fear that this contraceptive technology will encourage, enable, and condone (young) women's sexual impulses. Hinging on popular and ideological assumptions of neutrality and freedom from bias, a discourse of science still works to position EC within a moral conceptual terrain as it articulates women as (appropriately) sexually disciplined, whose behavior is suspended, and indeed separate, from the availability of certain contraceptives.

Indeed, a rhetoric that frequently reverts to the exception disciplines reproductive bodies into traditional modes of maternity and proper feminine sexuality. As mentioned earlier, EC is clearly articulated as a form of birth control for emergency—and not ordinary—circumstances. Positioning EC as a method of *exception* allows for a circumvention of the problem of undisciplined or otherwise promiscuous sex, and renders EC compatible with mainstream, normative values regarding maternity and sexuality. In a particularly explicit example, EC is declared "not a form of birth control. It is there in case the birth control method fails. The condoms breaks, the diaphragm slips. A woman forgets to take her pills. Or she has sex when she wasn't planning on it" (Trafford, 2001, para. 7). In this moment, the use of EC designates extra care and responsibility in pregnancy prevention. Simultaneously, a variety of exceptional circumstances are identified so as to underscore an overwhelming presence of discipline and normative family planning measures within these scenarios, consequently recasting women's use of EC as similarly disciplined and normative. Implicit is the suggestion that EC is the "non-choice" that resides between the selection of a regular method of birth control, and the politicized right to an abortion—in other words, EC becomes the inevitable (and *responsible*) middle ground between one choice eclipsed and another suspended altogether. The discourse of emergency, then, works to articulate EC to extraordinary circumstance and, in so doing, disciplines its use (and women themselves) into normative codes of sexuality and "responsible" choices.

Discourses of science and the logic of emergency extend beyond a demonstration of individual restraint, however, and are implicated in the process of differential biopolitics. Science is mobilized in such a way that the fear of sexual excess is not simply deflated or minimized, but is entirely eclipsed by the circulation of a related, differentiated fear—that of reproductive excess. In other words, scientific studies of EC prove not only women's sexual restraint, but focus specifically on the potential of EC to address large scale social ills of unwanted or unplanned pregnancies and abortion. This repeated emphasis on reducing "unwanted" pregnancies effectively relocates concern from the *sexual* excess of women to the *reproductive* excess of certain women—namely, young, unmarried, and/or low-income women.

This troubling pattern is far from anomalous, but rather, is thoroughly embedded within broader cultural attitudes and public policies regarding reproduction. Historian Rickie Solinger (2005) points out that:

> Official discussions about reproductive politics have rarely been women-centered. More often than not, debate and discussion about reproductive politics—*where the power to manage women's reproductive capacity should reside*—have been part of discussions about *how to solve certain large social problems facing the country*. (p. 4; emphasis original)

EC adheres to this trend. First and foremost, it is contextualized in broad cultural terms, and is clearly aimed at relieving the large-scale social ills of "unwanted" pregnancy and abortion. The logic of emergency once again infuses discussions of EC's potential, which center on its ability to address these broader cultural concerns. Prior to the arrival of the over-the-counter debate in the U.S., early reporting focused on the loosening of restrictions to EC access in Europe and was framed in this manner:

> In the last decade, Britain has experienced a steady increase in the number of teenage pregnancies, unwanted pregnancies and abortions. In 1998, the last year for which figures are available, 22 percent of pregnancies ended in abortion. In addition, in a country struggling to promote a family-based agenda, 51.2 percent of new babies were born to unwed mothers. (Lyall, 2001, para. 5)

While this statistic was corrected a week later (the correct percentage of single mothers being 37.8), the anxiety expressed here is palpable; EC is explicitly imagined as redress for widespread and pressing social emergencies—specifically, the reproductive excesses of certain women. There is a rather frank articulation of which trends are deemed problematic—in this case, teenage and single mothers are isolated demographics amongst otherwise "unwanted" pregnancies and the overall rate of abortion. Indeed, single motherhood is cast in glaring opposition to the meaning of family itself.

Identifying and demonizing young and/or single women is neither unprecedented, nor should it be surprising when located within a history of reproductive politics in which certain women (mostly young, low-income, and/or of color) are socially and discursively figured as "unfit" mothers. Feminist scholars like Solinger (2001, 2005) and Dorothy Roberts (1997) have documented with painstaking precision the relationship between pregnancy and power in U.S. history, and the multiple histories of reproductive politics that are consistently overwhelmed by racism, classism, and sexism. From the earliest moments of the slave trade—when parental status was legally codified to privilege the economic interests of white slave owners over those of the bonded African women who bore children, many times as a result of rape—to the forced sterilization of low-income women, women of color, women with disabilities, queer women and/or immigrants through state funded programs throughout most of the twentieth century, what is made abundantly clear is that pregnancy—and maternity itself—are race and class privileges.

As a particular faction within broader reproductive politics, contraception is no exception. As Angela Davis (1981) explains, "class bias and racism crept into the birth control movement when it was still in its infancy. More and more, it was assumed within birth control circles that poor women, Black and immigrant alike, had a 'moral obligation to restrict the size of their families.' What was demanded as a 'right' for the privileged came to be interpreted as a 'duty' for the poor" (p. 210). In its function and potential use, EC may depart from contraceptive history in significant ways, and still, it is simultaneously disciplined and discursively located within the same tradition of managing social ills through women's bodies, and more insidiously, in attempts to manage the reproduction of certain populations in particular. Questions concerning contraception, reproduction, and who may or may not become a mother, are not bereft of politics; they are immersed within social relationships of power and privilege. Here, then, I wish to question which pregnancies are coded as "unwanted" and precisely who is allowed to name them as such, to underscore and interrogate the social and rhetorical articulation of EC as a solution to a set of moral and/or cultural problems. It becomes necessary to ask what kind of inclusions/exclusions the "emergency" delineates, which "choices" are deemed responsible and thereby defensible, and whose interests are being served.[7]

The use of science, its role in figuring excess and disciplining reproductive bodies, carries substantively distinct implications for women given social location—in other words, age, race, class, income, and marital status matter. Differential biopolitics can account for this reproductive stratification in the context of contemporary biopolitics; it provides a means of grappling with the complex ways in which women are differentially disciplined into normative codes for behavior. For women of race and class privilege, the central concern with sexual and moral purity is tamed through scientific demonstration of discipline and responsibility. "Rights" to EC are then properly conferred. Simultaneously, scientific justifications for EC that center on its macro implications—its potential capacity to reduce unwanted pregnancy and abortion—promises to harness the reproductive excess of "unfit" mothers, thus eclipsing rights and assigning responsibilities for women marginalized by age, income, race, and/or class. EC, whether through the differential biopolitics of reduction or investment, enables a strict enforcement of traditional "family values," while simultaneously disciplining "choice" back into white, middle-class, mainstream frameworks, an argument to which I now turn.

## DIFFERENTIAL DISCIPLINE AND THE DISCURSIVE LIMITS OF CHOICE

Thus far, I have focused on the public imagining of EC, the contingent and nebulous ontological terrain it is thought to inhabit, and the precarious relationships among excess, morality, and science it is thought to traverse and resolve through a logic of exception and emergency. Here, I turn to the specificity of this negotiation as it relates to the notion of choice and its implications for reproductive politics more broadly.

Rhetorics of choice are largely absent within the contentious debates that ensued regarding Plan B's over-the-counter application. This noteworthy departure from mainstream frameworks for birth control and abortion is perhaps less surprising upon close examination. Choice is politically and culturally incompatible with a method of contraception that is already marked by superfluous individual control. That is, in the midst of heightened cultural anxieties regarding the sexual and reproductive excesses of women, what became necessary was not a defense of choice, but a demonstration of discipline. The discourse of emergency properly circumscribes EC within "acceptable" use. To the extent that EC is constituted through a logic of exception and emergency, as a reasonable and responsible attempt to avoid having to choose abortion, EC is disciplined and legitimized as a "choice." At best, then, choice is culturally palatable and socially defensible only to the degree that it is wed to planning, responsibility, and normative sexuality and reproduction. Or perhaps, more insidiously, the logic of exception mobilizes a *suspension* of reproductive freedom and choice. EC is subsequently ontologized within this space as the *non-choice of necessity*. In either instance, the debates concerning EC's over-the-counter status lay bare the more problematic complexities and discursive limits of an "inalienable right to choose."

While the EC debates illustrate well the discursive limits of choice, it is hardly an aberration with the broader context of reproductive politics. Rather, it provides yet another example of the inability of "choice" to fully encapsulate and advance full reproductive autonomy and dignity for all women. Choice has been critiqued along these lines by feminist scholars and activists alike (see, for example, Davis, 1983; Mamo & Fosket, 2009; Roberts, 1997, 2009; Samerski, 2009; Solinger, 2001, 2005). As a discourse of consumption, choice is troubled in at least two ways. First, in lieu of possessing a claim to inalienable rights or justice, women's reproductive decisions are easily trivialized and denied through the language of choice. "Choice" is easily reduced to whimsical behavior or brash decision-making, as opposed to being located within a myriad of social and political structures that sharply delineates its borders. For Solinger (2001), choice is, at best, a *derivative* of rights—a kind of "rights lite": "by the end of the 1970s, fathers were recognized as having rights, fetuses were granted rights, and 'children's rights' were newly and broadly acknowledged. Women, on the other hand, were accorded only 'choice'" (p. 193). Thus, in the realm of reproduction, women's claims to autonomy, freedom, and/or protection under the law are rhetorically and materially relegated to a kind of peripheral status, subsumed within a discourse that assigns rights to every imaginable party within the process of conception and childbearing except the woman herself. Unlike possessing a claim to reproductive *rights*, *equality*, or *justice*, women's reproductive *choice* is rendered vulnerable to market analysis, public scrutiny, and social judgment. This marginalization enables the wholesale denial of reproductive choice for many women. Like any other consumptive practice, subject to the inequities exacerbated through free market capitalism, choice is accorded through one's ability to pay. Roberts (1997) refers to this as a negative conception of liberty, which allows states to guarantee legal, but not economic, access to reproductive choice. As such, women's decisions are largely determined by income: wealth equals access to a range of maternal and reproductive options; poverty or a reliance on public funding for health care translates into governmental regulation of one's reproductive health-care decisions.

Second, within the context of contemporary biopolitics and neoliberalism, the language of choice itself has been effectively co-opted and used against women. Silja Samerski's (2009) study of genetic counseling examines the use of "choice" to cover over a kind of "compulsory self-determination": "the call for responsible decision-making under the shadow of genes and risks must be understood as a social engineering technique . . . [that] makes women powerless while holding them responsible" (p. 744). Furthermore, Samerski argues: "Freedom, choice, and autonomy are being redefined in a way that requires scientific input and guidance services in order for them to be appropriately exercised" (p. 755). In other words, "choice" no longer means the same way. Mainstream feminisms of the 1960s and 1970s claims to a "woman's right to choose" is, and has been, easily absorbed and appropriated by a broader discourse of consumption and responsibility that troubles inclusion and solidarity within feminist communities, and the very notion of reproductive autonomy itself.

In this way, the EC debates offer another demonstration of the ease with which choice is adapted within dominant ideological frameworks and used to reinforce the status quo. In the case of the EC over-the-counter debates, these vulnerabilities are revealed and exacerbated to the extent that a "morning-after" contraceptive always already invites the assumption of carelessness and promiscuity from the night before. Choice, in this context, becomes difficult to defend and maintain. Indeed, what becomes exceedingly clear in these debates is that choice is only culturally legible and defensible to the extent that it is sutured to notions of planning and responsibility, terms clearly imbued with a kind of *doxa* that excludes the possibility of sex, reproduction, or maternity outside of culturally legitimate and authorized settings. Access to EC over the counter is subsequently bracketed by a narrow set of circumstances that are rhetorically clarified through a logic of emergency, with differential biopolitical implications. Some women are accorded rights, others responsibilities—distinctions that continue to deepen, rather than redress, divisions between women within the context of reproductive politics. At best, choice is inadequate in securing reproductive rights for all women; at worst, it works to reinscribe the very inequities and disparities it ought to dismantle, all under the banner of feminism.

For far too long women's access to sexual, reproductive, and maternal rights have hinged on race, class, and other forms of privilege. To the extent that a concern for all women's health and lives are not located at the center of mainstream debates concerning reproductive justice, to the extent that public discourse is centered on addressing broader social issues through the management of pregnancy and women's bodies—we continue to dwell in this treacherous terrain. Indeed, these debates exemplify the discursive limits of "choice" as a framework to secure all women's access to health and justice. Perhaps in an era of choice, then, our ability to interrogate and problematize discursive apparatuses that privilege some women at the expense of others, to explore, imagine, and articulate alternative possibilities, will bring us one step closer to a more radically inclusive maternal and reproductive dignity.

## REFERENCES

A public health victory. (2003, December 18). *New York Times*, p. A42. Retrieved April 7, 2009, from LexisNexis Academic database.

Adams, K., & Crumley, B. (1997, March 10). Health report. *Time, 149*, p. 24. Retrieved March 31, 2009, from Academic Search Premier database.

Bjerklie, D., Park, A., & Song, S. (2004, January 19). A to Z guide. *Time, 163*, pp. 120–32. Retrieved March 31, 2009, from Academic Search Premier database.

Davey, M., & Belluck, P. (2005, April 19). Pharmacies balk on after-sex pill and widen fight. *New York Times*. Retrieved April 7, 2009, from LexisNexis Academic database.

Davis, A. Y. (1983). *Women, race, and class*. New York: Vintage Books.

Feenberg, A. (1991). *Critical theory of technology*. New York: Oxford University Press.

Feenberg, A. (2003). Democratic rationalization: Technology, power, and freedom. In R. C. Scharff & V. Dusek (Eds.), *Philosophy of technology: The technological condition*. Malden, MA: Blackwell Publishing.

Foucault, M. (1990). *The History of Sexuality, Volume 1: An Introduction* (R. Hurley, Trans. Vintage Books ed.). New York: Vintage Books.

Goodman, E. (2004, February 29). A workable plan for fewer abortions. *Washington Post*, p. B7. Retrieved April 7, 2009, from LexisNexis Academic database.

Gordon, L. (2007). *The moral property of women: A history of birth control politics in America*. Chicago: University of Illinois Press.

Harris, G. (2005, September 1). Official quits on pill delay at the F.D.A. *New York Times*. Retrieved April 7, 2009, from LexisNexis Academic database.

Hartouni, V. (1997). *Cultural conceptions: On reproductive technologies and the remaking of life*. Minneapolis: University of Minnesota Press.

Johnson, J. A., & Burrows, V. K. (2007). *Emergency contraception: Plan B*. Washington, D.C.: Congressional Research Service: Report for Congress.

Kaufman, M. (2005, August 27). FDA Delays Decision on Plan B Contraceptive. *Washington Post*, p. A1. Retrieved April 7, 2009, from LexisNexis Academic database.

Kolata, G. (2003a, December 12). Debate on selling morning-after pill over the counter. *New York Times*, p. A1. Retrieved April 7, 2009, from LexisNexis Academic database.

Kolata, G. (2003b, December 17). A contraceptive clears a hurdle to wider access. *New York Times*, p. A1. Retrieved April 7, 2009, from LexisNexis Academic database.

Lyall, S. (2001, January 15). Britain allows over-the-counter sales of morning-after pill. *New York Times*, p. A4. Retrieved April 7, 2009, from LexisNexis Academic database.

Mamo, L., & Fosket, J. R. (Summer 2009). Scripting the body: Pharmaceuticals and the (re)making of menstruation. *Signs: Journal of Women in Culture and Society, 34*(4), 925–49.

Marvin, C. (1988). *When old technologies were new: Thinking about communications in the late nineteenth century*. New York: Oxford University Press.

Projansky, S. (2007). Mass magazine cover girls: Some reflections on postfeminist girls and postfeminism's daughters. In Y. Tasker & D. Negra (Eds.), *Interrogating postfeminism: Gender and the politics of popular culture*. Durham, NC: Duke University Press.

Redfearn, S. (2002, May 21). Preparing for a mistake: For emergency birth control, plan ahead. *Washington Post*, p. F1. Retrieved April 7, 2009, from LexisNexis Academic database.

Rein, L., & Timberg, C. (2001, February 21). Emergency birth control approved; Bill calls for access without prescription. *Washington Post*, p. A1. Retrieved April 7, 2009, from LexisNexis Academic Database.

Roberts, D. (1997). *Killing the black body: Race, reproduction, and the meaning of liberty*. New York: Pantheon Books.

Roberts, D. (Summer 2009). Race, gender, and genetic technologies: A new reproductive dystopia? *Signs: Journal of Women in Culture and Society, 34*(4), 783–804.

Rogers, A. (1999, Spring/Summer Special Edition). Options beyond the pill. *Newsweek, 133,* p. 39. Retrieved March 31, 2009, from Academic Search Premier.

Rose, N. S. (2007). *The politics of life itself: Biomedicine, power, and subjectivity in the twenty-first century*. Princeton, NJ: Princeton University Press.

Rose, N., & Miller, P. (2008). *Governing the present: Administering economic, social and personal life*. Cambridge: Polity Press.

Samerski, S. (Summer 2009). Genetic counseling and the fiction of choice: Taught self-determination as a new technique of social engineering. *Signs: Journal of Women in Culture and Society, 34*(4), 735–61.

Sharma, S. (2009). Baring life and lifestyle in the non-place. *Cultural Studies, 23*(1), 129–48.

Shorto, R. (2006, May 7). Contra-contraception. *New York Times Magazine, 48.* Retrieved April 7, 2009, from LexisNexis Academic Database.

Slack, J. D., & Wise, J. M. (2005). *Culture and technology: A primer*. New York: Peter Lang Publishing Inc.

Sloop, J. M. (2000). Disciplining the transgendered: Brandon Teena, public representation, and normativity. *Western Journal of Communication, 64*(2), 165–89.

Solinger, R. (2001). *Beggars and choosers: How the politics of choice shapes adoption, abortion, and welfare in the United States*. New York: Hill and Wang.

Solinger, R. (2005). *Pregnancy and power: A short history of reproductive politics in America*. New York: New York University Press.

Spigel, L. (2001). *Welcome to the dreamhouse: Popular media and postwar suburbs (Console-ing passions)*. Durham, NC: Duke University Press.

Stepp, L. S. (2004, February 10). With birth control, Plan B is topic a. *Washington Post,* p. C1. Retrieved April 7, 2009, from LexisNexis Academic database.

Trafford, A. (2001, May 15). Second opinion. *Washington Post*, p. T4. Retrieved April 7, 2009, from LexisNexis Academic database.

Vasquez, E., & Hammer, K. (2006, August 26). Easier access to Plan B pill evokes praise, and concern. *New York Times,* p. B3. Retrieved April 7, 2009, from LexisNexis Academic database.

Zernike, K. (2003, May 19). Use of morning-after pill rising and it may go over the counter. *New York Times,* p. 1. Retrieved April 7, 2009, from LexisNexis Academic database.

## NOTES

1. In using this term, I explicitly draw on the work of Sarah Sharma (2009). Sharma theorizes a differential biopolitics" in order to account for complexity, multiplicity, and nuance within the form and functioning of contemporary biopolitical power formations. Her work readily informs my analysis, and will be more thoroughly explored within this chapter.

2. The author would like to thank J. Robert Cox, Sarah Sharma, Billie Murray, Julia T. Wood, Lynn O'Brien Hallstein, and Sara Hayden for their valuable insights and generous feedback on this manuscript.

3. Emergency Contraception is a method of preventing pregnancy after unprotected sex. There are distinctions between various methods of EC. The most common method is an oral medication that consists of concentrated doses of birth control hormones. It can prevent pregnancy up to five days after unprotected sex. Until 1997, the only oral EC available to women was an off-label use of the pill that some physicians would prescribe in particular circumstances. At the invitation of the Food and Drug Association (FDA), two small drug manufacturers developed medications specifically for "emergency" use—Preven (approved for sales in the United States in 1998) and Plan B (approved in 1999). Preven was recently removed from the market; Plan B is at the center of the over-the-counter (OTC) debate and thus the focus of this study. The second form of EC is a copper IUD, which must be inserted by a medical doctor shortly after unprotected sex. This method is not nearly as common.

4. The FDA does not intervene in the practice of medicine, but rather regulates which medications are available for sale in the United States, and how they are to be distributed (over the counter, or by prescription only). An off-label use of a drug, then, refers to "use for an indication, dosage form, dose regimen, population or other use parameter not mentioned in the approved labeling" (Johnson & Burrows, 2007, p. 3).

5. Primary sources include all articles having to do with EC published in the *New York Times*, the *Washington Post*, the *New York Times Magazine*, *Time*, and *Newsweek* during the specified ten-year timeframe.

6. Mifepristone is used to terminate a pregnancy within the first forty-nine days of gestation (this is the FDA's recommended guidelines for use; many medical facilities will use mifepristone within the first sixty-three days of gestation). While entirely distinct from EC in its synthetic composition and use, mifepristone is also (perhaps obviously) used after unprotected sex and was approved for sale in the United States in September 2000, just over a year after Plan B. Confusion of these medications in mediated and public forums abound.

7. Perhaps not surprisingly, the final ruling on Plan B's OTC application was an unprecedented one. EC was made available behind-the-counter without a prescription, to women eighteen and older. Pharmacists were authorized to dispense Plan

B to adult women, leaving pharmacists in a powerful position to determine who is ultimately provided access to EC. The history of pharmacist dispensing of EC is, itself, mired in controversy over "conscience" clauses and the right of a pharmacist to refuse women's requests. While these issues extend beyond the scope of this chapter, I explore this as a form of ethopolitics more thoroughly in my longer study of emergency con(tra)ceptions.

3

# POLITICIZING PERSONAL CHOICES?

## The Storying of Age-Related Infertility in Public Discourses

*Jennifer J. Bute, Lynn M. Harter, Erika L. Kirby, Marie Thompson*

Public discourses about age-related infertility (ARI) have been readily available in mainstream outlets since the controversial publication of Sylvia Hewlett's (2002) *Creating a Life: Professional Women and the Quest for Children*, which was accompanied by the author's many talk-show appearances and various articles "sound-byting" her book. The book itself and much of the resulting media coverage featured the personal narratives of women who waited until their late thirties and beyond to have children and then faced the devastating nature of ARI. Around the same time that Hewlett's book caught the public's attention, the American Society for Reproductive Medicine (ASRM) introduced the "Protect your Fertility" campaign, which included ads highlighting the correlations between infertility and smoking, obesity, and sexually transmitted infections. Perhaps the most striking ad of the campaign focused on ARI, offering the image of an upside-down baby bottle in the shape of an hourglass with the text "women in their twenties and thirties are most likely to conceive."

As public discussion of Hewlett's book and the ASRM campaign unfolded, much of the debate centered on the notion of choice, more specifically the choice to delay childbearing and the concomitant consequences of this choice. Hewlett, members of the ASRM, and journalists drawing attention to ARI envisioned their rhetoric as a public service to guide women in making informed choices in the midst of widespread confusion about infertility. A case in point: in a survey conducted by the American Fertility Association (AFA), only 13 percent of respondents knew that fertility generally begins to decline at age twenty-seven, and close to 40 percent thought it declined at age forty (cited in Seward, 2002, para. 12). In the wake of such confusion, experts sought to warn women to consider the potential implications of their choices. For example, an April 2002 cover of *Time* posed a naked baby on a piled-high inbox and asked "Babies vs. careers—Which should come first for women who want both?" The accompanying article (Gibbs, 2002) chronicled Hewlett's thesis of the "creeping non-choice" that occurs for women who put their careers first, wait until it is "too late" to have a baby, and subsequently experience the "despair" of ARI. Early in her text, Hewlett argued, "It behooves the next generation to pay attention. By doing so, twenty-something women might be able to avoid the cruel choices that dogged the footsteps of their older sisters" (p. 35). While the book got a "glowing, almost uncritical reception . . . from the media" (see Walsh, 2002, para. 5), Hewlett's efforts came under fire from feminists for at best oversimplifying a complex issue and at worst "calling for a retreat to hearth and home, where motherhood comes before every other role" (Gibbs, 2002, p. 54). Meanwhile, ASRM members expressed frustration about the ineffectiveness of their campaign: "Six years ago, the American Society for Reproductive Medicine tried to warn women that they were waiting until too late to have children," shared Dr. Marcel Cedars, a reproductive endocrinologist, "women just didn't get it" (National Public Radio [NPR], 2008, p. 2).

Indeed, as public discourses about ARI persist, most experts and commentators continue to bemoan the choice to delay childbearing. In this way, the concept of reproductive choice is pervasive in public discussions and media coverage of ARI. Primary themes woven throughout Hewlett's book, mediated commentary on the book, and ongoing responses to ASRM educational efforts, have centered on individual decisions regarding whether and when to have children. These personal choices are framed almost exclusively as choices made by women who eventually regret choosing too late to start a family. As a result, women then face what Hewlett calls a "creeping non-choice" in which biological realities limit the possibility of producing offspring, sometimes making pregnancy an impossible goal to achieve. As such, women are encouraged to make smart choices (e.g., by planning their childbearing strategically) to prevent such catastrophe.

Inspired to investigate the discursive framing of choice in ongoing discussions of ARI, we use a poststructural feminist reading to explore the discursive moves through which ARI and related reproductive choices have been storied in public discourses. Our central purpose is not to argue whether or not ARI is a physiological reality. This would be a formidable task, as it is difficult to find medical professionals who disagree with the assumption that women (and men) are indeed more likely to conceive and carry a child to term before their late thirties. Rather, our primary goal is to interrogate the ways in which the notion of choice is socially constructed and imbued with cultural values as authors, medical experts, journalists, and commentators ponder ARI in public debates. We recognize that human experiences are simultaneously material and corporeal, on the one hand, and instilled with culturally defined meaning on the other. As poststructural feminists, we seek to understand how discursive practices construct beliefs and inform cultural practices and to illuminate means whereby we can contest prevalent meanings of a social order.

In taking a discursive turn, we focused on "the range of symbolic activities by which members of a culture name, legitimize, and establish meanings for social organization" (Wood, 1994, p. 123). Through our analysis of discourses we asked: How is Hewlett's work, and the personal stories therein taken up and played out in other mediated discourses? What is gained and lost when the political nature of individual reproductive choices is minimized as personal stories move through public domains? What is emphasized, what is not, and what are the potential consequences of these representations? As we present our analysis, we first position infertility as a salient issue for poststructural feminists and then outline our theoretical and methodological approach to analyzing ARI public discourses. Through our analysis, we illustrate the general failure of these personal stories to politicize the sociohistorical, institutional, and material nature of ARI specifically and reproductive choices more broadly. We conclude by noting the limits of narratives as rhetorical resources in feminist movements and public health initiatives when attention does not extend beyond individual expressions and choices to redress forces that shape and constrain human agency.

## AGE-RELATED INFERTILITY AND REPRODUCTIVE CHOICE AS A POSTSTRUCTURAL FEMINIST ISSUE

As the "waves" of feminism evolve, the importance of reproductive choice remains central to women's empowerment in public and private spheres. Since feminist history is a process perpetually in motion (Siegel, 1997), these issues have taken several forms in the United States across generations. In the early 1900s, Margaret Sanger connected reproductive rights to women's economic and social equality, and by 1942 the Birth Control League (later to become Planned Parenthood) was established (Lunardini, 1994). In 1960, the Federal Food and Drug Administration approved "the pill," and in 1973 the *Roe v. Wade* Supreme Court decision legalized abortion (Weatherford, 1994). At the same time, we have witnessed changing demographics in workplaces and legislative and employer initiatives aimed at helping employees (usually women) negotiate the increasingly complex responsibilities of work and family (Kirby & Krone, 2002). Due in large part to these processes and outcomes generated by first and second wave feminists, the ability to control one's fertility through a range of reproductive choices has become a taken-for-granted part of life for many women of the "third wave" in the United States. Not surprisingly, then, the recent public debate about ARI and its implications for "women" as they perform work and family refocused sharp attention on reproductive choices.

Public discourses about ARI also speak to the importance poststructural feminists place on "everyday discourses" (Aldoory & Toth, 2001). Alfonso and Trigilio (1997) asserted that to go beyond the limits of academic feminisms, we need to address the "socio-political problems ordinary women of different races, classes, sexualities, ethnicities face in their everyday lives" (p. 10). Whether or not women are personally coping with ARI, most have considered what is at the heart of this debate—whether and when to have children, whether and when to work outside the home, and how these life priorities can coexist. Reproductive rights and choices represent continuity throughout the "waves" of western feminisms even as these issues take unique forms across time and space. In the next section, we articulate our theoretical standpoint and how this shaped our reading of the discourses.

## A Poststructural Feminist and Narrative Standpoint

Drawing inspiration from Foucault (1972, 1980, 1973/1984), among others, poststructural feminists emphasize the constitutive power of discourses in ordering relational and communal life—arrangements that come to be perceived as normal, natural, and often incontestable (e.g., Weedon, 1987; Fraser, 1989). From a poststructural feminist standpoint, discourses make possible (and discourage) patterns of relating and organizing, and are materially grounded in the practices of everyday life. To participate in communal life, individuals depend on a general knowledge of shared signifying systems. Over time, routines develop and understandings solidify about "how things are done" and "what things mean."

A key task of the critic is to explore the situated, interrelated, and multivocal discourses through which power and control are continually constructed, masked, and contested (Dow & Condit, 2005). We rely on poststructural feminist theory and several key Foucauldian concepts to explore the historically contingent and socially constructed nature of gendered-power relations. Foucault offered an understanding of power not as a possession but as a *process*—dispersed and evident in discourses and inscribed in social practices. As Foucault (1980) argued: "There are manifold relations of power which cannot themselves be established, consolidated nor implemented without the production, accumulation, circulation and functioning of a discourse" (p. 93). Power is present in every relationship, unavoidable, and productive as well as repressive. Contemporary poststructural feminists explore power relations of everyday life by focusing on connections between signifying practices, subject positions, and subjugated knowledges (e.g., Ashcraft & Mumby, 2005; Buzzanell & Liu, 2005; Weedon, 1987). In particular, our analysis of ARI discourses draws on poststructural and Foucauldian sensibilities to underscore how the social construction of personal choice reflects individualistic ideologies and reinscribes gendered-power relations at work in our culture.

Poststructural feminists agree that *narratives* remain primary rhetorical resources through which some subject positions are legitimized and privileged (e.g., to be a woman is to be a mother) while others are disqualified or denied expression (e.g., to be infertile is the result of bad choices). Feminists rely on storytelling to raise consciousness about lived inequities and emphasize that the personal is political, meaning, among other things, that personal experience is inescapably social, and social experience is inescapably political (Fixmer & Wood, 2005).

The social world is a world of narrative forms and formulas that summon multiple forms of privilege and exclusion through their tenacious familiarity (e.g., metanarrative of technology as progress; Harter, Japp, & Beck, 2005). Poststructural feminists encourage attention to how personal lives are embedded in larger narrative landscapes—times and spaces that shape our lives and how we story them (e.g., Trethewey, 2001). In turn, poststructural feminists focus attention on the ideological nature of storying our lived experiences with an eye toward social, political, corporeal, and economic consequences. Storytelling is not a benign process—narratives are inherently partial and imbued with cultural values and struggles. History cannot escape the perspective that dominates its narrative expression, and ARI discourses are no exception. Poststructural feminists ask how "needs" are defined and interpreted, by whom and for whom and with what consequence? Whose ARI narratives are told? Why are narratives, and the choices discussed therein, framed the way they are and to what ends? A defining feature of poststructural feminist work is the inclination to ask: which personal and whose politics?

Finally, cultural stocks of meaning are neither static nor fixed. Narrative sensemaking is an indeterminate process. Rather than representing the inner state of a narrator, meaning is coconstructed between people. Much to the contrary of dominant literature, narratives are rarely self-contained and structured linguistic events (i.e., beginning, climax, end; Boje, 2001). Stories unfold as fragments and are challenged and changed to meet institutional and individual needs. Stories evolve across time as different constituencies take up and play out others' stories. A dialogic perspective permits movement from a message production standpoint (i.e., storyteller as sole owner of story) toward one that recognizes how narratives are fluid, coconstructed, meaning-centered productions of experience achieved in particular contexts and subject to varying frames of intelligibility. From this perspective, it is critical to explore the discourses of Hewlett and the ASRM and those who furthered the public conversation about ARI.

Drawing on poststructural feminist and narrative theory, we problematize the discursive framing of ARI. We collected discourses by performing a search for ARI in newspapers, magazines/journals, and news broadcasts archived in LexusNexus Academic Universe. The search was limited to the years 2002–2008 to restrict the data to articles relevant to analysis of Hewlett's (2002) work, the ASRM campaign and pamphlets surrounding ARI (ASRM, 2002, 2003), and much-publicized medical studies focusing on ARI in women (e.g., Bewley, Davies, & Bruade, 2005) and men (e.g., Lewis, Legato, & Fisch, 2006). Across obtained discourses, there were periods of intense discussion (e.g., April-May 2002; September-October 2005; summer 2008) and then months with little or no attention to the topic before a resurgence in public conversation. In total, the database included Hewlett's (2002) book, Fisch's (2005) book, several network television programs (*60 Minutes*, *Oprah*), organizational websites (e.g., ASRM, NOW), and sixty-eight articles (a complete list of discourses we analyzed is available from the authors). Although much of the mediated discourses we examined occurred in response to Hewlett's book, we also analyzed more recent articles and broadcasts that grappled with the issue of ARI (e.g., the 2008 NPR broadcast).

Once we collected discourses, we read them with poststructural feminist and narrative sensibilities. We approached narrative from an explicitly broad vantage point, casting a wide net that included autobiographical stories, institutional plots, and societal scripts. We continually moved between the personal stories of ARI, and the dominant narrative script of ARI—a master narrative that was shaped by personal narratives. We unpacked the aspects of personal narratives that gave rise to the dominant script of ARI, and the dimensions left in the shadows of the hegemonic plot. Finally, we explored how these discursive moves shaped possibilities for political action and fixed meaning in particular ways. Our analysis is organized around: (a) the plotlines of personal choices in ARI discourses; (b) whose choices are discussed and neglected in the cast of characters and narrators featured in stories of ARI, and (c) the (un)politicizing of personal choices in ARI narratives. In reporting the findings of our analysis, we focus not only on Hewlett's book as a source of discourse but also on the key themes from her book that were taken up in public discussions. In addition, we include in our analysis themes from media debates surrounding published studies of ARI and continuing discussions of ARI as a public health issue.

## PLOTLINES OF PERSONAL CHOICES IN ARI DISCOURSES

Early in her book, Hewlett (2002) thanked the women of the "breakthrough" generation who shared the "rare gift" of their stories with her, explaining, "The plotline of these lives is important: what worked, what went wrong. But the emotional arc is crucial as well. It is profoundly important to understand what these women now regret, and what they glory in" (p. 36). Throughout her volume, Hewlett highlighted the regretful personal choices made by women who prioritized their careers and neglected starting a family. She began her first chapter with the poignant, regret-filled narrative of Wendy, a talented playwright who struggled to get pregnant for ten years before finally getting a child "in under the wire" (p. 36). Hewlett recounted Wendy's agonizing journey, including years of unsuccessful fertility treatments, and noted how Wendy's decision to focus on her career "hindered her ability to have a family" (p. 41), a theme echoed in the stories of other women throughout the book.

Rearticulations of Hewlett's (2002) text and coverage of the ASRM campaign, and ARI in general, in the popular media brought women's narratives of choice to a broader audience and introduced new stories into public conversations about ARI. Newspaper accounts, magazine articles, and television shows featured ARI as a topic of interest and often included summaries of Hewlett's book and references to the ASRM campaign.

Indeed, Hewlett herself became the public face of ARI in 2002 as she made the television talk show circuit and was featured in numerous articles after the release of her book. As Hewlett became a lead character in the dominant public narrative of ARI, other women shared their own experiences. In May 2002, *The Oprah Winfrey Show* dedicated an entire episode to the discussion of ARI. The episode included an interview with Hewlett as well as segments featuring women coping with ARI, like Diana, who married her husband at age thirty-six, bought a six-bedroom home, and at age thirty-nine had yet to become pregnant. As Diana showed Oprah's viewers the room she decorated for a nursery, she explained her feelings of pain and disappointment: "I feel like I've hit a wall. I'm angry at my body. It's as if my body is betraying me" (p. 14). Like the women in Hewlett's text, Diana shared a story of grief, anguish, and regret.

In the emergent dominant script of ARI, choices regarding reproduction and work/life balance were discursively positioned as women's issues, as illustrated in headlines like this from the *Houston Chronicle*: "In the struggle to balance career and motherhood, many women are left wondering if they waited too long; Is time running out?" (Fergus, 2002, L-1). Women's choices and life plans were continually questioned and condemned, even as individual woman shared poignant stories with a captivated audience. Hjul (2002) described the dominant narrative of ARI constructed by Hewlett as an "alarmist story which implies that all ambitious, successful females must be aching inside, clutching their barren bellies and regretting the day they chose boardroom over labor rooms" (p. 14). Hewlett and various commentators presented the emotionally compelling stories of women who have experienced the creeping non-choice as tales of loss, despair, grief, struggle, resentment, and regret. Sue, for instance, shared the following story:

> You know, whenever you think you've come to terms with it—this business of not having children—it crops up again in another form. I try not to think about it, but when my parents die, I'll have to deal with not having kids yet again. I now see it as a rolling loss. (Hewlett, 2002, p. 72)

One of Hewlett's (2002) expressed goals in sharing these stories was to educate young women so that they don't make the same "mistakes" (i.e., poor choices) as women of the breakthrough generation. Indeed, many of the women Hewlett interviewed explicitly articulated desires to advise young women about making smart choices. A prominent theme throughout Hewlett's text, as well as subsequent public commentaries (e.g., Bewley et al., 2005), is to compel younger women to be as intentional and strategic in planning their personal lives as they are in planning their professional lives. Likewise, the ASRM campaign relied on visual and verbal narratives to raise consciousness and remind women to make smart choices by keeping their plans to have children in mind.

In some ways, the storytelling turn by activists who want to promote "better" choices is a smart move given that narratives can function as cultural markers of concern and move people to action. Indeed, this was Bewley and colleagues' intent when they published a 2005 editorial in the *British Medical Journal* warning women about ARI: "All we're saying is, if you saw a herd of people traveling north, you'd say, 'It's getting colder, take some warm clothes!' There's a herd of women drifting into a hazardous state. We are picking up the pieces" (in Williams, 2005, para. 8). By representing particular events, characters, obligations, and choices, these stories display for audience members what one "ought" to do. Feminist responses to these discourses have been varied. Kim Gandy of the National Organization for Women (NOW) cautioned that "the idea that you can choose what age you'll be to have your children is a ludicrous proposition for most women" (Kalb, Springen, Scelfo, & Pierce, p. 40). Yet "third wave" feminist advocate Amy Richards refuted accusations that such information makes women feel guilty or puts pressure on them to leave the workforce—she argued, "what is really antifeminist is withholding information from women on the grounds that they will then make the wrong choice" (as cited in Miller, 2008, para. 9). Cottle (2002a) agreed that:

> [W]hile we certainly don't want to scare 22-year-old gals into having kids before they're ready, neither should we keep assuring 39-year-olds they have all the time in the world. They don't. You can get as outraged as you like about that fact, but it is a biological rather than a social injustice—and thus not particularly prone to political pressure. (para. 5)

Some medical experts have even suggested that in the spirit of guiding smart decisions, ARI should become a part of sex education curricula; as argued by Lisa Jardine of the Human Fertilization and Embryology Authority (HFEA): "instead of all the teaching at school being about how to stop getting pregnant, someone had better start teaching about how you do get pregnant, because there are going to be a lot of extremely disappointed people out there" (Lewis, 2008, para. 3). Throughout mediated discourses of ARI, and particularly in the personal, painful narratives of individual women, alarm about the creeping possibility of a non-choice and advocacy for making smart choices work together to warn women about the dangerous consequences of choosing too late.

Such narratives reveal the harsh realities for some women facing ARI, and we honor and respect these women for sharing their stories. The personal has always been the material of feminist theory and practice. Indeed, these stories couple congenial faces and names with an otherwise distant and, often times medicalized, set of experiences. Even so, the stories of these women have been aestheticized; they "invite us to share in the private lives and problems of likable characters" (Condit, 1994, p. 220). As a result, it is tempting to accept their accounts of ARI as typical. We engage these storied discourses from a sympathetic yet critical standpoint. An enriched and complicated feminism is one that recognizes a *plurality* of perspectives and the political underpinnings of personal life. In the next section, we interrogate the relative homogeneity of personal choices as reinscribed in ARI discourses, and draw attention to choices and agents rendered invisible.

## THE CAST OF CHARACTERS AND NARRATORS

What is deeply unsettling about the flurry of ARI public discourses is the absence of diverse characters and narrators. In many ways, what is *not* being said, by whom, and about whom is as interesting (and problematic) as what is articulated. Differences and multiplicities within and between women are at best ignored and at worst dismissed. As such, some women's reproductive choices are condemned and criticized while other women, and men, are completely ignored. This is particularly problematic given contemporary feminist agendas that seek to "build a new kind of solidarity that recognizes and brings together blurred, overlapping, and sometimes contradictory facets of women's identities" (Fixmer & Wood, 2005, p. 237). We highlight the select voices in Hewlett's work and the broader conversation, and discuss the notably absent standpoints of men and non–"high-achieving" women, which resulted in a particularly narrow framing of reproductive choice.

### The Presence (and Absence) of Women

Hewlett's (2002) efforts began as a celebration of the breakthrough generation—women who became powerful figures in fields previously dominated by men. Unexpectedly, Hewlett discovered many of the characters she labeled as "high-achieving" were without children as "career constraints and relationship difficulties gradually squeezed the possibility of having a child out of her [women's] life" (p. 3). Hewlett herself narrated from a privileged position, and the characters in her script embodied similar socio-economic standpoints.

In identifying "high-achieving women," Hewlett focused on highly-educated women earning substantial incomes. In partnership with Harris Interactive and the National Parenting Association, Hewlett targeted the top 10 percent of women in corporate America measured in terms of earning power. High-achievers were defined as those women earning over $55,000 or $65,000 depending on age or who have a doctoral or professional degree in medicine, law, or dentistry. While race was not explicitly mentioned by Hewlett, her criteria for defining high-achieving women increase the likelihood for a primarily Caucasian-American sample. "High-potential women" were defined as highly qualified women who have left their careers, mainly for family reasons. Unfortunately, Hewlett's focus on "high-achieving women" created a narrow understanding of how upper-class women narrate ARI and their careers and make choices to delay childbearing.

In fact, Hewlett's (2002) work specifically and the public conversation more generally failed to call attention to the diversity of women's economic, social, and political realities. We do not hear the voices of women who struggle to pay bills, let alone infertility treatments. We do not hear the voices of women who are homosexual, medically diagnosed as disabled, happy with the choice to be childless, at peace with infertility, or who choose to adopt. As a result, some choices are promoted and valued in these discourses (e.g., prioritizing family over career) while others (e.g., remaining voluntarily childless) are not. Underscoring the importance of these absent voices is how much public attention this homogenous set of voices has generated. Journalists, talk show hosts, newscasters, and columnists have invoked Hewlett's work and the stories therein when framing ARI and its tragic consequences for women.

Perhaps what is most disturbing is how the experiences of women who comprise the upper-echelons of monetary and educational achievement in America have been privileged. Because the dominant metanarrative of ARI arose from a narrow and elite group of personal stories, the hegemonic script did not accommodate multiple and intersecting positionalities lived by women. The notion of reproductive choice in light of ARI plays out much differently for women who have access to social and material resources, like costly fertility treatments and the option to be stay-at-home-mothers, than it does for women who live paycheck-to-paycheck and for whom choosing not to work is simply not a viable option. If reproductive choices are considered only in the context of the privileged few, it becomes difficult, then, to fashion a coalition inspired by both difference and commonality when discourses that mark subjects are neither inclusive nor elastic.

## The Absence (and Presence) of Men

Also noticeably absent from ARI public discourses are men's reproductive choices. ARI and childlessness have been cast as problems created by and affecting women while discourses largely neglect that men, like women, delay childbirth, experience infertility, and have vested interests and meaningful parts to play in struggles to balance work and family. As Harris (2007) noted about her two male friends who just turned forty, "No one's tsking or ticktocking them to get their sh_t together and knock someone up already, quick, before their swimmers slow down and/or start causing trouble" (para. 4). Yet magazine and newspaper headlines such as "Delaying motherhood ignores hard realities" (Hart, 2002), "Women warned of risks in 'epidemic' of late childbirth," (Hall, 2005) and "Is there a 'right time' for a woman to have a baby?" (Yarbrough, 2002) were pervasive, tightly coupling delayed parenthood with women's choices.

Recent research suggests the age of fathers, as well as mothers, is going up (Mundy, 2002). Yet little serious treatment is given to the circumstances in which men may opt to delay fatherhood and the voices of men who do so. Mundy attributed the failure to ponder men's choices, in part, to the women's movement: "For so long, feminism has stressed women's choices, women's autonomy, women's right to control the childbearing process, is it any wonder that the public assumes, these days, that the choice is always and entirely the women's?" (p. W21). But in an op-ed piece, Williams (2005) furthered: "Having children is no more a 'woman's' decision than buying a house is . . . essentially, this cannot be undertaken without the willing participation of a man, and therefore it is a joint decision. Haranguing women over it seems nonsensical" (para. 4).

A pervasive notion that the responsibility for making difficult life decisions regarding career and family belongs solely to women permeated these discourses. Cottle (2002b) acknowledged this, and chastised journalists for "the shameful way in which the whole baby vs. career conundrum stubbornly remains a 'woman's issue'" (p. E-1). Men were rarely identified as characters obligated to choose between career and children or balance professional and parental roles. Public discourses warned women about squandering their fertility as authors invoked references to women's ticking biological clocks (e.g., Hall, 2005), and the expiration dates of women's eggs (e.g., Kalb et al., 2001). Pamela Madsen, former executive director of the American Fertility Association (AFA), suggested "[w]omen's eggs are like milk; they have a freshness date" (Liddane, 2002, p. L6).

Yet, research suggests that male fertility also declines with age and that men, too, have a biological clock (Hassan & Killick, 2003; Lewis et al., 2006; Rochebrochard & Thonneau, 2003). And medical authorities have argued "women should thus no longer be viewed as solely responsible for age-related fertility and genetic problems" (Lewis et al., 2006, p. 2369). The issue of male ARI has garnered some attention recently with Dr. Harry Fisch's (2005) book *The Male Biological Clock: The Startling News about Aging, Sexuality, and Fertility in Men*. Pamela Madsen (AFA) praised the book in a press release:

> Considering the age of our male partners as a factor when starting or growing a family has most likely never crossed anyone's mind. It's always been about the eggs. . . . Until now, however, we have lacked evidence that a man's advancing age may have an impact on his ability to conceive and may affect the health of the child.

Despite the increased attention paid to the male biological clock, there is evidence to suggest that many people remain unaware of the effects of aging on male fertility. In a 2005 poll conducted by RESOLVE, the national infertility association, just months after the AFA's press release lauded Fisch's book, only 55 percent of respondents understood that age is an issue for men when it comes to infertility, but 80 percent realized that age is an issue for women.

Overall, male ARI has received relatively scant attention in comparison to that given to similar research documenting ARI in women. Meanwhile, the absence of male narrators in these discourses illustrates the sheer tenacity of other social scripts. For example, reproductive choice is often narrated as an individual experience (read: female) rather than a partnered experience (see also Britt, 2001), and the responsibility for negotiating work-family responsibilities rests primarily with women (see Kirby, Golden, Medved, Jorgensen, & Buzzanell, 2003). The texts we analyzed reinscribed these archetypal plots, framing women as solely responsible for reproductive decisions and keeping individuals anchored to stories that generally limit rather than enlarge pathways of action for women and men alike.

## (UN)POLITICIZING PERSONAL CHOICES IN ARI NARRATIVES

Finally, in addition to framing ARI narratives in terms of personal choices and focusing only on the choices of a narrow group of women, public discourses about ARI almost universally failed to address the organizational and structural forces that shape and constrain reproductive decisions. Much of the expert advice is targeted at individual women, and choosing the "right ordering" of when to have a career versus when to prioritize having a mate and procreating. Yet as Goldberg (2002) noted, Hewlett's (2002) book is "bifurcated" between such "reactionary personal advice" and "serious, feminist-minded policy recommendations" (para. 23). Hewlett's storied portrayal of ARI concluded with policy recommendations (in the final "Solutions" section of the book) that advised readers on coping with the "time crunch" in their quest to "have it all." Hewlett offered a set of work/life policy guidelines for employers "that would make it much easier to get off the conventional career ladders and eventually get back on" (p. 267). The work/life package would include benefits such as a bank of paid leave time that working parents could use throughout a child's life, "high-level" jobs that provide flexible hours, and "off-ramps" and "on-ramps" that would allow working parents, particularly women, the opportunity to put a temporary hold on their careers to have children. Hewlett also pushed for government initiatives that would extend the Family Medical Leave Act (FMLA) to workers in small companies and turn it into paid leave, provide tax incentives for companies with family-friendly work/life packages, and promote legislation to reduce incentives for long workdays.

Curiously, public discourses about ARI, even media reports inspired by and focused specifically on Hewlett's book, rarely acknowledged or elaborated upon this extensive set of thoughtful policy recommendations. As Walsh (2002) noted, "Hewlett is spot on when it comes to indicting the workplace and government policies that keep career-minded women from having children, and child-minded women from having careers. . . . To be fair, Hewlett can't control what the media does with her book" (para. 21–22). As a few examples, a discussion of these recommendations is entirely absent from the *Oprah Winfrey* episode on which Hewlett appeared, and policy considerations were not discussed at all during Hewlett's 2002 interview with Lesley Stahl on *60 Minutes*. A few accounts of Hewlett's book mentioned policy recommendations in passing without elaboration. For instance, Cooke's (2002) review of the book included the following nod: "Hewlett reminds us how woefully inadequate maternity benefits continue to be" (Cooke, 2002), but Cooke leaves it to readers to ponder why precisely these benefits are inadequate and what changes we can make to improve them. Some commentators even articulated a disturbing backlash against Hewlett's suggestions. Hart (2002) wrote:

> Hewlett suggests lots of policy "solutions," like mandatory paid parental leave, that would really do little but make women of child-bearing age less attractive to business. It may come down to the fact that—gasp!—no one has a "right" to have it all on her terms, or to force the working world to change just so parents don't have to make choices. (p. 33)

A few journalists did highlight Hewlett's (2002) proposed solutions in their accounts of the book. Giese (2002), for example, noted:

> Much of the book is a very serious-minded and compelling argument for the U.S. to adopt a European model of family supports that includes benefits such as paid leave, reduced working hours for parents, and subsidized daycare. But forget about finding that policy discussion in any of the media reports. (p. A27)

Indeed, media reports of Hewlett's solutions are few and far between. Journalists and public figures paid much less attention to her policy recommendations than to the emotive and aesthetically compelling stories of grief and despair. Likewise, the ASRM's ongoing "Protect Your Fertility" campaign focused entirely on individual choices, reminding women "Your decisions now can impact your ability to conceive in the future."What is gained and lost when the political nature and implications of personal stories are minimized as stories move through public domains? In short, Bakhtin (1981) teaches us that retellings transform meaning. Consumers of Hewlett's (2002) text rewrite and reenvision ARI. Hewlett's storied portrayal evolved as journalists spun it out in the political, social, and economic contexts of their work, leaving some elements of the original narratives (i.e., structural constraints) in the shadow of other elements (i.e., poignant fears, difficult "choices," and painful regrets).

One disturbing implication of the focus on individual choices rather than societal orientations to health and careers is the tendency to ignore the organizational and structural influences that constrain reproductive choices. Public discourses and campaigns urge women to be smart, or in Hewlett's (2002) words "strategic," when planning their personal lives. Yet, how are women to be strategic when their choices are limited by lack of access to paid time off, inadequate child care, or fear of losing their jobs? Although many legislative initiatives have been advanced, women continue to be paid less for their labor and limited by glass ceilings and walls—especially after maternity leave. Meanwhile, men struggle to take paternity leave due, in part, to the value of "presence" at work (Kirby & Krone, 2002).

To Hewlett's (2002) credit, *Creating a Life* did tease out policy recommendations and actions for private corporations and governmental consideration. Yet, she was not the only actor making rhetorical choices in narrating ARI. As journalists and talk show hosts spun out and developed the metanarrative of ARI, the second part of Hewlett's text was all but ignored. Instead, "rolling, palpable losses" for women became the climax of the dominant metanarrative. The dominant narrative of ARI is an emotionally laden story of woe with little attention to structural constraints and strategy. Nearly every "news" story contained at least one woman's story of ARI, though such narratives were noticeably absent in the scant press coverage of male ARI. The dominant script remains stuck in one dimension—that of woe versus strategy. When such emotional appeals are privileged at the expense of structural and political forces, there is diminished potential for social change. Ultimately, ARI discourses offered up emotionally compelling autobiographies but left intact many institutional forces and patterns that shape choices and actions.

## CONCLUSION

This manuscript was inspired in part by the airing of an NPR broadcast on May 8, 2008, just before Mother's Day, entitled "For prospective moms, biology and culture clash." During the morning edition of NPR news, health experts and women alike agreed "women are waiting a little too long to have their children" (p. 1). Six years after the launch of the ASRM campaign and the publication of Hewlett's text, personal stories of ARI as narrated by a homogeneous group of women linger in public discourses—including the recent NPR broadcast. Personal narratives offer pathways to action that guide the development of individuals' identities and relationships, and can give rise to organizational and governmental policies. As poststructural feminists, we believe that storytelling is a powerful vehicle for simultaneously revealing and obscuring, disrupting and reifying, power relations that guide everyday life. From this perspective, we explored the discursive framing of ARI in public discourses and anticipated the consequentiality of these discourses. In this final section of our chapter we return to the questions that guided our reading of ARI discourses: How are Hewlett's work and the personal stories therein taken up and played out in other mediated discourses? What is gained and lost when the political nature of individual reproductive choices is minimized as personal stories move through public domains? What is emphasized, what is not, and what are the potential consequences of these representations?

First, we note that, as personal stories took center stage in Hewlett's book and most of the ongoing discourses, the social construction of choice, imbued with cultural values and meanings, also became a primary focus. As such, reproductive choice in the context of ARI , in this case delayed childbearing, was repeatedly framed as a personal decision made by privileged women who came to regret the decision to wait too long as they suffered the consequences and eventual non-choice. The career choices of high-achieving women were persistently portrayed in opposition to personal and family goals. Choices made by men and other women from diverse backgrounds remained conspicuously absent. And as experts urged women to make better choices, few of these discussions adequately acknowledged the structural constraints that shape reproductive decisions.

Yet, by including the voices of high-achieving women throughout her book, Hewlett legitimated the experiences of some women by bearing witness to their stories, rendered credible experiences that were previously silenced, and raised societal awareness about reproductive issues in the "service" of educating primarily young women. In fact, *Creating a Life* is a compelling text in which to witness feminist tendencies to rely on narrative resources to recount events, depict characters, suggest causes for events, and represent the passage of time. The ordering impulses of narratives allow humans to take stock of turning points even as they offer ways to consider what one "ought" to do or "should have" done. As such, narratives are instruments of self-knowledge and communion with others and provide pathways to action. Women took stock of events befalling them in light of life's temporal horizons. The plots we encountered were irrevocably about their endings—the inability of women to get pregnant and/or carry a child to term. Hewlett, like any good narrative detective, did not stop at the obvious storyline. In her initial text, she dug deeper and offered varied diagnoses whose treatments involved individual, corporate, and governmental interventions.

How did people enter into the portrayal of ARI offered by the ASRM and Hewlett in order to make meaning? Just as personal lives are (re)constructed through storytelling, narratives remain a staple of journalistic form. Journalists and lay individuals furthered the emergent dominant script of ARI, directing attention to some elements of the original stories (e.g., despair resulting from poor choices) to the detriment of narrative fragments that pointed toward systemic change. As with feminist attention to personal narrative, both Hewlett's and the media's attention to narrative is problematic in the same ways that Fixmer and Wood (2005) argue about feminist use of narrative. Fixmer and Wood (2005) identified a larger problem in contemporary feminist discourses that position "personal experience as a focus in its own right and not as a route to theoretical insights and structural change" (p. 248). We affirm the micropolitics of resistance that can occur when individuals (re)narrate their experiences. Even so, when the focus on personal choices and decisions remains disconnected from institutional forms of power and politics, storytelling may have limited impact in instigating consequential shifts in ideologies that order everyday lives in significant ways. Based on our reading of ARI discourses, we urge feminists to contextualize personal stories in political contexts in order to connect seemingly individual experiences to institutional sources of marginalization.

Ultimately, these discourses illustrate that multiple realms of our everyday life—including our health and career choices—have both personal and political dimensions. Yet there are limits to narratives as rhetorical resources in feminist movements and public health initiatives when attention does not extend beyond individual expressions to redress forces that shape and constrain human agency. When prominence is not given to policy proposals and initiatives that counter lived inequities, the aesthetic and emotive dimensions of storytelling are privileged too easily at the expense of social change. It is presumed that (many) women had another choice they could have made by trying to have children earlier. Likewise, when the issues are privatized, as they are in almost all public discussions of ARI, organizational structures and governments are absolved of responsibility. We must look for spaces where we, for the benefit of ourselves and others, need to contest social orders and politicize the personal.

## REFERENCES

Aldoory, L., & Toth, E. L. (2001). The complexities of feminism in communication scholarship today. In W. Gudykunst (Ed.), *Communication Yearbook 24* (pp. 345–61). Thousand Oaks, CA: Sage.

Alfonso, R., & Trigilio, J. (1997). Surfing the third wave: A dialogue between two third wave feminists. *Hypatia, 12*(3), 7–16.

American Society for Reproductive Medicine. (2002). *Protect your fertility*. Retrieved from http://www.protectyourfertility.org

American Society for Reproductive Medicine. (2003). *Age and fertility: A guide for patients*. Retrieved from http://www.asrm.org/Patients/patientbooklets/agefertility.pdf

Ashcraft, K. L., & Mumby, D. (2005). *Reworking gender: A feminist communicology of organization*. Thousand Oaks, CA: Sage.

Bakhtin, M. (1981). *The dialogic imagination: Four essays* (C. Emerson & M. Holquist, Trans.). Austin: University of Texas Press.

Bewley, S., Davies, M., & Bruade, P. (2005, September 17). Which career first? The most secure age for childbearing remains 20–35. *British Medical Journal*, 331, 588–89.

Boje, D. (2001). *Narrative methods for organizational and communication research*. Thousand Oaks, CA: Sage.

Britt, E. C. (2001). *Conceiving normalcy: Rhetoric, law, and the double binds of infertility*. Tuscaloosa: University of Alabama Press.

Buzzanell, P. M., & Liu, M. (2005). Struggling with maternity leave policies and practices: A poststructuralist feminist analysis of gendered organizing. *Journal of Applied Communication Research, 33*, 1–25.

Cooke, R. (2002, May 27). Fertility fears. *New Statesman*, n.p.

Condit, C. M. (1994). Hegemony in mass-mediated society: Concordance about reproductive technologies. *Critical Studies in Mass Communication, 11*, 205–30.

Cottle, M. (2002a, April 24). Feminine mistake. *New Republic* online. Retrieved from http://209.212.93.14/doc.mhtml?i=express&s=cottle042402

Cottle, M. (2002b, April 28) Dads are parents, too. *Pittsburgh Post-Gazette*, p. E-1.

Dow, B. J., & Condit, C. M. (2005). The state of the art in feminist scholarship in communication. *Journal of Communication, 55*, 448–78.

Fergus, M. A. (2002, June 30). In the struggle to balance career and motherhood, many women are left wondering if they waited too long; Is time running out? *Houston Chronicle*. p. L-1.

Fisch, H. (2005). *The male biological clock: The startling news about aging, sexuality, and fertility in men*. New York: Free Press.

Fixmer, N., & Wood, J. T. (2005). The personal is still political: Embodied politics in third wave feminism. *Women's Studies in Communication, 28*, 235–57.

Foucault, M. (1972). *The archaeology of knowledge and the discourse on language* (trans. by A. M. Sheridan Smith). New York: Pantheon.

Foucault, M. (1973/1984). *The birth of the clinic: An archaeology of medical perception* (trans. by A. M. Sheridan Smith). New York: Pantheon.

Foucault, M. (1980). *Power/knowledge: Selected interviews and other writings, 1972–1977* (trans. by C. Gordon, L. Marshall, J. Mepham, & K. Soper). New York: Pantheon.

Fraser, N. (1989). *Unruly practices: Power, discourse and gender in contemporary social theory*. Minneapolis: University of Minnesota Press.

Gibbs, N. (2002, April 15). Making time for a baby. *Time, 159*, 48–54.

Giese, R. (2002, May 30). Flawed logic obscures messages on having kids. *Toronto Star*, p. A27.

Goldberg, M. (2002, April 23). It's been 12 years since "Backlash"—It must be time to scare women into domestic submission again. Salon.com. Retrieved from http://dir.salon.com/story/mwt/feature/2002/04/23/childless_women/

Hall, C. (2005, September 16). Women warned of risks in "epidemic" of late childbirth. *Daily Telegraph* (London), news p. 5.

Harris, L. (2007, December 5). Their 40s just seemed to sneak up on them. Salon .com. Retrieved from http://www.salon.com/mwt/broadsheet/2007/12/05/moms_over_40/

Hart, B. (2002, April 14). Delaying motherhood ignores hard realities. *Chicago Sun-Times*. p. 33.

Harter, L. M., Japp, P. M., & Beck, C. S. (2005). *Vital problematics about narrative theorizing about health and healing*. In L. M. Harter, P. M. Japp, & C. S. Beck (pp. 7–30). Mahwah, NJ: Lawrence Erlbaum.

Hassan, M. A. M., & Killick, S. R. (2003). Effect of male age on fertility: Evidence for the decline in male fertility with increasing age. *Fertility and Sterility, 79*, 1520–27.

Hewlett, S. A. (2002). *Creating a life: Professional women and the quest for children*. New York: Talk Miramax Books.

Hjul, J. (2002, May 2). Is there any hope for single career women? *Scotsman*, p. 14.

Kalb, C., Springen, K., Scelfo, J., & Pierce, E. (2001, August 13). Should you have your baby now? *Newsweek*, 40.

Kirby, E. L., Golden, A. G., Medved, C. E., Jorgenson, J., & Buzzanell. P. M. (2003). An organizational communication challenge to the discourse of work and family research: From problematics to empowerment. In P. Kalbfleisch (Ed.), *Communication Yearbook 27* (pp. 1–43). Mahwah, NJ: Lawrence Erlbaum Associates.

Kirby, E. L., & Krone, K. J. (2002). "The policy exists but you can't really use it": Communication and the structuration of work-family policies. *Journal of Applied Communication Research, 30*, 50–77.

Lewis, B. H., Legato, M., & Fisch, H. (2006). Medical implications of the male biological clock. *Journal of the American Medical Association, 296*(19), 2369–71.

Lewis, J. (2008, June 8). Infertility: The lesson that comes too late. *Sunday Telegraph* (London), p. 20.

Liddane, S. (2002, May 26). Fertile at 40? Maybe not. Conceiving a mid-life baby is harder than many women think. *Seattle Times*, p. L6.

Lunardini, C. (1994). *What every American should know about women's history*. Holbrook, MA: Bob Adams.

Maheshwari, A., Hamilton, M., & Bhattacharya, S. (2008). Effect of female age on the diagnostic categories of infertility. *Human Reproduction, 23*, 538–42.

Miller, C. (2008, June 8). Scary rise of the "sanctimommy." *Washington Times.* n.p.

Mundy, L. (2002, March 17). The late shift. *Washington Post,* p. W21.

National Public Radio. (NPR). (2008, May 8). For prospective moms, biology and culture clash. *Morning Edition.* Retrieved from http://www.npr.org/transcripts/

RESOLVE. (2005). *National survey results reveal startling lack of awareness of infertility even as numbers climb to 7.3 million* (RESOLVE Press Release).

Rochebrochard, E. de la, & Thonneau, P. (2003). Parental age >40 years: An important risk factor for infertility. *American Journal of Obstetrics and Gynecology, 189,* 901–5.

Seward, H. (2002, April 11). Time—and Fertility—Waits for No Woman. *Free Republic.* Retrieved from: http://www.freerepublic.com/focus/f-news/731854/posts

Siegel, D. L. (1997). The legacy of the personal: Generating theory in feminism's third wave. *Hypatia, 12*(3), 46–75.

Stahl, L. (2002, April 7). The biological clock. *60 Minutes.* CBS Worldwide, Inc.

Trethewey, A. (2001). Reproducing and resisting the master narrative of decline: Midlife professional women's experiences of aging. *Management Communication Quarterly, 15,* 183–226.

Walsh. J. (2002, April 23). The baby panic. Salon.com. Retrieved from http://dir.salon.com/story/mwt/feature/2002/04/23/hewlett_book/

Weatherford, D. (1994). *American women's history: An A to Z of people, organizations, issues and events.* New York: Prentice-Hall.

Weedon, C. (1987). *Feminist practice and poststructuralist theory.* Cambridge: Blackwell.

Williams, Z. (2005, October 1). Interview with Melanie Davis and Susan Bewley. *Guardian* (London), final edition, p. 3.

Winfrey, O. (2002, May 1). When should you have a baby? *Oprah.* Harpo Productions, Inc. Burrell. Retrieved from http://www.oprah.com

Wood, J. T. (1994). *Who cares? Women, care, and culture.* Carbondale: Southern Illinois University Press.

Yarbrough, M. (2002, May 20). Is there a "right time" for a woman to have baby? *Jet,* 60.

# Section II

# Choice in the Public Sphere

4

# REPRODUCTIVE FREEDOM: TRANSFORMING DISCOURSES OF CHOICE

*Catherine H. Palczewski*[1]

In the 1970s, women of color and poor women challenged the primarily white middle-class women's movement to expand its advocacy for women's reproductive autonomy from an exclusive focus on abortion choice to a demand for reproductive freedom. Reproductive freedom[2] positions the right to have children as equally important as the right not to have them, and demands social justice in order to parent well. Marlene Gerber Fried's (1990) compilation of primary documents, *Transforming a Movement: From Choice to Reproductive Freedom*, chronicles the advocacy that led to this formulation of reproductive freedom which, in the early 1990s, was institutionalized by organizations that used to exclusively advocate abortion choice. Planned Parenthood, the National Abortion Rights Action League (NARAL), and the Religious Coalition for Abortion Rights (RCAR) revised their missions. In two cases, name changes accompanied the mission changes; RCAR is now the Religious Coalition for Reproductive Choice (RCRC) and NARAL became the National Abortion and Reproductive Rights Action League.[3]

During this transition, mainstream news media stories treated *choice* and *reproductive freedom* as synonymous (e.g., Elvin, 1991; "More Threats," 1990; Tribe, 1990) or described the shift as a strategic one meant to counter pro-life activities (e.g., "Abortion Rights," 1994; "Expanding," 1994).[4] Even Communication Studies scholar Celeste Condit (1990) dismissed the import of the call for reproductive freedom in a footnote to her comprehensive analysis of the abortion controversy. Although Condit may be correct that middle-class women's articulation of abortion rights largely shaped public discourse with its focus on *choice*, she is not correct in her descriptions of *reproductive freedom*. The phrase was not merely the creation of "activist and academic feminists, working largely outside the public arena" (pp. 76–77, n. 25). It was a term created and embraced by women of color and poor women who were challenging white middle-class women's control over the public vocabulary (Nelson, 2003; Silliman, Fried, Ross, & Gutiérrez, 2004). Even if *reproductive freedom* has not risen to the stature of *choice* within the public arena, it has reconfigured the discourses surrounding maternity and reproduction.

Reproductive freedom should not be dismissed as merely strategic or marginal in analyses of abortion discourse. Instead of viewing the shift as a response to pro-life discourse or as not rising to the level of public significance, the shift can be read as a demand by women of color and poor women on pro-choice organizations to account for the interests and needs of *all* women. The goal of reproductive freedom advocates was not only to challenge the dominant political climate or the pro-life movement, but also to challenge the pro-choice movement's stranglehold on public discourse. As a comprehensive study of women of color organizing for reproductive justice points out, even as they resisted the government and private population control organizations' oppressive reproductive restrictions, "they also had to contend with those white pro-choice activists in the mainstream movements for contraception and abortion who have been unable to see how what may be reproductive freedom for them is reproductive tyranny for others" (Silliman et al., 2004, p. 11).

Women of color have long critiqued the women's movement for being primarily focused on the identity, interests, and needs of white and privileged women (Hull, Scott, & Smith, 1982; Joseph & Lewis, 1981; Ruiz & DuBois, 1994). Women's movements' focus on abortion choice is one such example (Davis, 1981/1983/1990; Roberts, 1997). If a woman has the luxury of access to pre- and postnatal care, to medical care, to food, shelter, and clothing, then the primary concern is not having healthy babies who can survive infancy and childhood, but is instead avoiding unwanted pregnancies. Poor women and women of color still do not have this luxury, and long faced the additional threat of "systematic and widespread sterilization abuses practiced by the U.S. government and by private doctors (who were more often than not subsidized by the U.S. government)" (Silliman et al., 2004, p. 9). These abusive practices resulted in sterilizations of 35.3

percent of Puerto Rican women of childbearing age by 1968 and 24 percent of Native American women of childbearing age by 1976 (CARASA & Davis, 1988, p. 28; Davis, 1981/1983/1990, p. 218). White women may have fought compulsory motherhood, but women of color have had to fight for the right to procreate, and to procreate on their own terms. Recognizing this, groups like the National Black Feminist Organization, Committee Against Sterilization Abuse, Combahee River Collective, Women of All Red Nations, Native American Women's Health Education Resource Center, National Black Women's Health Project, National Asian Women's Health Organization, National Latina Health Organization, International Women's Health Coalition, and Women of Color Partnership Program created a new inclusive movement for reproductive freedom (Nelson, 2003; Silliman et al., 2004).

In this chapter, I explore the implications of the call for a shift from choice to reproductive freedom on the topography of the abortion argument and on social protest theory. First, I explain why counterpublic sphere theory can explain better the significance of the reproductive freedom movement than traditional movement studies. Second, I analyze the emergence of reproductive freedom as an alternative to choice to advance two arguments: (1) degrees of counterpublicity exist, as counterpublics themselves must be countered when they replicate exclusionary practices of the dominant public, and (2) the target of protest is not necessarily the establishment or opposing movements, but may be other counterpublics.

## PUBLICS AND COUNTERPUBLICS

The controversy over abortion rightly has been a central topic in the study of social protest and rhetorical movements. Despite this sustained attention, only one article in *Communication Studies* journals discusses the shift of focus from *choice* to *reproductive freedom* (Hayden, 2009). One explanation for this lack of attention is movement studies have tended to use an establishment vs. movement model that foregrounds confrontation between the two (e.g., Bowers, Ochs, & Jensen, 1993; Cathcart, 1978). This model ignores the role of hegemonic social forces (Murphy, 1992) and privileges the study of instrumental rhetoric targeted at the establishment in dominant public sphere discourse, consummatory and empowerment rhetoric studies being notable exceptions (e.g., Campbell, 1973; Lake, 1983). However, confrontational and instrumental rhetoric does not spring fully formed from subordinate groups. Attention to *how* marginalized groups develop counterdiscourses is necessary. Counterpublic sphere theory offers one way to explore how oppositional groups develop discourses that challenge the dominant public and the replication of hegemonic forces by other counterpublics.

As an alternative to Jürgen Habermas's (1989) unitary public, Nancy Fraser (1992) offers a conception of multiple counterpublics, defined as "parallel discursive arenas where members of subordinated social groups invent and circulate counterdiscourse to formulate oppositional interpretations of their identities, interests, and needs" (p. 123). Counterpublics expand not only the space for argument, but also what counts as argument because "assumptions that were previously exempt from contestation will now have to be publicly argued out" (p. 124). Literary theorist Rita Felski (1989) highlights how counterpublics particularly "contest the basis of existing norms and values by raising alternative validity claims" (p. 12). For Felski, counterpublics' power comes not only from the way they challenge the dominant public, but also from how they operate outside of the dominant public sphere; they engage in a "series of cultural strategies which can be effective across a range of levels both outside and inside existing institutional structures" (p. 171).

Counterpublics possess distinct functions when enclaved and when oscillating to a dominant public. When enclaved, counterpublics create safe spaces in which participants: (1) develop alternative validity claims; (2) elaborate alternative norms of public speech and styles of political behaviors; (3) regenerate their energy to engage in argument in the political and public spheres; (4) construct cultural identities through idiom and style; and (5) formulate oppositional interpretations of identities, interests, and needs through the creation of new language. Writer bell hooks (1989) explains the particular importance of developing a language: "The most important of our work—the work of liberation—demands of us that we make a new language, that we create the oppositional discourse, the liberatory voice" (p. 29). Enclaved moments of counterpublicity are necessary for the possibility of oppositional ideas and actions in the dominant public.

However, if a counterpublic remains enclaved, its participants run the risk of speaking only to each other and "do not learn how to put what they want to say in words that others can hear and understand" (Mansbridge, 1996, p. 58). Thus, oscillation outward to argue and engage with those with whom one disagrees is essential to a healthy counterpublic. Oscillation also carries with it practical benefits. Daniel C. Brouwer's (2001) study of ACT UP and its participation in congressional AIDS hearings identifies a number of them. Oscillation (1) can garner national attention for a group and enhance its credibility; (2) opens a forum for the repetition and recognition of the group's message; (3) can push for implementation of the group's recommendations that require institutional support; and (4) enables the counterpublic to "push for access to strong publics" (p. 132, n. 1). What repeatedly needs to be made explicit, however, is that not only may counterpublics oscillate toward the public, but also toward other (more dominant) counterpublics. In other words, social movements may seek to *move* other movements, not just the establishment. As scholars theorize this process, we need to attend to Pheadra C. Pezzullo's (2003) call to "pay attention to power relations and to the various types of publics that form in one's society" (p. 348) and Robert Asen's (2000) warning not to oversimplify the relations among counterpublics.

Although women's movements constitute a counterpublic, so, too, do the movements of women of color. Although women's movement discourses generated by predominantly white middle-class women may function as a counter to the dominant public, they unfortunately replicate racist hegemonic elements that need to be countered. Although women of color played a vital role in women's movements across their waves,[5] the foci of women's movements did (and does) not always address the concerns of women of color or poor women. The essentialism of the so-called mainstream women's movement created what Jane Mansbridge (1998) calls a falsely universal *we* that encourages subordinated groups' identities, interests, and needs to remain inchoate (pp. 143, 152). Not only does the comprehensive public sphere render the reproductive concerns of poor women and women of color inchoate, but so too does the dominant feminist sphere when their deployment of "we women" includes only the concerns of middle-class white women. Thus, women of color and poor women's demand for reproductive freedom can be read as a challenge to a feminist counterpublic.

## FROM ABORTION CHOICE TO REPRODUCTIVE FREEDOM

Typical approaches to the abortion controversy cast it as an irreconcilable divergence in beliefs, with the debate stalemated between two diametrically opposed sides, represented by two ideographs: *choice* and *life*. With the elevation of these two ideographs debate is truncated so that the ultimate question is whether women's choice to have an abortion outweighs the potential risk that a fetus is a human being (Condit, 1984, pp. 59–73, 159). Unfortunately, continuing to read the controversy this way renders the concerns of poor women, young women, and women of color inchoate[6] and ignores the calls for broader reproductive freedoms for women (and men).

To understand how the *choice* focus deflected women of color and poor women's concerns, a recapitulation of the controversy is required. Condit (1984), in her article detailing the contemporary U.S. abortion controversy up to the mid-1980s, argues that the argument can be read as moving through seven stages: (1) the professional stage, identified by argument in a nonpublic arena that sets the ground for a move into public argument; (2) the narrative phase, in which stories of the horrors of illegal abortion were recounted; (3) the auxiliary ideographic stage, which focused on the discriminatory elements of abortion policy by drawing on the discourse of the Civil Rights Movement; (4) the intrinsic ideographic stage, in which *choice* became the central term of the movement advocating abortion access; (5) the normalization stage, in which abortion was both worked into the daily understandings of U.S. people and when opposition began to escalate; (6) stalemate, when two mature ideological components presented themselves to the public and compared values; and (7) fragmentation, which occurred as ideologies became less and less univocal.

Building off of and responding to Condit (1984, 1990), I argue a parallel rhetorical trajectory began in the 1970s in the rhetoric of those who advocate reproductive freedom, situating abortion as one within a constellation of rights and freedoms, and generated the creation of an eighth stage in the early 1990s in which dominant abortion rights groups began to embrace what had been the auxiliary ideograph of discrimination. These parallel/new stages in the controversy represent the effects of counterpublic sphere dynamics. The women's movement marginalized women of color, thus replicating the structures of the dominant public sphere, when it relegated *discrimination* to the role of an auxiliary ideograph and decided to elevate *choice* as an intrinsic ideograph. This marginalization created the necessity for the emergence of a parallel stage beginning in the 1970s and reaching fruition in the 1990s when the auxiliary ideograph of *discrimination* motivated the creation of a new intrinsic ideograph: *reproductive freedom*. This shift alters the fragmentation created in stage seven; instead of fragmentation increasing between advocates, the elevation of discrimination allows for the cohesion of diverse groups, including: women of color, international women, lesbians, gays, and poor women. Using arguments about how abortion laws disproportionately (and, hence, in a discriminatory manner) affect women of color and poor women, these groups argue the mainstream choice agenda must be broadened beyond the focus on abortion to include a full range of reproductive freedoms. To enable this, women of color and poor women participated in an enclaved counterpublic in which a distinctive articulation of their identities, interests and needs could be formulated.

## Poor Women and Women of Color Articulate Reproductive Freedom Interests and Needs

A quick review of Supreme Court decisions clarifies why the simple call for abortion choice did not address the concerns of women of color or poor women. After abortion choice was constitutionally protected as a privacy right in *Roe v. Wade* (1973), access to abortion and reproductive services for poor women was limited in *Harris v. McRae* (1980) which denied poor women the ability to exercise that right by denying them access to Medicaid funding (MacKinnon, 1987). The end result of this ruling was identical to the end result of illegal abortion: "back alley" abortion and the death of women (Frankfort, 1979). While *McRae* allowed the denial of Medicaid funding, *Webster v. Reproductive Health Services* (1989) set the stage for restrictions at state funded health care facilities and *Rust v. Sullivan* (1991) allowed the denial of information at federally funded clinics. *Planned Parenthood v. Casey* (1992) also would disparately impact poor women. The Court's "essentialism in considering women's lives" resulted in the lack of judicial protection for "the most disadvantaged women in society" who were disproportionately affected by waiting periods; poor women cannot afford multiple trips to faraway clinics and women victimized by domestic violence may not be able to explain multiple trips to an abusive partner (Colker, 1994, p. 90). Added to these Supreme Court decisions are numerous lower court decisions allowing forced cesareans, primarily on poor women and non–English-speaking women (Daniels, 1990; Roberts, 1990).

At the same time that the focus on abortion was insufficient to meet the needs of women of color and poor women so, too, was it too expansive. Poor women and women of color fought against forced sterilization and forced abortion and demanded access to pre- and postnatal care, health care, adequate food and housing. Legal scholar and activist Dorothy Roberts (1990) synthesized the distinctive identity, interests, and needs of poor women and women of color:

> This connection between denying reproductive choice and oppression will necessarily be the sharpest for poor women and women of color. Because of

> poverty, these women have fewer real options and are dependent on government funds to realize the decisions they make. Because the government is more involved in their lives, through their use of public facilities and bureaucracies, they are more susceptible to government monitoring and supervision. Because it is harder for them to meet the ideal middle class standard of what a woman or mother should be, society is more likely to approve of, or overlook, punishing them for making reproductive decisions. Because they have less access to lawyers, the media and advocacy organizations, and because society has convinced many that they are powerless, they are less likely to challenge government restrictions of their rights. Reproductive freedom is a right that belongs to all women; but, its denial is felt hardest by poor and minority women. (pp. 61–62)

These concerns were not noted solely by academics, but by women themselves.

As early as 1971, the mainstream women's movement was critiqued because of its failure to address the interests and needs of all women. In a "Letter from a Welfare Mother" (1971) written to *Women: A Journal of Liberation* (and later sent to NOW, see Chappell, 2002), the author challenged the movement's focus on choice:

> How dare you mention freedom and sit up there and talk that shit about free 24-hour child care centers and free abortion on demand when we're worrying whether our children will live? Talking about control over our own bodies when we don't have the right to even keep our bodies from being hungry. . . . I'm begging for the privilege of Motherhood. I already have free abortion on demand, lady—they do the demanding. I just want a healthy baby. . . . You murder me, womens' [*sic*] liberationist, every bullshit demand you make; not because what you ask for is wrong, but because of what you leave out. (Underline in original, pp. 50–51)

She proceeds to outline how the women's movement focus on abortion choice deflected concern from issues such as forced sterilization, access to pre- and postnatal care, health care, adequate food and housing, access to quality education, and the right to be sexual.

Recognizing that reproductive freedom necessarily entails sexual freedom, the author challenges the sexual double standard that describes privileged women's sexuality as "free" and poor women's sexuality as "loose":

> When you make love, it's meaningful, it's exploring alternative life styles, it's individual freedom, breaking the shackles of Freudianism, and Judeo-Christian morality. It's finding yourself, discovering your sexuality. When I

> screw, it's immoral, irresponsible, decadent, evil, promiscuous, casual, low, wrong. (p. 51)

Ultimately, the author calls for a focus not only on abortion (the right not to mother) but also on the right to mother and to mother well. Freedom, for her, includes (but is not limited to): "having healthy children . . . hot school lunches . . . being able to want a baby, and not feeling guilty about bringing him into the world to suffer and make the other kids poorer. . . . I could send you a dozen pages about how our freedom consists of things you take for granted" (p. 51). The freedom from forced abortion and sterilization is one of those taken-for-granted freedoms.

Forced abortion and sterilization have long been used against women of color and poor women (CARASA, 1979; CARASA & Davis, 1988; Nelson, 2003; Silliman et al., 2004). Reacting to U.S. government sterilization of women in Puerto Rico, Dr. Helen Rodriguez Trias[7] was a founding member in 1972 of the Committee to End Sterilization Abuse (CESA) and in 1977 (in the wake of the Hyde Amendment restrictions on Medicaid funding) of the Committee for Abortion Rights and Against Sterilization Abuse (CARASA). Both committees placed equal importance on the right to choose not to have a child and the ability to have a child. Both groups also sought to differentiate a reproductive rights agenda from population control (Nelson, 2003).

Latinas articulated this same expansive agenda (Silliman et al., 2004). Teresa Lujan (1993), of the Comisión Femenil Mexicana Nacional, writes: "Reproductive choice is a broad issue for Latinas. 'Choice' means little to women without access to quality health care" (p. 8). She continues,

> For our community, being pro-choice is more than being pro-abortion. Choice means: 1) the right to good, accessible child care; 2) the right to information on sexuality that is culturally relevant and in a language we understand; 3) the right to pre-natal care so that we can have healthy babies; 4) access to information regarding contraception, so that abortion will not be our only option; and 5) freedom from forced sterilization and other reproductive abuses. (p. 8)

The right to have a child is as important as the right not to.

Asian American women also focus on basic reproductive freedoms and define abortion as something much more than a choice (Keju-Johnson, Eknilang, & Palacios, 1990). Echoing Alice Walker's (1989) naming of abortion "an act of mercy, and an act of self-defense" (p. 692), one Asian American activist casts reproductive issues as "survival issues," arguing the "right to have an abortion is . . . a right to survival in this country if you are a poor, uneducated, non–English-speaking immigrant" (Chan, 1990, pp. 175–76).

Once their interests and needs were identified and named, women of color and poor women demanded their recommendations be implemented and institutionalized in reproductive rights advocacy organizations. They made clear the conditions under which they would cooperate with other women's organizations. At the close of the April 1989 "In the Defense of Roe" conference cosponsored by the RCAR Women of Color Partnership[8] and the ACLU Reproductive Freedom Project, women of color explained:

> Until we focus on quality of life, quality of care, survival, and access issues, women of color will not automatically endorse organizations or actions. This is the context within which we will work on any issue of women's reproductive health and freedom such as access to abortion and health care, publicly funded abortion, services within and controlled by our community, forced sterilization, access to reproductive technologies that deal with infertility, infant mortality, pre-natal health, HIV testing, and forced cesarean sections. (As cited in Baehr, 1990, p. 53)

The expanded agenda was further developed by the Women of Color Partnership Program in a 1991 pamphlet defining reproductive freedom.[9] Reminding readers of the denial of reproductive freedom to African American women under slavery, the front of the pamphlet shows three African American women in front of a backdrop of chains. Inside the pamphlet, the group argues that reproductive freedom, "to choose and to exercise our choices," is a matter of "survival" (see also Avery, 1990). The pamphlet concludes with an explanation of what reproductive freedom means:

> 1) The right to comprehensive, age-appropriate information about sexuality and reproduction, 2) The right to choose to have a child, 3) The right to good, affordable health care to assure a safe pregnancy and delivery, 4) The right to health services to help the infertile achieve pregnancy, 5) The right to choose not to have a child, 6) The right to the full range of contraceptive services and appropriate information about reproduction, 7) The right to choose to end an unwanted pregnancy, 8) The right to safe, legal, affordable abortion services, 9) The right to make informed choices, 10) The right to easily accessible health care that is proven to be safe and effective, 11) The right to reproductive health and to make our own reproductive choices. ("We Remember," circa 1991)

It is important to note the "right to choose to have a child" is second in the list, while "The right to choose not to have a child" is fifth.

The broader agenda of reproductive freedom was institutionalized in 1990 by women of color when leaders of major African American groups decided that the term *reproductive freedom* "best described their pro-choice position" (White, 1990, p. 8). Reporting on the "Sisters in Session, About Our Reproductive Health" conference, Lisa Diane White (1990), Program Developer at the National Black Women's Health Project, explained the rationale for the selection of the phrase:

> Not all Black women's organizations are ready to embrace the term "reproductive rights" because it is interpreted by many to be limited to abortion rights. Reproductive freedom is more inclusive, including the right to have a child, the right to good affordable health care and the right to make informed choices about our reproductive health. . . . (p. 8)

While the pro-choice movement challenges the norms and values that position pregnancy and childbirth as definitive of womanhood, the reproductive freedom movement challenges the essentialist assumptions of the pro-choice movement—assumptions that all women have the same interests and needs. Reproductive freedom challenges the exclusions not only within the dominant public, but also the exclusions replicated by the feminist counterpublic. After years of advocacy by poor women and women of color targeted at abortion choice advocacy groups, change began to happen.

## The Pro-Choice Movement Moves

Since the 1970s women of color and poor women have called for an expanded agenda of reproductive freedom, during the 1980s the feminist counterpublic sphere began to incorporate that agenda in its understanding of reproductive freedom, and in the 1990s advocacy organizations would institutionalize those demands as part of their agenda when they oscillated to engage the dominant public. Longtime activist and sociology professor Margaret Cerullo, in a 1989 speech at a rally in response to *Webster v. Reproductive Health Services*, outlined the broad areas of change needed in the choice movement. In a particularly self-reflective speech, she argues:

> At this moment, we must turn a critical eye on our own movement. We must ask, who has defined and who will define the reproductive rights agenda that we will fight for? Those of us who have been in control of this movement, in control of its national organizations, must move over and share power with the young women who are coming into the struggle; those of us who are white must move over and share power with women of color; those of us who are middle class must move over and share power with poor women; and those of us who are straight must publicly recognize the presence of lesbians and,

> increasingly, of gay men in this movement. We must include in our agenda the right of every woman to become pregnant in whatever way she chooses, and to parent with whomever she decides. And we cannot allow the public face of this struggle to remain a battle between two groups of white people—with the bodies and lives of women of color caught in the crossfire. We must expand our strategies and our agenda. (p. 8)

Others noted the beginning of this change.

Rosalind Petchesky (1990), one of the premiere researchers on the abortion controversy and an activist herself (she was a cofounder of CARASA), notes the change: "Happily, a new political movement based on a broader array of forces than feminism has yet known is beginning to emerge under the vocal leadership of black feminists active in the reproductive rights struggle" (p. 734). Nina Baehr (1990), in her radical history of the abortion movement, writes: "One of the most exciting things about the current movement for reproductive freedom is the sense that it will be more inclusive than the early pro-abortion movement and the recent pro-choice movement" (p. 53). Kathryn Kolbert (litigator in *Planned Parenthood v. Casey*) (1989/1990) endorsed the notion that freedom includes not only choice, but the ability to exercise choice: "True reproductive freedom . . . includes much more than the legal right to choose abortion. It includes the right to decide whether, when, with whom, and under what conditions women will have children, and envisions a world in which women will have both the economic means and the social conditions to effectuate whatever moral decisions they make" (p. 3).

CARASA's own shift from 1977 to 1988 reflects this broadening of agenda (for a history of CARASA, see Nelson, 2003). In its initial iteration of reproductive freedom in its 1979 pamphlet, *Women under Attack*, the group (primarily composed of socialist feminists) defined it as women having

> the possibility of controlling for themselves, in a real and practical way—that is, free from economic, social, or legal coercion—whether, and under what conditions, they will have children. . . . *Genuine control over one's own reproductive life* must mean, among other things, the universal availability of good, safe, cheap birth control; and adequate counseling for *all* women and men about *all* currently existing methods. It must mean adequate abortion services and an end to involuntary sterilization. It must mean the availability to *all* people of good public childcare centers and schools; decent housing, adequate welfare, and wages high enough to support a family; and of quality medical, pre- and post-natal and maternal care. It also must mean freedom of sexual choice, which implies an end to the cultural norms that define women in

> terms of having children and living with a man; an affirmation of people's right to raise children outside of conventional families; and, in the long run, a transformation of childcare arrangements so that they are shared among women and men. Finally, all these aspects of reproductive freedom must be available to *all* people—women, minorities, the disabled and handicapped, medicaid and welfare recipients, teenagers, everyone. (CARASA, 1979, p. 11)

CARASA reissued their pamphlet in 1988 and immediately recognized "our vision of reproductive freedom has broadened since 1979. . . . Our increasing understanding propels us to struggle around new issues of reproductive freedom: the new reproductive technologies and the possibilities of abortion and sterilization abuse related to AIDS" (p. 1). The pamphlet explicitly recognizes "women are not a homogenous group" and, thus, "have been subjected to vastly varied forms of oppression" (p. 3). Thus, reproductive freedom must include legal, safe, and accessible abortion; freedom from sterilization abuse; sexuality and lesbian rights; access to contraception and sex education; childcare and medical care; safe jobs paying living wages and affordable housing; reproductive technologies; and freedom from stereotyped gender roles (for parallel lists, see Kolbert 1989/1990, pp. 4–5; Fried, 1990; and Fried & Ross,1992).

The vivid articulation of the interests and needs of *all* women, and not just white middle-class women, influenced the mainstream organizations that have long dominated abortion advocacy. The Religious Coalition for Abortion Rights, in response to the work of its Women of Color Partnership Program (1988a, 1988b, 1989, 1990, 1991b), expanded its agenda. On December 13, 1993, RCAR announced in a news release that it had "expanded its focus beyond abortion to include full reproductive choice. The organization's broadened purpose is 'to ensure that every women is free to make decisions about when to have children according to her own conscience and religious beliefs, without government interference'" (RCRC, 1993). The release quoted Rev. Ragsdale, president of RCAR, describing the move as "putting abortion back where it belongs—in the context of women's full reproductive health." The new RCRC mission recognizes "Because women of color are disproportionately affected by restrictive laws and policies, the Coalition places particular emphasis on developing broad-based participation and leadership" (RCAR, 1993, p. 2). The new mission promises that its "work for reproductive choice must go beyond the single issue of abortion. We must defend the right of women *not* to have children, by ensuring accurate information and safe contraception, as well as abortion—*and* the right of women to *have* children, by ensuring adequate family planning and prenatal services and ending involuntary sterilization" (RCAR, 1993, p. 2). Along with the new mission, the group announced a new name: the Religious Coalition for Reproductive Choice (RCRC), which continues to be its name. When discussing the name change that attended the shift in mission, RCAR explained: "Changing our name *would* acknowledge that abortion cannot be taken out of context of a larger picture of reproductive decisions—and that women need to be free to make any such decisions . . ." (RCAR, 1993, p. 2).

In 1994, the National Abortion Rights Action League also changed its name to the National Abortion and Reproductive Rights Action League and expanded its mission so that its political and policy work would include "a range of reproductive health initiatives that can make abortion less necessary" (NARAL, 1994a). The January 14, 1994, news release announcing this change explained that NARAL "has adopted a broader agenda that includes safe and legal abortion, better sexuality education, more effective contraceptive methods, access to prenatal care, and healthy infants and children" (NARAL, 1994a).

*Promoting Reproductive Choices* (1994b), the sixty-page booklet that outlines NARAL's shift in name and mission, identifies five main goals: (1) protecting adolescent reproductive health, (2) preventing unintended pregnancy and sexually transmitted diseases, (3) ensuring access to safe abortion services, (4) eliminating coercive reproductive health policies, and 5) promoting healthy pregnancy and early child health (pp. i–iii). The report outlines a "new approach to reproductive health care—an approach that recognizes that genuine reproductive freedom requires the ability to make informed, responsible decisions about sexuality, contraception, abortion, childbirth and childrearing" (p. vi). Unfortunately, it seems NARAL refocused on choice in 2003 with the name NARAL Pro-Choice America and attendant campaign to make abortion a key issue in the 2004 election (Lee, 2003). Women of color would challenge NARAL on this during planning for the 2004 March for Women's Lives.

Women of color's threat to not participate in a narrow choice agenda was made real in 2003, when women of color initially refused to participate in the 2004 "March for Freedom of Choice" unless changes were made. Loretta Ross, an organizer of the SisterSong Women of Color Reproductive Health Collective annual conference, explained, "I didn't want our discussion derailed talking about white women again" (as cited in Kashef, 2004). During its 2003 conference, SisterSong laid out conditions for participation: "If the focus of the march went beyond abortion, if they included women of color on the steering committee and if they gave money to women of color to organize, then we'd be willing to participate" (Ross as cited in Kashef, 2004). The National Organization for Women, NARAL ProChoice America, Planned Parenthood and the Feminist Majority Foundation, the organizers of the event, agreed, and renamed the event the "March for Women's Lives." Ross explains why the name change away from choice was critical:

> "'Choice' is a problematic term in communities of color," says Ross. Faced with a lack of health insurance and health care access; immigration restrictions; and population control policies such as welfare reform "family caps" and sterilization abuse, many women of color health advocates don't see their communities as having choices. "To frame it as a liberal, individualistic choice message doesn't speak to the [lack of] control in communities of color," she notes. (Kashef, 2004)

The National Latina Institute for Reproductive Health and the Black Women's Health Imperative became members of the steering committee, and brought to the table a more holistic approach to reproductive freedom. However, the March still had a strong focus on choice and, even when its activities included reproductive freedom, "mainstream media persisted in characterizing the protest in terms of abortion rights" (Roberts, 2004, p. 539). As activist and scholar Dorothy E. Roberts (2004) notes, "the battle to expand the agendas of these [mainstream reproductive rights and women's] organizations and to transform their understanding of reproductive freedom is far from over" (p. 358).

## IMPLICATIONS

Women of color and poor women's call to shift focus from abortion choice to the larger social context in which reproductive and sexual decisions are made provides insight into the dynamics between counterpublics. The demand for a broader agenda was a demand from one counterpublic (women of color and poor women) to another (the women's movement). Once the agenda was expanded, then the coalition of forces could demand change by the establishment. This makes clear that the models of social movement that have long dominated the discipline are not adequate. Social movement research focusing on the dynamics between the establishment and the movement or between the movement and the countermovement miss an important rhetorical development. Counterpublic theory, with its emphasis on a multiplicity of publics, some of which are more marginalized from the establishment than others, can help highlight the unique contribution of women of color and poor women to discourses on maternity.

With a wider agenda, and with participation of diverse groups, the topography of the argument shifts beyond the simple weighing of women's choice against fetal life. Reproductive freedom elevates discrimination from being an auxiliary ideograph to being an intrinsic ideograph. Reproductive freedom demands examination of the differential effects of reproductive restrictions and opportunities on poor women and women of color to understand exactly what demands activists must make in order to ensure reproductive freedom for all women and men. A broad range of concerns that extends far beyond the initial privacy right recognized in *Roe* is publicly articulated. Such a shift is essential to move the debate beyond the constraints of hegemonic assumptions. Rosalind Petchesky (1990) remarks:

> The struggle to achieve women's reproductive freedom cannot succeed in the long run if conducted as a civil liberties struggle for individual privacy. . . . What is lost in the language of liberal privacy is the concept of social rights, familiar in most European social democracies: that society has a responsibility to ameliorate the conditions that make either abortion or childbearing a hard, painful choice for some women, and that the bearers of this right are not so much isolated individuals as they are members of social groups with distinct needs. (p. 734)

The fact is that women do, indeed, have children and a rights analysis premised on equal treatment is unable to account for that. The dominant discourse, bounded by abstract notions of equality, is unable to recognize the substantive inequalities created by neutrality. By explicitly introducing the concerns of particular groups, no longer is neutrality and abstraction a possibility.

Communication studies scholars, in particular, recognize the power of language to direct people's attention, to shape the way people understand the world. Reproductive freedom is a vivid example where a shift in terminology has the potential to shift the debate, and activists, feminists, and public policy-makers should embrace it. This is not an argument to avoid or evade the fraught debates over abortion choice (especially at a time when the House just passed a health care reform bill with the Stupak-Pitts amendment attached), but to recognize that places for common ground do exist, and that to truly secure all women's (and men's) reproductive freedom, a broader scope of discussion is needed. Thus, attention to reproductive freedom asks activists not only to be outraged over the Stupak-Pitts amendment, but also to ask if the health care reform bill guarantees broad reproductive coverage for all.

Choice, meaning abortion choice, alone as a focus is extremely problematic. As women of color have made clear, an agenda defined by it is not one in which they will participate. It frames the debate in such a way that not only are concerns of women of color and poor women marginalized, but it also frames the debate in a way that has proven irresolvable. Perhaps broadening the scope of the debate can tap into the broader argument to, as the RCRC asks, "Trust women." Thus, people concerned about building coalitions, and working in a women's movement that truly moves the world in a direction beneficial to all women, need to consider embracing this terminological shift.

Unfortunately, even when activists fully integrate *reproductive freedom* into their vocabulary, they are not always heard. Despite activists' clear articulations of a unique reproductive freedom agenda, those in power often still hear it as merely a mask for abortion advocacy. One example comes from my own experiences. In the early 1990s, while working at a Catholic university, I was approached by a group of students who wanted to create a group called Advocates for Reproductive Freedom (ARF). Although the group clearly articulated a broad agenda, the administration declared ARF was merely a pro-choice group and overruled the student government's recognition of the group. Even though the group's agenda did not center around abortion choice, which meant most of the agenda was consistent with Catholicism, the school's administration refused to believe that reproductive freedom was distinct from choice.

Ultimately the shift from choice to reproductive freedom is one that holds out the possibility for an expansion and reinvigoration of public discourse on maternity and reproductive justice, even if that shift is not an easy one to effect. Much as Fraser (1992) predicts, "the proliferation of subaltern counterpublics means a widening of discursive contestation, and that is a good thing in stratified societies" (p. 124). Reproductive freedom as articulated by women of color and poor women provides an excellent mechanism by which the limited agendas of apparently radical groups can be challenged for their failing to account for privilege. As we contemplate maternity, we should contemplate it from the perspectives of all women.

## REFERENCES

Abortion rights and real choice [editorial]. (1994, January 1). *Washington Post*, A26.

Asen, R. (2000). Seeking the "counter" in counterpublics. *Communication Theory*, *10*, 424–46.

Avery, B. (1990). A question of survival/A conspiracy of silence: Abortion and Black women's health. In M. G. Fried (Ed.), *From abortion to reproductive freedom: Transforming a movement* (pp. 75–82). Boston, MA: South End Press.

Baehr, N. (1990). *Abortion without apology: A radical history for the 1990s*. Boston, MA: South End Press.

Bowers, J. W., Ochs, D. J., & Jensen, R. J. (1993). *The rhetoric of agitation and control* (2nd ed.). Prospect Heights, IL: Waveland Press.

Brouwer, D. C. (2001). ACT-ing UP in congressional hearings. In R. Asen & D. C. Brouwer (Eds.), *Counterpublics and the State* (pp. 87–110). Albany: State University of New York Press.

Campbell, K. K. (1973). The rhetoric of Women's Liberation: An oxymoron. *Quarterly Journal of Speech*, *59*, 74–86.

CARASA. (1979). *Women under attack: Abortion, sterilization abuse, and reproductive freedom*. New York: CARASA.

CARASA, & Davis, S. E. (Ed.). (1988). *Women under attack: Victories, backlash and the fight for reproductive freedom*. Boston, MA: South End Press.

Cathcart, R. S. (1978). Movements: Confrontation as rhetorical form. *Southern Speech Communication Journal*, *43*, 233–47.

Cerullo, M. (1989, August). We won't go back. *Sojourner*, 8.

Chappell, M. (2002). Rethinking women's politics in the 1970s: The League of Women Voters and the National Organization for Women confront poverty. *Journal of Women's History*, *13*, 155–79.

Chan, C. S. (1990). Reproductive issues are essential survival issues for the Asian-American community. In M. G. Fried (Ed.), *From abortion to reproductive freedom: Transforming a movement* (pp. 175–78). Boston, MA: South End Press.

Colker, R. (1994). *Pregnant men: Practice, theory, and the law*. Bloomington: Indiana University Press.

Condit (Railsback), C. (1984). The contemporary American abortion controversy: Stages in the argument. *Quarterly Journal of Speech*, *70*, 410–24.

Condit, C. M. (1990). *Decoding abortion rhetoric*. Urbana: Illinois University Press.

Daniels, J. A. (1990). Court-ordered caesareans: A growing concern for indigent women. In M. G. Fried (Ed.), *From abortion to reproductive freedom: Transforming a movement* (pp. 255–62). Boston, MA: South End Press.

Davis, A. (1981/1983). Racism, birth control, and reproductive rights. *Women, race and class*. New York: Vintage. Reprinted in M. G. Fried (Ed.) (1990). *From abortion to reproductive freedom: Transforming a movement* (pp. 15–26). Boston, MA: South End Press.

Elvin, J. (1991, September 27). Nation: Inside the beltway. *Washington Times*, A6.

Expanding the meaning of choice [editorial]. (1994, January 17). *New York Times*, A16.

Felski, R. (1989). *Beyond feminist aesthetics*. Cambridge, MA: Harvard University Press.

Frankfort, E. (1979). *Rosie: The investigation of a wrongful death*. New York: Dial Press.

Fraser, N. (1992). Rethinking the public sphere. In C. Calhoun (Ed.), *Habermas and the Public Sphere* (pp. 109–42). Cambridge: MIT Press.

Fried, M. G. (Ed.). (1990). *From abortion to reproductive freedom: Transforming a movement*. Boston, MA: South End Press.

Fried, M., & Ross, L. (1992, April 5). *Reproductive freedom: Our right to decide*. Westfield, NJ: Open Magazine Pamphlet Series. Pamphlet released for the 1992 March on Washington.

Habermas, J. (1989). The public sphere. In S. Seidman (Ed.), *Jürgen Habermas on society and politics: A reader* (pp. 231–36). Boston, MA: Beacon Press.

Hayden, Sara. (2009). Revitalizing the debate between <life> and <choice>: The 2004 March for Women's Lives. *Communication and Critical/Cultural Studies, 6*, 111–31.

hooks, b. (1989). *Talking back: Thinking feminist, thinking Black*. Boston, MA: South End Press.

Hull, G. T., Scott, P. B., & Smith B. (Eds.). (1982). *But some of us are brave: All the women are white, all the blacks are men.* New York: Feminist Press.

Jamieson, K. H. (1992). *Dirty politics*. New York: Oxford University Press.

Joseph, G. I., & Lewis, J. (1981). *Common differences: Conflicts in black and white feminist perspectives.* Boston, MA: South End Press.

Kashef, Z. (2004, December 22). Toward reproductive freedom: If women of color can frame reproductive rights as both health and social justice issues, that would be one of the most significant outcomes of the historic March for Women's Lives. *Colorlines Magazine*. Retrieved from http://www.thefreelibrary.com/

Keju-Johnson, D., Eknilang, L., & Palacios, C. (1990, Fall). Pacific women speak. *Woman of Power, 18*, 36–41.

Kolbert, K. (1989). A reproductive rights Agenda for the 1990s. *Yale Journal of Law and Feminism, 1*, 3–5. (Reprinted in M. G. Fried (Ed.) (1990). *From abortion to reproductive freedom: Transforming a movement* (pp. 297–306). Boston, MA: South End Press.

Lake, R. A. (1983, May). Enacting Red Power: The consummatory function in Native American protest. *Quarterly Journal of Speech, 69*, 127–42.

Lee, J. (2003, January 5). Abortion rights group plans a new focus. *New York Times*. Retrieved from http://www.nytimes.com

Letter from a welfare mother. (1971). *Women: A Journal of Liberation, 2*, 50–51.

Lujan, T. (1993). "Latinas speak out for choice." *RCAR Newsletter, 20*(2), p. 8.

MacKinnon, C. A. (1987). *Feminism unmodified*. Cambridge, MA: Harvard University Press.

Mansbridge, J. (1996). Using power/fighting power: The polity. In S. Benhabib (Ed.), *Democracy and difference: Contesting the boundaries of the political* (pp. 46–66). Princeton, NJ: Princeton University Press.

Mansbridge, J. (1998). Feminism and democracy. In Anne Phillips (Ed.), *Feminism & Politics* (pp. 142–58). New York: Oxford University Press.
More threats to a woman's liberty. (1990, June 26). *New York Times*, A22.
Murphy, J. M. (1992). Domesticating dissent: The Kennedys and the freedom rides. *Communication Monographs*, *59*, 61–78.
NARAL. (1994a, January 14). Leading pro-choice group adds sexuality education, contraception and prenatal care to its agenda [news release].
NARAL. (1994b). *Promoting reproductive choices: A new approach to reproductive health*. Washington, DC: NARAL Foundation.
Nelson, J. (2003). *Women of color and the reproductive rights movement*. New York: New York University Press.
Petchesky, R. (1990, May 28). Giving women a real choice. *Nation*, 732–35.
Pezzullo, P. C. (2003). Resisting "National Breast Cancer Awareness Month": The rhetoric of counterpublics and their cultural performances. *Quarterly Journal of Speech*, *89*, 345–65.
RCAR. (1993). RCAR in the '90s: A redefined mission, A new name? *Newsletter*, *20*(2), p. 2.
RCRC. (1993, December 13). Religious Coalition for Abortion Rights broadens mission, changes name [news release].
Roberts, D. E. (1990, Summer). The future of reproductive choice for poor women and women of color. *Women's Rights Law Reporter*, *12*, 59–67.
Roberts, D. E. (1997). *Killing the Black body: Race, reproduction and the meaning of liberty*. New York: Pantheon.
Roberts, D. E. (2004). [Review of the book *Women of Color and the reproductive rights movement*, by J. Nelson]. *Journal of the History of Sexuality*, *13*, 535–39.
Ruiz, V. L., & DuBois, E. C. (Eds.). (1994). *Unequal sisters: A multicultural reader in U.S. women's history* (2nd ed.). New York: Routledge.
Silliman, J., Fried, M. G., Ross, L., & Gutiérrez, E. R. (2004). *Undivided rights: Women of Color organize for reproductive justice*. Cambridge, MA: South End Press.
Smith, A. (2005). Beyond pro-choice versus pro-life: Women of color and reproductive justice. *NWSA Journal*, *17*(1), 119–40.
Springer, K. (2002). Third wave black feminism? *Signs*, *27*, 1060–82.
Staggenborg, S. (1991). *The pro-choice movement: Organization and activism in the abortion conflict*. New York: Oxford.
Tribe, L. H. (1990, July 2). Will the abortion fight ever end? A nation held hostage [Editorial]. *New York Times*, A15.
Walker, A. (1989, May 22). What can the white man . . . say to the Black woman? *Nation*, 691–92.
We remember: African American women are for reproductive freedom [pamphlet]. (Circa 1991). RCAR. Reprinted by Women of Color Partnership, RCRC, circa 1994.
White, L. D. (1990, September/October). Sisters in session. *New Directions for Women*, *8*.

Women of Color Partnership Program (RCAR/RCRR). (1988a, April). *Common Ground—Different Planes.* [newsletter].

Women of Color Partnership Program (RCAR/RCRR). (1988b, December). *Common Ground—Different Planes* [newsletter].

Women of Color Partnership Program (RCAR/RCRR). (1989, August). *Common Ground—Different Planes.* [newsletter].

Women of Color Partnership Program (RCAR/RCRR) (1990). Vision statement: Women of Color Partnership program. In M. G. Fried (Ed.), *From abortion to reproductive freedom: Transforming a movement* (pp. 293–94). Boston, MA: South End Press.

Women of Color Partnership Program (RCAR/RCRR). (1991a, Summer). *Common Ground—Different Planes.* [newsletter].

Women of Color Partnership Program (RCAR/RCRR). (1991b). Reproductive health among Black women in the U.S. [pamphlet].

## NOTES

1. An earlier version of this chapter was presented at the 1994 Speech Communication Association Convention, held in New Orleans, LA. The author thanks Randall Lake, Ph.D., for his thoughtful comments then and Robert Asen, Ph.D., for his feedback on counterpublic theory more recently.

2. In contemporary usage, *reproductive freedom*, *reproductive rights*, and *reproductive justice* are used interchangeably (Silliman et al., 2004, p. 4).

3. In 1969, NARAL was founded as the National Association for the Repeal of Abortion Laws. In 1973, after the *Roe v. Wade* decision, it changed its name to the National Abortion Rights Action League. In 1993, it again changed its name to the National Abortion and Reproductive Rights Action League but kept the same acronym. Then, in 2003, it became NARAL Pro-Choice America.

4. Jamieson (1992) argues that media focus on the strategy of political campaigns instead of on the substance of policy differences. A similar dynamic is in operation here. Even some academic studies of the expanded focus minimize the role of women of color and focus on it as a strategic move by mainstream pro-choice groups (e.g., Staggenborg, 1991).

5. Even the concept of *waves* itself can be exclusionary as it "obscures the historical role of race in feminist organizing" (Springer, 2002, p. 1061). For example, even before such a thing as a women's movement existed, "enslaved women actively resisted rape, forced pregnancy, and separation from their children on plantations. Through natural abortion methods and fighting back against nonconsensual sexual relations when they could, they enacted an early form of feminist resistance to distinctly gendered oppression aimed at women" (p. 1062).

6. Andrea Smith (2005) offers a vivid analysis of how the choice/life paradigm marginalizes women of color. She is skeptical of any attempt to simply broaden the

pro-choice agenda. Instead, she argues a reproductive justice agenda can only be achieved as the result of a nationally coordinated women of color movement that positions reproductive justice within a larger social justice agenda.

7 For more information on Trias, see Mississippi appendectomy: a developing online archive of information about women of color and coercive sterilization at http://mississippiappendectomy.wordpress.com/2007/11/25/sterilization-abuse/

8. RCAR created the Women of Color Partnership Program in 1985 as "a vehicle through which African American women, Latina women, Asian/Pacific Islander women, Native American women and all women of color in this country can become actively involved, as decision makers, in the reproductive choice movement" (Women of Color Partnership Program, 1991a, p. 8).

9. The internal text originally was written by Marcia Gillespie in the summer of 1989, but the list of freedoms was added to the circa 1991 pamphlet, of which 250,000 were distributed (see http://www.ourbodiesourselves.org/book/companion.asp?id=31&compID=41). RCRC reformatted and redistributed the pamphlet circa 1994.

5

# THE COMMODIFICATION OF MOTHERHOOD

## Surrogacy as a Matter of Choice

*Charlotte Kroløkke, Karen A. Foss, and Jennifer Sandoval*

Surrogate motherhood first was brought to the public's attention during a 1987 custody case of a baby girl known as "baby M." The public was confronted with the story of William and Elizabeth Stern, both professionals, who desired a child genetically related to one of them. Simultaneously, the public was introduced to Mary Beth Whitehead, a working-class mother with two children who agreed to enter a surrogacy contract with the Sterns. During the pregnancy, however, she realized she wanted to keep the baby. This ignited a long custody battle over baby M. In the courts, the surrogacy contract first was validated and then invalidated by the New Jersey Supreme Court. In both decisions, custody was given to the biological father, William Stern, and visitation rights granted to the biological mother, Mary Beth Whitehead (Markens, 2007).

Surrogacy raises a wide range of questions related to our understanding of reproductive choice and the making of motherhood. In the midst of commercial surrogacy how do we understand reproductive choice, for example? How do we come to understand motherhood when the product of one woman's egg or womb is intended to make another woman a mother? New reproductive technologies have reconceptualized motherhood into separate components such as social and biological motherhood. Gestational surrogacy blurs the lines between biological and social motherhood even further. The gestational surrogate is connected to the embryo through her blood system, yet another woman's ova are used to create the embryo, granting couples more options. They can possibly create a child genetically related to (one of) them or custom-pick the ova, sperm, and carrier needed to create the baby (Strathern, 1988).

In this chapter, we examine the choices that are constructed around and play out in the various discourses surrounding surrogacy. We are interested in highlighting the discursive frames within which surrogacy is constituted, mediated, and understood. To address these concerns, we first present two dominant framings typically offered up in regard to choice and surrogacy—gift-giving choice and commercial choice—discussing the mechanisms of agency and constraint that each choice offers. We then turn to four surrogacy websites to examine whether and how choice plays out in the marketing of surrogacy.

## PERSPECTIVES ON CHOICE

As in any commercial or capitalistic system, the question of how choices are made and who gets to make them is in the forefront. Matters of choice—and in particular choices regarding the female body and reproductive processes—historically have sparked debate about systemic constraints that limit full agency. Traditionally, feminist discourse has followed the dominant line of freedom versus emancipation (Mies & Shiva, 1993). This dualistic perspective, however, does not allow for the complexities in women's lives to be fully taken into account—complexities that allows for both the ability to choose as well as multiple constraints on those choices. This contradiction can be seen in the framing of surrogacy as both the product of scientific advancement and a new choice as well as a practice constrained in a number of ways.

Within the rapidly changing global body economies, the material conditions of individuals and their positionalities are critical to understanding how choice and constraints are experienced by the various decision-makers. These changes create "new planes of dis/empowerment" unique to this moment in history (Shome & Hegde, 2002, p. 175). As couples turn to surrogates to have children they consider "their own," the medical, legal, and governmental communities increasingly regulate the industry and with it women's bodies.

The legislation of the female body in relation to reproduction creates additional constraints on women's choice particularly in regard to the rights afforded a fetus. Pregnancy is no longer a process a woman experiences where the fetus is part of the body; rather the woman's body becomes both separate from the fetus and an incubator for a baby. One such example is the *Lynch v. Lynch* case, in which the court upheld the right of a child to sue its mother for damages, holding her responsible for an injury the child incurred in the womb due to a car accident (Karpin, 1991). The pregnant body is inseparable from the fetus as well as distinct from and responsible for it. The issue of choice is not easily simplified into "being controlled" versus "being in control." Partial agency allows for a more complex view of the way women are able to make choices under structural or cultural constraints. Subjects enact some kind of agency even if the meanings applied to that choice "depend on the ways of interpreting the world and on the discourses available to them at any particular moment" (Canning, 1994, p. 377).

## Gift-Giving Choice

Gift giving traditionally has been studied in opposition to commodity exchange. "Gift" and "commodity" typically "form a single cultural pair" within Western discourses of economy (Strathern, 1988, p. 18), with the notion of "exchange" considered "natural" and placed in counterpoint to gifts (Strathern, 1988, p. 9). Thus, while gifts have been studied extensively in anthropology, in part because gifts tend to be the economy of families, small groups, and tribes (Damon, 1983; Feil, 1984; Hyde, 1983; Josephides, 1985; Mauss, 1990; Titmuss, 1997), Western categories that privilege systems of exchange have constrained if not dictated the terms of those discussions.

Feminist scholars are among those who have provided critiques of Western notions of exchange and who have elaborated what gift giving as a system has been and can be (Strathern, 1988). Genevieve Vaughan is perhaps the most prolific feminist thinker who has systematically explored gift economies (1999, 2002, 2004). She suggests that gift giving as a way of getting needs met in a society has not been allowed to develop because of the dominant ideology of patriarchal exchange systems—but that in fact such a system is and always has been available in the practices embedded in mothering (Vaughan, 2004, p. 1). At the core of Vaughan's conceptualization of a gift economy modelled on mothering is "unilateral gift giving" or "the unilateral satisfaction of another's need." While considerably more complex in agrarian societies in which children play an important role in daily work activities, contemporary Western formulations of motherhood demand that the woman gives "without a return of a self-interested kind" (Held, 1990, pp. 297–98; Vaughan, 1999).[1]

In addition, gift giving is creative, other oriented, and communicates value to the other. In the process of giving a gift, the "giver attends to the needs of the other and finds or creates something" that will satisfy that individual specifically while the giver receives something "appropriate to her needs" (Vaughan, 2004, p. 5). As a result, a relationship or connection is established that not only binds the two together but transfers value from the giver to the receiver: "if the receiver were not important to the giver, she would probably not be satisfying the need" (Vaughan, 2002, p. 1). Mauss, in his classic book on the gift (1990), suggests that the gift creates obligation precisely because it "still possesses something" of the giver: "to make a gift of something to someone is to make a present of some part of oneself" (Mauss, 1990, p. 12).

Not surprising, given its associations with motherhood, the notion of gift giving, as metaphor and reality, is prominent in both discussions of biological reproduction and in alternate and technological approaches to motherhood. The child as gift is a common framing—babies are described as "gifts from God," and mothers sometimes talk of giving a gift of a child to the child's father (Layne, 1999). In other cases, such as when a child has disabilities or special needs, the child is often described as a gift to the parent, offering life lessons about appreciation and unconditional love (Landsman, 1999). Even when monetary exchange is involved—breast milk donation (Weaver & Williams, 1997), foster parenting (Wozniak, 1999), adoption (Modell, 1999), sperm/egg donation (Kroløkke & Foss, 2007), and surrogacy (Ragoné, 1994, 2000)—the metaphor of the gift dominates the discourse: an individual is able to give something to another—sperm, egg, womb, child—to help another become a parent.

While altruism seemingly is present to a large degree in reproductive "gifts," altruism also masks the complexity of this issue for women. This is particularly true of egg donation and surrogacy. That it is women who give of their reproductive capabilities (sperm donation is the only exception) goes largely unexamined, perhaps because, as Raymond (1993) argues, it is part of a long and accepted tradition of giving women and their bodies away. Gift-giving rhetoric also disguises the commercial gains made by agencies and other "baby brokers" who instead of "selling babies" now are fulfilling the ultimate dream of parenthood and providing services in the process (Markens, 2007).

The degree to which a woman is making a truly self-determined choice when she gives of her reproductive capability is difficult to determine (Raymond, 1993, p. 52). Ragoné (2000) is particularly critical of altruistic surrogacy because despite the rhetoric of the gift, monetary exchange is still involved. Doctors, lawyers, and other fertility experts clearly receive fees for their services, so "elevating" surrogacy to a gift—one far too profound to conceptualize in commercial terms—is to ignore other important commercial aspects of the process (Ragoné, 2000). The fact that surrogates frequently come from less privileged socioeconomic backgrounds is masked, for example, when surrogacy is discursively presented and privileged as a gift. Further, the constraints of traditional definitions of how women should feel may impact the way that they talk about their choices (Elgin, 1999). Gift giving, then, is a common way of framing surrogacy, but it is a frame wrought with contradictions and complexities.

## Commercial Choice

Despite the tendency to frame surrogacy in gift terms, there is no denying that in contemporary culture surrogacy shares all the facets of a marketplace (Spar, 2006). The market consists of consumers (intended parents), commodities (babies), reproductive workers (surrogates), legal documents (surrogacy contracts), supervisors (doctors), and owners (fertility clinics/consumers). Not surprisingly, however, the commodification of baby making is highly controversial; no one likes to think of babies as a business (Spar, 2006).

Several factors have contributed to the development of what is now a global and highly specialized fertility market. First, infertility in the West has been constructed as a problem of almost epidemic proportion (Raymond, 1993). Because infertile individuals from Western nations have been willing and able to dig deep into their pockets to have a baby genetically related to them, they have moved out of the patient position and into the position of consumers. Secondly, developments within reproductive technologies have enabled infertile clients to purchase whatever "part" is missing. Sperm may come from a Danish donor, the egg from an Ivy League student, while the surrogate may be from India or the Ukraine. Thirdly, different national legislative restrictions have motivated parents desperate for a baby to cross national borders. In combination, these factors constitute the prime ingredients of what is now a growing and profitable global fertility industry, all made even more accessible by the development of the Internet.

Given the market dynamics at play, the work of consumer theorists is particularly insightful (Baudrillard, 1998; Featherstone, 1991; Lury, 1996). Consumer theorists note the symbolic and cultural practices inherent in new reproductive practices. Sperm is selected, for instance, not just because of its motility, but because of what it signifies: athletic, Christian, intelligent future babies (Kroløkke, 2009; Kroløkke & Foss, 2007). Surrogates are chosen on the basis of a healthy lifestyle, youth, and attractiveness, for example. Allowing commercial transactions to make families also challenges conventional understandings of gender, parenting, and the family (Mamo, 2007; Moore, 2007; Thompson, 2005). Purchasing sperm, for instance, may disrupt conventional ideas that reproduction takes place within the confines of a committed, heterosexual relationship. New reproductive technologies deconstruct essentialist notions of maternity, in the process allowing for new family constellations to emerge.

While much feminist critique links commercial choice and exploitation, others disagree. For instance, Spar (2006) critiques the exploitation argument, asking why it is problematic for Third World women to make the choices that First World women can make? Maternal labor should, in this framing, be commercially compensated and an option available to all women. Feminist scholars, however, tend to refute the critique by asking whether the choice to engage in commercial surrogacy truly empowers women as a group (Raymond, 1993). Fuelled by patriarchal and late-capitalist forms of oppression, commercial surrogacy, for these scholars, is cast as a choice growing out of economic despair rather than a choice springing out of self-determination.

The debate regarding the extent to which women are empowered is present in the surrogacy discourse in the same way it has been part of the pornography and prostitution conversation. Can women willingly enter into these professions as an economic opportunity? The so-called choices that are available to women are cast within the context of a larger social system that necessitates certain actions for survival or, as noted by Raymond: "The ease with which the right to choose shrinks to the right to consume should make us examine carefully the consumer-designed context of the new reproductive supermarket" (1993, p. 88). Although women are by no means passive actors in the business of surrogacy, the necessity for income combined with limited economic alternatives cannot be left out of the equation, and the considerable benefit to those engaged in the business of surrogacy cannot be completely ignored.

Commercial choice is indeed messy business. While surrogacy assists in constructing new definitions of the family, it also raises a series of complex questions: Who are the reproductive laborers? Who profits? How are women's wombs marketed and rented? And how is (in)fertility constructed, mediated, and consumed?

Ultimately, contradictions and tensions are present in each framing of choice, and feminist scholars can be found on both sides of the debate. Similarly, the position of surrogates themselves and the structures that monitor and regulate the surrogacy industry are in flux. These are tied to the context, positionality, and subjectivity of each actor and contribute to different understandings of providing or preventing women with access to choice.

## SURROGACY WEBSITES

To examine the particular ways choice plays out in surrogacy, we have chosen four websites to serve as the basis of our analysis. We are interested in how the notion of choice becomes part of the discourse of surrogacy and the degree to which there is a consistent framing of choice around this issue. To this end, we chose a variety of websites related to surrogacy that are directed toward Western couples, seeking a representative look at the issue of choice: Circle Surrogacy, Surrogacy India, International Surrogacy Partners, and Surrogate Mothers Online.

Circle Surrogacy is a U.S.-based fertility clinic (www.circlesurrogacy.com) that markets itself as a successful surrogacy and egg-donation clinic. Our second website is Surrogacy India (www.surrogacyindia.com), a UK- and Mumbai-based surrogacy center, catering to U.S. and European clients. International Surrogacy Partners, our third website (www.surrogateagency.com), is based in the United States but uses surrogates from the Ukraine (surrogateagency.com). It is also distinctive in billing itself as a not-for-profit agency. Finally, we have included one website for surrogate mothers themselves; Surrogate Mothers Online is a virtual meeting place for U.S.-based surrogate mothers (www.surromomsonline.com). In combination, this blend of surrogacy websites illustrates the transnational context of choice and the complexity with which it is negotiated.

Our analysis of these websites is informed by Nathan Stormer's notion of the body as a rhetorical situation. Viewing the body as a situation, Stormer (2006) argues, involves diverse ways of becoming that evolve over time and invoke gendered speaking positions.[2] Bodies are called into existence rhetorically and in relationship (or flows) with other bodies. The rhetorical situation, as articulated by Stormer (2006), concerns a situation in which an exigence or problem exists that is capable of being addressed by a particular rhetor and audience.

What this means for the processes of surrogacy we examine here is that we see the speaking subject and audience as simultaneously constructing and responding in particular gendered and rhetorical ways to the series of exigencies offered by the surrogacy experience. At the core is the surrogate's body, which responds literally to the exigence of another body's infertility by carrying a child. The infertility clinics and their websites provide information and services in response to the exigence of a need for action experienced by the intended parents—"there has to be something that can be done" to overcome infertility. Cultural discourses of pronatalism serve as yet another layer of exigence; having children is seen as an important and essential life experience, an exigence that propels many to seek out surrogacy. Individualism, self-determination, and pro-choice rhetorics are additional cultural discourses that play into this experience as well: the ability to make your own choices in life and to be able to succeed with those choices is the quintessential American dream. "Experience and embodiment and theorizing are mutually defining aspects of "becoming" (Stormer, 2006, p. 257). Thus, with the notion of human embodiment as situation, it is possible to understand how a person becomes a subject at one moment in response to one exigence but to a lesser degree in another. We will explore how the body as a situation helps explain shifting possibilities for choice that emerge in the surrogacy experience as described in four websites. The examination of the negotiation and management of choice will contribute to an understanding of choice as it meets new reproductive technologies and new mediated formats.

## ANALYSIS

### Circle Surrogacy Website

Circle Surrogacy, with headquarters in Boston, is an agency with an international clientele. In existence since 1995, Circle Surrogacy reportedly has helped individuals from over 30 countries, bringing approximately 300 babies into the world. President of the agency, John Weltman, a parent of two surrosons himself as well as an attorney of reproductive law, promotes surrogacy as a legitimate alternative to adoption. The agency's slogan, "Making Miracles Happen," is presented along with photos of two (white) children, a boy and a girl, playing by the water. The image reinforces the idea that surrogacy enables the making of happy, healthy, (white) families.

The website is set up with three different parties in mind: intended parents, egg donors, and potential surrogates. Fully incorporating all of the new media technologies, the agency engages the intended parents on the website, on Facebook, and in videos on YouTube. As Weltman notes, intended parents are in control: "You (intended parent) have had them both (the surrogate and the egg donor) completely psychologically reviewed" ("Screening and matching surrogates with intended parents," YouTube video, www.circlesurrogacy.com).[3] While previous birth history, home state, medical history, and support networks are all key ingredients in the choices that the agency makes, intended parents are free to set other requirements for the surrogate as well.

The agency disguises the intended parents' control over the process when it frames surrogacy as a gift-giving choice enabling the surrogate to put her own mark on the world. As noted on the website: "Being an egg donor or a surrogate mother is the greatest gift you can give to a childless couple and one for which you will be remembered as a valuable member of that family for generations to come." Pictures of pregnant surrogates along with happy parents create an image of a mutually empowering and enriching choice. This image is reiterated in the Circle Surrogacy YouTube videos in which surrogate mothers frame surrogacy as "a calling" and something "just meant to be." Weltman reinforces this image when he frames surrogates as extraordinary "goddesses,"disguising, in the process, the mercenary transactions and employee-employer relationships within which surrogates also are positioned ("Surrogacy for Gay Israelis," YouTube video).

Circle Surrogacy highlights the progressive potential of new reproductive technologies. We hear, for instance, of gay couples from Texas, Belgium, Israel, and Sweden, and about a gay dad just returning from Afghanistan. Weltman's own story as a gay, white male who, with his long-term partner, contracted with a surrogate for two surrosons testifies to the idea that more (gay) men are turning to surrogacy to fulfill their dreams of becoming fathers. In this manner, Circle Surrogacy embraces the making of families outside of the paradigm of heterosexual married relationships yet mimics heteronormative and, in fact, quite conservative values in its choice to focus on committed, gay couples and in stipulating the desire for children as "natural."

Stories from surrogates and parents are included on the website, but only pictures and short biographies are offered of egg donors, including a brief overview of their ethnic lineage, height, weight, education, and fertility success along with a facial photo. This is, as Weltman notes, the most important choice that intended parents have to make. The agency promises swift egg-donor matching while also encouraging intended parents to meet both egg donors and "carriers" (surrogates). Egg donors come from various ethnic backgrounds, yet they are frequently college students—fit and young. Surrogates, on the other hand, are valued for their lifestyle and birthing histories, most notably their ability to successfully carry a baby to term. The company's choice to frame surrogates as "carriers" further positions the surrogate within the employer-employee relationship. Weltman highlights this when he points to the advantages of gestational surrogacy: U.S. courts are not likely to grant gestational surrogates visitation or custody rights ("Surrogacy for Gay Israelis," YouTube video).

Circle Surrogacy effectively combines consumer choice with the potentials of new reproductive technologies. Intended parents are reassured of their agency and control while surrogates are doubly positioned as both "goddesses" and "carriers." Efficiency, expediency, and quality characterize the agency's self-presentation. Surrogacy seminars in London as well as Stockholm and Weltman's own background as a Harvard and Oxford graduate combined with an elaborate range of media coverage reaffirm the agency's positioning of itself as an international, high-quality agency.

## Surrogacy India Website

Surrogacy India bills itself as the "first and only third party Surrogacy agency in India" dealing professionally with surrogate mothers and egg donors. Three sets of pictures dominate the website, each with a link directed at potential clients, whether parents, surrogates, or egg donors. The first picture, over the link to "Surrogates," is of a very pregnant white woman with her shirt raised to show her pregnant belly; around her waist is a carpenter's tool belt, with children's toys spilling out of it. The second picture is of a seated, nonsmiling couple—the "Intended Parents" link. The third picture, representing "Egg Donors," is of a woman holding out an open hand into which a chicken egg is being placed. Intended parents, donors/surrogates, and the agency itself become the main characters in this website, each exercising choice and control in different ways (surrogacyindia.com).[4]

The agency itself is the starting point for the choices that are presented on the Surrogacy India website. Surrogacy India presents itself as the agency to choose for infertility issues because of its professionalism, perseverance, and complete and efficient services for parents. That representatives of Surrogacy India will even travel to the homes of intended parents, anywhere in the world, with what they call their program of "premium privileged parenthood"[5] is an indication of the lengths to which they will go to provide for their clients. Surrogacy India, then, is both distinguished by the features that construct its highly professional image and constrained by them: in order to preserve this image and gain future clients, they must maintain this level of professionalism, efficiency, and success.

The agency exercises choice at another level as well: they get to choose which clients to accept. In a list of procedures required of intended parents, the agency clearly is in control: "Our doctor team will review you and your spouse with the help of your previous medical records"; "Our fertility physicians will guide you with the best treatment options available"; and "You need to be with us now. Pack your bags to be here latest by day 6 of stimulation." On one hand, the agency presents itself as having to live up to the highest standards, with not much margin for error and not much choice in how it manages its clients and services. On the other, it exerts considerable control over the clients, dictating every aspect of the process. Not surprising, financial gain is not mentioned as a motivation for the agency; instead, the exigence to which the agency responds is the "pain, anguish, suffering which the hoping parents and families go through, to see a joyful little face" that is the agency's stated reason for being.

The intended parents might be assumed to have ultimate control with their choices at Surrogacy India; after all, they are the ones who get to choose to work with Surrogacy India to obtain a child. In addition, they choose the surrogate mother and/or the egg donor and thus choose, to some degree, the characteristics of their child. The website describes the intended parents as having "equal opportunity" to choose from a "huge" database of egg donors, and the choice of surrogate is "totally your prerogative."[6] But beyond these choices, the parents-to-be are operating within the requirements of the agency. They must meet the requirements for infertility, submit the proper paperwork and medical records, travel when told to, and pay the appropriate fees.

The surrogate mother/egg donor's contribution is framed as privileged. Her contribution is labelled "altruistic," "priceless," "invaluable," "self-sacrificing," and "brave." Her contribution is described as the "most rewarding act of kindness in the history of human mankind." She is referred to repeatedly as a "Special Woman" for her ability to give happiness to an infertile couple: "It's 'YOU' who can give happiness and smiles to the other couple." That the agency selects "only a few" surrogates makes her even more special. And while the language of the gift plays large in the presentation of the surrogate's motives, it is also raised as an issue for intended parents as well: what the surrogate offers is a gift that needs to be "acknowledged" by the intended parents for the "sisterly love, godly act, and mothering care" the surrogate provides.

The surrogate also has another important choice to make—how much compensation to ask for: "It's not us, it's you who decide the compensation package for yourselves." Thus compensation is discussed openly in terms of choice, although financial gain is always last on lists of a surrogate's motivations.[7] The choice of compensation is offset to some degree by the fact that certain characteristics make her more or less desirable as a surrogate and thus affect the amount of compensation she is likely to receive. These factors include whether she has had an intellectually gifted child in the past and her genetic background. In this sense, she is controlled not only in terms of payment but in terms of requirements during the pregnancy, such as where she lives: "we ensure a separate accommodation along with a caretaker during the surrogacy process." The constraints placed on her by the agency are offset by "monthly financial assistance, regular visits to the hospital, legal expenses, medical insurance," but these are minimized in comparison to her ultimate sacrifice and sense of agency. The surrogate, then, is described as having considerable control in this choice-making process: she has the choice of whether to become a surrogate and can negotiate the amount of payment.[8]

With Surrogacy India, the website emphasizes that the three parties involved—agency, parents, surrogate—are a "unified dedicated team," each with an important role to play in "making motherhood possible." The agency creates "the liaison, monitoring you and your surrogate, bringing together and ensuring the dream is made a reality, making baby a possibility." The logo emphasizes this as well: an abstract blue number 3 is shadowed by a line of pink, standing for the surrogate. Within the 3 are a plus and an arrow in circles—abstract references to male and female symbols. For the agency, however, the "plus" stands for "the value we add to you" while the arrow "indicates our aspiration to move right up." In the end, the agency remains in control, determining the value added and making sure that all parties "move right up" with them to successful parenthood.

### International Surrogacy Partners Website

International Surrogacy Partners is a Northern California based not-for-profit company that works exclusively with surrogacy clinics in the Ukraine. The website is relatively small, but offers an "Introduction to Surrogacy Pack" with application materials to begin the communication process with company representatives. The website's home page is simple in design with pictures of an infant's face and of a woman holding a baby nose to nose, with both mother and baby grinning. Next to the images is the quote: "Making the decision to have a child—it's momentous. It is to decide forever to have your heart go walking outside your body" (www.surrogateagency

.com).[9] While emotional in appeal, the quote centers the issue of decision-making in the surrogacy process.

International Surrogacy Partners began in 2007 to provide alternatives to families who experienced challenges with international adoption. According to the website, the same year their organization was founded, over 150 foreign couples successfully completed a surrogacy pregnancy in the Ukraine. It claims to be the first surrogacy company in the United States to partner with an Eastern European country, although surrogacy has been known throughout Europe for some time.

The website promotes the ease of working in the Ukraine and focuses on efficiency and on the commitment to helping intended parents get a child. It invokes the idea that working with a European country, unlike India, for instance, is more reliable and thus preferable. The intended parents have a large amount of choice in the process, including the selection of the surrogate mother. They are able to preselect from the United States, and if they are not satisfied when they meet the surrogate on their first trip to the Ukraine, they can select an alternate. There is no information about the surrogate's power to veto or opt out in the selection process. In addition, the intended parents can select the sex of their intended child by having gender determined prior to the implantation of an embryo. If they wish to try for the opposite sex, they start the process over and do not have to proceed with implantation until they are satisfied.

The agency presents its program as having exclusive rights to work with the Human Reproduction Center, a full-service infertility clinic in the city of Kharkov, where over 400 in vitro children were born in the last decade, as well as the International Surrogate Motherhood Center, which claims to have "the largest and most carefully selected databank of surrogate mothers, egg donors and sperm donors." The Surrogate Motherhood Center also handles all the legal aspects surrounding the surrogacy agreement and the child. The reasons for working with Eastern European partners are described pragmatically: legislation that does not allow a surrogate mother to keep the child; costs that are 50 to 60 percent lower, due to standard and cost of living compared to Western countries; the lack of waiting time; and the availability of "healthy surrogate mothers" all under the age of thirty.

International Surrogacy Partners does have some restrictions in terms of who can become a client. Intended parents must be English speaking and between the ages of twenty-two and fifty-eight. A single intended parent must be able to supply his or her own egg or sperm. Additionally, the total cost for the surrogacy process exceeds $50,000, thus requiring the intended parents to make a significant monetary investment in the birth of a child.

While the agency appears to focus on the wide range of choices its services provide for intended parents, as an organization it already has made many of the large decisions. The agency has selected only one location and clinic with which to work and has requirements for who qualifies to use its services. The agency also makes the first round of selection of potential surrogates and/or egg donors from which intended parents can choose while requiring two trips to the Ukraine—one for screening of surrogates and/or donors and one to pick up the baby. In many ways, International Surrogacy Partners constrains choice for intended parents at the same time it creates a new option for them.

Although the agency stipulates that surrogate mothers should be treated with respect and dignity, the surrogates themselves are relatively absent on the site. This absence would appear to imply that the surrogates do not have a great deal of control and decision-making power, if any, in the process. The surrogate mother is mentioned when discussing the monthly pregnancy-status reports the intended parents will receive. These involve not only medical updates but updates on the surrogate's emotional health, including visits to a psychologist who may also communicate with the family "to ensure that SM's overall environment and family life is healthy." The choice to focus on fetal development, for instance, further erases the surrogate (as a person) and reduces her body to a container of sorts. The additional needs and subsequent services provided to the surrogate mother may in fact be necessary and important, but they also imply a high level of monitoring of the surrogate's lifestyle.

Ultimately, the intended parents are privileged on the site for International Surrogacy Partners. The agency makes clear the importance of a user-friendly service that provides "the right to happiness through parenthood." The agency highlights its ability to make the process as smooth and easy as possible for intended parents and provide them with the largest amount of commercial choice. The surrogates are positioned as particularly constrained given their lack of presence in the site's description of the process and the fact that the agency "speaks" for them instead of giving them the literal and rhetorical space to do it themselves.

## Surrogate Mothers Online

Surrogate mothers share their stories, thoughts, and experiences with surrogacy on the website, Surrogate Mothers Online; the website also serves as a personal link between intended parents and surrogates as manifested in the many personal ads listed on the site. Several consistent themes appear:

pregnancy is defined as a "journey," birth is framed as a "privilege," and the act of surrogacy is labelled "babysitting" and a "gift-giving" choice (www.surromomsonline.com).[10] Surromoms define pregnancy as a metaphorical journey to be shared with the intended parents. Frequently, no agency is involved and regular contact with the parents is preferred. A one-on-one, personalized contract (and contact) between the surrogate and intended parents is created. While surromoms describe their own pregnancy histories, physical health, and marital status, they also articulate expectations of the intended parents in their surrogate ads related to both personality (sincerity), sexual orientation (gay or heterosexual couples), as well as age or marital status.

Pregnancy and the ability to give birth are cast as particularly privileged experiences. As noted by a surromom in her online story: "I am one of the lucky ones. Conception is easy and pregnancy is successful." While the surrogate here frames herself as an efficient assembly line of sorts, infertility is conceptualized as an almost unimaginable trauma. Although financial compensation is required by almost all surromoms, their ability to perform surrogacy, not the money involved, is rhetorically privileged in their personal ads as well as in the stories available in the online forum. Surromoms are in the business of "making families." The choice to become a surrogate, although infused with financial compensation, is importantly also framed as an altruistic one.

Surrogacy is overwhelmingly defined as a gift-giving choice and as an extended form of babysitting. In an online story, one gestational surrogate states:

> I will hold their little embryo deep inside my body, nourish it, warm it, and keep it safe for nine months. I will sing to it, rock it, read to it, and feel it move. I will love the gift that I am giving, but not like my own children. It is a spiritual love that will heal a family full of pain. I feel so special to be trusted with such a precious cargo.

The surrogate performs many of the traditional roles of the babysitter, mother, or caretaker. Yet, the embryo is distinctly not hers, and in describing the embryo as "their embryo" and her love toward it as "spiritual," she reassures the intended parents that they are the "real" parents.

Motherly love is both privileged and naturalized. One surromom notes: "knowing the love a mother has for a child makes me believe that every woman should have a chance at feeling the love for their own." The surrogate mother's choice to become a surrogate is not only honored, but also cast as a particularly privileged choice. Altruistic and spiritual giving are the focus for the moms on this website, with financial compensation mentioned only in light of the number of successful births, including previous surrogate children. The surrogate's competencies and experiences as a surrogate determine the compensation, something she alone stipulates. It is not surprisingly the special blend of love for pregnancies, the plight of infertility, and the desire to complete another family—and not the hormonal injections, pregnancy nausea, or failed inseminations—that is presented on this site.

## CONCLUSION

This analysis of surrogacy websites suggests the privileging of different types of choice and constraints. On the websites we examined, there is no consistency in terms of whether intended parents, surrogates, or the agency itself is positioned as having most control over choice. On two sites—Circle Surrogacy and International Surrogacy Partners—the intended parents are featured in the privileged position, while surrogates themselves are privileged on the Surromoms website, and the agency itself is presented as most in control on Surrogacy India. The sites share, however, conventional pronatalist values in which women are positioned as service providers while also rearticulating—not necessarily heterosexual families—but traditional, heteronormative, nuclear family values as desirable, thus, providing claim for Judith Butler's (2004) question "Is kinship already always heterosexual?"

The surrogate is spoken into existence in two recognizably gendered ways: Firstly, as a privileged giver, a "surromom," who stipulates her own demands and secondly, as constrained by employer and client stipulations, an employee and "carrier." The choice to frame the surrogate as a "goddess" or a privileged "giver" and pregnancy as a "calling" calls upon stereotypical gendered discourses and disguises the market dynamics at play. Strikingly absent in the marketing material is any discussion of the physical or psychological discomforts or dangers that surrogates experience as a result of their profession. Avoiding the critique that surrogacy is a form of "baby selling," the agencies frame—not surprisingly—their economic interests as almost "missionary services" motivated by the "plight of infertile (Western) couples." In the process, they silence the financial and material conditions that encourage some women to become surrogates.

Considering the body as a rhetorical situation—whether the bodies, in this case, are literally those of the surrogates, the intended parents, the unborn child, or even the "body" that is the agency—demonstrates that choices and constraints shift and change, creating hybrid in-between-zones of partial agency and constraints. The rhetors involved are sometimes exercising a great deal of control and at other times ceding to other dynamics, needs, and options in the situation. What is needed is a more direct examination of the surrogacy process in order to fully sort out how choice functions for the parties involved in it.[11]

While the reproductive technologies and websites that make fertility tourism possible are still new, the feminist implications are well-known. Does surrogacy simply reveal another instance of a feminist dilemma—where the certain conditions that constitute choice for one group—the desire (and assumed right) to be fulfilled as a mother, for instance—are seen as the very conditions that reinstate a gendered transnational economy in which some women (mostly poorer women in developing countries) provide their bodies as services to other women (mostly white, wealthier, Western women)? There are no easy answers, as always is the case for motherhood in any of its iterations, but there is no doubt that, as Haraway puts it, "addressing the question of where babies come from" puts women "at the center of the action in the New World Order" (Haraway, 1997, p. 187).[12] What remains uncontested is that motherhood is always under scrutiny; there probably is no cultural construction approached with as much concern and criticism, commentary and critique as motherhood. As reproductive technologies continue to develop, we can only expect such scrutiny to increase, placing women once again at the heart of social controversies of choice.

## REFERENCES

Baudrillard, J. (1998). *The consumer society: Myths and structures.* Thousand Oaks, CA: Sage.

Butler, J. (2004). Is kinship already heterosexual? *Differences: A Journal of Feminist Cultural Studies, 13,* 14–44.

Canning, K. (1994). Feminist history after the linguistic turn: Historicizing discourse and experience. *Signs, 19,* 368–404.

Circle Surrogacy. Retrieved May 13, 2009, from www.circlesurrogacy.com

Damon, F. H. (1983). What moves the Kula: Opening and closing gifts on Woodlark Island. In J. W. Leach & E. R. Leach (Eds.), *The Kula: New perspectives on Massim exchange* (pp. 309–42). Cambridge: Cambridge University Press.

Elgin, S. H. (1999). *Láadan: The constructed language in Native Tongue.* http://www.sfwa.org/members/elgin/Laadan.html.

Featherstone, M. (1991). *Consumer culture and postmodernism.* Thousand Oaks, CA: Sage.

Fiel, D. K. (1984). *Ways of exchange: Te enga "tee" of Papua New Guinea.* St. Lucia: University of Queensland Press.

Grosz, E. (1999). *Becomings. Explorations in Time, Memory, and Futures.* Ithaca, NY: Cornell University Press.

Haraway, D. J. (1997). Modest_witness@second_millenium.FemaleMan_meets_OncoMouse: *Feminism and technoscience.* New York: Routledge.

Held, V. (1990). Mothering versus contract. In J. Mansbridge (Ed.), *Beyond self-interest* (pp. 287–304). Chicago: University of Chicago Press.

Hyde, L. (1983). *The gift: Imagination and the erotic life of property.* New York: Vintage/Random House.

International Surrogacy Partners. Retrieved May 13, 2009, from www.surrogateagency.com

Josephides, L. (1985). *The production of inequality: Gender and exchange among the Kewa.* London: Tavistock.

Karpin, I. (1991). Legislating the female body: Reproductive technology and the reconstructed woman. *Columbia Journal of Gender and the Law, 3*, 325–49.

Kramarae, C. (1980). *Women and men speaking.* Cambridge: Newbury House.

Kroløkke, C. (2009). Click a dad: Commercial masculinity on the line. *Journal of Consumer Culture, 9*, 7–30.

Kroløkke, C., & Foss, K. A. (2007). Sørg hellere for en solid tremmeseng. Feministiske udfordringer til retorikken ["You'd better build a strong crib": Feminist challenges to rhetoric]. *Rhetorica Scandinavica, 42*, 5–19.

Landsman, G. (1999). Does God give special kids to special parents? Personhood and the child with disabilities as gift and giver. In L. L. Layne (Ed.), *Transformative motherhood: On giving and getting in a consumer culture* (pp. 133–66). New York: New York University Press.

Layne, L. L. (Ed.). (1999). *Transformative motherhood: On giving and getting in a consumer culture.* New York: New York University Press.

Lury, C. (1996). *Consumer culture.* New Brunswick, NJ: Rutgers University Press.

Mamo, L. (2007). *Queering reproduction: Achieving pregnancy in the age of technoscience.* Durham, NC: Duke University Press.

Markens, S. (2007). *Surrogate motherhood and the politics of reproduction.* Berkeley: University of California Press.

Mauss, M. (1990). *The gift: The form and reason for exchange in archaic societies.* (W. D. Halls, Trans.). London: Routledge.

Mies, M., & Shiva, V. (1993). *Ecofeminism.* London: Zed Books.

Modell, J. S. (1999). Freely given: Open adoption and the rhetoric of the gift. In L. L. Layne (Ed.), *Transformative motherhood: On giving and getting in a consumer culture* (pp. 29–64). New York: New York University Press.

Moore, L. J. (2007). *Sperm counts: Overcome by man's most precious fluid.* New York: New York University Press.

Ragoné, H. (1994). *Surrogate motherhood: Conception in the heart.* Boulder, CO: Westview Press.

Ragoné, H. (2000). Of likeness and difference: How race is being transfigured by gestational surrogacy. In H. Ragoné & F. W. Twine (Eds.), *Ideologies and technologies of motherhood* (pp. 56–75). New York: Routledge.

Raymond, J. G. (1993). *Women as wombs: Reproductive technologies and the battle over women's freedom.* North Melbourne: Spinifex Press.

Shome, R. & Hegde, R. (2002). Culture, communication and the challenge of globalization. *Critical Studies in Media Communication, 19*, 172–89.

Spar, D. L. (2006). *The baby business: How money, science, and politics drive the commerce of conception.* Boston, MA: Harvard University Press.

Stormer, N. (2006). A vexing relationship: Gender and contemporary rhetorical theory. In B. J. Dow and J. T. Wood (Eds.), *The Sage handbook of gender and communication* (pp. 247–62). Thousand Oaks, CA: Sage.

Strathern, M. (1988). *The gender of the gift: Problems with women and problems with society in Melanesia.* Berkeley: University of California Press.

Surrogacy India. Retrieved May 13, 2009, from www.surrogacyindia.com

Surrogate Mothers Online. Retrieved May 13, 2009, from www.surromomsonline .com

Thompson, C. (2005). *Making parents. The ontological choreography of reproductive technologies.* Cambridge: MIT Press.

Titmuss, R. M. (1997). *The gift relationship: From human blood to social policy* (Rev. ed., A. Oakley & J. Ashton, Eds.). New York: New Press.

Vaughan, G. (1999). *Mothering, co-muni-cation and the gifts of language.* Paper presented at the Enigma of the Gift and Sacrifice Conference, Rice University, Houston, TX.

Vaughan, G. (2002, Summer). *The gift economy.* Paper presented at the Women's Worlds Conference, University of Makerere, Uganda.

Vaughan, G. (2004). *Gift giving as the female principle vs. patriarchal capitalism.* Unpublished manuscript.

Weaver, G., & Williams, A. S. (1997). A mother's gift: The milk of human kindness. In R. M. Titmuss, *The gift relationship: From human blood to social policy* (pp. 319-32). (Rev. ed., A. Oakley & J. Ashton, Eds.). New York: New Press.

Wozniak, D. F. (1999). Gifts and burdens: The social and familial context of foster mothering. In L. L. Layne (Ed.), *Transformative motherhood: On giving and getting in a consumer culture* (pp. 89–132). New York: New York University Press.

## NOTES

1. The unilateral nature of the gift is particularly true in the early years of raising a child. Of course, in the past, children constituted a labor force for the family,

so there was an expectation of return. In many cultures today, parents expect their children to take care of them in their old age. Again, these forms of reciprocity occur when the child is older and may not always be realized.

2. Stomer is here inspired by Elizabeth Grosz's (1999) reworkings of Deleuze and Merleau-Ponty.

3. All references are from www.circlesurrogacy.com, retrieved May 14, 2009.

4. All references are from www.surrogacyindia.com, retrieved May 13, 2009.

5. This program is only for "select clients with valid clinical/medical problems who wish for us to travel to you to make babies possible"; while cost is not mentioned, it probably is considerable, so an unstated criterion is also the financial means to be able to afford this service.

6. Nowhere does the website indicate whether the surrogate has similar veto power over the parents.

7. Interestingly, nowhere on the website is the cost to intended parents mentioned.

8. How a surrogate is presented on a website is an entirely different matter, of course, than what sense of control and agency she may feel in fact. We will return to this issue in our concluding comments.

9. All references are to surrogateagency.com, retrieved May 13, 2009.

10. All references are from surromomsonline.com, retrieved May 13, 2009.

11. An ethnographic or fieldwork-based approach would create a more sophisticated understanding of the dynamics at play.

12. Haraway uses the phrase the "New World Order" to refer to an imaginary configuration of a world that carries many material and semiotic markers of the world of contemporary techno-science (1997, p. 2).

6

# LAWS, POLITICS, AND REPRODUCTIVE CHOICES

*Jennifer Emerling Bone and Beth Meyers-Bass*

U.S. women who came of age in the late twentieth century grew up believing that reproductive decision-making is a political right; however individuals' right to choose motherhood cannot be taken for granted. In her book, *Woman's Body, Woman's Right: Birth Control in America*, Gordon (1990) argues that the question of birth control, or "voluntary motherhood" was being debated by different organizations in the 1870s. Yet, it would take an entire century from the time voluntary-motherhood advocates articulated "a political statement about the nature of *involuntary* motherhood and child-rearing in women's lives" until birth control was legally available to single women, illustrating the political system's ability to affect which choices women can make regarding family planning (Gordon, 1990, p. 93).

This chapter explores how seven U.S. court decisions from the twentieth and twenty-first centuries have affected women's reproduction and family planning. It begins with the 1918 New York court decision that allowed physicians the right to provide information about contraception to married patients whose health required such information, and continues through the United States Supreme Court's ruling to uphold the ban on late-term abortions in *Gonzales v. Carhart* (2007). The first set of cases focus specifically on the arguments surrounding access to birth control and contraception. The New York case, *Sanger*, 222 N.Y. 192, 118 N.E. 637 (often referred to as the Crane decision) was the first to rule on a physician's ability to provide birth control to married women whose health required it. In *United States v. Dennett* (1930) and *United States v. One Package of Japanese Pessaries* (1936), the courts ruled in favor of allowing birth control information and devices to be transported via the mail. In 1965, the United States Supreme Court declared state statutes prohibiting married couples from accessing birth control unconstitutional (*Griswold v. Connecticut*). These cases set a precedent for future rulings on women's access to birth control. The second set of court cases pertain to women's reproductive choices on abortion-related issues. Although there are a number of significant court decisions related to abortion, we strategically selected *Roe v. Wade* (1973) since it was the first Supreme Court ruling on abortion, *Harris v. McRae* (1980), the case that affirmed the legality of the Hyde Amendment, the first Congressional ruling to limit funding for abortion services, and *Gonzales v. Carhart* (2007), the case that supported the federal ban on late-term abortion and the most recent abortion-related decision. We recognize many additional court decisions have had a significant impact on women's reproductive choices (e.g., *Webster v. Reproductive Health Services*, 492 U.S. 490 (1989), *Hodgson v. Minnesota*, 497 U.S. 417 (1990), *Planned Parenthood of Southeastern Pa. v. Casey*, 505 U.S. 833 (1992); however, we selected seven court decisions to better understand how women's choices in regards to birth control and abortion services have been impacted by courts' rulings over a century of time.

Our chapter includes personal testimonies from physicians and women themselves that illustrate a range of experiences from obtaining contraception, to seeking abortions in early and late-term pregnancies, to choosing adoption services. These stories come from anthologies, magazines, and interviews to represent reproductive discourses of the time. Because most early twentieth-century women did not have access to publication outlets, the first series of testimonies are from physicians' and birth control advocates' observations rather than the women themselves. The second set of testimonies come from anthologies that provide women's discussions of their individual and unique experiences grappling with unintended pregnancies. MariAnna (2002) states her motivation for writing the book, *Abortion: A Collective Story*, was her desire to hear other women's abortion stories. She argues it is "clear that personal stories are important and constitute the ground of a narrative tradition that is a rich source of information and knowledge about women's varied lives" (p. xiii). Findlen (2001) adds that hearing women's voices creates a "visible, public forum for . . . young women to explore their ideas and hopes and struggles" (p. xiii). Finally, Bonavoglia (2001) explains that the purpose of her book, *The Choices We Made*, is to share stories about the human experience. She maintains that the stories contained "in the book—told primarily in each person's words, as oral history—provide valuable documentation of the circumstances under which women had illegal abortions" (p. xxv).

Condit (1990) argues that mass media's stories of women's experiences with abortion often provide a narrow perspective and thus, do not "take into account the full range and complexity of individuals' lived experiences" (p. 177). Of course, there is no way that we can address the full range of women's experiences with reproduction and abortion in a project of this scope; nonetheless, we sought to select stories that illustrate the personal, and often complex, challenges some women face as they make decisions about reproduction within the confines of the court of law. The stories are chronologically consistent with each case discussed to represent how laws have impacted a woman's choice and experience with family planning. We believe hearing women's personal accounts of their (in)ability to make family choices due to the laws in place provides a better understanding of how courts have impacted women's reproductive freedom.

## THE CHOICE TO NOT CONCEIVE

Although the 1873 Federal Comstock Act was not the first case to look at obscenity charges, it was one of the most influential acts prohibiting the public discussion and medical prescription of birth control. Anthony Comstock, a member of the Young Men's Christian Association, worked tirelessly at the end of the nineteenth century to reinstate Victorian moralist principles. He sought legislation banning literature that he believed was responsible for corrupting the minds of America's youth. The Federal Comstock Act made it a felony to:

> Offer to sell, or lend or give away, or in any manner exhibit . . . publish or offer to publish in any manner, or . . . have in [one's possession], for any purpose or purposes, any obscene book, pamphlet, paper, writing, advertisement, circular, print, picture, drawing or other representation, figure, or image on or of paper or other material, or any cast, instrument or other article of an immoral nature, or any drug or medicine, or any article whatever for the prevention of conception, or for causing unlawful abortion, or . . . advertise same for sale. (Cited in Tobin, 2001, pp. 3–4)

This decision ultimately gave the post office the authority to ban material deemed inappropriate from the mail and request violators be prosecuted by the United States District Attorney (McFarlane and Meier, 2001).

During the beginning of the twentieth century, physicians, midwives, nurses and other health care professionals witnessed the harmful results that came with the limitation on prevention information. In his book, *Birth Control or the Limitation of Offspring* (1938) William J. Robinson, M.D., describes the atrocities associated with the silence surrounding birth control. He contends, "in many cases an unexpected pregnancy, an undesirable child was considered the most terrible calamity that could befall the family. I saw, as a result of it, the deepest anguish, the most acute suffering; I saw physical, mental and economic ruin; and I saw death—death by infection and death by suicide" (Robinson, 1938, preface). Yet, Robinson knew providing his patients with contraceptive information could result in fines and jail time. Most physicians were not willing to risk their careers; rather, they had to witness the torment that many women endured. Robinson (1938) explains how some women responded to the death of a parent, spouse, or child, realizing there would be one less mouth to feed:

> Here is a woman, of whom I heard recently, who on the eighth anniversary of her marriage was expecting her eighth child. Now she lies in the hospital, having had several miscarriages since then. When her seventh child was born, they were so poor that she had to get up the next day. Her husband earned only $4.50 a week and her own mother was lying sick in the next room, where she remained helpless for nine months until she died. Another, with eleven children, thanked God when her drunken husband on one of his sprees walked off a pier into the East River. The assurance that she would never have to bear another child made the prospect of merely supporting the eleven she already had comparative Heaven [sic]. It sickens one to think what love and home means to these poor wretches and what life will do to their children, yet these cases are typical of thousands. (pp. 190–91)

Not only did the censorship of birth control information lead to socioeconomic problems, for many mothers, multiple pregnancies with little healing time in between brought about significant physical harm. Margaret Sanger, an obstetrical nurse and birth control advocate, recounts many stories of helping women deliver their babies at home. These mothers often begged Sanger for information on how to control their fertility. Yet, due to the laws in place and lack of information on birth control, Sanger was unable to answer these inquiries. Instead, Sanger witnessed many accounts of poverty, child labor, and abuse. Sanger (1918) reminisces:

> I recall the death-bed scene, when the patient, a woman of twenty-six, passed away during the birth of her seventh child. Five out of the seven were girls,

> the eldest being about ten years old. Upon the death of this woman, this girl began to assume the duties of her mother and later, I found this girl suffering from the ravages of syphilis, although she had only just entered the period of puberty. She told me she could not remember when she had not dressed before the roomers, and on winter nights she often slept in their beds. She was already old—old in ignorance, in vulgarity, in degeneracy. ("Morality and Birth Control," Feb. 1918)

The stories of women dying during childbirth propelled Sanger into the fight against Anthony Comstock and the obscenity laws. On October 16, 1916, Margaret Sanger opened America's first birth control clinic in the Brownsville section of Brooklyn, New York. The clinic provided an estimated 400 women with information on the female reproductive system and instructions on how to use various contraceptives. On November 16, 1916, Margaret Sanger, her sister and registered nurse, Ethel Byrne, and interpreter Fania Mindell, were arrested and charged with violating section 1142 of New York State's Penal Code, which prohibited dissemination of contraceptive information. All three women were tried and convicted. Sanger appealed her conviction, which eventually led to a slight change in the standing obscenity laws (Sanger, 1938).

In January 1918, the New York Court of Appeals upheld Sanger's conviction; however, Judge Frederick Crane included a more liberal interpretation of New York's Penal Code which prohibited information on contraception to be shared by anyone, including medical professionals. Instead, Crane's ruling gave physicians the right to legally provide birth control information and prescribe contraception for the "cure or prevention of disease" to *married* women. The term "cure or prevention of disease" continued to restrict doctors from freely prescribing birth control. Moreover, in 1927, the Committee on Maternal Health (CMH) argued that contraceptives should only be prescribed in cases of "active disease" necessitating "therapeutic abortion" (McCann, 1994, p. 92). Therefore, women in New York gained little reproductive knowledge and rights after the *Crane* (1918) decision.

## One Package That Changed Legislation

At the time Margaret Sanger was opening America's first birth control clinic, Mary Ware Dennett was also challenging the courts' interpretation of obscenity and trying to provide reproductive information to the general public via the postal service. Dennett had created and mailed the first edition of a pamphlet titled, *The Sex Side of Life: An Explanation for Young*

*People* (1919), which was eventually deemed "obscene, lewd, lascivious, filthy, vile and indecent" for containing information on sex organs, intercourse, and reproduction (Chen, 1996). Yet, the pamphlet also contained information on relationships and family. Dennett had included her definition of what family should be: "a man and a woman feel that they belong to each other in a way that they belong to no one else; it makes them wonderfully happy to be together; they find they want to live together, work together, play together, and to have children together, that is, to marry each other; and their dream is to be happy together all their lives" (Dennett, 1919, p. 8). Dennett was found guilty of violating the Comstock Act and fined $300. The case was appealed and in 1930, the United States Circuit Court of Appeals reversed the decision (*United States v. Dennett*, 39 F. 2d, 564, 1930). Although the decision allowed *The Sex Side of Life* and other pamphlets like it to be transmitted via mail, the Comstock law still prevented birth control devices from being sent through the postal service. As such, many women were still not able to secure the type of birth control needed to control their family size.

In 1932, a package of contraceptive devices sent to Margaret Sanger by a Japanese physician was confiscated by U.S. customs. To prove the Comstock Act still contained provisions excluding the interstate transportation of contraception, Sanger had the contraceptives mailed again, only this time to a physician. The case, *United States v. One Package* (1936), finally declared the right to provide contraceptive information and supplies via mail to physicians. Yet, not all states willingly complied with the new decision or helped fund clinics that provided contraception to patients. The *One Package* decision "removed all federal legal bans on birth control. But it did not touch state legislation against birth control" (Gordon, 1990, p. 317). Some states had a limited number of clinics and physicians providing birth control to patients. In addition, during the Great Depression, the cost associated with obtaining contraception was too high for many women and public health facilities to afford. Finally, "those who did not have access to private doctors regularly were effectively deprived of contraception information [and] clinics served only a negligible fraction of the population" (Gordon, 1990, p. 316). Women living in rural and small-town communities lacked the information necessary to control their family size due to their limited access to clinics.

Although the American Medical Association approved the study of contraceptive practices in 1937, it would take years before all married women in the United States were eligible to receive reliable information and supplies. The *One Package* decision was originally thought to have ended Comstockery, yet, some states continued to have statutes prohibiting prescription birth control. Connecticut was one state that continued to enforce its 1879 anticontraception law, which prohibited physicians from providing birth control information and contraception to married patients. Johnson (2005) argues the law's continued "presence on the statute books likely had a chilling effect on the provision of birth control information by some Connecticut physicians, and, perhaps, kept some of the state's women—particularly those of lower socioeconomic statutes—from realizing that contraceptive counseling was available" (p. 15). Moreover, the courts upheld the statute several times between 1936 and 1965.[1]

In 1953, Estelle Griswold, a certified medical technologist, began working as the executive director of the Planned Parenthood League of Connecticut (PPLC). At this time, counseling women on how to use a diaphragm was in violation of the General Statutes of Connecticut Section 53–32 that stated "any person who uses any drug, medicinal article or instrument for the purpose of preventing conception shall be fined not less than fifty dollars or imprisoned not less than sixty days nor more than one year or be both fined and imprisoned" (Johnson, 2005, p. 6). In order to provide women contraceptive devices, Griswold would have to challenge this statute directly. On November 1, 1961, the PPLC moved its state offices to New Haven, Connecticut, and began providing contraceptive services to married women, purposely violating state law. Three women agreed to release their medical records to state prosecutors upon request to provide evidence for the courts. On November 10, 1961, Griswold and Lee Bruxton (the physician working at PPLC) were issued arrest warrants. During her trial, Griswold testified that birth control should be made available to married women "in order that they might protect their health as mothers, the emotional and economic stability of their families, and promote responsible motherhood" (Johnson, 2005, p. 87). The defendants were found guilty and fined $100 each. The case eventually made it to the United States Supreme Court, which determined the statute violated the constitutional rights of married persons (*Griswold v. Connecticut*, 381 U.S. 479, 1965).

By 1965, the United States Supreme Court and Court of Appeals granted all married couples the right to access reproductive and birth control information and supplies; thus, shaping the discourses of choice that surrounded family planning during the early- to mid-twentieth centuries . Embedded in these early court decisions was an assumption that *married* women *should* choose motherhood. In 1918, the lower courts limited a woman's ability to choose motherhood by only allowing married women with medical conditions access to such information. Physicians were the only ones granted, by law, the right to disseminate birth control. Even then, information was only to be distributed to married women in poor health. Embedded in the *Crane* decision is the assumption that healthy women should have children, and only unfit or "feeble-minded" women should use birth control to prevent conception entirely.[2] Thus, courts provided women very limited control over choosing their family size.

Discourses of choice eventually shifted from choice provided only to patients whose health required such information, to choice provided to married women who sought to control the spacing between children. The ideology of "family" during the early- to mid-twentieth centuries was made clear by the courts' decisions. Courts ruled in favor of married couples having access to birth control, but prohibited that same right to single women. Perhaps Anthony Comstock's desire to retain Victorian moralist principles lived on through the courts' decisions to provide contraception only to married couples. Yet, another battle was brewing during the middle of the twentieth century between women and courts. Instead of focusing on the choice to prevent conception, courts began looking at a woman's choice to terminate a pregnancy.

## THE CHOICE TO ABORT

By 1910, abortion was illegal in most states. With few physicians willing to risk their careers by practicing abortion procedures, many women took it upon themselves to end unwanted pregnancies. In 1938, birth control advocates were engaged in an unsuccessful campaign to convince the government to support women's access to birth control by funding contraceptive clinics. Part of their argument was based on the Children's Bureau's conclusion that "25–30 percent of maternal deaths occurred as a direct result of illegal abortions" (McCann, 1994, p. 198). The Planned Parenthood Federation of America, created first in 1939 as the Birth Control Federation of America, also could not persuade policy-makers to support birth control clinics, even though more than 800 birth control clinics existed nationwide in 1945 (McCann, 1994, p. 218). Although these clinics provided counseling and contraceptive services, abortion procedures were considered a dangerous, and still illegal, practice. Therefore, many women seeking abortion services from clinics were denied such requests, forcing them to find other options (Gordon, 1990).

Sarah Weddington recounts her own experience of traveling across borders to obtain an abortion. In 1967, Weddington was a graduate student in

Texas. When she learned of her pregnancy, she knew she would have to obtain an abortion outside of her home state. Her partner heard about a doctor in Piedras Negras, Mexico, who had some medical experience performing abortions. Although abortion was illegal in Mexico, Weddington assumed the doctors paid the police to keep things quiet. She writes:

> We left Austin early on a Friday morning in fall, drove to Eagle Pass, checked into a motel, and went across the border to the meeting place. I was scared of the unknown, but mercifully I had been spared the horror stories I was later to hear from so many women. I can still see Ron [Weddington's partner] and me following a man in brown pants and a white guayabera shirt down dirt alleys to a small white building, two young Americans trying unsuccessfully to blend into the background. . . . I was one of the lucky ones. (Weddington, 2002, p. 14)

Pregnant women like Weddington went to extreme, and often dangerous, measures once they made a decision to not choose motherhood. Other women decided against traveling across state or national borders and instead chose to terminate their pregnancies at home. In her book, *Articles of Faith: A Frontline History of the Abortion Wars*, Gorney (2000) provides doctor and patient narratives of their abortion experiences. The first story, set in the early 1960s, involves the experiences of Dr. Duemler, a physician who delivered babies at a Catholic Hospital in Sedalia, Missouri. Gorney describes the scene Dr. Duemler encountered upon arriving to work one day:

> When Duemler walked into the emergency room, what he saw, in more places than he would have thought possible, was blood. There was blood on the walls. There was blood on the floors. There was blood on the gurney and blood on the towels and on the hands and arms of the emergency crew. . . . Beneath them lay a woman whose skin had gone pallid and slack, and when Duemler lifted her legs he saw that someone had pushed inside her vagina with a sharp instrument and aimed it at the cervix and thrust upward. . . . The husband told Duemler they had five children already. (cited in Gorney, 2000, pp. 16–17)

Unlike Dr. Duemler's experience, many abortions taking place prior to 1973 were performed secretly in the back office of a medical facility (and not necessarily in a back alley). Claderone (1960) estimated that 90 percent of all abortions taking place prior to legalization were performed by doctors (p. 949). Yet, similar to Duemler's patient, these practices have not always been safe.

The case *Sylvia Redman v. State* (1955) describes the death of Betty Ledel, a young woman who died as the result of an abortion. Although the doctor claimed to have treated her for a misplaced uterus, not an abortion, Ledel died due to the procedures implemented. The doctor was found guilty of murder by attempted abortion and was sentenced to four years in a penitentiary. Ledel was one of thousands of women who died as the result of a mishandled abortion (*Sylvia Redman v. State*, 162 Tex. Crim. 524, 1955). The 1968 "Federal Constitutional Limitations on the Enforcement and Administration of State Abortion Statutes" states:

> mishandled criminal abortions claimed the lives of an estimated ten thousand American women each year. The vast majority of these individuals were married—wives and mothers. Legal hospital abortions, on the other hand, presently account for the termination of only eight to nine thousand pregnancies yearly. (As cited in Hull, Hoffer & Hoffer, 2004, p. 94)

To avoid such private devastation, Norma McCorvey challenged the laws preventing abortion in hopes of securing women a safe place to seek this type of medical procedure. Norma McCorvey reveals in her narrative that she had a difficult life. She had not completed high school, worked as a waitress to support herself, and already had two daughters, one raised by McCorvey's mother, and the second by her father. In 1969, McCorvey learned she was pregnant again. She remininces:

> When I got pregnant with the *Roe* baby, I knew I couldn't take care of a child. I wasn't working at the time. I lived with my dad. I wasn't really destitute—I had food to eat and a roof over my head—but I didn't have any jingle in my pocket, and I really didn't have a whole lot of ambition. I went to an abortion clinic, an illegal abortion clinic, in Dallas. Actually, I believe it was a dentistry clinic, and they were using the back portion of it to do abortions. I got real bad vibes when I walked up to it, but then I was scared as hell, too. The place had been busted. It was abandoned. There was still some stuff there, but no people. It was very eerie. So, I had no choice at all. I stood there maybe fifteen minutes or so, and I cried. I don't know why—just being scared, just wanting something to happen that I knew would never happen. (Cited in Bonavoglia, 2001, pp. 138–39)

McCorvey, known by the courts as "Jane Roe," filed suit against the district of Dallas, Texas, in 1970. Roe's attorney, Sarah Weddington, argued, "because of economic hardships and social stigmas involved in bearing an illegitimate child, Plaintiff [Jane Roe] wished to terminate her pregnancy by means of an operation, generally referred to as an abortion, performed by a competent, licensed physician, under safe clinical conditions" (Weddington, 1992, p. 55). On January 22, 1973, the Supreme Court decided that Texas's (and nearly all other states') criminal abortion statutes were unconstitutional. This ruling provided women the freedom to choose to terminate a pregnancy during the first trimester. If a woman was in her second trimester, a physician's consultation and approval would be necessary, and the court stated the third trimester was essentially banned from any sort of abortion procedure with the exception of when the mother's life was in danger. Furthermore, writing for the majority, Justice Blacknum maintained:

> Maternity, or additional offspring, may force upon the woman a distressful life and future. Psychological harm may be imminent. Mental and physical health may be taxed by child care. There is also the distress, for all concerned, associated with the unwanted child, and there is a problem of bringing a child into a family already unable, psychologically and otherwise, to care for it. In other cases, as in this one, the additional difficulties and continuing stigma of unwed motherhood may be involved. (*Roe v. Wade* [10] 410 U.S. 155)

The scope of the *Roe v. Wade* decision surprised those closely watching the case unfold,[3] and allowed greater freedom for women (single and married) to have a choice about motherhood. Even married women who identified as queer felt the impact of the decision. One woman who goes by the alias "Paula" describes her sense of relief knowing she had an option to end a pregnancy. Paula began her story by stating, "I never knew whether I wanted to be married or not. I always knew that I was woman-identified. Even as a young person. The only word I knew was 'queer,' and I knew that I was one" (cited in MariAnna, 2002, p. 48). At the time she discovered she was pregnant, Paula was married with two children and in the process of getting a divorce. Paula was also preparing to come out as a lesbian. She and her husband both agreed to terminate the pregnancy. Paula describes her immense relief once she had woken from the procedure. MariAnna (2002) opines, "had legal abortion not been available, [Paula's] story might have been a very different one" (p. 47).

Although some women express their sense of relief at the opportunity to terminate a pregnancy, the choice can be an agonizing one for other women. Inga Muscio shares her experiences with multiple unintended pregnancies. She writes:

> The first time I got pregnant, I was nineteen. I lived in California and was within weeks of moving away from home for the first time in my life, to Seattle. The idea of making such a major move with a tiny human growing

> inside me seemed a pretty contradictory way of setting off on my own, so I went to Planned Parenthood. In the waiting room were fifteen to twenty other women. Each had a horror-stricken look on her face. It was one of those situations where you can assume that you have the same expression as everyone else without having to look in the mirror. . . . In the U.S., we don't (and we're also not encouraged to) look inside ourselves for healing or for finding truths or answers. If you want to know something, you find out what the Person In Charge Of This Area says. The weather is not to be discerned by looking at the sky or the mountains in the distance or by listening to the song of the wind. You will find it in the Report of the Meteorologist. Likewise, if you are pregnant and don't want to be, you don't look at yourself and the resources in your immediate world, you pay a visit to the Abortionist, who will subsequently predict the climate in your body for nine days to two weeks, guaranteed. (Findlen, 2001, pp. 113–16)

Muscio articulated the difficulty some women experience in following through with the decision to legally terminate a pregnancy; for others, the cost of an abortion procedure adds to their despair.

In 1965, Congress created a Medicaid program to provide federal funds to states supporting health care for their citizens. Five years later, federal funds were used to provide birth control counseling and family planning options to women seeking such services. Yet, the program contained restrictions that many women believed would limit their ability to receive federal funds. In *Abortion: A Collective Story*, "Karen" describes how her financial situation impacted her decision to have an abortion. She had been raped by her boyfriend's acquaintances, and was unsure if she was pregnant by her boyfriend or by the rape. Karen had access to a safe abortion, but not enough money to pay for it. The procedure cost approximately $400 and Karen arrived at the clinic with only $100. She decided against filling out the paperwork for Medicaid believing she would likely be denied funding. Fortunately, the doctor was understanding and worked with her on a payment plan (MariAnna, 2002). Karen had the choice to apply for Medicaid funding, but in 1976, women lost that choice through the Hyde Amendment.

Henry Hyde, a member of Congress who opposed the *Roe* decision, successfully argued to ban federal funding for abortions except when a mother's life was in danger, or in cases of rape and/or incest that had been properly reported to authorities. Medicaid recipients filed suit in New York to challenge the funding restrictions of the Hyde Amendment. The case became a class-action suit "on behalf of all pregnant or potentially pregnant women eligible for Medicaid in New York State who choose to seek an abortion and all abortion service providers, and it granted an injunction against enforcing the law, pending a full hearing" (Baer & Goldstein, 2007, p. 398). Eventually, the case was heard by the Supreme Court and the 5-4 ruling to overturn the injunction on the district court's ruling allowed the Hyde Amendment to take effect (*Harris v. McRae*, 448 U.S. 297, 1980). Medicaid recipients were no longer eligible for federal funding for non-therapeutic abortions. Writing for the majority, Justice Stewart maintained that a woman's freedom of choice did not carry with it "a constitutional entitlement to the financial resources to avail herself of the full range of protected choices" (*Harris v. McRae*, 448 U.S. 297, 1980). Not all Justices agreed with the decision; some argued that the ban directly impacted poor women. In his dissent, Justice Marshall wrote:

> The Court's opinion studiously avoids recognizing the undeniable fact that for women eligible for Medicaid—poor women—denial of a Medicaid-funded abortion is equivalent to denial of legal abortion altogether. By definition, these women do not have the money to pay for an abortion themselves. If abortion is medically necessary and a funded abortion is unavailable, they must resort to back-alley butchers, attempt to induce an abortion themselves by crude and dangerous methods, or suffer the serious medical consequences of attempting to carry the fetus to term. (*Harris v. McRae*, 448 U.S. 297, 1980)

As indicated in the dissenting opinion, poor women found the decision-making process on motherhood to be even more complicated and difficult under the Hyde Amendment.

Allison Crews, the daughter of a pro-life advocate, found her own ability to choose motherhood especially difficult. For Crews, the funding necessary to terminate a pregnancy was not her biggest worry. Rather, Crews was a teenager who grew up in a household that publicly advocated against abortion. When Crews discovered she was pregnant during her sophomore year of high school, she remembers feeling scared about her impending decision. She describes:

> I scheduled three consecutive abortion appointments and systematically canceled each one. With each new appointment, my due date grew closer, the price of an abortion higher, and the distance that I would have had to travel for the procedure grew longer. . . . Whatever the reasons, whether they were beyond my control or self-created, I did not abort my pregnancy. Perhaps because I was not sure of the choice to abort, I delayed my appointments at Planned Parenthood. Perhaps because I was scared of making the wrong choice, I purposely showed up late to appointments at the social services

> office, knowing that I would then need to reschedule. After much prayer and divination, many tears and several horrible poems, I made a choice to bear a child. (Findlen, 2001, p. 145)

Crews gave her son up for adoption and experienced firsthand the joys and pains that surround a woman's ability to choose motherhood. She now believes that no matter what choice a woman makes, she needs a community of people to provide physical, mental, and emotional support.

The women's stories presented above illustrate diverse experiences with choosing motherhood. Age, sexual identity, sexual abuse, marital status, and family size all influence a woman's decision to have a child—as long as the decision is made early in the pregnancy. Gina Gonzales's story is different; she tried for years to get pregnant. After three miscarriages, treatment for endometriosis and a uterine polyp, doctors told Gina she could finally carry a pregnancy to term. When she found out she was pregnant with twins, she was overjoyed. Then, Gina's life changed dramatically. In April 2000, Gina and her husband, John, learned at the twenty-week ultrasound appointment that their twins had life-threatening illnesses. The doctors informed the couple that more tests were necessary, but that the results did not look good. Gina writes:

> Driving home, I tried not to cry, but I felt like my world was crumbling. John was trying to be strong, but I could tell he was holding back tears. . . . My husband and I are devout Christians, and during that time we prayed and prayed, believing that God was going to heal our girls. Instead, the new prognosis was even grimmer than we had anticipated: The twins' conditions were actually growing worse. Savanna's fluid had spread around her abdomen, signaling a condition called ascites, which has a wide range of consequences, including putting additional pressure on the organs, thereby causing respiratory distress and heart failure. Sierra had a leaky heart valve. The doctor also suspected that they were developing Twin to Twin Transfusion Syndrome, which meant that Savanna was taking blood from Sierra through their shared placenta. Sierra's chance of survival outside the womb hovered at around 5 percent—and she was the healthier of the two girls. (Yeoman, 2001, p. 204)

The doctor recommended that Gina terminate the pregnancy, a recommendation that infuriated Gina. She remembers thinking there was just no way she could abort the pregnancy. She wanted her twins to live, but John reminded Gina that when Savanna died, she would take her sister with her. In addition, Gina's doctor confirmed that Savanna's illness could trigger a rare syndrome in Gina, one that put her health at risk, as well. She knew at that point what they had to do. She recalls:

> I went in for the procedure. For three days, the medical staff dilated me with the natural substance laminaria to ensure that there would be no injury to my cervix, and I stayed in a hotel at night. When I was ready for the surgery, I was given an anesthesia, and while I slept, the physician terminated the pregnancy and then carefully removed Sierra and Savanna from my body vaginally. After I awoke, the nurse brought my daughters in so that my husband and I could hold and bond with them. Seeing them, I almost forgot they were dead. They weren't perfect, but to me they were beautiful. . . . I didn't know much about abortion before all of this. I didn't even realize that most women who have abortions don't get to hold their babies. But I'd had an intact dilation and evacuation (D&E), in which the fetuses were removed whole. It makes so much sense: If you can give a grieving mother a baby to hold afterward, you give her a more healing way to end a wanted pregnancy. (Yeoman, 2001, p. 270)

Gina was able to legally obtain a late-term abortion, a procedure she prayed she would not need. Yet, the risks involved for Gina to continue the pregnancy were far too great.

Three years after Gina and John obtained a D&E, federal legislation deemed late-term abortions illegal and sought charges against physicians who performed the procedure. Any physician accused of such practice may arrange a hearing with the State Medical Board to determine if the physician's conduct was necessary to save the life of the mother. Although late-term abortion accounts for only 0.17 percent of all abortions performed in the United States, the Supreme Court upheld this legislation and criminalized "partial birth abortion" in *Gonzales v. Carhart* (2007).

Choosing whether or not to terminate a pregnancy can be difficult. Some physicians are willing to respect the choices made by women to not choose motherhood; yet, the legislature and courts are still influencing and seeking to (re)shape laws surrounding women's choices. Since *Roe v. Wade*, court cases have challenged the right of a woman to choose pregnancy termination. From banning federal funding (Hyde Amendment) to the late-term abortion ban (*Gonzales v. Carhart*, 2007), women continue to struggle with limitations placed on their reproductive rights.

## LAWS, POLITICS, AND REPRODUCTIVE CHOICES

At the beginning of the twentieth century, courts limited women's ability to choose motherhood by prohibiting public access to contraceptive information and devices. Religious and societal norms placed expectations on married women to bear children, even when financial and/or health risks were evident. Working-class families were especially impacted by such expectations, leading to an increase in poverty, physical and mental illness, and child labor (Gordon, 1990). As courts continued to silence the discussion on family planning, working-class families faced the prospect of infant and/or maternal mortality, disease, starvation, prostitution, and even suicide. Instead of being overjoyed with the prospect of another baby, Robinson (1938) maintains many working-class women viewed undesirable children as the most terrible calamity that could befall the family; many working women (and many women from all socioeconomic classes) desired small families, and many women sought to delay or prevent conception altogether. Women dreamed of "family" consisting of men and women being happy together, having only the number of children they could support, spaced years apart, educated, and healthy. The law, however, deemed reproductive information obscene and therefore forbidden. Thus, many families turned out to be large in number, unhappy, uneducated, and unhealthy.

The United States Circuit Court of Appeals decision in *United States v. Dennett* (1930) that allowed birth control information to be sent through the postal service, and the passage of the *One Package* decision in 1936, provided women some hope that they would be able to control their family size. Yet, not all women benefited immediately from this decision. Many societal norms and conditions kept women from receiving adequate information and birth control. The depression made it difficult for women and clinics to obtain necessary funds to purchase supplies. Women living in rural areas did not have access to clinics. And, it took decades from the *One Package* (1936) decision until all states allowed married women access to birth control as ruled in *Griswold v. Connecticut* (1965).

In 1973, women secured additional reproductive rights. The Supreme Court ruled in *Roe v. Wade* that women had the legal right to terminate a pregnancy in the first trimester, but placed further restrictions during second and third trimesters. In *Harris v. McRae* (1980), the Supreme Court upheld the Hyde Amendment that placed additional limitations on poor women's ability to access the abortion services, making the decision to safely terminate a pregnancy more complicated. Finally, *Gonzales v. Carhart* (2007) continues to limit women's reproductive choices, specifically disallowing late-term abortions. Yet, the reasons for pregnancy termination are both varied and complex. As illustrated in the stories provided above, many women who choose early abortions are often facing an unintentional pregnancy, or perhaps they believe they are not emotionally, physically, or financially ready or able to care for a child. Some women, like Gina Gonzales, who make the difficult choice to terminate a wanted pregnancy in the third trimester, do so based on the potentially fatal health condition of the child(ren).

Reproductive choices are heavily influenced by the political system. Women of all ages, races, ethnicities, classes, genders and sexualities are expected to make choices about family planning within the confines of the law. At the beginning and middle of the twentieth century the courts began to rule in favor of providing women more choice over reproduction and family planning. With additional information and access to birth control, women were granted the political right to choose to have control over their family size. However, not all women have health insurance or the financial resources to afford the costs associated with obtaining birth control. In 2009, the census bureau reported that approximately 20 percent of women of reproductive age are uninsured, and thirteen states continue to allow "private insurance companies that cover prescription drugs to exclude coverage for FDA-approved contraceptives (cited in "Facts and Figures," 2009). Moreover, Myra Batchelder, the director of the low-income access program for the National Institute for Reproductive Health, reports that "12 percent of women of reproductive age depend on Medicaid for their health care. However, the birth control options that state Medicaid programs provide are not always adequate to meet women's needs. Emergency contraception, of instance, is not covered by all state Medicaid programs" (2008, para. 2). Hence, women's ability to make reproductive choices may be limited based on whether she has health insurance and the quality of her health insurance policy.

Although *Roe v. Wade* granted women the right to choose to terminate a pregnancy during its early stages, the policies regarding abortion are being continually revisited and revised. Limiting funding for abortion services and placing restrictions on late-term abortions are curbing women's abilities to make personal, private choices. These political decisions illustrate how fragile choice is for women, and highlight the power differences between legal systems and women's voices.

Reading women's narratives provides insight into the difficult, and often painful, choices and experiences women have in making reproductive decisions. As stated by Maxtone-Graham (1973) in her book *Pregnant by Mistake*, "stories are unlikely to change people's convictions about themselves in their own situations, but I sincerely hope they will make for greater understanding of *other* people in *other* situations" (p. ix). As courts continue to decide cases that impact women's ability to make reproductive choices, we hope that one day the voices of women will influence courts to rule in favor of granting more, not fewer, choices for women.

## REFERENCES


Baer, J. A., & Goldstein, L. F. (2007). *The constitutional and legal rights of women: Cases in law and social change,* 3d edition. Los Angeles, CA: Roxbury.

Batchelder, M. G. (2008). *Low-income women's access to birth control.* Retrieved from http://apha.confex.com/apha/136am/techprogram/paper_187529.htm

Bonavoglia, A. (2001). *The choices we made.* New York: Four Walls Eight Windows.

Calderone, M. (1960). Illegal abortion as a public health problem. *American Journal of Public Health, 50* (7), 948–54.

Chen, C. M. (1996). *"The sex side of life": Mary Ware Dennett's pioneering battle for birth control and sex education.* New York: New Press.

Condit, C. (1990). *Decoding abortion rhetoric: Communicating social change.* Chicago: University of Illinois Press.

Crews, A. (2001). And so I choose. In Findlen, B. (Ed.), *Listen up: Voice from the next feminist generation* (pp. 142–59). New York: Seal Press.

Dennett, M. W. (1919, self-published pamphlet). *The sex side of life.* New York.

Findlin, B. (2001). *Listen up: Voices from the next feminist generation.* New York: Seal Press.

*Gonzales v. Carhart.* (2007). 550 U.S. 124.

Gordon, L. (1990). *Woman's body, woman's right.* New York: Penguin Books.

Gorney, C. (2000). *Articles of faith: A frontline history of the abortion wars.* New York: Simon & Schuster.

*Griswold v. Connecticut.* (1965). 381 U.S. 479.

*Harris v. McRae.* (1980). 448 U.S. 297.

Hull, N. E. H., Hoffer, W., & Hoffer, P. C. (Eds.). (2004). *The abortion rights controversy in America.* Chapel Hill: University of North Carolina Press.

Johnson, J. W. (2005). *Griswold v. Connecticut.* Lawrence, KS: University Press of Kansas.

MariAnna, C. J. (2002). *Abortion: A collective story.* Westport, CT: Praeger.

Maxtone-Graham, K. (1973). *Pregnant by mistake: The stories of seventeen women.* New York: Liveright.

McCann, C. R. (1994). *Birth control politics in the United States, 1916–1945.* Ithaca, NY: Cornell University Press.

McFarlane, D. R., & Meier, K. J. (2001). *The politics of fertility control.* New York: Seven Bridges.

Muscio, I. (2001). Abortion, vacuum cleaners and the power within. In Findlen, B. (Ed.), *Listen up: Voices from the next feminist generation* (pp. 112–17). New York: Seal Press.

National Women's Law Center. (2009). *NWLC facts and figures*. Retrieved from http://www.nwlc.org/reformmatters/facts.html

Robinson, W. J. (1938). *Birth control or the limitation of offspring*. (48th ed.). New York: Eugenics.

*Roe v. Wade*. (1973). 93 S. Ct. 705.

Sanger, M. (1918, February). Morality and birth control. *The Birth Control Review*.

Sanger, M. (1938). *Margaret Sanger: An autobiography*. New York: W. W. Norton.

*Sylvia Redman v. State*. (1955). 162 Tex. Crim. 524.

Tobin, K. A. (2001). *The American religious debate over birth control, 1907–1937*. Jefferson, NC: McFarland & Company.

*United States v. Dennett*. (1930). 39 F. 2d 564.

Weddington, S. (1992). *A question of choice*. Harmondsworth, Middlesex, England: Penguin.

Yeoman, Barry. (October 2001). I had an abortion when I was six months pregnant. *Glamour, 99*, pp. 204, 206, 270.

## NOTES

1. For more information on Connecticut's court decisions, see *State v. Nelson* (1940), *Tileston v. Ullman* (1942), *Poe et al. v. Ullman* and *Buxton v. Ullman* (1961).

2. The idea that birth control should be used to limit offspring by the "feebleminded" was also argued by eugenics proponents. Many eugenics proponents failed to understand the discriminatory nature of such arguments.

3. *Roe v. Wade* was not the only case reviewed by the United States Supreme Court during the 1970s. *Doe v. Bolton*, 410 U.S. 179 (1973), challenged the abortion statutes in the state of Georgia. Also, *Thompson v. State* (Ct. Crim. App. Tex. 1971) declared that Texas had reason to protect fetal life; thus, the state's law did not violate the federal Constitution.

# PART II

# EXPERIENCES OF CHOICE

# Section 1

# Pregnancy and Choice

7

# MY EYES CRY WITHOUT ME

## Illusions of Choice in the Transition to Motherhood

*Elissa Foster*[1]

As I sit down to write this chapter I think, "This could be a big mistake." I know that the topics of infertility and miscarriage are underresearched areas, especially within communication studies. A keyword search of *Communication and Mass Media Complete* database retrieved only seven articles with *fertility* or *miscarriage* in the subject terms and *communication* in the abstract—two of which were from a special issue of *Women's Studies in Communication* from summer 2008 discussing mothering in the academy. Further searches of the National Communication Association (NCA) publications database returned one article from 1975 identifying the impact of mass media on the nations' fertility rates, and one article (Stone, 1991) related to infertility discourse. A search of the journal *Health Communication* for the terms *fertility* or *infertility* produced no citations. Compared to the flood of popular press books and articles about motherhood that began around 2002, communication scholars have been relatively quiet on questions related to fertility and reproduction. Even so, as I write I am acutely aware that this cannot be a purely academic activity for me and that my motives for writing are complex.

As a woman who has "postponed motherhood" (Poelker and Baldwin, 1999) and at the time of writing this chapter is actively seeking to conceive, I recognize the capacity of my contemporaneous personal account to provide unique insight into processes and relationships that may otherwise be artificially smoothed and simplified by the availability of a more distanced stance. However, by attempting to write about this subject matter while I am in the midst of it, I struggle between the visceral impact of my "chaos narrative" (Frank, 1995) and my belief that, if I am to be a trustworthy author, then I must make sense of my story and present coherent conclusions. As I sit to untangle the threads of the story and arrange them for my reader, I am caught in a moment of ethnographic vacillation. Crawford (1996) describes such a moment during his fieldwork, in which "Hard distinctions softened. Category systems dissolved. The interpersonal dynamics . . . seemed so fluid at times, the variables so numerous, that a cogent approach to rendering them intelligible was little more than a pipe dream" (p. 162). Thus, I offer this early warning that the resulting text will be as "messy" (Denzin, 1997) and potentially as uncomfortable as the experiences it represents.

Autoethnography is no longer a newcomer to the compendium of methodological tools available to communication researchers. Early autoethnographic publications in communication studies date from the mid- to late-1990s (e.g., Crawford, 1996; Corey and Nakayama, 1997; Ellis, 1998; Tillmann-Healy, 1996; Trujillo, 1998), mostly from the fields of performance and cultural studies. In the new millennium, autoethnographies became increasingly common and included reflections on pedagogy and the life of the academic (Alexander, 1999; Pelias, 2000; Pineau, 2000; Spry, 2000). Three books by Art Bochner and Carolyn Ellis reflect the development of autoethnographic inquiry both within communication studies and across other disciplines: *Composing Ethnography* (1996), *Ethnographically Speaking* (2002), and *The Ethnographic I* (2004). Most recently, Tillmann (2009a, 2009b) published both an update of her autoethnographic research on bulimia from 1996 and an introductory essay (re)introducing autoethnography to readers of the *Journal of Applied Communication Research*. Although as a method autoethnography has been tested by its critics (e.g., Shields, 2000; Taft-Kaufman, 2000), it continues to gain ground as an appropriate means to investigate aspects of experience that cannot be as effectively accessed through second-order representations such as interviews or questionnaires.

For those not familiar with the tenets of this approach, autoethnography combines practices of evocative narrative writing and introspection (Ellis, 1991) to provide a "full accounting for and utilization of the researcher's personal body and felt experience as research instrument" (Banks and Banks, 2000, p. 234). An important goal of autoethnography is to write in order to reveal "the researcher's vulnerable selves, emotions, body, and spirit; the production of evocative stories that create the effect of reality

. . . the examination of how human experience is endowed with meaning . . . [and] a focus on helping us to know how to live and cope" (Sparks, 2002, p. 210). In the autoethnographic narrative that follows, as the storyteller I am at various times an aging woman, a patient, a partner, a cultural critic, and a vulnerable participant in a reproductive journey. The common ground between autoethnographic and ethnographic practices is that they are both concerned with the revelation of cultural experiences; in the case of autoethnography, the researcher's practice includes cycles of looking outward for a sense of place and identity, then turning reflexively inward to the self as a site wherein culture is internalized and interpreted (Neumann, 1996).

In the text that follows, I begin with the narrative details of my story, rendered evocatively as a point of entry for others to enter the experience, and punctuate the narrative with reflections on research literature, cultural analysis, and popular press texts related to (in)fertility. In keeping with the themes of this edited collection, the analytical commentary of this chapter queries the concept of "choice" as an artifact of second wave feminism, and a concept I uncritically embraced until faced with the transition to motherhood. Born in 1970, I was the beneficiary of a set of related feminist ideals—equality, freedom, self-determination—that meant I could choose from an almost infinite set of options and exert control over the contingencies that might threaten the attainment of my dreams. On the topic of motherhood, the message I internalized was that having children was simply one of those options that I could select whenever and however I chose to do so. As I have come to realize, however, unlike the feminist stories of education and career success that guided my life choices in the first three decades of my life, feminist stories of successful conception, childbirth, and child rearing were absent from the discourse. Perhaps I assumed that this was because having children was so "natural" that it did not warrant much discussion; what I have learned was that second wave feminism was silent on the subject (O'Brien Hallstein, 2008) and left its daughters—like me—to make sense of the transition to motherhood on our own.

## PART I: FERTILITY

### Pregnancy Diagnosis

*July 2008.* By the time I test for pregnancy I am already well practiced in the art of what I call simply "peeing on a stick"—so practiced, in fact, that I can do it in the semidark before I've put in my contact lenses. Using between three and twelve ovulation predictors every month for the last two years—along with the occasional pregnancy predictor when warranted by a late period—the sticks are a mundane feature of my morning ritual. Admittedly, by calling the modern plastic wonder "a stick" I deliberately downplay the vast medical technology apparatus of which it is a component part, and I deliberately resist the power that its blue (or pink) lines seem to hold over my state of mind. Middle of the month, two pink lines, ovulation, equals possibility and hope. End of the month, two blue lines, not pregnant, equals disappointment and, increasingly, frustration. After three unsuccessful cycles of our first-line reproductive procedure, the IUI (intra-uterine insemination), this morning I am hopeful but not expectant.

I wait the required minutes and then peer down to see the blue plus sign that has appeared on the stick like an apparition appearing from the mist. I blink, grab the box and then double check to see that I have interpreted the results correctly. Blue plus sign equals pregnant.

Anticipating this moment over the past two years, I imagined I would be overcome with stronger emotions—elation, excitement, flooding relief. Instead, I feel happy, cautiously optimistic, a little nervous, and a little guilty for feeling nervous after wanting this for so long.

I walk back to the bedroom and show Jay, my partner, the stick.

"What does it mean?" Jay asks sleepily, a hopeful smile animating his features.

"It guess it means happy anniversary," I reply, drawing his attention to the date of our commitment ceremony five years ago this week. I begin to laugh.

"Oh, baby, baby, baby!" Jay gathers me in his arms and pulls me back onto the bed. It occurs to me that he could be referring to us—me and *our baby*—and not just me. We initiate what would become a ritual for us; mornings and evenings spent spooning with Jay's hand on my belly. We savor the moment and anticipate the months between now and next spring.

A week later I am at my doctor's office to have my initial pregnancy visit. In the year that I have worked in the department of family medicine residency program Holly, one of the physician faculty members, has become a good friend in addition to being a wonderful doctor. Today, she is the consummate professional as she confirms my pregnancy, modestly celebrates the news, and then turns to the business of advising me about diet, exercise, symptoms of pregnancy, and the sobering statistics related to miscarriage. Although rates of miscarriage are reported differently by different sources, there is consensus that rates increase exponentially by age. A sample of these statistics include: (a) maternal age twenty-five to twenty-nine years 10 percent of pregnancies end in miscarriage, at thirty to thirty-four years the rate is 11.7 percent, at thirty-four to thirty-nine years it is 17.7 percent, and at forty to forty-four years it is 33.8 percent (Rosenberg and Epstein, 2001, p. 345); (b) miscarriage ranges from about 12 percent of pregnancies in twenty-year-olds to 25 percent in a forty-year-old woman (Shanahan, 2000, p. 57); (c) when counting both confirmed and unconfirmed pregnancies, as a woman approaches thirty-five extremely early miscarriages occur more frequently and by forty years of age "the average woman may face a 50 percent miscarriage rate" (Weschler, 2002, p. 177). Holly does not go into detail about these statistics, but she presents the early term miscarriage as something that is both part of normal reproductive life and emphasizes that if it is going to happen there is nothing that I can do or not do to prevent it.

"I'm going to give you orders for an ultrasound in about three weeks," Holly explains as she turns toward the computer in the exam room. She begins to type and then turns back to me with a rueful smile.

"You're not going to like this," she preempts, "but I think you'll appreciate it given your expertise in communication."

"What is it?" I'm intrigued.

"Well," Holly explains, "In your note you will be classified as an *elderly primigravida.*"

"I beg your pardon?" I exclaim in somewhat exaggerated horror.

"I know," Holly empathizes. "It's awful. It goes along with many other terrible and outmoded clinical terms that we have for women's conditions—like *incompetent cervix*. Anyone who is over thirty-five and pregnant for the first time is, clinically, an *elderly primigravida.*"

I retort, "I was getting used to the idea of being an 'older mum,' but *elderly? Really?*"

"Just try to think of it as a lingering linguistic dinosaur of medical discourse," Holly suggests. "It doesn't make it right, but it helps not to take it too seriously."

I happily take my orders for the ultrasound, anticipating the reassurance of being able to confirm the pregnancy by *seeing* it. At barely five weeks, before morning sickness and weight gain, it is challenging for me to relax in the knowledge that our longed-for baby is on its way. I wonder when I became such an empiricist; shouldn't I just *know* and trust that I am pregnant?

Sylvia Ann Hewlett's (2002) book, *Creating a Life* generated an avalanche of popular press attention on what has come to be known as age-related infertility; Hewlett's book and accompanying rhetoric surrounding age-related infertility are investigated elsewhere in this volume by Bute, Harter, Kirby, and Thompson. In April of 2002, *Time* magazine ran a cover story that scared or depressed many academic women (Gibbs, 2002). Inspired by Hewlett's book, Gibbs (2002) put together a series of interviews and statistics, graphically arguing that women who waited for children faced rapidly declining chances of conceiving, rapidly increasing chances of miscarriage, ectopic pregnancy, and chromosomal abnormality (pp. 52–53). Also in 2002, Mason and Goulden published their study of family and academic life, producing the statistic that, twelve to fourteen years out from the Ph.D., 62 percent of tenured women in the humanities and social sciences do not have children (see also Mason and Goulden, 2004). Combine this with the now "common knowledge" truth that "academic women have the lowest fertility rate of women in any of the professions" (Goodman, 2005, para. 1), and one gets a sense of the confusing and hostile culture around delayed conception.

Following the publication of an editorial in the *British Medical Journal* (Davies and Bewley, 2005) the delayed pregnancy debate was sparked in the UK. Although Davies and Bewley, obstetricians in maternal-fetal medicine and gynecology respectively, protest that they are speaking *for* women (their patients!) and not against them (Williams, 2005), their editorial pushes many cultural hot buttons. As Williams (2005) points out, having a child is not solely a woman's choice, the delaying of pregnancy and childbirth is not simply a reflection of women's desires to "have it all," and language such as "an epidemic of pregnancy in middle age" and "deferring [pregnancy] defies nature and risks heartbreak" (Davies and Bewley, 2005, p. 589) is obviously inflammatory. As a consumer of these messages and others about the appropriate timing of motherhood, I feel chastised and more than a little anxious; ironically, the very emotion that Davies and Bewley identify as a complicating factor in the later-life pregnancy.

I deeply question whether I actually *chose* to postpone pregnancy. I reflect on the course of my life—my extended education, the meeting of my life partner in my thirties, the necessary steps of an academic career. It is only now that I am faced with the label of "elderly primigravida" that I feel the first twinges of doubt that I have taken the "right" steps given that I have always wanted to be a mother. Indeed, this is the first time that I begin to see my education and career as "choices" at all, because the discourse implies that I could have lived my life differently by undertaking the more timely work of reproduction. Having become pregnant at the age of thirty-eight, I wonder if I should be grateful to have evaded the consequences of procrastinating childbirth in favor of my career. By being a "good feminist" and striving to develop my identity as an accomplished and empowered member of society, I wonder if I have been a "bad woman" by failing to understand and respond to the realities of my body.

### The First Ultrasound

*August 2008.* Holding hands with Jay in a darkened exam room; staring at a large flat screen monitor high on the opposite wall; lying prone beside an enormous piece of computer equipment. The technician gently folds down my trousers and folds up my shirt.

"This may be a bit cold," she says, and squirts gel onto my lower abdomen. "You're only eight weeks along, so we may not be able to find the baby from the outside."

I shoot a look at Jay. I didn't know there was an alternative. The "inside" version of the ultrasound is never shown in the movies or on TV.

She pushes the transducer impossibly low and I can see why they ask women to empty their bladders. In seconds, she is clicking the computer to show us our baby. After three years of "trying"—the moment feels both unreal and intensely real.

"There's the Cheerio!" Jay exclaims. Although the baby is now the size of a bay shrimp, the size analogy in our pregnancy book for week seven—when the baby was "the size and shape of a Cheerio cut in half" (Shanahan, 2000, p. 48)—was so surprising that the name stuck. Jay grins and squeezes my hand. Our eyes focus on the center of the "body," where a butterfly appears to flutter its wings in happy agitation.

"Ready to hear the heartbeat?" she asks and, before we can respond, half the screen fills with pulsating lines as the room beats with an insistent, rapid rhythm.

"Chill out dude!" Jay urges.

"Actually, 170 beats per minute—that's perfect," she says.

I don't say anything. I just try to absorb the "otherness" of this little being—that heart beat, coming *from* me but not *of* me. I think, "You *go* little Cheerio! You *go.*"

### The Second Ultrasound

*September 2008.* Three weeks after the initial ultrasound I walk a short block to the clinic, grateful to have a doctor who is also a friend. Holly is not seeing patients today, but after four days of slight bleeding and "watchful waiting" she asks me to come for an exam.

"It doesn't sound like there's anything to worry about, but let's just have a look and see what might be going on."

This week, I searched my pregnancy books to find information about spotting. I turned from one book's index to the indicated page to find myself in a chapter called "Dashed Hopes" (Shanahan, 2000, p. 55), which indicates that 80 percent of miscarriages occur before the eighth week, but that 20 percent will occur later. I skillfully compartmentalize my reaction to this text and wait for information that is not based on statistics but is specifically about me.

Holly is in charge of the family medicine maternity care curriculum, so I expect that I will experience the definitive gyn exam—feet in the footrests ("Not stirrups," she explains, "No one's riding a horse here"), announcements of every step, slow and reassuring. My cervix is "closed," she tells me, so it's not clear what the bleeding portends.

"Let's have a listen," Holly suggests, picking up the handheld Doppler ultrasound that she used during last month's exam. She listens intently and for a long time as she moves the transducer across my belly. Last month it was too early to hear the heartbeat and I remember this as she continues the exam. "Come on little Cheerio!" Holly says quietly, and something in the tone of her voice ignites the tinder of anxiety that I had not yet acknowledged.

Holly turns off the Doppler saying, "Why don't you get dressed and I'll be back in a moment?" I hear her speaking to someone outside but only one phrase distinguishes itself from the others—"if the pregnancy is still viable."

Reentering the room she asks, "What else do you have going on today?"

I quickly dismiss my next meeting. She explains that not finding the heartbeat is "a bit concerning," so she has arranged for us to go to the women's center at the hospital across the street for a more complete ultrasound, just to be sure.

"But what do *you* have going on today?" I ask.

"*This* is what I have going on today," Holly smiles and dissolves any protest.

After a short wait, a dark-haired technician escorts us back to an exam room larger but quite similar to the one that Jay and I visited only a few weeks ago.

The technician asks, "How are you feeling?"

"A little nervous," I admit. "I *am* an elderly primigravida," I note, only semiseriously. She smiles kindly.

I lie back and feel the gel, followed by the transducer moving fairly quickly across my abdomen. My eyes are focused on the wall monitor, so I'm surprised when the technician stops and says, "*I'd* feel better if we do this transvaginally."

"Have you had one of these before?" she asks. I shake my head; she holds up the clearly phallic transducer and declares seriously, "As you can see, it's nothing too different from what you would have already experienced."

I laugh; grateful for some levity. The technician raises an eyebrow.

I go to the adjacent change room and disrobe from the waist down. I return and quickly position myself on the exam table. Holly stands beside me—ready.

The exam proceeds and I am, again, transfixed by the screen, strangely oblivious to the presence of the transducer between my legs. Holly takes my hand. I watch as this technician, like the first, identifies the baby and clicks the computer to record measurements. No one speaks. I stare at the screen and wonder why it looks like the baby has turned its back on us and, at the same moment, I realize that the butterfly is gone. Tears escape across my temples as I turn my face to the ceiling. An intense internal struggle begins as I tell myself that "no one has said anything yet; I don't really know anything," and yet, somehow, my eyes continue to cry.

Like before, the technician flips a switch but, this time, there is no insistent rhythm and the lines on the screen are flat.

"You can get dressed now," the technician says quietly. I go into the change room and dress in a fog, refusing to allow any thoughts to form in my mind. My body, in contrast, is internally frenzied as my pulse roars and my hands shake.

Holly turns as I emerge from the change room. "It's not good news," she says.

Holly holds me. The technician leaves the room. I wail with abandon as I feel the stories, plans, and hopes we have constructed for our family dismantled and discarded by waves of realization—"It's over. It's over. It's over."

I regain enough composure to ask Holly, "What happens now?"

Holly explains that she can schedule a D&C (dilation and curettage) or that I can wait for the miscarriage to happen on its own.

"When will it happen?" my voice is small, like a child's.

"There's no way to know exactly," she tells me gently, "But if it doesn't happen in the next five days, we'll need to schedule the D&C anyway." As she continues to explain the details, I note that Holly uses the term "products of conception" to describe what will be "passed" during the miscarriage or D&C. So quickly, we have moved on from referring to "the baby." The Cheerio has disappeared.

When we leave the exam room, the technician is right outside the door. "I'm so sorry." She reaches out to hug me and whispers in my ear, "Please don't despair."

In the days and weeks to follow, I ponder my response to the ultrasound image and the struggle between my body's realization and my mind's refusal to accept the evidence that our baby was lost. Some of the most powerful research we have that theorizes the body as a site of meaning comes from performance studies, including reflections on mothering, identity, and grief (e.g., Holman Jones, 2005; Pineau, 2000; Spry, 2000). I will only visit this idea briefly; I feel compelled to note the power of speech act theory (Austin, 1983) to explain my response at this point in the narrative. Although psychologists might call it "denial," there are realities (e.g., "I declare you husband and wife," "The defendant is guilty") that occur through the speaking of the words that declare them to be. The "reality" of my condition had existed for untold days before the diagnosis, the ultrasound was the confirmation for my physician, but I waited for her words to define the reality. As a communication scholar, it is profound to realize that Holly's words marked the end of the pregnancy and the beginning of our grief even more tangibly than the physical loss which was to come.

## Aftermath

After consulting with Holly and Jay, I decide to "allow Mother Nature to take her course" (Shanahan, 2000, p. 61) rather than scheduling a D&C, imagining that this course of action will be more faithful to our goals of having, eventually, a birth experience relatively free of medical intervention. In the first of many such ironies that would occur in the following months, Jay and I head out for supplies—ibuprofen and maxi pads—and absentmindedly enter the store via the entrance that takes us past the baby products on our way to the pharmacy section. As we check out, we note the pregnant belly of the woman ahead of us in line and instinctively reach for each others' hands. Later that night, and for many nights and mornings to come, the ritual of spooning with Jay's hand on my belly elicits floods of grief from both of us.

Although I have rehearsed the possibility of a pregnancy loss in my mind and have even published reflections about a close friend's miscarriage (Foster, 2005), I am woefully unprepared for the event when it occurs the morning after the ultrasound. As Holly explains later, like birth every miscarriage is different, yet I am confronted by the consequences of knowing so little of the stories of miscarriage, especially when compared to what I know of the exertion and the journey of birth. I resent that I am caught off-guard because miscarriage remains "an unrecognized loss" (Renner, Verdekal, Brier, & Fallucca, 2000) in our culture. The loss of a first pregnancy is complicated by the implications it often holds for the mother regarding her fertility and ability to carry and give birth to a child (Gerber-Epstein, Leichtentritt, and Beyamini, 2009). In addition, miscarriage after infertility, which Rosenberg and Epstein (2001, p. 339) call "the cruelest loss of all," retains particular meanings. Or as Domar and Lesch Kelly (2002) put it:

> Miscarriage after infertility is incredibly brutal. It is the loss of an extraordinarily desired baby. And it also represents a loss of innocence for you and your husband [*sic*]. Once you have a miscarriage, you know that you can get pregnant, but you know also that you can lose your baby. It can be given to you, but it can also be taken away. (p. 229)

Reading these texts, I feel confirmed in my experience of loss and grief, yet somehow I want to resist the subtle pull of what seems to be a canonical story—that of the tragic, infertile woman. I resist the construction of that stereotype and its application to me even as I feel comforted by the suggestion that the grief and rage I feel is "normal."

The final medical visits of my now-ended pregnancy involve blood work to ensure that my hormone levels are returning to normal. In a sadder reflection of her earlier conversation about medical terminology, Holly turns to me before giving me the orders for the pathologist.

"I hate this," she sighs and stops typing to look at me. "I have to write something on the order, but I want you to know in case you see it and it comes as a shock."

"Okay," I respond and brace myself.

"Your diagnosis is *spontaneous abortion*. It's an ugly term, I know, and it probably brings up a lot of feelings for you. I wish I didn't have to write it."

"I understand," I reassure her, not really sure that I do understand. "I think I've heard that term before, I just wasn't thinking about it in relation to what I've just experienced."

"I know; that's why I wanted you to know," Holly puts her hand on my knee briefly before turning back to the computer.

As a feminist who fully supports reproductive choices for women, including the choice to terminate their pregnancies, I feel caught in a web of signification. I struggle between my longing to be a mother, my rejection of any association with the idea that my pregnancy was aborted, and my shame that my reaction feels more aligned to the attitudes of pro-lifers than the feminist scholars I admire. I recall my own argument about the public-private dialectic (Foster, 2005). It is possible to defend the public rights of all women to access abortion while resisting the discursive violence of a clinical term that denies the private and unique meanings of my loss. As I consider the semantic weight of the word "abortion," I realize that the term and its associated political and material conflicts also denies the individual stories of the women who undergo the procedure—my mistake is in assuming that they *chose* and I had *no choice* when, in fact, they may have felt as helpless in the face of their circumstances as I did. Echoing my resistance to the idea that I "chose" to postpone pregnancy, I understand that even those acts that imply agency (e.g., terminating a pregnancy) cannot be adequately rendered by the term "choice" if there is no accompanying recognition of and access to alternate courses of action.

## PART II: INFERTILITY

### The Belly of the Machine

> Among the tribes of northern Natal in South Africa, the most common greeting, equivalent to "hello" in English, is the expression: "Sawu bona." It literally means, "I see you." If you are a member of the tribe, you might reply by saying, "Sikhona" or "I am here." The order of the exchange is important: Until you see me, I do not exist. It's as if, when you see me, you bring me into existence. (Senge, Ross, Smith, Roberts, & Kleiner, 1994, p. 1)

*January 2009.* Four months have passed and Jay and I agree to seek a second opinion from a fertility specialist. Although I became pregnant on our fourth "try" with IUI, my hormones have been fluctuating unpredictably since the miscarriage, so I want to know if there's another step that we can take to get us back on track. Dr. W comes highly recommended and is the quintessential specialist—efficient, armed with data on bar charts, and a terrible listener.

> Me: See? I can get pregnant. And it really only took four tries. That's good, right?

The Voice of Biomedicine: No. Forget all that. You are thirty-eight years old.

Me: Right, so we don't want it dragging out. I just think we need a little help to make it happen sooner rather than later.

The Voice of Biomedicine: Don't be stupid. According to the statistics you only have a 10 percent chance of getting pregnant. At this rate, it will never happen.

Me: But, in a way, I've had four chances to get pregnant and it worked once!

The Voice of Biomedicine: I told you. Forget that! The evidence says that IVF is the only reasonable option. Do you want to have a baby or not?

Me: I do. I do! Of course!

The Voice of Biomedicine: Well then?!

The physical exam is the second leg of a three-hour appointment sandwiched between the consultation and the financial counseling. The nurse invites me to sit on the examining table and Jay to sit on the chair in the corner. It occurs to me that this is an apt reflection of where he gets relegated much of the time—there, but peripheral to the process. Why is that? She instructs me to disrobe and put on "the drape" that is behind me. I stand, turn, and look for the drape. Nothing.

"It's there," she says, and points to where I'd been sitting.

I pick up the small square of paper and ask, "You mean this paper towel? This napkin?"

She laughs as she walks out the door, "It does fold out!"

After disrobing, I unfold the square and discover she's right. It's a small paper tablecloth, not a napkin. I stand corrected.

Dr. W arrives with another person. Is this a resident? I wonder. A medical assistant? I may never know. Dr. W picks up the transducer of the sonogram machine and with the briefest of preambles ("You'll feel some pressure.") inserts it. It occurs to me that, if I hadn't had one of these before, I would be both appalled and mortified. It also occurs to me that the only other time I had an internal ultrasound I learned that the baby I was carrying was no longer alive. If Dr. W had taken time to ask, she would know that. Instead, she calls out numbers that indicate the size of my ovaries, my uterus, and how many follicles she sees. I have no idea whether these numbers are good or merely normal, or whether normal is the most good I can hope for. I also don't know why, as an educated and empowered woman, I don't speak up, interrupt, and ask the questions I want to ask. Even in this context where the stakes are so high for me, I fail to be unruly.

The light goes on and, just as I begin to sit up, Dr. W exclaims, "The catheter test!"

Although I have had four IUI procedures already, it is apparently necessary for Dr. W to "try out" my cervix for herself to see how easy it is to penetrate my uterus. I note that the basics of the IUI are far more unpleasant when there is no chance of a baby at the end of it.

"What a horrific experience that was!" Jay exclaims as we leave the offices following a disastrous meeting with a nurse and our "financial counseling."

"I think I want to do the tests they recommended and send all the results back to our other doctor," I say quietly.

"Absolutely," Jay agrees. "We are *not* going back there."

Tears fall furtively as I listen, feeling panic rising in my chest and yet knowing that we have just been manipulated by a well-oiled baby-making machine. "I feel awful."

When I settle back at my desk and Jay is about to return to his, he looks me in the eyes and whispers, "I see you."

I whisper back, "I am here," and immediately fall apart. I begin to sob—as quietly as I can so that no one in the office will hear me. My face in my hands, I feel my shoulders heaving as I cry and cry. I feel completely erased by the experience—not simply dehumanized but completely erased—as if my body, my desires, my faith are just so many obstacles to be swept away by the force of medical *truth* and *science*. I am nothing, but if I put myself in their hands, they may just be able to salvage the mess that I have made of my reproductive dreams.

"You have every right," I hear Jay say as he stands beside me. "You have every right to feel the way you're feeling. They are assholes."

I laugh sobbingly at Jay's classic bottom-line, which is exactly what I need to hear.

## Illusions of Choice

In February, we choose to undergo diagnostic procedures—a hysterosalpingogram (HSG) and a saline sonogram.

In March, we choose to return to our original clinic and agree to try fertility medication.

In April, the day before our baby would have been due, we discover that I have ovarian cysts which disqualify me from taking the medication; we choose to go on birth control to try to get rid of the cysts (imagine the irony of taking birth control pills and prenatal vitamins at the same time).

In May, we choose to begin fertility medication and undergo an IUI for the first time in six months.

In June, having been unsuccessful, we choose to "rest."

In July, we choose to try medication again and repeat the IUI—without success.

In August, I am diagnosed with a large ovarian cyst and am again disqualified from using the medication. We choose to try again "on our own," and are unsuccessful.

In September, we choose to go on birth control again. We choose to investigate our options for financing IVF. We choose to consider only the clinic we have been working with even though it is not covered by my insurance. We choose to look into adoption.

At some point, choosing to have a baby became a matter of a hundred choices in a quest to ensure, to *control*, the attainment of our dream. As Domar and Lesch Kelly (2002) point out, we grow up feeling "completely confident that if we're smart about contraception we'll maintain complete control of when we will or won't get pregnant—we believe that it's all solidly in our own hands" (p. 10). Now, having slipped from fertility to infertility, the only control we have is to say "yes" or "no" to the next intervention proposed by our physician—but this control does not bear up under scrutiny. It is nonsense to speak of choice when "no" means moving away from our heart's desire and "yes" means no guarantee whatsoever that we will "achieve" (Weschler, 2002) our goal.

## PART III: A MESSY SYNTHESIS AND CONCLUSION

As a critical scholar, I can turn my attention relatively easily to the rampant, *disciplining* hegemony of cultural discourse surrounding (in)fertility and reproduction. I see the ways in which I, by reporting rates of miscarriage by age in this chapter, by giving a platform to the already-privileged medical voices in my narrative, and by presenting rather than problematizing my changing attitudes toward fertility medication I have put myself in a rhetorically untenable situation. I want to argue that the discourse of "age-related infertility" is socially constructed and serves the purposes of a powerful biomedical industry. And yet, when I turn to the particulars of my personal story—delayed conception, miscarriage, and failure to conceive for twelve months following the loss of the pregnancy—I am faced with the limits of critical thinking to help me make any sense of it. Thematically, when biology and biography meet biomedicine, I find that I am called to question the limits of all three, because they fail to help me make sense of my subject position as a woman who is (in)fertile-not-yet-pregnant-and-still-trying.

Stone (1991) proposes a powerful framework for understanding how reproductive medicine and associated technologies function as cultural mechanisms; specifically, through analysis of media from the 1950s through the 1980s, she identifies how women have increasingly become the targets of messages around fertility. In these media, women are admonished to "protect" (p. 317) their fertility before there is even a problem, to "prepare" (p. 318) themselves for conception through diet, exercise, safer sexual practices, and regular medical care, and to plan for a postponed pregnancy by arming themselves with information to help them "'fight' infertility once it has been perceived as a problem" (p. 319). The overarching theme that Stone identifies in these articles is the disciplining of the female body and mind, such that everything that occurs (or fails to occur) in a woman's reproductive life is her responsibility. Stone notes "Americans' willingness to employ a type of technical rationality in their personal lives in order to conceive" and notes, "In the area of human reproduction, submitting oneself to 'control and dependence' seems to be an acceptable behavior, especially for heterosexual women, because it redeems their 'rights' to conceive and bear children" (p. 319). Reading this article sheds some light on the uneasiness I sense as I move forward in my reproductive journey.

I am aware that in this chapter I have quoted uncritically from three of the top selling, popular press books in the fertility literature: *Taking Charge of Your Fertility* (Weschler, 2002), *Conquering Infertility* (Domar and Lesch Kelly, 2002), and *Getting Pregnant When You Thought You Couldn't* (Rosenberg and Epstein, 2001). Even glancing at the titles, one gets a sense that the content will be more boot camp than bucolic retreat. Despite the best intentions of the authors, and testimony from readers and reviewers, I have read all three with an increasing sense of bewilderment at the sheer volume of information and range of activities I am expected to perform in order to fully participate in this project of making a baby. What I bought when I obtained these texts was a promise that I could choose to actually *do* something to affect the outcome of our reproductive efforts. What I got when I read them was the sense that I must be disciplined, vigilant, and dedicated toward this outcome—even to the point of managing my emotions including hope, despair, and overall stress. And I can't help wondering if what I have chosen to invest in is the illusion of control, because choosing to have a baby is not really an option—I can only choose to *try*.

Many competing discourses clamor in the arena of infertility. On the one hand, women are admonished to plan pregnancies, to make good choices about when to begin a family, and to reproduce in a way that does not burden others, including coworkers, taxpayers, or insurance plans. On the other hand, there is a not-so-subtle condemnation of women who encounter age-related infertility and enlist help from reproductive technologies. In this discourse, we are blamed for wanting to "have it all" and prioritizing career over family; essentially (the argument suggests) we have brought our infertility on ourselves through careless procrastination instead of procreation. Underlying these discourses is the assumption that we have choices about when to reproduce, and that we will be able to have a baby if we time our choice appropriately.

By emphasizing life activities *other than* motherhood, second wave feminist discourse around women's education, career, and reproductive rights inadvertently supports the notion that motherhood will come naturally with a simple choice rather than active efforts like those devoted to career (O'Brien Hallstein, 2008). The notion of choice is also promoted by the industries of reproductive technologies, which thrive on success stories of women—mostly white, middle-class, educated, "older"—who deliver babies after years of struggle. (Sylvia Ann Hewlett, author of *Creating a Life,* delivered a child at the age of fifty-one.) In the context of infertility, what challenges these ideas is that choice is meaningless in the absence of knowledge about one's conditions and options. Specifically, to the extent that the majority of women cannot know their reproductive capacity until they try to conceive, the notion that we *choose* to postpone pregnancy or *choose* to have children is highly problematic. In addition, choice cannot be understood outside the mechanisms of social production that allow women like me—white, middle-class, educated, "older"—access to the kinds of resources and medical support that will allow me to have a child one day. . . . I hope.

## FINAL THOUGHTS

I fear that I cannot leave this chapter without some attempt to resolve the narrative with a sense of forward movement and the potential for transformation that we look for in narrative projects like this (Bochner, 2000). As

I write the final paragraphs of this chapter, I anticipate the one year anniversary of our miscarriage in two weeks' time. Today, I am in a difficult place, so I offer the following thoughts from a performance I presented at a conference in May (Foster, 2009). I invite the reader to touch down on these sentiments with me as a testament that hope can take many forms and can offer us a story we can live with.

It is common in our culture to speak of not only *having* children, but of *making* them. "Where did I come from, Mummy?"—"I made you." Well, I can no longer think in terms of "making" a baby; making is something that one *does* which implies a degree of control over the process that I believe is an illusion. To me, this feels more like a quest, a seeking, with no degree of certainty whatsoever. As the ground continues to shift under my feet, I am no longer trying to *make* a baby I am trying to find our child . . . who is also, I imagine, waiting for us.

## REFERENCES

Alexander, B. K. 1999. Performing culture in the classroom: An instructional (auto)ethnography. *Text and Performance Quarterly* 19, 307–31.

Austin, J. L. 1983. *How to do things with words*. London: Oxford University Press.

Banks, A. P., and Banks, A. 2000. Reading "The Critical Life": Autoethnography as pedagogy. *Communication Education* 49, 233–38.

Bochner, A. P. 2000. Criteria against ourselves. *Qualitative Inquiry* 6, 266–72.

Bochner, A. P., and Ellis, C. (eds.). 2002. *Ethnographically speaking: Autoethnography, literature, and aesthetics*. Walnut Creek, CA: AltaMira.

Corey, F., and Nakayama, T. 1997. Sextext. *Text and Performance Quarterly* 17, 58–68.

Crawford, L. 1996. Personal ethnography. *Communication Monographs* 63, 158–70.

Davies, M., and Bewley, S. 2005, Sept. 17. Which career first? The most secure age for childrearing remains 20–25. *British Medical Journal* 331, 588–89.

Denzin, N. K. 1997. Interpretive ethnography: Ethnographic practices for the 21st century. Thousand Oaks, CA: Sage Publications.

Domar, A. D., and Lesch Kelly, A. 2002. *Conquering infertility: Dr. Alice Domar's mind/body guide to enhancing fertility and coping with infertility*. New York: Penguin.

Ellis, C. 1991. Sociological introspection and emotional experience. *Symbolic Interaction* 14, 23–50.

Ellis, C. 1998. What counts as communication scholarship: An autoethnographic response. *American Communication Journal* 1(2). [Electronic publication].

Ellis, C. 2004. *The ethnographic I: A methodological novel about autoethnography*. Lanham, MD: AltaMira.

Ellis, C. and Bochner, A. (eds.). 1996. *Composing Ethnography: Alternative forms of qualitative writing* (pp. 172–98). Walnut Creek, CA: AltaMira.

Foster, E. 2005. Desiring dialectical discourse: A feminist ponders the transition to motherhood. *Women's Studies in Communication* 28, 57–83.

Foster, E. 2009. Tales of the not-yet-pregnant. Performance presented at the Fifth International Congress of Qualitative Inquiry, Urbana-Champaign, IL, May 20–23.

Frank, A. W. 1995. *The wounded storyteller: Body, illness, and ethics*. Chicago: University of Chicago.

Gerber-Epstein, P., Leichtentritt, R. D., and Beyamini, Y. 2009. The experience of miscarriage in first pregnancy: The women's voices. *Death Studies* 33, 1–29.

Gibbs, N. 2002, April 15. Making time for a baby. *Time Magazine* 159(15), 48–54.

Goodman, E. 2005, January 23. Can women have it all? *Boston Globe* [Electronic version]. Retrieved January 28, 2006 from www.boston.com/news/globe/editorial_opinion/oped/articles/2005/01/23/can_women_have_it_all?mode=PF.

Hewlett, S. A. 2002. *Creating a life: Professional women and the quest for children*. New York: Hyperion.

Holman Jones, S. 2005. (M)othering loss: Telling adoption stories, telling performativity. *Text and Performance Quarterly* 25, 113–35.

Mason, M. A., and Goulden, M. 2002. Do babies matter?: The effect of family formation on the lifelong careers of academic men and women. *Academe* [Electronic version]. Retrieved January 29, 2006 from www.aaop.org/publications/Academe/2002/02nd/02ndmas.htm.

Mason, M. A., and Goulden, M. 2004. Do babies matter (Part II)?: Closing the baby gap. *Academe* [Electronic version]. Retrieved January 29, 2006 from www.aaop.org/publications/Academe/2004/04nd/04ndmaso.htm.

Neumann, M. 1996. Collecting ourselves at the end of the century. In C. Ellis and A. Bochner (Eds.), *Composing Ethnography: Alternative forms of qualitative writing* (pp. 172–98). Walnut Creek, CA: AltaMira.

O'Brien Hallstein, D. L. 2008. Silences and choice: The legacies of white second wave feminism in the new professoriate. *Women's Studies in Communication* 31, 143–50.

Pelias, R. 2000. The critical life. *Communication Education* 49, 220–28.

Pineau, E. 2000. Nursing mother and articulating absence. *Text and Performance Quarterly* 20, 1–19.

Poelker, D. A., and Baldwin, C. 1999. Postponed motherhood and the out-of-sync life cycle. *Journal of Mental Health Counseling* 21, 136–47.

Renner, C. H., Verdekal, S., Brier, S., and Fallucca, G. 2000. The meaning of miscarriage to others: Is it an unrecognized loss? *Journal of Trauma and Loss* 5, 65–76.

Rosenberg, H. S., and Epstein, Y. M. 2001. *Getting pregnant when you thought you couldn't: The interactive guide that helps you up the odds* (Rev. ed.). New York: Warner.

Senge, P. M., Ross, R., Smith, B., Roberts, C., and Kleiner, A. 1994. *The fifth discipline: Fieldbook*. New York: Broadway Business.

Shanahan, M. K. 2000. *Your over 35 week-by-week pregnancy guide: All the answers to all your questions about pregnancy, birth, and your developing baby*. Roseville, CA: Prima.

Shields, D. C. 2000. Symbolic convergence and special communication theories: Sensing and examining dis/enchantment with the theoretical robustness of critical autoethnography. *Communication Monographs* 67, 392–421.

Sparks, A. C. 2002. Autoethnography: Self-indulgence or something more? In A. P. Bochner and C. Ellis (eds.), *Ethnographically speaking: Autoethnography, literature, and aesthetics* (pp. 209–32). Thousand Oaks, CA: AltaMira.

Spry, T. 2000. Tattoo Stories: A postscript to Skins. *Text and Performance Quarterly* 20, 84–96.

Stone, J. L. 1991. Contextualizing biogenetic and reproductive technologies. *Critical Studies in Mass Communication* 8, 309–32.

Taft-Kaufman, J. 2000. Critical claims, critical functions: Autoethnography and postscholarship. *American Communication Journal* 4(1) [Online Journal].

Tillmann, L. M. 2009a. Speaking into silences: Autoethnography, communication, and applied research. *Journal of Applied Communication Research* 37, 94–97.

Tillmann, L. M. 2009b. Body and bulimia revisited: Reflections on "A Secret Life." *Journal of Applied Communication Research* 37, 98–112.

Tillmann-Healy, L. M. 1996. A secret life in a culture of thinness: Reflections on body, food, and bulimia. In C. Ellis and A. Bochner (eds.), *Composing Ethnography: Alternative forms of qualitative writing* (pp. 76–108). Walnut Creek, CA: AltaMira.

Trujillo, N. 1998. In search of Naunny's grave. *Text and Performance Quarterly* 18, 344–68.

Weschler, T. 2002. *Taking charge of your fertility: The definitive guide to natural birth control, pregnancy achievement, and reproductive health*. (Rev. ed.). New York: Quill.

Williams, Z. 2005, October 1. Family: Interview Melanie Davies and Susan Bewley cause uproar with the British Medical Journal editorial demonizing late motherhood. *Guardian (London)*. Retrieved from LexisNexis database November 20, 2007.

## NOTE

1. Elissa would like to acknowledge essential developmental feedback on this chapter provided by Jay Baglia and Krista Hirschmann, and by the other members of the motherhood quartet—Sara Hayden, Lynn O'Brien Hallstein, and Suzanne Daughton—who have accompanied me on this intellectual and emotional journey these many years.

8

# TWO WOMEN, TWO STORIES

## Complicating Our "Right to Choose"

*Summer R. Cunningham and Amy R. Pearson*

In this piece, we explore the ways we (two young, white, educated females) made different reproductive decisions amidst discourses of family, religion, feminism, academia, and motherhood, amongst others. We tell our stories in the hopes of complicating and expanding contemporary understandings of reproductive "choice." Our intention in this chapter is to use our stories to illustrate how discourses of choice presented by various social institutions (i.e., family, religion, feminism, academia, motherhood) can be interpreted and embodied in different ways.

As feminists, we believe that focusing on lived experiences and the knowledge obtained through such experiences is critical for understanding the politics of reproductive choice. Furthermore, our theoretical backgrounds in feminism and organizational communication have instilled us with a desire to explore the complex, dialectical relationships between discourse and materiality, power and resistance and the various ways these forces impact, organize, and structure various facets of our lives. Indeed, the writing of our narratives for this chapter were specifically informed with these dialectics in mind, particularly as discussed in Ashcraft and Mumby's (2004) text *Reworking Gender: A Feminist Communicology of Organization*. However, we have made a conscious decision to exclude a theoretical analysis of our narratives in this piece. Rather, we have chosen to employ an autoethnographic approach to this topic, allowing our narratives to speak to issues of contemporary reproductive choice(s) and the powerful discourses which constrain and enable those choices.

Autoethnography is a particularly effective methodological form for tapping into and exploring the subtle complexities of lived experience (Pearson, 2009; Ronai, 1995; Stewart, 2009). Ellis and Bochner (2000) argue that stories "create the effect of reality, showing characters embedded in the complexities of lived moments of struggle" (p. 744). In order to best implicate the broader social discourses surrounding our choices and to most effectively illustrate the complexities behind our decisions, we tell our stories here. In doing so, we attempt to explicate the very feelings and material circumstances which simultaneously inform and draw from contemporary discourses of reproductive choice (Ashcraft and Mumby, 2004).

Allowing our narratives to remain stories is important for two main reasons. First, we want readers both familiar and unfamiliar with the theoretical concepts that informed this piece to appreciate some component of our stories. Second, we believe the juxtaposition of our narratives illustrates the complexity and distinctiveness behind every reproductive decision while concurrently highlighting the fundamentally social aspects of our choices. Despite the fact that feminist rhetoric has traditionally foregrounded women's personal narratives in discussions of reproductive rights, we find that scholarly dialogue underscoring the simultaneously personal and collective nature of the discourses we embody and that inform our choices are largely absent from contemporary discussions of reproductive choice. This move is important both conceptually and personally. Conceptually, we must remember that discourses are not abstract or detached from us (Ashcraft and Mumby, 2004). Though we often note this in our scholarly work (Ashcraft, 2005; Mumby, 2005), it is generally discussed in abstract, theoretical terms. This chapter demonstrates the ways similar discourses are embodied, lived out, produced, modified, and reproduced differently as individuals navigate socially developed discourses (Giddens, 1984). Personally, this move is important in terms of forming feminist solidarity (Foss, 1996). By locating points of commonality among our differences, we begin to see the ways each of our choices intersects with the choices of everyone else. In this way, we hope our stories continue to push us toward an even richer appreciation of the different reproductive decisions that are made and for the women who make them.

In this chapter, we draw attention to a number of key discourses surrounding Amy's reproductive choice to have an abortion and Summer's reproductive choice to have a child. In particular, we highlight such issues as our relational statuses, our relationships with our families, our positions as academic students, our relationships to feminism, and the influence of religion, among other things. Through our stories, we attempt to highlight and explicate the ways our relationships to these discourses merged with the material circumstances of our lives such that we made particular choices (Ashcraft and Mumby, 2004). In keeping with much feminist and autoethnographic scholarship though, we hope that our stories do more to demonstrate the messiness involved in the intersection(s) between our theoretical concepts and the actualities of our lives than a traditional analysis might do (Ellis and Bochner, 2000). Further, we hope the interchange between our stories points to the interchange between ourselves as women making individual choices and the ways our choices are also always collective choices shaped by and also shaping, changing and perpetuating reproductive discourses available in contemporary society. We organize our chapter according to broad similarities in theme, but like most autoethnographic research, we leave space for you to make sense of and draw connections between our stories as we weave back and forth between different periods of our lives to show how broader social discourses informed, but were informed by, our decisions (Ellis, 2004). We conclude with some final thoughts on reproductive choice in modern times.

## AMY

I was leaving Ted's after doing the dishes so his mom would like me. I told his parents it was nice meeting them, and hopped on my pink ten-speed. Biking across town, I noted the old brick apartment buildings, the wide streets, the open, twilight sky, the intensifying pangs in my stomach. I biked faster. I sang a song at the top of my lungs. I felt sad and I felt happy and I let my feet move the pedals, and the bike kept moving forward.

Earlier, I was sitting at Denny's with my three brothers and my sister who were in town for her tennis tournament. My mom called two days earlier to say they were coming, but that my sister didn't want to see me so I shouldn't come to watch her play. The afternoon she said that, I climbed up the backside of Mt. Sentinel and let my body get whipped by the trees so that the cuts were bleeding. They called at the last minute to invite me for dinner before leaving town. No one spoke to me, but I sat there with them.

My place on 3rd street was a last minute find after my husband said he thought that I should leave. I bounced from couch to couch at friend's places until the apartment emerged. The woman showing it told me she thought I should live there because it had a safe and healing capacity. She had lived in the attic space for two years following her divorce. I did not tell her I was divorcing. I met her in her small house on 5th to sign the paperwork and noticed her long fingers and the empty, lonely feeling of her place; one tabby cat, a plastic Christmas tree, tinsel, blue ornamental bulbs.

I was pedaling mindlessly and I was thinking about my sister, how she wouldn't look me in the face or stand near me. And I was watching the tree boughs wave in the May evening air, and the moon was only a sliver. And then I was on the ground, in the dirt. The wheels of my bicycle were spinning in the air. It was dark and I couldn't see. There was a big, bloody gash on the side of my leg. My stomach was aching again. I didn't want to get up, and I didn't want to stay there. So I crawled. Crawled to the house, up the stairs and into the old bathtub. I let the water get really hot and I sat in it. The water filled up all around me, and I washed the wound. I clutched my legs to my stomach, and looked at my body. I let myself cry and the tears mixed in with the blood and the dirt and the water. And I felt really sad and simultaneously clean and dirty, and I tried to wish away what I knew in my body.

## SUMMER

I was born in 1979. The landmark Supreme Court ruling on *Roe v. Wade* afforded my legal right to choose years before the first breath of oxygen ever crossed these lungs. Growing up, my perception of reproductive choice was so slight. I had no or very little grasp of the significance of reproductive rights for women on a large scale much less the significance in my personal life. Perhaps, the fact that I had the legal right to choose didn't mean much to me because my right to choose, as a teenager, wasn't yet my own. I was a minor. My rights were limited. So, even though I considered myself a feminist from a very young age, for me reproductive choice was not something that featured prominently on my feminist radar.

Until I found out I was pregnant. That's when the politics hit me.

It's hard to make an informed decision or even perceive the fact that you have choices when the dialogue itself is constantly pushed under the rug, when you have limited access or education about your choices. Teenage sex, pregnancy, and its various related outcomes were issues I was aware of, yet they were both real and unreal. They evoked feelings and images that were scary. As a teenager, my impression of pregnancy was that it ruined your life and made you disappear. This impression came largely from the way teenage pregnancy was addressed on television, in my home, and around me in my daily life.

This doesn't make sense, so let me show you what I knew about pregnancy, tell you about some of the impressions I remember getting.

## AMY

"Why can't a woman be president of the United States?" I asked my parents on the way to church.

"Well, the president of our country has one of the most important leadership roles in the world," said Mom.

"Yes?"

"Women aren't supposed to serve in leadership roles."

"Why?"

"Men are the head of the household," said Dad.

"Yes?"

"Women are too emotional to handle the responsibilities of that position."

"Hmm."

"Plus, women have children, and they need to take care of them."

"Hmm."

When I was eleven years old, my mom took me aside and said she thought I might be becoming curious about sex. We went out to the back living room and sat on the gray seventies felt couch with orange and black flowers. She pulled out a small book called *Almost Twelve* and quietly guided me through the workings of the female body.

"This is the vagina," she whispered. (You don't touch it, and neither does anybody else.)

"These are breasts. Your body will change, like this, and you will develop breasts," she whispered. (You don't touch them, and neither does anybody else.)

"In a few years, you will start to bleed from your vagina because your body will be preparing itself to have babies. Of course, your body won't need to use that blood until you get married and start having sex."

When I started growing armpit hair at age thirteen, I thought there was something wrong with me.

## SUMMER

We didn't talk about sex in my house. I'm not sure why. It could've been that my parents, consumed by midlife crises, failed to realize the timely importance of discussing sex with their children. It could've been that they were in denial of my blooming sexuality and found it easier and more convenient to think of me as asexual. It could've been that they believed that the religious exposure they provided (only) during my earliest years of childhood would provide enough of a moral compass to steer me away from sex. It could've been that they believed that if they simultaneously treated me like a good girl (who would never have sex) and like a little harlot (who needed to be kept under close supervision) the opportunity for any sexual encounter would remain beyond my reach. It could've been that my parents simply didn't know how to talk to us about sex.

It could've been *any* or *all* of those reasons, but we didn't talk about sex or even hint at the possibility of pregnancy in my parent's house with three daughters and no sons. I suppose you could say that the family discourse about pregnancy was hidden, bordering the line of nonexistence.

The lack of attention given to this issue in my home stood somewhat at odds with the reality of the issue in other facets of my life. At first, sex, reproductive choice, teen pregnancy, and teenage parenting were mainly issues that I was exposed to on television. For example, I remember watching the television series *90210*. There was an episode where Brandon dates a teenage mother who held aspirations of attending one of the Ivies.

Juggling a baby, academic responsibilities, and a boyfriend was too much. By the end of the episode, she's denied admission into Harvard due to her single motherhood, decides she can't date Brandon for related reasons, and isn't even sure if she can be a mother. Neither the baby's father nor his academic aspirations are featured in the episode. He is absent, presumably free to date whomever he wants and to attend college without the burden of parenting on his back.

*How ridiculous,* I remember thinking. *Why should she have to choose between being a mother and obtaining an education?* In hindsight, I see that the writers were probably trying to illustrate the challenges faced by teenage mothers, but that's not the message I received.

And still, this situation was so far removed from my reality. At least for a little longer, until people I knew began to have sex, and eventually I was one of those people. And the pregnancy and parenting part, that became a bigger part of my reality as well, when people I knew began to get pregnant.

## AMY

We had waited all week for this ceremony. It was legendary. An excuse to talk about sex. And in the public arena. As usual, my cousin Jenny and I sat on chairs in the back, perched expectantly on our knees so we could see. The final song faded into the old wood of the tabernacle, the worship band dissipated, and the district youth director moved slowly to the center of the room, his round body sluggish.

"We've got a special night planned for you," he began. "Pastor Nick from New Hope Church is here to talk to you about sex and sexual sin. At the end of the night, you'll have the opportunity to purge yourself of some of the terrible sins you have committed against our Lord Jesus Christ. It's going to be an incredible night here at Bugle Bible Camp! Let's welcome Pastor Nick."

"Turn to Genesis 1. God created man in his own image. Male and female he created them, and blessed them and said, go now, be fruitful and multiply upon this earth . . ."

"I have been married for ten years, and sex, boy, it is great! It is a wonderful blessing from God, one of God's greatest gifts."

A muffled laugh ran through the auditorium.

"My wife and I were both virgins when we married. In fact, we saved our first, passionate kiss for our wedding day."

One hour later.

"And I know some of you have regrets because you did not follow God's plan for you and your body. But God can restore you. He can turn you back into a virgin. He can clean away all your sin, and make you whole again."

Soft music started playing in the background. Quiet sobs could be heard throughout the room. The young woman next to me moved off her chair to the floor and put her head in her hands.

"Come back to Jesus," the music leader urged. "Join me in front for special prayer."

Teenaged boys and girls filtered out of their seats to the front of the room to kneel at the altar. Some stood with their arms outstretched, tears pouring down their faces. Adults gathered around them, bowing their heads, and extending their hands. The music played louder and louder and people were singing and praying out loud. The murmur in the room increased to a drone of simultaneous voices. I watched adult men lay their hands on teenaged women as they prayed. I watched young men and adult men watching young women out of the corner of their eyes as they stood singing, arms outstretched to heaven.

## SUMMER

Sarah and I were freshmen in high school when she got pregnant. She hid her pregnancy under baggy clothes. She hid it from other students, school administrators, and mostly her parents. It worked—some days I didn't even believe she was really pregnant. She was so afraid to tell her parents that she just pretended it wasn't real until she literally went into labor.

She called her mom at work:

"Mom, I'm having a baby."

"Okay, Sarah. We'll talk about it when I get home."

"No, Mom, I'm having a baby. Right now."

The last time I saw Sarah was when I dropped by her home to visit her and her one-month-old daughter. She had her baby and then she disappeared.

A few months later I had my own pregnancy scare. I remember consulting with my friend's older sister about what to do. She'd once been pregnant too. There was a knowing between us, a bond shared silently about things that were unspeakable. Perhaps for this reason, she assumed that I would automatically get an abortion as she did.

"Figure out which parent you can tell. Whoever will freak out the least. You only need one parent to sign the paperwork. And don't tell anyone else. No one."

It's not like I wanted to advertise my situation or make a formal public announcement, but I didn't want to have to hide it either. I remember feeling so angry that there was shame associated with it, at the realization that I could be shamed in the eyes of my parents and my peers. Shamed, not necessarily because I was having sex, but because I was pregnant—the obvious sign that one was having intercourse.

Fortunately, I didn't end up having to make a decision about pregnancy at that time. I didn't have to make such a decision until I was seventeen.

## AMY

"You can do either a surgical or a medicinal procedure, but with the medicinal procedure, you need at least a week of recovery time because your body will be aborting the child," the woman (from a large corporation) said over the phone.

Ted leaned over and whispered, "My friend's girlfriend did the medicinal route. It was terrible. Ben said Sarah had to just sit around and wait while her body caved in on itself. She was so sad."

"Do you have any openings for a surgical procedure?"

"You could have an operation in Billings in three weeks."

I looked at Ted and hung up the phone.

I called the *other* clinic and left a message: "I'm defending my thesis next week. I'm moving to Glacier Park the next day. Can you help?"

Their response: "We can get you in Monday morning. It's $500 cash. Come early to do paperwork. Don't mind the protestors."

The night before the procedure, I bought two pints of Ben and Jerry's, a pizza, and two films. All of my furniture was packed in storage since I was moving away. I spread out the blue quilt from my grandmother and lay in a patch of sunlight on the floor. I stared at the ceiling. It felt like slow motion. It felt like a non-choice. It felt like a real choice.

## SUMMER

*July 1997*. I don't remember what was going on politically. But I remember what was going on personally. I had officially graduated high school just two months earlier and was dating one of my colleagues from work. It wasn't serious. He was older than me by nearly seven years which was great because he could buy cigarettes and alcohol. My plan was simply to have a good time before returning to school in the fall where I would embark on my coursework at the local community college.

Although I was not yet eighteen, I wasn't living at home for reasons that mostly involved a contentious, unhealthy, and sometimes abusive relationship with my father. I rented a room for $250 a month from my supervisor and her husband. It was a good deal, especially since I was only making ten cents above what was then the minimum wage of $5.15 an hour. Even working forty hours a week, I was barely clearing $300 every two weeks after taxes.

When I first noticed my period was late, I didn't panic right away. I figured there could be a million different reasons for such an occurrence. I kept waiting for it to come, diligently checking my panties for spots every time I went to the restroom.

It didn't come.

*Shit,* I thought.

Pregnancy didn't figure into my plans for the fall or anywhere in my future. I didn't want children. Ever.

## AMY

I was sitting on my boyfriend's lap and we were kissing. He had brown hair and brown eyes. He played guitar in a band. I was eighteen years old. On Monday nights we went to College Campus Ministries. On Tuesday nights we went to College Campus Ministries at the other university. On Wednesday nights I facilitated a church group for junior high girls. After church with his family on Sundays, we'd go over to their house for dinner. His mom made casseroles and bought prepackaged lettuce from Albertson's. My mom said she was lazy.

We were in the living room at his aunt and uncle's up the street. I was living in a basement bedroom in their mansion for $50 a month. No one was home, so we were kissing on the couch upstairs. Then, his mother and sister came in the front door. They said they were looking for a vacuum cleaner. They saw me sitting on Calvin's lap.

~

"I like your sweater," I told his sister.

"Thanks," she said mildly.

"When does the football game start?" I asked his dad.

"Should be about half an hour," he said staring at the television.

"Can I help with dinner?" I asked his mom.

"No."

~

"My parents want us to meet with the church counselor," Calvin announced later.

"Why?"

"They just want to make sure we're pursuing a Godly relationship."

"Why is that of their concern?"

"They're my parents and they love us."

"I'm not going to do that."

"They only want what's best for us."

"I'm not going to do that."

"Do it for me."

"Why?"

"Pray about it."

## SUMMER

I didn't want to believe it, but I did. Didn't want it to be true, but it was. The pregnancy tests only confirmed this truth. Yet, despite the fact that I felt in my heart and elsewhere (like my cramping uterus and my convulsing stomach) that the results were correct, I denied them mentally. It was too heavy to comprehend. Too unreal.

I remember walking into my sister's room.

"I'm pregnant."

She and her girlfriend looked up at me. I could see in their faces that my statement had the same impact on them as the extra blue line had on me when it appeared before me on the pregnancy test. They knew it was true, but the magnitude of the truth I'd just spoken was far too intense for any of us to comprehend in a tangible way. After all, we were teenagers. We were invincible. We had our entire lives ahead of us. We were all devout followers in the church of "it won't happen to me."

## AMY

Calvin's father cleared his throat, announced: "The Bible is very clear about its stance on sexual sin. I'm just going to read here what it says in 1st Corinthians. Flee from sexual immorality because your body is a temple of the Holy Spirit. Now, I don't know about you, but it seems to me like sexual sin is more than the act of actual intercourse."

"Tell me about your goals for this relationship," said the counselor.

"We want to create a pure and holy relationship," said Calvin.

"Any romantic relationship not geared toward marriage is useless in God's eyes," said his mom.

"What do you see as the end goal of your relationship?" asked the counselor.

"Uh . . ."

"We want to be married one day, probably soon," said Cal.

"Turn with me again to Corinthians. I think the Bible is pretty clear that if sexual behaviors are transpiring, the relationship is already tainted," his dad said.

"I saw Amy sitting on Calvin's lap," said his mom.

The counselor looked at us.

"I think it's clear what needs to happen here. Amy and Calvin need to break up," said his dad.

"One other thing, I saw Amy flirting with other guys. Do you even love Calvin?" his mom asked.

I threw a box of Kleenex across the desk. The counselor looked at me.

"There are obviously some significant issues here."

## SUMMER

The first thing I had to do at my gynecological appointment was to pee in a cup. After depositing my cup through the slot marked "urine" I waited in a cold examination room, scared to death, never having seen this kind of doctor before.

I was alone.

I was alone in all of the decisions I made about this pregnancy. (But not really, because there were a lot of "voices" telling me what I ought to do.)

"Do you know that you're pregnant?" the nurse practitioner asked.

"Yes, that's why I'm here. I think I'm miscarrying. I've been bleeding and cramping."

(I hoped I was miscarrying.)

"Well, let's complete the exam, and then we'll send you down for an ultrasound to see what's going on."

(She thought I might be miscarrying, too. Whew.)

I only had to go a couple of doors down to get the ultrasound. Alone.

The technician couldn't find the baby.

(Relief; I was miscarrying.)

No, I was just barely pregnant. She would have to use special equipment to locate the fetus. Some kind of vaginal probe.

The vaginal probe was this awful thing that looked like a giant dildo with a camera on the end. The technician stuck the giant, cold, phallic-like camera inside of me and I wanted to scream and cry. It hurt and was unbearably uncomfortable. I felt like I was being molested, raped. I felt so alone. But this was all in the name of medical practice and it was for my health, so I wasn't being violated, right?

Then, there on the screen in front of me was a little dot.

"That's the baby," she said.

And I wasn't alone anymore.

## AMY

I mailed them a letter because how do you tell your parents who you love very much that you have decided that you don't want to be married anymore. That you have decided that you need to be free. That you have decided this is not for you. That you are unhappy and you are tired and you want to make all your own decisions without ever considering him again. And how do you tell your parents who you love very much that there are things that you value more than their feelings, and more than their religion, more than your extended family, more than your new home, more than your friendships, more than their community, the local school board.

He was never home during that period of time. He was out hunting wild game. He was out at the bar with his new work colleagues. He was beyond cellular service.

What I might have written in that letter:

Dear Mom and Dad,

I moved into town and I'm homeless. I hang out at coffee shops all day. At night I sleep wherever I can. I went home the other day to get some things. There was a photograph of a beautiful blond woman I have seen before in a bikini on his new dresser. It sounds funny, but it wasn't.

Love you, Amy

P.S. We're getting divorced.

Memorable phone conversations:

Father: "You are not getting divorced."

Amy: "I am."

Mother: "There is nothing like the love of god and a husband to fill the ache inside a woman's heart."

Amy: "I've no ache."

Memorable one-liner:

Sister: "Your voice will no longer resonate inside my head."

## SUMMER

Choices. This conception involved several choices:

*The choice to have sex knowing that if it resulted in pregnancy my body and my life would bear the weight of that pregnancy, regardless of the fact that there was another person involved.*

*The choice to abort, adopt, or keep a "child."*

*The choice to tell or not tell the other parent.*

And, now, I had a decision to make.

I knew the decision was mine and mine alone. Or at least, I felt that it should be. But I also remember that it seemed as though the whole world, from my closest friends to the feminist movement at large, had a stake in this decision.

I was terrified. And sick in my soul. None of my options seemed like good choices. Based on what I knew of teenage pregnancy my life after this moment was ruined no matter what I chose to do.

If I chose to have an abortion, I would be ridiculed by some as a murderer. Even though, technically, that choice was completely legal. And how would I *feel* if I terminated my pregnancy? What would it be like to spend the rest of my life wondering "what if"?

If I chose to give the child up for adoption I would have to live with another person inside me for ten months. Inside me. Inside me and closer to me than any other living person on this earth has ever been before. Then I would have to give that person away and possibly never see them again.

But, if I chose, as I did, to have the child, there would be consequences as well. Some of which I realized at the time, some of which I didn't.

I knew I would be ridiculed as a sinner who had sex outside of marriage.

I knew I would be seen as a promiscuous teenage slut who got what she deserved and would spend the rest of her life on welfare because she couldn't keep her legs crossed. I knew that the other person involved would not bear the same stigma or be destined for such a failed future.

I knew that some would see me as a failed feminist[1] who gave up her hopes, dreams, and future to become just another faceless statistic of teenage pregnancy in America.

What I didn't know was that even though I chose "life," even as I struggled to pay my bills, to purchase health care, to find childcare, I would also be looked down upon for choosing to have a child when I was young and unprepared.

I didn't know that the presence of this child in my life would result in my absence elsewhere.

I couldn't win.

## AMY

I thought it would be very complicated, and I thought I would have many qualms about it. But I was sick and throwing up early that morning when it was still dark. I was leaning over the toilet at Ted's place and I could hear his roommate getting ready to head out for the day.

I was wearing gray mountaineering pants and a long-sleeved olive green shirt with flowers on it because they were loose. I hadn't wanted to see anybody. I noticed myself walking carefully, almost on tiptoe, with an arch in my back, like a hunchback. I avoided my stomach, a foreign object. I was carrying the whole world, in my stomach. Its arms were stretching my whole body. I wanted to notice, and forget it. I wanted to know how your body could be someone else's. I wanted these feelings over.

## SUMMER

I had conversations with various members of my family. Each eerily similar, yet different:

Me: I'm pregnant and—
Mother: Oh, you have to keep the baby. I'll adopt it. Just don't have an abortion.
Me: It's my choice, not yours. It's my kid, not yours. You are not going to adopt it.

Me: I'm pregnant and I am keeping this baby.
Grandmother #1: I'm so sorry.

Me: I'm pregnant and I am keeping this baby.
Sister: You just ruined your life; I'm so disappointed in you.

Me: I'm pregnant.
Grandmother #2: I can't believe you had sex out of wedlock. You're going to hell.
Me: Well, then, if I have the abortion I won't go twice, will I?

Me: I'm pregnant.
Dad: (Silence.)

## AMY

In the back room, the nurse pricked my finger to make sure I was pregnant. It was the fourth time. But I knew before the first time, because suddenly, I had wanted to treat my body tenderly. I had stopped riding my bicycle. My breasts felt heavy and obvious. I carried them like a secret.

"Tell me how you're feeling about the procedure," the social worker goaded.

I looked at her.

"Fine."

She waited.

"I'm feeling fine."

"You don't have any religious or moral issues?"

"No."

The doctor's hands were cool. Before he came in, I heard him talking with the nurses.

"She's about to start her Ph.D."

## SUMMER

My vision of a carefree future involving education, friends, travel, and joy crumbled. I felt my life turning 180 degrees from the future I'd known, propelling me toward a horizon of foreboding uncertainties and dismal realities. As my friends went away to school, attended parties, and explored "the real world," I battled morning sickness, attended obstetrical appointments, and tried to figure out how I was going to make it in the world, for real.

I was depressed, lonely.

No longer able to relate to my friends, I stopped talking to them. I saw practically no one for the entire duration of my pregnancy.

But I couldn't relate to other pregnant women or mothers either.

All the literature I read about pregnancy, all the images of pregnant women on TV, movies, commercials, and various other forms of media showed pictures of women who were not me. They were financially secure, supported by devoted husbands, and excitedly looking forward to a future with their bubbling baby. They were happy.

That was not me. I was consumed with fear and utterly miserable. I couldn't even see into my baby's future or mine for that matter because I was so afraid that we wouldn't have one that was anything more than grim.

The other images of pregnant women, those who were like me, were teenagers who dropped out of school, continued to have more children—usually with multiple partners—and lived off of welfare. That's the future that seemed inevitable.

I didn't want that future. That wasn't me.

## AMY

Afterward, the social worker asked if I'd like to invite Ted into the room. He almost fainted when he walked in, and I laughed.

"She's under medication," the social worker explained. "Are you feeling alright?"

"I feel great!"

They left me alone in a small room next door. There were two reclining chairs, some fashion magazines, and a journal with entries from other women who had had abortions. I read some of the entries, and waited. I couldn't write that I felt sad like the other women had. I couldn't write anything.

We went directly to the grocery store. I walked the aisles and felt like I was floating. I felt like I was skipping, but didn't have legs. I wanted to greet every person. I wanted to call my mother. I wanted to eat everything. I had a sandwich, and felt happy.

## SUMMER

I walked around campus, unsuccessfully trying to hide my pregnant belly from onlookers who either looked at me with disdain or as if I was some kind of a freak of nature. I encountered professors who were sympathetic to my situation and others who flat out told me that I should drop out of school because "there were places for girls like me."

*Girls like me? What kind of a girl was I?*

A slut. An irresponsible whore. An unwed teenage mother. A statistic. A future, lifetime welfare recipient. A white-trash, single mom.

I worried a lot. I was afraid for my future and afraid for my son. Would I be able to take care of him? Would he be punished because I decided to have a child at such a young age? Would he be better off with someone else, parents who were prepared to take care of him?

At least once a week I found myself paging through the phonebook under "A."

"A" for adoption agency.

"A" for answers.

"A" for ambivalence.

"A" for alienated and alone.

"A" for absent.

I was unable to comprehend or enjoy the fact that there was a life growing inside of me because I was so focused on what kind of a life we were going to have after the pregnancy.

## AMY

Last weekend, I sat in the back row with my arms crossed as my twenty-year-old sister said her wedding vows. It was eerily familiar. She married on the farm, late August, homegrown flowers, rehearsal dinner barbecue, no one knew the groom. She put a yellow flower in her hair and everyone smiled like marriage at twenty was expected.

At toast time, the best man took the microphone and said that he wasn't concerned about the ages of the bride and groom because of their solid maturity in the Christian faith. When he finished speaking, the minister (our uncle) invited anyone who wanted to say something to speak. I stood ten feet from the microphone. Two friends in back pointed at me vehemently. Other relatives urged me toward the stage. I stood there.

Later, my cousin Jenny asked me why I didn't speak.

"Because," I said, "I had nothing to say."

On the way over to the neighbor's house to get more pint-sized jars for flowers, my mother sighed, "Sorry this is hard for you. Is this hard for you? This must be hard for you."

I turned my head and looked at her.

It was a beautiful wedding.

## SUMMER

I looked forward to my Women's History class most. It was the class where I felt least self-conscious of my progressively protruding midsection, but I was still self-conscious. It was impossible to ignore the fact that as we moved from suffragists and abolitionists to second wave women's libbers, my stomach moved from a little bump to a hump so large I could no longer squeeze it into the all-in-one, chair-desk combo seating accommodations of the classroom.

Like many other aspects of my freshman year in college, the room was not designed with pregnant students in mind.

One day as I sat sideways uncomfortably stuffed in my chair-desk, our class—which consisted of about twelve presumably middle-class, white twenty-something females and one white twenty-something male—became engrossed in a discussion about the contributions second wave feminism made with regard to women entering the workforce. This discussion was notably absent of any talk of glass ceilings and paid no consideration to working-class women who had no choice but to work. Indeed, the general consensus seemed to be that the issue was simple: women in the workforce were *always* a good thing. Furthermore, women who *chose* to stay home and raise children were antifeminists.

There it was. That familiar yet elusive feminist dogma, that ironic unspoken doctrine that told me at once that: feminism was about the right to choose, but some choices were valued more than others. Only certain choices were truly feminist.

I sat there unable to hide behind my growing belly. Unable to hide *because* of my growing belly. I sat there as a representative of all the failed feminists who'd made the wrong "choices." Though my decision not to have an abortion was somewhat different than the decision other women made when they chose not to enter the workforce after having children, we shared some common ground. There were other women, other feminist women, who could not, would not appreciate our decisions. We were rejected feminists.

I was speechless and disheartened. Thankfully, my instructor cut in:

"Do you hear yourselves? For this movement to be considered successful, in order for feminism to endure, we need to support one another. That means respecting the decisions of other women, even when and often especially when they make choices that you wouldn't have made for yourself."

## AMY AND SUMMER: TWO WOMEN, TWO STORIES

Summer finishes the last few words of her performance and stares out at a classroom of graduate students who return her glaze blankly. *Does anyone get it?* She wonders. *Do they understand the complexities of the "choice" that was made? Can they begin to understand its consequences?* Doubtful and disappointed, she returns to her seat.

After class, Amy approaches Summer. She looks at Summer deeply, her blue eyes searching, brow furred in compassion.

"I wanted to tell you that your piece really resonated with me," Amy begins, "I recently had an abortion."

Confused, Summer wonders how and why her choice to have a child as a teenager resonates with a woman who chose to terminate her pregnancy. She meets Amy's eyes. She's compelled to embrace the woman standing before her, to thank her for saying *something*, for acknowledging the experience. She wants to thank Amy for being with her, occupying that strange space of confusion, contradiction, alienation. They agree to get together and talk about their experiences.

Weeks pass. The women meet for coffee, exchange emails, share phone conversations about the circumstances surrounding their decisions. The (lack of) complication. The (ir)rationality of it all. Summer listens as Amy explains how she felt liberated after making her decision. Amy listens as Summer explains how she felt abandoned after making hers. As they sit together and share their experiences, so similar, so different, something changes for the women. For the first time in eleven years, Summer feels liberated in her choice. For the first time, she *feels* that she too made a feminist decision. And after months of loneliness and quiet, Amy feels supported in her choice. She has found a friend who understands.

## CONCLUSION

As feminists we believe that the legal "right to choose" continues to be a critical component of women's liberty; however, we also believe that discourses—above and beyond those of a legal origin—play a powerful role in constituting our reproductive freedom. It is important for feminists to critically and reflexively consider the stories of "choice" we construct and perpetuate at both macro- and microlevels, and to be aware of the "complicated ways in which discourses get appropriated, adapted, invented, enacted, and so forth toward coherent and conflicted effects" (Ashcraft and Mumby, 2004, p. 180). The juxtaposition of our stories demonstrates some of the ways in which discourses, feminist discourses included, can both empower and disenfranchise, liberate and alienate, enable and constrain. However, in sharing our story, we aim to do more than get at the complex relationships between discourse and materiality. We relay a story of solidarity. We show two stories of reproductive choice merging together into a larger story, a feminist story, about two women who made two different decisions coming together in the mi(d)st of their choices to find common ground and appreciation for one another and their decisions. Indeed, we came together because of difference, which is really just another commonality.

## REFERENCES

Ashcraft, K. L. 2005. Resistance through consent? Occupational identity, organizational form and the maintenance of masculinity among commercial airline pilots. *Management Communication Quarterly* 19, 67–90.

Ashcraft, K. L., & Mumby, D. K. 2004. *Reworking gender: A feminist communicology of organization*. Thousand Oaks, CA: Sage.

Ellis, C. 2004. *The ethnographic I: A methodological novel about autoethnography*. Lanham, MD: AltaMira.

Ellis, C., & Bochner, A. P. 2000. Autoethnography, personal narrative, reflexivity. In Denzin, N. K., & Y. S. Lincoln (eds.). 2000. *Handbook of Qualitative Research* (2nd ed., pp. 733–68). Thousand Oaks, CA: Sage.

Foss, S. K. 1996. *Rhetorical criticism: Exploration and practice*. Prospect Heights, IL: Waveland Press.

Giddens, A. 1984. *The constitution of society*. Berkeley: University of California Press.

Mumby, D. K. 2005. Theorizing resistance in organization studies: A dialectical approach. *Management Communication Quarterly* 19, 19–44.

Pearson, A. R. 2009. Scenes in the life of a woman. *Qualitative Inquiry* 15, 1448–51.

Ronai, C. R. 1992. The reflexive self through narrative: A night in the life of an erotic dancer/researcher. In C. Ellis and M. G. Flaherty (Eds.), *Investigating subjectivity: Research on lived experience* (pp. 102–23). Newbury Park, CA: Sage.

Stewart, K. 2009. How do I remember you?: A narrative of memory, loss, and Alzheimer's Disease. *Qualitative Inquiry* 15, 201–13.

## NOTE

1. In theory, feminism would tell us that we are liberated because we have the right to choose what is best for us as individuals with different life circumstances and aspirations. However, somewhere in the background, I heard loud whispers of a "true feminist choice." Perhaps they weren't whispers. Perhaps they were the voices of my feminist sister and feminist friends telling me: "Choose *you*. Abort, abort." From where I stood, I could see quite a gap between feminist theory and feminist practice.

9

# THE IN/FERTILE, UN/NATURAL BODY

## Ecofeminism, Dis/Embodiment, Technology, and (the Loss of) Choice

*Tracy Marafiote, Ph.D.*[1]

> Today's reproductively challenged woman may pack a basal body thermometer and hypodermic needles instead of intoning incantations over goat bladders, but despite the obvious technological advancements, in many ways we haven't come very far; the barren-woman stigma seems as powerful as ever. (Rosenberg, 2008, p. 53)

*Month 11, Year 2.* We get out of the car into the ubiquitous bone-chilling, damp grayness of a late western New York autumn and scurry into the refuge of the building. This place doesn't feel like a sanctuary, though; it's a typical office building: cold glass, hard brick, and inexpensive linoleum floors. Nothing about it sooths the adrenaline that I realize is starting to seep through my limbs, making me feel edgy as we scan the lobby directory board. Standing there, I recall that, unlike other nearby businesses, the roadside sign had listed only the doctors' names rather than the title of the business we are seeking. My first reaction is to be indignant; I frown self-righteously at the thought that they are hiding something. Yet, although I've been to similar places before, as my husband and I climb the stark staircase I'm slightly relieved that there's no one in the hallway to see where I'm headed and know why I'm here. At the top of the stairs, the door is closed with little hint of what's behind it. If someone should mistakenly get this far, or even enter the office, they'd have no idea whether it's another dentist, an ophthalmologist, or . . . what it really is. I know, however; and, as I enter the door and see the other couples waiting in the room, they know too. They look at me and know. I avert my eyes and wonder if it is my shame or theirs that I wish to disregard. *No*, I insist, *it's not shame; it's consideration for their privacy. No,* I acknowledge, *it's my own disgrace.* Because I'm a failure in accomplishing the most fundamental of female functions, I have an appointment at an infertility clinic.

We all have some narrative in our heads as we approach our research; some personal connection to the subject, some back-story about our own engagement with or enmeshment in the topic that most typically goes unstated. This particular chapter, however, began as a narrative as, across the course of over three years, I chronicled some of my personal experiences with in/fertility and choices related to maternity in an effort to make sense of and gain control over them, my emotions, and, in some odd way, my relationship with my body. The choice to become pregnant entailed for me a process that was characterized by a numbing ambivalence about maternity and was both fiercely embodied and disconcertingly disembodied. Learning that I am infertile (that still feels uncomfortably revealing to state so frankly) involved an unsettling grappling with reason and emotions related to pronatalist societal norms as well as my private assumptions and the very core of my sense of self. Both of those events compelled a reframing of personal choice: what was and was not an actual option for my future.

As a feminist and a cultural studies scholar who situates herself firmly in environmental communication, making sense of these tensions begged for an ecofeminist framework, which provides avenues for a qualitative examination of ways in which female bodies are, on the one hand, essentialized as *natural* and, on the other, simultaneously inherently (as are all bodies) *of nature* (see Burns, 2008; Curtain, 1997; Sturgeon, 2009). More specifically, ecofeminism is a lens through which to examine constructions of fertility and infertility as natural or deviant within a social framework that stigmatizes the nonmaternal woman. In doing so, I intersperse ecofeminist theorizing with excerpts from my journaling of my experiences with the inability to conceive, the discovery and denial of infertility, the labor (pun intended) to resist and overcome that pronouncement, and a loss of reproductive choice.

Narrative has been widely used in ecofeminist literature (see Filemyr, 1997; Gardner and Riley, 2007; Wagner, 2008) although few overtly discuss the method, as if there is no need to defend or explain the utility of first person accounts. Indeed, in the mid-1990s, McAndrew (1996) delineated ecofeminist methodologies, which privilege situated, lived experience uncovered through qualitative methods, including autoethnography and first-person narrative. Narrative, such as that used in this chapter, is an element of authoethnography that "strive[s] to show life's complexity and fragility in depth and detail" (Tillmann, 2009, p. 95). These methods are effective means by which to achieve the ecofeminist goal of examining the significance of personal, lived experience and the constructedness of knowledge.

Fertility, the possibility of biological maternity, is a condition that most women take for granted; likewise, the choices related to motherhood—to have or not to have biological children, how many of them to have, and when to have them—are typically simply assumed to be the birthright of females in a developed nation. For me personally, as well as in ongoing feminist political battles, fertility, women's bodies, and choice have been intimately entwined. Upon contemplating choice, I realized that it was about far more than merely the ability to select some given option. Choice entailed the perception of a range of alternative paths for my current and future practices that I could freely and feasibly select. Choice was about not just choosing but *achieving*, and not just the *possibility* of achievement, but *actual success*. Indeed, it was not only the unforeseen realization of constraints on my maternal options and the ability to choose from among them that was so shocking, but that I could not expect to attain a goal that I had chosen to pursue—especially because the limitations were not truly "external" but were imposed by my own being. In short, infertility did not just take away the choice to pursue conception; it reframed *not* conceiving as no longer one possible viable option but, instead, as a failure.

In reviewing my journaling for use in this chapter, I came to see the female body as a battleground upon which cultural skirmishes are waged in relation to woman, maternity, nature, technology, and, fundamentally, choice. The sites of these struggles are multiple, as deliberated within each of the three sections of this chapter. Specifically, first, as I examine ecofeminism and embodiment, academic clashes ensue as various types of feminisms express disparate views about the relationship of women's bodies with nature—a tension mirroring my own vacillation between feeling physically embodied and rationally disembodied as I thrashed my way through the thickets of infertility. In the next section, the un/natural body and choice, I consider discord surrounding constructions of the female body as "naturally" fertile (or unnaturally infertile), and the impact of such views on women's actual and perceived choices (and their loss) as related to feminism, identity, age, and maternity. Finally, I explore ways that reproductive technologies position female bodies as sites of battles wherein the meaning of technology is itself contested and in which subjectivity and agency emerge and are subjugated in an often relentless pursuit for victory over the unnatural, infertile female body.

## ECOFEMINISM AND EMBODIMENT

Ecofeminism or ecological feminism is, at its core, a view that there is a link between social and political frameworks that contribute to the oppression of women (as well as people of color, the underclasses, developing nations . . .) and the domination of the natural world (Sturgeon, 2009; Warren, 1997). Here, I explore the oppression present in the relations between women, women's bodies, and reproductive technologies. Feminist literature from several camps has painstakingly theorized the cultural positioning of female bodies in general, and technology and female bodies in particular, and this work has much to contribute to the issues in this chapter. While drawing on these, I nonetheless emphasize an ecofeminist viewpoint because, more so than other feminisms, ecofeminism has "refute[d] the liberal feminist advice of transcending the female body and bodies in general" (Twine, 2001, p. 33). Here, too, women's bodies are the site of battle as, in struggling to overcome entrenched, hierarchical dualisms, feminists have frequently dissociated women from nature or the body in order to contest the historical articulation of men with the more valued culture, mind, and reason. In contrast, ecofeminists resist arguments that the physical/human being is distinct from nature—viewing that position as one that reinforces a potentially damaging culture-nature dichotomy. For me, the stance that the body, my body, is of nature has become even more strongly embedded through my experiences with infertility.[2]

Nonetheless, warranted critiques of ecofeminism include the charge that it tends toward the mystification of women and nature or the condensing or marginalizing of complex social politics and relations with the natural world into (reductive) metaphors of maternalism (Alaimo, 1994, 2008; Moore, 2008; for example, see King, 1993). The most common concern surrounding (especially early) ecofeminist writing was that in challenging the culture-nature dualism, it tended toward essentializing women/the female body, as somehow closer to nature than men/the male body. This strain of ecofeminism cultivated the idea that *as women* we have an intrinsic relationship with that which is "natural," an inherent sensibility or intuition that men do not; that we "know" in particular, innate ways outside of cultural constructions. There are many obvious problematic implications of stances linking women (as opposed to humans in general) and nature, especially hinging upon ways this reinforces hierarchical cultural binaries related to gender, and these have been assessed at length by ecofeminist authors such as Val Plumwood (see, for instance, Plumwood, 1993) and Carolyn Merchant (see Merchant, 1996). This standpoint is also a precursor to pronatalism—an ideology, policy, or practice that encourages childbearing and embraces a patriarchal and paternalistic view of women's bodies and motherhood. It is an easy turn from notions of women having a natural affinity for motherhood/maternalism, to it being feminine nature to be mothers, to it therefore being our female nature to give birth. On this slippery slope, consequently, women who do not conceive embody a questionable femininity.

For obvious reasons, I am dismayed by the social, personal, and political implications of such reductions. Yet, although often painful, my quest for conception made me reevaluate my sense of embodiment, of being in my body, as well as my hounding sense of disembodiment, a psychological distance from my physical being. Although, often, the two coexisted and skirmished for supremacy in my psyche.

> *Monthly, Years 2 and 3.* As I sleepily drag myself from my bed, eyes half closed against the morning light, brain not yet engaged, I'm aware that my stomach feels . . . just not quite right. I feel a little thrill in my core. Quickly, I try to tamp down any anticipation; I've had this hope so many times. *We did a hard run yesterday and it was really hot out, I'm probably just a little dehydrated. . . . But maybe . . . !* My brain instantly switches to the second person: *Stop it, you do this every month. It. Is. Not. Happening.* Still, I furtively knead my breasts willing there to be some revealing tenderness.
>
> For several days I'm even more hyper-aware of every internal twinge and surge, and am immediately attentive to a slight pressure in my abdomen. Within hours I spot the telltale dark red stain when I use the bathroom: my period. I bite my lip and exhale sharply—*I will not cry this time.* Taking a deep breath, I repress the ballooning disappointment, mentally squeezing it into a tight, controlled ball in my chest where it will linger until next month, always threatening to rupture into a tempest of frustration, shame, and sadness.

Throughout this journey, it has been common to vacillate abruptly between feeling deeply embodied and coolly disembodied, especially falling back on the latter, the rational mind, when the emotional and psychological pain of my near-obsession with my physical being became too difficult. The distance proved to be a safe removal from myself by placing the fault elsewhere: the problem was not *me* but my body. While perhaps "safe," the body/mind rupture impacts our sense of agency, our ability to choose, with the body becoming the oppressor of the mind, an external force preventing "me" from accomplishing my goal.

Ironically, upon choosing and then beginning the quest for maternity, I struggled with intense ambivalence—being a parent is far too daunting an undertaking for me to not question my readiness and qualifications. I was unprepared, therefore for the intensity of my grief at the loss of this possibility. It is one thing to be unsure about one's goal, it is quite another to be informed that it is not available to you, and it is common for couples to desperately mourn the child they are unable to have (see Higgins, 2003). And, in part, we may also grieve the loss of our own perpetuation, the ability to recognize oneself in another being, the realization that the continuation of our identity cannot be taken for granted (Raphael-Leff, 2003).

I became suddenly cognizant of the engulfing arms of identity reaching both backwards and forwards when I recently posted some old family photos on a social networking site. A friend immediately commented, "Is that a little Tracy? How cute! You look a lot like your Mom from what I can tell." It made me smile—while also evoking an unexpected, stabbing sadness. My whole life people have commented on how much like my mother I look; something that has always (except perhaps for a few years in high school) given me a great deal of pleasure and somehow made me feel closer to her. Although there are of course no guarantees that one's child will favor them in any way, the idea that I cannot reproduce and know I will never have that type of connection with my child is a personal and deeply painful loss that at times feels as if it engulfs my body and being, overwhelming any possible "safe" divide between physical body and rational mind. As depicted so poignantly by novelist Hilary Mantel (2003) in her chapter in *Inconceivable Conceptions: Psychological Aspects of Infertility and Reproductive Technology*,

> If the chain that links you to "biological destiny" is severed, you are left winded and bruised on the road, the casualty of an accident. You come up hard against the question: what's the use of me? . . . The intellect can make guesses about what the loss will do to the spirit. But what afflicts the intellect—the thing that makes it suffer—is the lack of freedom and capacity, the lack of choice, the knowledge that the incapacity is absolute, that nature has made a choice and made it against you. (pp. 21, 22)

And that is the crux of it—feeling as if you have been singled out for some unspeakably cruel persecution that has denied your aberrant body and your very self the ability to choose its future. Ironically, not only has choice been taken from you but your damaged, "unnatural" body makes you unable to make your own choices.

## THE UN/NATURAL BODY AND CHOICE

Historically, social frameworks have developed in order to manage natural bodily development, creating tacit cultural standards for appearance, size, behavior, and other embodied characteristics. And in large part, we understand our identities in relation to the extent to which we satisfy or deviate from these social norms (Foucault, 1995). Bodies meeting the mandate go unnoticed as normative and "unmarked" while those failing to fulfill social expectations are "marked" and devalued (Twine, 2001). Conventionally, the marginalized, marked body has been that which is embodied rather than intellectual, closer to nature than culture, and of course exemplifies femininity as opposed to masculinity; that is, the female body.

Nonetheless, there exist ideals and norms within each cultural category, and for women, the centered, unmarked body is the one that exhibits the ultimate standard of femininity: childbearing. Ironically, in enacting its femininity, the fertile, pregnant body is centered, unmarked, and *natural*, at once representing and reinforcing cultural norms and approved gender-related patterns. Unnatural, infertile bodies, then, call into question conventional dualisms and are branded as abnormal and marginal. As a woman who is infertile and who, despite my critical scholarship, has in many ways internalized social ideals, I reflexively scrutinize myself and realize how I have marked my own body as inferior and my infertility as unnatural, malfunctioning, a source of ignominy. Revisiting my journaling of my experiences, I found it disturbing to see this self-evaluation so evident in my own language:

> *Years 1, 2, and 3.* It's my own *disgrace* . . . I'm a *failure* in accomplishing that most fundamental of female functions; I [hide] my *shame* and shock; I've *failed, ruined* our chances, *let* [my husband] *down*; an effort to . . . avoid *my culpability, my shame, my blame*; technology makes it more clearly *my fault*.

Of course, I know rationally that infertility (especially, perhaps, as one drifts into her fourth decade) *is* "natural," like farsightedness or bunions or the eventual sneaky proliferation of gray hairs. But this is the dilemma: if I do not view it as natural, then I must view it as an aberration, a failure. Yet to say it is natural is really to say that such flaws in physiological functions are normal—but they are still defects, a failure of the expected functioning, are they not? Either way, so powerful are the narratives of feminine maternity that, despite, the prevalence of difficulties with fertility[3] the infertile body is nonetheless framed as deviant both socially and personally. One way of disciplining this digression from the norm is through the use of reproductive technology to comfortably reposition women where and as they should be, a process I consider further in the third section of this chapter. Technology can also be a means by which those battling infertility desperately seek to recapture choice.

## (The Loss of) Choice

What, then, do these constructions of the un/natural body mean for choice? The significance and centrality of choice for women has been shouted across the decades: the right to choose something different, the right to choose to continue with or terminate a pregnancy, the right to choose career and—or career *over*—family. For many of us brought up with this empowering message resonating in our (raised) consciousnesses, the biological clock metaphor was a tired hoax used to pressure women into denying the choice of alternative life paths from those of our mothers and grandmothers: we were sure/assured that we had plenty of time. (As a friend who struggled (happily for her, successfully) with infertility in her late thirties wryly observed: "to think we had spent our entire adult lives trying to avoid getting pregnant!") For me and others who were the privileged recipients of decades of feminist battles and perhaps ambivalent about parenting—there was no need, we believed, to decide *right now*—choice also meant opting to postpone decisions about maternity, selecting to achieve other goals first. To have that belief, that right, that choice denied felt for me like a betrayal of a core promise of an unquestioned feminist life.

Indeed, O'Brien Hallstein (2008) posits that feminist successes in the 1970s were in some ways related to the problems that many women of my era experience with age-related infertility. She contemplates the "often unstated feminist assumption about women and motherhood that as long as a woman is viewed first and foremost as a person rather than as a mother then motherhood will 'naturally' occur for most women" (p. 146). In fact, current feminism, for instance in the form of National Organization for Women's (NOW) vehement responses against campaigns to educate women about age constraints, has continued to sustain this notion. Clearly, there are strong reasons to be wary of movements that perpetuate frameworks that reify women-as-childbearers. Nonetheless, it is also relevant for women to know sooner rather than later that, as Rosenberg (2008) pithily put it, "eggs do get old" (p. 54). Indeed, as she further maintains, for those (feminist or otherwise) experiencing age-related infertility, this recognition could have minimized the need or desire for the very reproductive technologies that many feminists so harshly critique (2008).[4]

Knowing that at one time I could conceive yet chose not to be a parent, and that my current infertility is most likely age-related only layers a gnawing guilt on top of the already heavy deposit of shame. This is not just guilt toward one's partner—that you are responsible for preventing them from achieving biological parenthood—but guilt about knowing that you *could have* chosen otherwise; that when you were younger and still fertile, still a complete woman, you purposefully and deliberately (and selfishly?) made other choices. My rueful confession of a desperate ambivalence about parenting only intensifies that guilt; perhaps I didn't want it badly enough, or for the right reasons . . .

> *Month 9, Year 2.* I am sobbing. I'm surprised how difficult it is to write this even though I can't stop myself. The longing aches, the humiliation pierces, the frustration wears me down.
>
> And still, some detached part of me wonders if it is all about the baby? Or, it slyly asks, *is it because you—the driven one, the achiever, the perfectionist, the "A" work-personality—you can't tolerate not accomplishing what you set out to do?* I shock myself and pause, wondering if I can accept how even this possibility seems to cheapen my desire for a child. I lower my eyes and resist deleting this paragraph. Even though this isn't the whole truth, can it ever not be some part of it?

Self-reproach can deeply impact even those of us who once vacillated about maternity as we battle with ourselves over our choices. Certainly those choices were made without being fully informed but guilt is not rational. Choice, however, implies reasoned deliberation as if we come up with a plan, take appropriate action, and achieve our goals. So when we are unable to achieve such a goal, to discover that our ability to choose has been retracted, the burden of our own actions is crushing.

> *Month 9, Year 1.* We've been trying to conceive for 9 months and I'm getting anxious, so my husband and I go to the clinic to meet the doctor and discuss our fertility test results. There are couples with babies in the waiting room. I eye them with satisfaction, anticipation, and slight uncertainty: *Soon, I'll be one of you; I will be a member of your exclusive club . . . if I choose to.*
>
> When we enter the doctor's office, however, his expression is not reassuring. He explains that my FSH (follicle stimulating hormone) levels are through the roof—double the desired level—and the likely cause is not treatable: my age. My eggs are, quite simply, no longer viable. *You can have more tests*, he skeptically offers, *but as it stands we will not be able to work with you.*
>
> I'm stunned, horrified. My voice breaks as I try to ask questions, even though I can no longer hear the answers. Still, I hold it back, push it down and somehow tears are repressed until I rush out of the clinic, past the smug women and their babies, into a seating area near the elevator. As my body quakes and tears stream down my face, I stare out of a window overlooking the vast parking lot; its lack of any life seemingly mocking my own newly-discovered barrenness. I keep my back to the public area, hiding the sloppy

wetness of my face, hiding my shame and shock. *How can it be? It just really can't be right. Me? My body?* My husband lays a tentative hand on my shoulder as it shudders through a fresh surge of grief.

I am suddenly very aware that I am older than he is—perhaps if he had a younger wife this wouldn't have happened to him. In a small shaky voice, I apologize, feeling that I've failed, ruined our chances, let him down. *Would it be easier if it was me?* he gently asks. I barely pause and realize that, yes, it *would* be easier. It would be fine with me if it were him—that I could work with. Instead, it's me: my age, my flaw, my fault, my failing.

Most of us unreflectively assume our own fecundity and to be assailed by a pronouncement of infertility is shocking; a personal assault on our sense of self, to our gendered identity. And in an era in which deviations from the natural condition are routinely contained and corrected, it is common for those experiencing infertility to seek to discipline their unruly bodies through the use of reproductive technologies.

## TECHNOLOGY AND THE UN/NATURAL BODY

Ecofeminists and feminists of many other varieties have voiced drastically varying views on reproductive technologies, which have been summarized by multiple feminist writers (see, for instance, Brakman and Scholz, 2006; Rosenberg, 2008; Sandilands, 1999). The most common of these perspectives are some variation of the argument that reproductive technologies constitute a "misogynistic violence" (Daly, cited in Sandilands, 1999, p. 9) toward women as they provide a patriarchal industry leverage over one process that has been the primary sphere of femininity, thereby threatening to conquer reproductive freedom (Rushing and Onorato, 2003). Indeed, McAndrews (1996) asserts that one of the six tenets of ecofeminism is that "science and technology are tools of patriarchal dominance" (p. 371). Other feminists assert, for instance, the "inappropriateness" of controlling one's own body through the use of reproductive technologies due to its contributions to reifying cultural dualisms (Hadd, 1991). Reflecting the academic battles over the relation of women's bodies with nature, unfortunately, some of these feminist standpoints come perilously close to blaming women for their infertility. Rosenberg (2008) laments that,

> Underlying the feminist judgments . . . is a suspicion, perhaps, that women who can't get pregnant are not quite women. [Yet,] Women who can't attain pregnancy are seen as selfish and unnatural when they pursue the genetic link

> through ART [assisted reproductive technology]. . . . We can't win for losing. (p. 56)

It is rarely cut and dried; in my choices surrounding maternity and infertility, I have felt ambivalence about the use of reproductive technologies. In general, my qualms fall into at least three forms—yet each is also mitigated by conflicting views and ways in which I desire, for too many complex and self-interested reasons, the both reassuringly and offensively authoritarian touch of technology on my unmanageable and withered ovaries.

## Un/Natural In/Fertility

The first is an issue with which I have struggled and yet been fully complicit: the reification of the lack of conception as unnatural (Alaimo, 1994; Britt, 1998). Paralleling and strengthening this view is the mapping of technology as distinctly in opposition to nature. Yet I maintain (perhaps self-centeredly) that rigid definitions of technology should be viewed with skepticism. "Reproductive technology" as used in eco/feminist, scientific, and other literature is imbued with an invasive quality, typically implying some procedure or process that manipulates or causes a divergence from extant bodily function. Although typically considered outside the realm of the term, by these rules, I was utilizing technology when taking my temperature in the mornings or timing our lovemaking to coincide with ovulation. I was also, theoretically, using reproductive technology when, after being rebuffed by the doctor at the fertility clinic, I sought out alternative options.

> *Month 2, Year 2*. Dr. Ming turns off the light and partially closes the door, leaving me lying in a darkened examination room with nearly two dozen slender metal needles penetrating my face, chest, hands, abdomen, legs, and feet. Unable to comfortably move, the acupuncture forces me to lay still and I actually find myself breathing gently and relaxing into the dimness. *If I get nothing else from this*, I persuade myself, *being forced to unwind can only help my fertility*. Despite Dr. Ming's grandmotherly attention and enthusiasm, I have mixed feeling about whether acupuncture really can help me conceive—but I feel like I can't *not* do it. *After being turned away by that bastard at the fertility clinic, I don't really have any other options open to me*, I rationalize. So I assure my husband that my twice-daily choking down of foul-smelling and -tasting Chinese herbal concoctions and twice-monthly appointments with these tingling needles are not reckless and improvident investments.

When debating what does or does not count as technology (and conversely, what is natural), many wouldn't hesitate to argue that doubling as a pin cushion is *un*natural. Yet, "alternative health practices"—especially Eastern ones with their "Oriental" mystique—are framed as more in tune with nature and therefore not "really" technology. Indeed, humans have been using (fully natural?) herbs in teas and tinctures to address physical conditions for thousands of years. The line, then, between what is natural and what is technology is blurry at best, and in contrast to some feminist viewpoints, I argue that framing them as dualistic is itself an essentializing construction that limits women's choices in relation to maternity.

Regardless of one's perspective on conceptive technologies, the hopefulness that they provide in the midst of self-doubt, shame, and despair is nearly irresistible. Although my husband and I knew on a rational level—reinforced verbally by both clinic's doctors—that it was mostly an exercise in futility, we tentatively decided to at least try a comparatively noninvasive fertility medication: Clomid (a brand name), an egg-stimulating chemical that is rather frequently prescribed for women having fertility issues. Ultimately, however, this flirtation with "real technology" was a choice I regretted. After two years, I had ceased my Chinese herbs and acupuncture and had even given up my daily habit of compulsively measuring, charting, and obsessing over my basal body temperature to determine when I was ovulating. At least on the surface, I had begun to accept that I could not conceive and the painful, monthly emotional ups and downs had begun to lessen—until I was suddenly offered choice: choice in the form of conceptive technology. And the temptation offered by that technology, that renewed hope that perhaps I still retained the right and ability to choose, proved too strong to resist. With this surrender, however, I was plunged back into monthly cycles of anxious hope cut short by powerless despair. Over the course of several attempts, the process went like this: wait for the perfect day of my cycle, take the drugs, wait a week, travel an hour for an ultrasound of the (successfully!) developing eggs, try (futilely) to reign in the excitement . . . return for a follow-up performed by a tellingly grim-faced nurse, face a (silent, anguished) long drive home. As I grieved despairingly in my journal, this, like every other effort, was "unsuccessful in coaxing life from my aged and emaciated eggs. To me, the promise of technology makes it more clearly *my fault*."

For many, in the face of desperation, reproductive technologies can become addicting: "With all of these miracle procedures available, how could I *not* conceive?" In many ways, social norms surrounding fertility position the relationship between those struggling with infertility and conceptive technology as less of a choice than a compulsion. Author Peggy Orenstein, in her revealing and touching memoir of her multiyear and multicontinent journey to motherhood writes:

> That's the insidious thing about infertility treatments: The very fact of their existence, the potential, however slim, that the next round might get you pregnant creates an imperative that may not have otherwise existed. If you didn't try it, you'd always have to wonder whether it would've worked. That's how you lose sight of your real choices, because the ones you're offered make you feel as if you have none. (Orenstein, 2007, p. 224)

In the context of infertility, my "real choices" had felt as withered and pathetic as my eggs. The idea of not becoming a parent—so real a possible option a few years prior—now loomed as no longer being a choice but rather as a humiliating failure. Infertility then, took away both the "choice" of being a mother and of not being one. In the face of the temptation of reproductive technologies, then, if I truly desired maternity, how could I not try?

Still, for several reasons my husband and I dismounted the fertility carousel after trying the Clomid, resisting hormone injections, egg donors, IVF, and the myriad other options. The pull of possible success is difficult to resist, though, and I still wondered many times if I "gave up" too easily. Perhaps I didn't want it badly enough? Yet, as women focus upon and seek to manipulate, medicate, and stimulate various organs, we dismember our bodies and foster a psychological and emotional detachment from ourselves.

## Dis/Embodiment

A second reason for my reservations about conceptive technology is that the processes by which it facilitates fertility can engage the physical body in ways that encourage that distance between mind and body. I believe that I am, that my body is, of nature (as are, equally, male bodies); I believe in the interconnectedness of the mind, body, and spirit. Yet, like many people whose careers are largely cognitively driven, it is easy to become withdrawn into the mind, the rational. The pain and shame of infertility can contribute to this mind-body rupture and disembodiment as the body becomes the perceived betrayer, obstructing my ability to choose. And to succeed.

> *Month 7, Year 2*. Infertility. Even now it's painful to write that word. It's been nearly two years since being "diagnosed" and it's still hard to accept, instigating

> a tightening in my gut and a burning behind my eyes. Will it change? Will I ever be able to think of it without anger, frustration, and the ever-present humiliation? Maybe. But right now I'm still in the midst of it, still hopeful that something—those nasty herbs, the acupuncture, the drugs, *something*—will make a difference; that somehow the tests are wrong and the eggs produced by my traitorous body are not dried up and lifeless like the hard, dusty raisins I imagine them to be. Right now I'm still somehow hopeful, in my silent, impotent (how ironic) rage at my myself, that my body—my body with which I regularly trail run, mountain bike, and hike, to which I feed healthful and nourishing foods, that still appears to be fairly youthful and vigorous—will realize how it's wronging me and summon, one last time, the vibrant, glowing, pink egg, throbbing with life, that will become my baby.
>
> I think about what I've just written and recognize how my words paint the distance I feel from my physical being; I don't feel embodied, I feel betrayed.

As I struggled to overcome my infertility—with the start of each period and the failure of each cycle of timing, charting, herbs, acupuncture, blood tests, chemicals, or ultrasounds—I felt betrayed by and crushingly, overpoweringly angry at my body. I did recognize, and was almost clinically intrigued by, this reaction. Journaling its disloyalty to me, I noted, "It's odd, disconcerting to read my own words about the concurrent radical physicality and distinct disembodiment of my own experiences. It's all about my body, yet it doesn't fully feel as if it's about *me*." This distancing from myself allowed me to more easily embrace mainstream conceptive technologies and even consider more invasive ones: it was something I was doing *for* me, *to* treacherous my body—a revenge that felt fair, that felt deserved. From a more neutral or a critical perspective, however, my objectification of my own body, which so closely mirrored the potential impersonal brutality of science, horrifies me.

## Technological Violence

The third area of misgivings about conceptive technology parallels this idea of acting on and objectifying one's own body and is most closely related to many of the feminist critiques mentioned above; that is, the always-present potential for gendered violence as female bodies are the sites of an oppressive, technological aggression. These include, for instance, serious health risks—such as increased rates of cervical cancer—from the excessive use of powerful hormones, as well as a common ecofeminist concern that it is yet another site of the domination of nature (the natural body) by patriarchal culture (technology). At the same time that a woman may distance herself from her own body, technology can encourage the positioning of a (female) human body as an object upon which to practice a procedure, the receptor of the site of indifferent masculine agency and force, rather than a responsive being with whom to work toward a goal. Such was my experience in my very first interaction with technology and the fertility industry.

> *Month 8, Year 1.* Before any other tests are done, the fertility clinic authorizes a standard procedure: an HSP (the contraction of hysterosalpingogram—how ironic that root word connection to hysteria now seems to me). *Just take a few ibuprofen beforehand,* a nurse suggests as I phone in for an appointment, *sometimes there can be slight cramping.*
>
> I arrive to meet the technician: a kind older woman who offers me a pair of unsightly, bright teal blue socks with white rubber non-slip dots on the sole. I wear them thankfully in the cold lab as I lay awkwardly waiting for a stranger to enter me. Several minutes pass before a pale, white-haired man comes in and introduces himself as the doctor, making a small effort to lighten the oddness of the situation. I am here because I have not been successfully fertile: his goal is to determine whether my fallopian tubes have become blocked, which can prevent eggs from being inseminated.
>
> He pulls out a long, thin, metal instrument with a camera on the end that will project images of my reproductive organs to a black and white screen and inserts it between my splayed legs into my vagina. As it passes the cervix, my uterus immediately tightens, fighting to reject the intrusion—*No! This foreign, unfamiliar tool is not welcome inside me.* My hips shift on the metal table as I try to make light of physical and psychological discomfort; after all, I have now been going to gynecologists for decades, this shouldn't be any different.
>
> I even manage a wry smirk as the pale man responds to the technician's suggestion about why my uterus is resisting with a snapped, *She's contracting because she has a virgin uterus!*
>
> *Hah,* I think, *I haven't heard that term used in reference to me in a long time.*
>
> The contractions increase but despite escalating signs from my body that his entering me is unwanted and intolerable, he thrusts ever more urgently to pierce my uterus and then fallopian tubes. My body begins to heave and writhe on the hard metal slab trying to end the intensifying, unbearable pain; I hear myself emit low groaning screams, *No! NO! STOP IT! STOP IT!*
>
> Despite my pleas he does not stop and his driving, unrelenting penetration seems endless until abruptly he achieves fulfillment. He has mastered the contraction of the fallopian tube, jamming his hard rod through my clenched-tight muscle and flesh. Having satisfied his need, he eyes me with a mix of anxiety and self-satisfaction. *Well, at least we opened the tube,* he offers rather feebly.

> In retrospect, I am oddly aware of his perspective: a clinical, detached being watching my body from a distance as it convulses uncontrollably on the cold stainless steel board, heavy shudders originating deep in my core and jerking their way through my limbs. In the moment, however, in my body, I feel the ache of torn flesh in my abdomen, a hot wetness in my eyes and hair and ears from unstoppable, streaming tears, the spasms engulfing my torso, head, arms, and legs, banging them against the unyielding table. Disoriented and frightened, I cry, *What's happening to me!?* Resorting to a primal defensive response to the extreme agony of metal ripping through sensitive, internal flesh, my body has gone into shock.
>
> Perhaps some part of the resisting contractions, the pain, the shock was body-memory. I had been penetrated before in a manner that was uninvited, forcefully entered, damaged by a man I barely knew, a man who also ignored my pleas to stop. Then, too, my body had been unsuccessful in resisting the intrusion. In fact, then, my body betrayed me in the opposite way that it does now. When I wanted nothing more than to forget the invasion, I discovered that my body had collected a memento of the trespass; then, my body had been able to conceive. The bitterest irony was that that initial violent attack on my body had led to another assault, a second undesirable penetration as the residue of the first was sucked from my teenaged womb. How could I ever foresee that over twenty years later, conception and a form of sexual violence would again come to the fore in my life? How could I have known that, despite the circumstances causing it, I would recall that telltale morning queasiness, the horrifying pink "+" on the little test-stick—and my ability to choose—with some envy (although never with regret)?

Mine was not a common reaction to an HSP; few women have such intense bodily responses or experience such physical (or emotional) trauma. Nevertheless, even when the reaction is, as the nurse had initially suggested to me on the phone, "minor cramping," it demonstrates how the actual physicality of one's body can become distanced from a vital goal: for the woman-patient, conception; for the partner, parenthood; for the physician, an open fallopian tube or whatever the objective for a given procedure happens to be. And, as in this case, the body is less a part of the process to be nurtured or seen as a part of a unified whole, than an impediment to the ultimate objective of fertility.

## CONCLUSION

This chapter used an ecofeminist lens to look at ways that, through social constructions of maternity and the use of technology, women's bodies, like nature, are still diminished and relegated to being objects that must be controlled and made to conform. It examines similarities between feminist constructions of fertility and choice and cultural constructions of fertility as natural and privileged, as well as their shared consequences. Fueled by the normalizing of maternity and choice, a mind-body binary is perpetuated by these logics, which have substantial consequences for women and women's relationships with their physical selves.

These relationships, like choice, are intrinsic to maternity, and have salient, emotional implications in relation to in/fertility. Despite, or perhaps because of received eco/feminist notions about women's bodies and choice, women like me have not, in fact, been able to "have it all." In reality, getting an education, pursuing a career, or simply following one's own (nonpatriarchally defined) path may be a right and a choice, but the presumption that we will then still have other choices—namely biological maternity—available to us may be wrong. In spite of the soundness of such a rationale, in fact, real bodies do age.

Choice is not just about the ability to say, "yes, I could do that if I wanted" but hinges upon the actual accomplishment; perhaps a perception of control over oneself and the expected life outcomes that have been chosen. As noted by Elissa Foster, who also writes about infertility in this text ("My Eyes Cry without Me"), even when we may have choice, control is an illusion; one that, for some of us, is part of the point of choice. This desire for control was in part what lead my husband and I to reject further forms of conceptive technology in favor of adoption: if we were taking the emotional (and financial) risks of further pursuing parenthood, we wanted to be guaranteed success. We wanted to know, definitely, that we would have a child—biologically linked or not—something that, despite its leading promises, conceptive technologies can never promise.

## Postscript

As noted in this chapter, after much deliberation, my husband and I made a different choice: adoption. It is a process that instigated a host of different challenges and complications related to choice, yet has ultimately been empowering. It allowed me to be confident that at some point, I could achieve my desired goal—the inability of which was, it seems, a significant source of my struggles with the loss of conceptive choice.

Nearly five years after deciding to pursue parenthood, we received an amazing Christmas gift when our beautiful son ignored my need to meet this text's editorial deadlines and was born a month premature. It is an important lesson, I think, on loosening my grip on expectations and recognizing that even when exercising choice, we cannot fully control the outcomes. My husband and I have been awed at finally becoming parents and the deep and passionate emotions this four pound, thirteen ounce being has elicited from us. Still, making the final edits with this perfect, tiny baby sleeping in my lap does not nullify what I have written here, or the pain and shame that were experienced; the stigma of infertility—and its consequences—are powerful. It does, though, convince me that the journey to parenthood, however fraught with difficulties, was a worthwhile choice for me.

## REFERENCES

Alaimo, S. 1994. Cyborg and ecofeminist interventions: Challenges for an environmental feminism. *Feminist Studies* 20(1), 133–43.

Alaimo, S. 2008. Ecofeminism without Nature? *International Feminist Journal of Politics* 10(3), 299–304.

Assisted Reproductive Technology: Home. June 30, 2009. Center for Disease Control and Prevention. Retrieved July 27, 2009, from www.cdc.gov/ART/.

Brakman, S-V., and Scholz, S. J. 2006. Adoption, ART, and a re-conception of the maternal body: Toward embodied maternity. *Hypatia* 21(1), 54–73.

Britt, E. C. 1998. Infertility as a medical problem: Recasting feminist accounts of nature, science, and the law. *Science as Culture* 7(2), 265–84.

Burns, K. A. 2008. Warren's ecofeminist ethics and Merlau-Ponty's body-subject. *Ethics & Environment* 13(2), 101–18.

Curtain, D. 1997. Women's knowledge as expert knowledge: Indian women and ecodevelopment. In K. J. Warren (ed.), *Ecofeminism: Women, culture, nature* (pp. 82–89). Bloomington: Indiana University Press.

Filemyr, A. 1997. Going outdoors and other dangerous expeditions. *Frontiers* 18(2), 160–78.

Foucault, M. 1995. *Discipline and punish: The birth of the prison*. 2nd ed., A. Sheridan, trans. New York: Vintage Books.

Gardner, C. V., and Riley, J. E. 2007. Breaking boundaries: Ecofeminism in the classroom. *Radical Teacher* 78, 24–33.

Griffin. 1997. Ecofeminism and meaning. In J. Warren (Ed.), *Ecofeminism: Women, culture, nature* (pp. 213–26). Bloomington: Indiana University Press.

Hadd, W. 1991. A womb with a view: Women as mothers and the discourse of the body. *Berkeley Journal of Sociology* 36, 165–75.

Higgins, R. 2003. One man's story. In J. Haynes and J. Miller (Eds.), *Inconceivable conceptions: Psychological aspects of infertility and reproductive technology* (pp. 27–30). New York: Brunner-Routledge.

King, Y. 1993. Where nature meets nurture: Reflections on ecofeminist motherhood. *Ms.* 4(1), 41

Mantel, H. 2003. Clinical waste. In J. Haynes and J. Miller (eds.), *Inconceivable conceptions: Psychological aspects of infertility and reproductive technology* (pp. 19–26). New York: Brunner-Routledge.

McAndrew, D. A. 1996. Ecofeminism and the teaching of literacy. *College Composition and Communication* 47(3), 367–82.

Merchant, C. 1996. *Earthcare: Women and the environment.* New York: Routledge.

Moore, N. 2008. Eco/feminism, non-violence and the future of feminism. *International Feminist Journal of Politics* 10(3), 282–98.

O'Brien Hallstein, L. 2008. Silences and choice: The legacies of white second wave feminism in the new professoriate. *Women's Studies in Communication* 31(2), 143–50.

Orenstein, P. 2007. *Waiting for Daisy: A tale of two continents, three religions, five infertility doctors, an Oscar, an atomic bomb, a romantic night, and one woman's quest to become a mother.* New York: Holtzbrinck.

Plumwood, V. 1993. *Feminism and the mastery of nature.* New York: Routledge.

Raphael-Leff, J. 2003. Eros and ART. In J. Haynes and J. Miller (eds.), *Inconceivable conceptions: Psychological aspects of infertility and reproductive technology* (pp. 33–46). New York: Brunner-Routledge.

Rosenberg, M. 2008. The scarlet I: Has the advent of assisted reproductive technology lessened the stigma of infertility—or added to it? *Bitch Magazine* 40, 53–57.

Rushing, B., and Onorato, S. 2003. Controlling the means of reproduction: Feminist theories and reproductive technologies. *Humanity & Society* 27(3), 393–413.

Sandilands, C. 1999. *The good-natured feminist: Ecofeminism and the quest for democracy.* Minneapolis: University of Minnesota Press.

Sturgeon, N. 2009. *Environmentalism in popular culture: Gender, race, sexuality, and the politics of the natural.* Tucson: University of Arizona Press.

Tillmann, L. 2009. Speaking into silences: Autoethnography, communication, and applied research. *Journal of Applied Communication Research* 37(1), 94–97.

Twine, R. T. 2001. Ma(r)king essence: Ecofeminism and embodiment. *Ethics & Environment* 6(2), 32–58.

Wagner, B. L. 2008. Ecofeminist action in the twenty-first century. *Canadian Dimension* 42(2), 40–43.

Warren, K. J. 1997. Introduction. In K. J. Warren (ed.), *Ecofeminism: Women, culture, nature* (pp. xi–xvi). Bloomington: Indiana University Press.

## NOTES

1. Many thanks to Alexandra (Lexa) Murphy for her unswerving friendship and contributions both in my initial struggles with infertility and with the refining of this chapter.

2. Like many ecofeminists, however, I unquestionably hold the position that there is no necessary distinction between the "naturalness" of women's bodies versus men's bodies (Griffin, 1997).

3. The Centers for Disease Control and Prevention ("Assisted Reproductive Technology," 2009) states that 7 percent (2.1 million) of married couples yearly meet their definition if infertile: failing to conceive after twelve months of attempting to do so.

4. I focus primarily on age-related infertility, recognizing, however, that infertility can be an incredibly painful circumstance for women or men of any age.

# Section II

# Working with Choice

**10**

# THE INVISIBLE POLITICS OF "CHOICE" IN THE WORKPLACE

## Naming the Informal Parenting Support System

*Julia T. Wood and Bonnie J. Dow*

1. *On a recent day, a male faculty member failed to attend a committee meeting that had been scheduled more than a week in advance. The committee, of which one of the authors of this chapter is a member, was informed by an administrative assistant that the colleague was not able to be on campus because he had no childcare for his nine-year-old, who did not have school that day due to a scheduled in-service training day for teachers. The chair of the committee nodded sympathetically and the meeting commenced. At the end of the meeting, the author, who had been taking notes for her own use, was asked to write up a summary of what had been accomplished and circulate it via email to keep the absent committee member apprised. That evening, the author ran into this same committee member in a local restaurant, where he was on a date (sans child).*
2. *Last fall, one of the authors of this chapter went to a staff member's office seeking information for a departmental report. The staff member tried to be helpful, but she was preoccupied with a ten-month-old baby a faculty member had asked her to watch while the faculty member taught a class. The faculty member had not brought a baby carrier, assuring the staff member that the baby would sleep on a pallet that she had provided. Uninformed of this, the baby was wide awake and active, so the staff member was compelled to hold the infant on*

*her lap. The staff member's mind was no more free than her hands to focus on departmental business.*

3. *One of the authors was part of a ten-person group of faculty that convened to discuss whether her university needs to do more to make the university family friendly. A faculty member who was in her midfifties and child free launched the discussion by stating that the university doesn't support her choices about priorities in her personal life so why should it support others' choice to be parents? "What makes some choices of how to invest our time more important, more worthy of university support and accommodation?" she asked. Another woman of about the same age stated she had two children before being tenured and just assumed it was up to her to make that work. A man in his late thirties with three children under twelve said he had found it extremely difficult to work toward tenure while being actively involved in his children's lives, but he was committed to doing both. The two untenured twenty-something members of the group, one female, one male, were quiet. However, as they left, together, the author overheard the woman say to the man, "I never knew so many faculty are antifamily."*

Much has been written about the burdens faced by parents who work in the paid labor force. By contrast, much less has been written about the consequences absorbed by others who accommodate parents' schedules and other constraints. We believe that the impact of parents' choices on others is elided by the neoliberal framing of reproduction and childrearing as "personal choices" (Vavrus, 2007). In emphasizing individuals' responsibilities for their lives, such framing not only obscures the need for structural solutions to the difficulties faced by working parents,[1] but also implies that those difficulties are faced only by parents. More specifically, we argue that a primary emphasis on choices made by parents functions to erase the involvement of colleagues in what we term the "informal parenting support system."

We wish to be clear that our concern here is not with the choice to have children; rather, we are focused on the ways that some working parents' childrearing choices can impact their colleagues in the workplace. We work with the assumption that parents make choices every day about how to manage the intersections of their work and their parenting, and we are primarily concerned with how those choices affect their colleagues in the workplace. Although we acknowledge that choices are variously constrained, we maintain a straightforward understanding of choice in this chapter: choice exists in those circumstances when more than one option is available. For example, the parents described in our first two anecdotes above each made a choice not to arrange for childcare during times that they had work commitments. They made a "choice," quite simply because they had more than one option for how to manage their responsibilities.

This chapter unfolds as a series of "snapshots" such as the three with which we opened. They are derived from our own experiences, and those of our colleagues, in departments at large, research-intensive universities that provide some structural support for parenting, such as parental leave, tenure clock extensions for parents, and, in some cases, on-campus childcare. These snapshots capture particular moments in our work lives that prompted us to pause, notice, and reflect on how parenting choices sometimes enter into the workplace in ways that are seldom acknowledged, much less discussed. Because our thoughts about these issues evolved episodically in response to particular incidents, we invite readers to think with us as we present each snapshot.

Our analysis is informed by grounded theory, which encourages attention to situated events and interactions as those are embedded in, and reflective of, cultural structures, practices, and ideologies. Geertz (1973) was one of the earliest advocates of detailed analyses of particular, concrete moments as a means of gaining insight into cultural life. Following Geertz, other scholars (Charmaz, 1983, 2004; Strauss and Corbin, 1998; Wood, 1992, 2004) have relied on grounded theory to illuminate the ways in which cultural values and understandings are constructed and sustained in particular episodes of human interaction. In this chapter, we analyze specific moments that reveal parenting preferences held and enacted by people in the paid labor force to tease out insights they offer into parenting, the workplace, and collegial relationships.

In presenting these snapshot moments and our analysis of them, we want to resist two inclinations. On the one hand, we eschew the simplistic tendency to hold parents, usually mothers, solely accountable for workplace complications that sometimes arise from parenting preferences (Goodman, 2008). On the other hand, we agree with but don't want to focus this chapter on criticism of the lack of institutional support for employees who choose to have children (Evans and Grant, 2008; Tracey, 2008; Vavrus, 2007). Instead, we wish to emphasize the consequences of the interaction between these two impulses. Attending to the dialectic of agency and structure in this context allows us to make visible a third set of stakeholders: the colleagues of working parents, many of whom are parents themselves, who often are caught in the gaps created by the imperfect fit between parenting preferences and institutional support.

In its broadest sense, our central thesis is that lack of structural support affects people other than specific parents who are making choices about how to care for their children while also participating in the paid labor force. Working parents' decisions about raising children sometimes also implicate people who compose an informal, often involuntary, and generally invisible support system for parents' "personal" choices. This system is informal in the sense that it is not established or maintained by organizational policies or official workers' rights. In the same sense, it can be considered largely involuntary because workers are rarely, if ever, consulted about their willingness to participate in the system. It is invisible to the extent that workers—both those providing support and those receiving it—do not call attention to the system or the expectations that inform it. Rather, they assume the system is normatively approved. This support system includes neighbors, friends, relatives, colleagues, superiors, and subordinates. Our focus is on the last three of these groups, as we are primarily concerned with the consequences that arise when working parents rely on an informal support system for accommodations in the workplace, particularly in academic workplaces and particularly from their female and feminist colleagues, superiors, and subordinates. We propose to make that reliance and those consequences visible in order to make the larger point that the choices involved in reproduction and childrearing are never wholly personal—they are inevitably and fundamentally social as well. In the pages that follow, we explore how these choices play out in the social space that exists between the personal and the institutional.

In making the social space our focus, we are in no way suggesting that institutions should not be expected to provide more support to workers, including but not restricted to parents. Many others have advocated more family friendly workplaces. What has not been addressed is how workers can best manage until and unless their workplaces effectively support a range of life commitments that people make. Our chapter seeks to begin addressing that issue through a focus on social means of addressing tensions and needs regarding parenting preferences.

We develop our argument in three parts. First, we analyze a series of snapshot moments to make visible various elements in the culture of entitlement that exists around the provision of informal support for workers' parenting choices. Second, we offer a rationale for naming the issue of informal support for parenting choices. Third, we offer preliminary suggestions for criteria that might be used to foster productive discussion among colleagues about the tensions surrounding workplace accommodation for nonwork commitments.

## MAKING THE INFORMAL PARENTING SUPPORT SYSTEM VISIBLE

The snapshots with which we opened this chapter show different permutations of the informal parenting support system as well as reactions to it. The first snapshot describes a situation that is somewhat typical in the authors' professional lives—a colleague forgoes a professional responsibility, claiming a lack of childcare as the reason, and assumes his colleagues' support for his choice. Importantly, however, that choice is presented as a kind of non-choice. That is, it is not so much that he does not have childcare (a somewhat passive phrasing that was recounted by the administrative assistant) as that he failed to *arrange* for childcare other than himself or failed to note that his child would not have school that day until it was too late to arrange childcare. Yet another choice not taken would have been to bring the child to campus and have him wait in his father's office during the forty-minute meeting. All of these thoughts danced through the author's head, but she knew better than to voice them lest she be branded as unsympathetic to a divorced dad who should be praised rather than censured for being dedicated to his child. Yet his choice to skip the meeting and to stay home with his son made more work for the members of the committee and for the author in particular. This outcome was made even harder to swallow when the author later realized that the faculty member had clearly planned well enough to obtain childcare so that he could go on a date the same night that he had skipped the meeting.

We want to make clear that this father's choice to skip the meeting is distinct from the choice of a parent to deal with a child's emergency or from that of a coworker who has to deal with any kind of emergency, for that matter. All workers are occasionally faced with unforeseen crises for which, by definition, they cannot have made advance plans. Whether these involve children or not, urgent matters in our nonwork lives occasionally intrude on the workplace. These rare emergencies are not what this chapter addresses; we assume all workers understand these will arise and are willing to help each other out. Rather, our focus is on parenting choices that are routine or that are not the result of unforeseeable circumstances. For instance, school holidays and teacher workdays are generally scheduled far in advance so that parents can make childcare plans.

The second snapshot provides a more obvious instance of the role that power inequities can play in maintaining the illusion that invisible, informal support systems are voluntary. Like the faculty member in the first anecdote, this one made the choice not to arrange childcare for a time she knew she had other obligations. Also like the faculty member in snapshot 1, this one conveniently assumed that others—the staff person and anyone who needed the staff person's professional assistance—would not object to infant care interfering with work. But this case is distinct in that the faculty member has more power (and job security) than the staff member. How free was the staff member to refuse a faculty member's "request" to watch a baby for an hour? We've seen graduate students and junior faculty placed in the role occupied by the staff member in this snapshot. In each case, the person being "asked" to watch the baby might legitimately perceive that refusing the "request" could result in undesirable consequences beyond the immediate consequence of making it impossible to focus on work.

The third snapshot is the most explicit in its foregrounding of the issues that interest us here. The conversation perhaps reflects the group's somewhat unusual composition: several members of this particular group had not had children and were now past child-bearing years, and other members of the group had chosen to have and raise children when nobody would have thought of asking for institutional support or informal accommodation from colleagues. Yet we are not willing to dismiss either the question raised by group members or the untenured woman's interpretation of those comments as evidence that "so many faculty are antifamily." The women and the man who objected to workplace policies that benefited only workers who are raising children were giving voice to a view that is often not expressed precisely because it leads to accusations of being "antifamily" or "not liking children." Rather than labeling it "antifamily," we suggest it may reflect the point that all workers have lives beyond work—lives that involve a range of commitments and constraints that matter to the workers. Yet only parenting and urgent medical needs are routinely considered to merit special accommodation and support from the workplace. In the United States, as well as some other countries, having and raising children are regarded as admirable, perhaps *the most* admirable ways to invest time, thought, feeling, energy, and money.

We agree that having and raising children are important activities; indeed, they are essential to cultural life. Yet our belief that parenting is a worthy commitment does not mean that we think it is the *only* worthy commitment or that it automatically justifies encroachments on the workplace. Workers make a range of commitments beyond those associated directly with their work. These might include volunteering with Hospice, fostering homeless animals, playing bridge competitively, leading civic groups, training for a marathon, gardening, tutoring at-risk youth, or traveling extensively to learn about other cultures. Obviously some of these other commitments are generally accorded more social respect (e.g., volunteering with Hospice, fostering homeless animals, tutoring at-risk youth) than others (e.g., gardening, playing bridge competitively), but regardless of the social merit attributed to the commitment, our point is that commitments other than parenting and personal medical needs are not perceived as meriting any workplace accommodation. These other commitments are respected *as long as* they do not interfere with an employee's doing her or his paid job. They are not accepted as excuses for not doing one's paid job, and they are not perceived as justifications for asking/expecting coworkers to adjust their schedules, work loads, and expectations of the worker. In contrast, questions are rarely asked when a colleague assumes that a parenting responsibility will lead to accommodation by those with whom she/he works. Phrased another way, we are arguing that expectations of assistance from coworkers are often one-sided. That is, some working parents expect and usually get accommodations for their childrearing preferences whereas workers who are not parents or who do not ask for their parenting preferences to be accommodated rarely get support for other life commitments.

Particularly troublesome to us is the perception that people are antichild if they question efforts to accommodate colleagues' parenting choices. For many who do question some workplace accommodations of parenting choices, the issue is not between valuing or not valuing children and their needs. Rather, it is the presumption that workers who claim parenting responsibilities are automatically entitled to singular accommodation and support from their colleagues and subordinates. The untenured faculty member's comment in snapshot 3 that she is surprised that "so many faculty are antifamily," is exactly the kind of unreflective reaction that some people have when anyone dares to question that children are the only worthy priority. As a result, many workers feel strong normative pressures to honor the parenting choices of colleagues but do not expect equivalent honoring of other commitments outside of work. As our fourth snapshot illustrates, even a mild suggestion that it might be worthwhile for colleagues to talk about ways that parenting choices affect the workplace can be treated as an attack on parenting and the value of children:

4. *One of the authors visited another campus to give a talk. After the formal presentation, several faculty members at the host institution took the author out for coffee and asked her about her new lines of research. She mentioned several, including this chapter, which she described as an effort to begin to think about how some workers' parenting choices assume colleagues' assistance and support. She had*

> *barely offered this general description when one of the host faculty said, "That sounds really antifamily." The author resisted that characterization, saying, "No, we're just trying to prompt more honest conversations about something affecting a lot of workers." The host faculty member responded, "But colleagues should want to support working parents. Gosh knows we parents are doing all we can to take care of the children and do our jobs too. Give me a break!" The author ventured that it might be that the working parents' colleagues are also doing all they can to balance their personal and professional lives. A second host faculty member asked, "When you say 'their personal lives,' do you mean their children?" The author replied, "Their personal lives could include children, but I wouldn't restrict it to that. I'm just saying that most workers have pretty full plates so it can be frustrating to be asked to take on more because a colleague doesn't want to teach morning classes or do committee work." "Well, they just need to suck it up," rejoined the first host faculty. "Let me tell you: I've had two children, and it's the most important and most difficult job in the world. If my colleagues can't cut me a little slack so I can do what I need to for my children, then I'll leave. You wouldn't understand because you don't have children."*

This snapshot exemplifies a lack of perspective-taking that we believe is common in occasional efforts to discuss how workers' parenting choices affect the workplace. The statement that parenting is "the most important and difficult job in the world" implies that all other jobs are trivial by comparison and, by extension, that lesser jobs should adjust to accommodate the greater job. Asserting that "You wouldn't understand because you don't have children" slams the door on conversation. Someone who does not have children of her or his own may understand well what it means to love and feel responsible for taking care of a dependent family member. Someone who does not have children may not have chosen that course. Someone who does not have children nonetheless may be deeply involved in the lives of children. But the comment, "You wouldn't understand because you don't have children" sharply dichotomizes those who do and do not have children and implies that the former are uniformly fond of children and sympathetic to working parents' requests for accommodations for childcare whereas the latter uniformly dislike children and are not sympathetic to such requests.

In fact, we both know parents who have found ways to avoid allowing their parenting choices to affect their workplace and are troubled by the behavior of colleagues who take a different approach. Working parents are stressed and they may worry that they aren't doing everything they once did in the workplace. In addition, they are often highly and understandably protective of their children and their parenting philosophies. Their colleagues may feel defensive about possibly being perceived as "antifamily," "antichild," or nonfeminist, yet also resent having to add more to their already full plates. The result is often avoidance of any discussion of this issue. When discussion does occur between working parents and their colleagues, it is often laced with the kind of defensiveness and distrust that surfaced in snapshot 4. Mutual defensiveness is poor soil for sustained, productive conversation.

We believe that the pressure to support parenting preferences is culturally based and not confined to particular workplaces, making it even more powerful. Recent feminist scholarship documents the ideology of "intensive mothering" (Hays, 1996) or the "new momism" (Douglas and Michaels, 2004), establishing that women, in particular, are expected to make their children the center of their lives, regardless of whether or not they also work for wages. O'Brien Hallstein (2008) summarizes this scholarship as follows: "children need and require constant and ongoing nurturing, . . . mothers must lavish enormous amounts of time and energy on their children, . . . [and] mothers should always put their children's needs above their own" (p. 143). Most importantly, she notes that all women are "disciplined into" this ideology, regardless of whether or not they actually practice it. We concur, and we further contend that this disciplining affects all of us such that colleagues are expected not only by others, but by themselves to respect all preferences made in the name of parenthood, particularly motherhood, and to put children's, including colleagues' children's, perceived needs above their own and above those of their workplaces. Consider our fifth snapshot:

5. *One of the authors had a colleague who delivered a healthy baby after a planned pregnancy. The institution had an on-campus childcare facility that took infants, although, like most such facilities, it had a waiting list. Yet the expectant colleague chose not to apply to the center or to arrange for other childcare, explaining that she and her partner (also an academic) wished to care for the baby themselves for its first year. The faculty member was on a research leave the semester that she delivered the child. When she returned to a full-time schedule the following term, she was able to teach her classes successfully, which she had scheduled for days that her partner cared for the child, but she was rarely in the office on days she did not teach. She ceased*

*attending faculty meetings and departmental events that occurred on days that she was caring for the child, and began asking graduate students to come to her home to meet with her so that she would not have to leave the baby.*

This snapshot describes a situation that is both common and frustrating for some colleagues of new parents. When the faculty member in question made a particular parenting choice—not to obtain childcare for her infant—she also made a choice that affected her colleagues, who felt powerless to question her decision. The faculty member's absence from department meetings and events became the subject of office discussion, particularly when it became apparent that her unwillingness to obtain childcare made it very difficult to schedule her for ad hoc meetings, including graduate student committee meetings. She became, in essence, a part-time worker for the purposes of the department and virtually ceased performing service (including advising) work, which was informally redistributed to her colleagues. A department chair who has written about his experiences with such a situation succinctly expresses our concern: "It is difficult to justify paying a full-time salary to someone who is fulfilling 75 to 80 percent of their job duties" (Kramer, 2008, p. 199).

The colleagues of the new mother in snapshot 5 did not feel comfortable speaking with her about this situation, because, in their minds, to do so entailed being unsupportive and critiquing her parenting practices. That mindset, however, shows that such practices are (mis)understood as purely personal, rather than social, choices. If her work performance had suffered for another reason—for example, because she had decided to train for a triathlon—her colleagues might have felt more comfortable speaking with her about it (although she might have been less likely to expect their unquestioning support as well). Yet, consistent with our understanding of the neoliberal framing of having and raising children, her colleagues understood the faculty member's choice to eschew paid childcare as a personal decision that could not be questioned.

Now we introduce two additional snapshots that offer further examples of both the existence and the assumption of informal support from colleagues and that are linked in ways that will become clear.

6. *A number of years ago, a junior colleague of one of the authors had a very difficult pregnancy. At month five and just one month into a new semester, her doctor told her that complete bed rest for the remainder*

*of the pregnancy was her only hope of delivering a healthy baby. At that time, the university had no parental leave policy, and the junior faculty member could not afford to give up her salary. Two of her colleagues agreed to take over her classes for no financial compensation, an arrangement that was handled informally so that the Faculty Payroll office was unaware of the change in her work and her paycheck and years of service were unaffected. After her child was born (healthy), the junior colleague sent a pro forma thank you note to each of the faculty members who had taught her classes for three months.*

7. *More recently the young son of a colleague of one of the authors developed an acute medical problem that required treatment over a two-week period. As in the foregoing anecdote, her colleagues volunteered to teach her classes for two weeks so that she could be with her son during his treatment. When she returned to work after her child had recovered, she gave each of the colleagues who had taught her classes generous gift certificates to an upscale restaurant.*

The first snapshot is perhaps a predictable consequence of endorsing an ideology of intensive mothering. Yet the second snapshot demonstrates that not all people—whether parents or not—subscribe unthinkingly to that ideology. The faculty member with the difficult pregnancy took for granted the informal network that preserved her income while shouldering her work responsibilities for the majority of an academic semester. Her casual treatment of extraordinary support vividly demonstrates the assumption that informal support for parenting is so expected that it barely merits mention. In the seventh snapshot, the faculty member recognized that her colleagues had helped her—though obviously less extensively than in snapshot 6—and she acknowledged their noncompulsory support generously. Our own experience and our impressions of colleagues' experiences is that the first case is more typical. Other than offhand "thank yous" in some cases, informal provisions for parenting choices are too seldom acknowledged by some of the people receiving the assistance. This underlines the expected nature of support for parenting choices—it is assumed that others will absorb work and adjust schedules to accommodate colleagues' parenting choices. Yet there are countless examples of faculty who take on time-consuming commitments outside of the work sphere for which they are not granted any special accommodations, and who, for the most part, know not to expect any accommodation for the priorities in their lives.

## NAMING THE ISSUE

As we experienced the snapshot moments that we have discussed, we did not feel free to discuss them with either our colleagues making the parenting choices or our colleagues in general. Other than expressing some irritation to close friends, we refrained from comment. Each of us felt we could not publicly question the impact on the workplace of parenting choices made by our colleagues. We were reluctant to speak up for two reasons. First, we are not antifamily or antichild, and we didn't want to be perceived as being so. To challenge the impact of childrearing practices on colleagues can be read—as in our third snapshot—as irrefutable evidence that the challenger dislikes children. In a related vein, to publicly criticize a parent's childrearing preferences or parenting philosophy—a frequent misperception that arises when attempting to discuss workplace ramifications of parenting choices—is a powerful taboo. Second, we are both staunch feminists, and we realized that raising the issues we foreground in this chapter runs afoul of what often appears to be the only acceptable feminist position: support the mother in her struggle to "make do" in a culture that does not offer enough structural support for parenting (Buzzanell and Liu, 2007; Rosen, 2007). We find it exceedingly uncomfortable to speak out in ways that are likely to be perceived as violating feminist solidarity. Yet, there are also feminist justifications for naming the issues.

We bring these issues up now because, after substantial reflection and conversation between ourselves, we feel compelled to call attention to a support system that has been overlooked and often unappreciated because it operates outside of the dualistic framing that posits the work/family balancing act as either a personal or an institutional concern. We see naming this informal parenting support system as consistent with other efforts to bring common problems into social consciousness. Betty Friedan (1963) did it when she wrote about the "problem that has no name," which she then named the feminine mystique. Feminists did it in the 1980s when they named sexual harassment into both social awareness and legal standing. Other experiences common to women that went unnamed for too long but were finally named include date rape, marital rape, and the second shift (Hochschild, 2003). Bonnie Dow first addressed the issue we elaborate in this chapter when she published "Does It Take a Department to Raise a Child?" (2008). Bonnie shared early drafts of that article with Julia who responded with support not just for Bonnie's ideas but also for the importance of expressing them, for the value of getting this issue out in the open where it can be addressed more directly and more honestly.

In naming this issue, we are attempting to bring it into social consciousness. In doing this, we are not arguing that parents and their colleagues (who may or may not be parents themselves) are necessarily adversaries. And we are certainly not trying to pit one group of women against another (Litwin and O'Brien Hallstein, 2007). In fact, quite the opposite: A key motive for writing this chapter is to find ways that workers with parenting responsibilities and their colleagues can work together with mutual respect and support and without tensions and resentments that grow out of not being able to discuss collegial working arrangements. Prerequisites for that are naming and discussing issues.

Most workplaces currently have some parental leave policy that specifies how much time is allowed when a worker gives birth or adopts, and whether the time is compensated; some parental leave policies also have provisions for time off if a worker needs to care for a child with a medical problem. Yet basic parental leave policies do not specify what, if anything, working parents are entitled to for all of the parenting activities beyond births, adoptions, and medical emergencies. As a result, informal social systems evolve to deal with what is not managed by the formal, institutional system. Those systems, and the reactions they generate, differ widely, as our various snapshots have illustrated.

Some parents ask for no accommodations because they assume it is their personal responsibility to manage their nonwork commitments in ways that don't interfere with the workplace. Other working parents assume the workplace should and will accommodate their parenting choices in a variety of ways from rearranging schedules and excusing them from service work to allowing staff to babysit while they are working. Some colleagues of working parents may assume they should, must, or are expected to understand when colleagues who are parents miss meetings or refuse certain schedules, whereas other colleagues may not assume they should understand. Further, workers who do not have parenting responsibilities or who choose not to ask the workplace to accommodate how they meet their responsibilities may resent colleagues whose requests for accommodation result in preferred schedules and other benefits. In fact, there is clear evidence that some workers do resent, often greatly, the benefits, both formal and informal, that are given exclusively to coworkers who are parents. Burkett's (2002) book, *The Baby Boon,* offers a particularly sustained argument that assistance for workers' parenting choices amounts to discrimination against workers who are not parents or who do not ask for special accommodations for their parenting choices. Despite the unfortunate tone and the excesses of Burkett's book, she advances both evidence and argument for widespread resentment of specialized support for working parents. Research by others such as Dunteman (2006) and Kirby and Krone (2002) provides additional evidence that resentment often accompanies accommodations of workers' parenting choices. Working parents may be perplexed that some colleagues seem to willingly adjust to meet their needs whereas other colleagues at least bristle and sometimes refuse to accommodate them.

When norms for workers' parenting choices are not clear, there is huge potential for misunderstanding, abuse, inequity, tension, and resentment, all of which undermine morale, healthy collegial relations, and productivity. For example, concerns about inequity emerge in Michael Kramer's (2008) reflections on chairing a department during a year when several faculty members gave birth. Although the story he tells is ultimately a positive one, in which, as he puts it, "we collectively managed the issues fairly well" (p. 201), he also contemplates the consequences of extensive accommodation for parenting:

> I also have to wonder about the equity of policies that favor faculty parents of newborns. I recently had a discussion with a male faculty member who considers many family-friendly policies discriminatory because they provide benefits to some employees but not to others; due to gender or lifestyles, some employees will never be eligible for a spousal accommodation, reduced teaching for maternity, or stop the clock benefits. Further, when faculty parents receive first choice in scheduling to accommodate small children, other faculty are often left with limited and less desirable choices. So the policies seem right to me from a human compassion perspective for faculty members who benefit, but they also can create resentment and inequities for others. (p. 200)

The potential for resentment is evident in comments on a recent Chronicle of Higher Education blog. Sara Goldrick-Rab (2009) posted a guest blog about her concerns as an untenured faculty member who was about to give birth to a second child and who wanted to nurse the child. Many responses to Goldrick-Rab's posting offered her support, asserting her department should accommodate her needs. Yet other responses evidenced resentment from faculty who resent what they perceive as inequities. One response, labeled #18 on the blog, asked four questions, each of which reflects skepticism about the appropriateness of accommodations uniquely given in response to workers' parenting choices:

1. Do academic women who decide to have a child at any given point in their careers do so voluntarily?

2. If academic women can't get their husbands/partners to assume an equitable share of childrearing tasks, should that become their institutions' problem?
3. Does a woman whose tenure clock is put on hold for a period of time because of childbirth, but who nevertheless manages to get substantial research done during the time the tenure clock is stopped have an advantage over a childless woman whose clock is not stopped?
4. Are there "work/life" balance issues for men who "want to have it all" and maintain some major nonacademic endeavor whilst being a professor, to which colleges should attend?"

Another respondent (#14) expressed bitterness over the inequity of accommodating parenting preferences but not other life commitments: "maybe i should post a picture of myself with my dying father on my tenure and promotion website. maybe that will get me special compensation or let me whine. everybody has something to deal with when having a professional and private life and it isn't always as socially cute as having kids. get over yourself."

Even more recently, responses to another blog about mothering and the academy on Inside Higher Ed reveal the even stronger emotions felt by some faculty members who perceive accommodations for parenting as a form of inequity. In a post on Mama Ph.D., blogger Libby Gruner praises attempts to accommodate parents, prompting the following response from CAprof:

> Accommodating work/life balance isn't just an issue for parents—although it is almost always framed as such. Those of us without children are always an afterthought and it's always assumed that we "might" have an elderly parent who needs care—and then the parents congratulate themselves for being sensitive. Most of the time though our request for schedule consideration is dismissed (as Mama Ph.D. dismisses it) as trying to protect prime research time. Ph.D. parents just can't wrap their head around the notion that (1) I don't care as much about their children as they do; (2) I have work/life balance issues that can't just be reduced to research time or "aging parent." If I accept a less than desirable schedule (in the coming semester that means an early 8 a.m. class *and* a night class—as well as one other in the late afternoon—I am on campus teaching three or four days a week) to help out the many parents in my dept. then my ability to also go to meetings to accommodate their schedules is reduced *and* it means that I am on campus all day, pretty much every day so that they don't have to be. I am expected to always be available if they are (because they are not that available and many, unlike Mama Ph.D.,

> refuse to ever pay for childcare to go to a meeting or stay late). So where's the balance in my work life if I never (and I do mean never) have control over my schedule because I'm accommodating yours? Your fifteen years of parenting might seem like it has whizzed by but those of us who have had our lives dominated by your needs, it has been a very, very long time. So far, I haven't seen those parents in the "post-parenting" phase rush to support the new parents in the dept. in the way they demanded to be supported—why should they? They've gotten used to the cushy schedules and the lack of engagement with or obligation to the dept.

As these postings reveal, resentments exist but they generally simmer below the surface in unhealthy ways. We believe that all workers—those who are and those who are not parents—would benefit from clear operating norms. Ideally, these would be arrived at through open discussion, leading to consensus. Yet even if there is not open discussion or full agreement, workers would benefit from clear guidance about what is expected and what is out of line in their workplace. Having this kind of clarity would allow everyone to navigate with greater assurance and effectiveness. All workers understand that their workplace has the right to establish and enforce policies and normative behaviors. Workers don't necessarily like all of the policies and normative expectations of their workplace, but they do accept these as a necessary part of collective enterprises and, for the most part, they conform to both the formal and informal rules of the workplace. In our final section, we offer some suggestions toward the development of the kind of guidelines we recommend, and we include additional snapshots that we believe illustrate the benefits of open discussion regarding workplace accommodations for life commitments.

## ADDRESSING WORKPLACE ACCOMMODATIONS OF LIFE COMMITMENTS

While we are surely not in a position to propose normative expectations for workers' parenting choices, we would suggest that development of effective guidelines might center on clear criteria that are understood by all members of a given workplace. For illustrative purposes, we identify four criteria that might be used when considering whether a worker's parenting preference should be accommodated. First, is the parenting preference a response to an emergency (a child who suffers an injury that requires immediate medical attention) or is it a response to a planned event (a child's annual physical exam)? Second, is the parenting preference rare (once a year attending a day-long event at the child's school) or routine (being home when the child returns from school each day)? Third, is the parenting preference one that the parent could have managed without affecting the workplace (scheduling a baby sitter on afternoons a committee meets) or one the parent could not have planned for (a babysitter cancels at the last minute)? Fourth, is discussion of whether to provide some accommodation squarely based on policies and normative practices that are clearly germane to the workplace and (all) workers (can the worker do what she or he wants without compromising workplace quality, creating inequity, or burdening colleagues) rather than on judgments about parenting styles and philosophies (Is the worker "overparenting")? In other words, colleagues and superiors have the right to assess work-related behaviors, but they have no right to judge workers' parenting philosophies. We see this last criterion as particularly useful because we have observed a tendency for working parents to perceive judgments of the impact of their parenting preferences on the workplace as criticisms of how they parent or as lack of support for good parenting. Shared understandings of criteria such as these—or many others that might be generated—would allow all workers to better understand how to behave in ways that are collegial, humane, and appropriate.

These same criteria—or, again, others that are generated collectively by members of particular workplaces—might prove useful for parents themselves. For example, parents might strive to keep in mind that what they perceive as insensitivity to their children's perceived needs might at least as accurately be perceived as a reflection of their colleagues' desire to have the norms of their workplace respected. Similarly, parents might ask themselves whether they have a routine expectation that their colleagues and subordinates will adapt to their parenting preferences without prior consultation. Our point is that the workplace functions better when expectations are at least understood and, ideally, consensually endorsed. Candid discussions that respect the perspectives of both workers who are parenting and their colleagues are a first and critical step in generating informal systems that allow all workers to understand and plan for what is expected and allowed.

So far, our snapshots have focused on the difficulties, resentments, and silences that sometimes surround operation of the informal parenting support system. Yet there are other possibilities that bespeak a sense of mutual and reciprocal accommodation among workers, and we now turn to those. One alternative is enacted by the many workers who strive to prevent their parenting choices from having detrimental effects on their colleagues and/or pursue their desire for accommodation for parenting in thoughtful ways that respect their colleagues and the norms of their workplaces. In some cases, they even find ways to make their choices benefit their colleagues, as in our eighth snapshot:

8. *The schedules of faculty members often vary from semester to semester, particularly in terms of course assignments and scheduling. One of the authors knows an untenured colleague with two children under the age of five who found these semester-to-semester shifts difficult to coordinate with her childcare provider. This colleague went to her department chair and proposed that, for the next few years, she be scheduled for the same teaching slots on Monday, Wednesday, and Friday afternoons each semester in order to create consistency in her childcare arrangements. At the faculty member's request, the chair consulted with other faculty members on this proposal because the norm in the department was for faculty members to trade off MWF and TR slots each semester in order to give everyone a chance at the most desirable days and times. Assent from the parent's colleagues came easily, probably because, in addition to their desire to support her, the teaching slots she proposed to take were generally considered the least desirable slots in a department where Tuesday-Thursday and midmorning teaching times were highly prized.*

Three aspects of this story are noteworthy. First, the faculty member recognized that she was asking for a special arrangement outside the norms of her department's approach to scheduling classes, and she designed her proposal such that it would cause the least inconvenience for her colleagues (rather than, for instance, asking for a Tuesday-Thursday schedule). Second, she requested that her chair poll her colleagues for their approval, making sure that they had the opportunity to weigh in on it. Third, she asked that the arrangement persist only until her children were both in full-time school (four years at the most), thus ensuring that it could be revisited at a future point. All three of these points are, in effect, choices that the working parent made—choices to be aware of and respectful of her colleagues' time, commitments, and right to be consulted. Importantly, those choices were guided by an awareness of the social implications of her request for an accommodation for parenting. Both authors have known parents who received preferential treatment when they had young children and who assumed the arrangement would endure indefinitely, often without any discussion with colleagues. Yet, the resolution of snapshot 8 was that everyone was included in the process, everyone compromised, and everyone benefited: the faculty member took a less desirable teaching schedule but solved her childcare problem, and her colleagues made an exception to their norms but gained additional Tuesday-Thursday slots each semester that the parent would not be using.

We wish to stress that we do not hold the perspective that colleagues should never be asked to accommodate their colleagues' nonwork commitments. Rather, we believe that accommodation of parenting choices should not be a routine expectation and that accommodation of life commitments other than parenting should not always be viewed as inappropriate or indefensible. Consider our ninth snapshot:

9. *One of the authors knows of a department in which the longstanding norm was for faculty meetings to occur at noon on Tuesdays, a time when no faculty were teaching. This time proved difficult for a faculty member with children who hoped to use her Tuesday lunch hour as the one time each week that she could pick up her youngest child from morning preschool herself. In this small department, rescheduling faculty meetings would not prove that difficult. Yet, while sympathetic to the faculty member's situation, the department chair was reluctant to adjust the meeting time to accommodate this one faculty member, who could, of course, make other arrangements to get her child from preschool. Another faculty member then came to the chair and revealed that the easiest time for him to work out at the campus gym was at noon on Tuesdays and Thursdays. Initially, the chair did not see this as relevant, as rescheduling a meeting for a workout seemed frivolous. Upon reflection, however, she questioned why she had more sympathy for the first situation than the second. Ultimately, both faculty members were simply seeking accommodation for nonwork commitments. The chair polled the entire faculty for alternative meeting times, found one that worked for everyone, and the meetings for that semester were rescheduled. Since then, the norm in the department has been that faculty meeting times are renegotiated each semester.*

We regard this as a positive story for three reasons. First, it demonstrates the possibility of understanding that colleagues can have a range of nonwork commitments for which they might seek accommodation, and it flattens the hierarchy that automatically puts parenting at the top of the list. This is an enactment of Nelson's (2005) suggestion for avoiding resentment over accommodations for workers' parenting choices: Give all workers equal access to a set amount of time off for personal reasons. Second, a solution was arrived at through group interaction and consensus. Third, the outcome provided a benefit for faculty other than those who sought accommodation. When faculty meetings ceased to occur only on Tuesdays, faculty who were teaching MWF during a given semester did not feel consistently disadvantaged because their nonteaching days were interrupted by a meeting several times during the term.

Snapshots 8 and 9 share some important features. First, in both of them, working parents' efforts to meet their parenting preferences reflected awareness of and consideration for both colleagues' rights and workplace norms. Second, in both snapshots all workers who might be affected were given a voice in decisions about accommodations. These and other means of showing respect and professional courtesy nurture the kind of climate conducive to finding creative solutions to tensions that inevitably arise when people who have full lives also participate in the paid labor force.

Lorraine Jackson (2008) offers an additional idea for equitable workplace accommodation of workers whose parenting choices make it difficult to meet the full complement of faculty responsibilities. She points out that at least one U.S. university has a half-time tenure track, which allows faculty to work half-time instead of full-time so that they may devote substantial time and energy to children while still meeting their job responsibilities. Another option is for all or a sufficient number of workers in a particular workplace to agree to operate according to a cooperative logic whereby all workers who join give and receive roughly equivalent "favors" so that each of them enables the others to invest in nonwork commitments. This arrangement might be modeled after neighborhood childcare co-ops that allow each parent some time without any children in exchange for some time taking care of others' children.

And there are surely other ways to address the dual needs for a productive, equitable workplace and caring for children. Those ways, however, are unlikely to be identified, much less put into practice, without the kind of honest, difficult, and sustained conversations that we encourage in this chapter. Candid dialogue among workers whose priorities and perspectives differ is a necessary precondition for finding ways for working parents to enact their preferences while also respecting the needs of the workplace and the rights of their colleagues. In the Mama Ph.D. posting prompting CAprof's response that we quoted at length above, Libby Gruner offers some closing thoughts that are congruent with the perspective we have advanced in this chapter:

> What I'd really like to see is an atmosphere of trust and collegiality that allows us to work these things out reasonably. If a chair sees that one colleague

has had a plum teaching schedule several semesters in a row—and someone else hasn't—it might be time to change things around. On-campus childcare, after-school transportation, and flexibility in the workplace (the last of which I have this summer) would also help. From my current vantage point, it seems that the time of needing accommodation is relatively short—I'm probably about halfway through my career, and I've really not needed it for a few years already. So maybe if we take the long view we can see that we'll all need help now and then, and the more we trust that we're all doing our jobs, the more we'll be willing to bend a little.

## CONCLUSION

We experienced more than a little trepidation when we decided to write this chapter. We know from experience—some of which we've shared in snapshots presented herein—that our argument for clear and agreed-upon norms for workers' parenting preferences will lead some readers to brand us antichild, antifamily, and/or antifeminist. Yet our experience has also taught us that the concerns we've voiced are not restricted to the two of us. As we have noted, our experiences are supported by ample research showing that many workers resent or are confused about workplace accommodations uniquely made for parenting, yet those same workers are unable or unwilling to speak out about their concerns in the workplace itself. In addition, at least some working parents appear unaware of the extent to which colleagues alter their own work schedules and responsibilities to accommodate parenting preferences. We believe that the silence that surrounds these issues obscures their impact on workers and does not contribute to healthy workplaces. We also believe that better choices tend to be conscious and informed. When workers who are parents are not aware of the ways their parenting choices affect coworkers, those choices are less than well informed. Similarly, when coworkers are not aware that they have options other than silently acquiescing to what they assume is expected, their choices aren't well informed.

Our guiding goal in this chapter is to improve workplace communication and collegial relations by naming an issue that has gone unnamed—the informal parenting support system—but that nonetheless operates below the surface of many workplaces. Giving the issue a name allows workers to begin discussing the issue, which is the first step in deciding how to manage it in ways that are respectful of the rights and priorities of all workers and of the functional needs of the workplace. Moreover, in making the informal parenting support system visible, we intend to place it in a broader perspective. This perspective recognizes that, in the life cycle of many—but not all—workers, parenting is one of many worthy life commitments that workers might make and that colleagues and the workplace might want to accommodate. The culture of respectful discussion that we advocate would begin with such a perspective, encouraging colleagues to develop communally agreed-upon strategies that address not only the interaction of parenting and work but also the possibilities of supporting a wide range of life commitments that workers make.

## REFERENCES

Burkett, E. 2002. *The baby boon: How family friendly America cheats the childless.* New York: Free Press.

Buzzanell, P. M. and Liu, M. 2007. It's "give and take": Maternity leave as a conflict management process. *Human Relations* 60, 463–95.

Charmaz, K. 1983. The grounded theory method: An explication and interpretation. In R. Emerson (ed.), *Contemporary field research* (pp. 109–26). Boston: Little, Brown.

Charmaz, K. 2004. Grounded theory in the 21st century: Applications for advancing social justice studies. In N. K. Denzin and Y. S. Lincoln (eds.), *The Sage handbook of qualitative research* (3rd ed., pp. 507–36). Thousand Oaks, CA: Sage.

Douglas, S. J. and Michaels, M. W. 2004. *The mommy myth: The idealization of motherhood and how it has undermined women.* New York: Free Press.

Dow, B. J. 2008. Does it take a department to raise a child? *Women's Studies in Communication* 31, 158–65.

Dunteman, D. 2006, October. Women vs. women. *Sacramento*, 184–95.

Evans, E., and Grant, C. (eds.). 2008. *Mama Ph.D.: Women write about motherhood and academic life.* New Brunswick, NJ: Rutgers University Press.

Friedan, B. 1963. *The feminine mystique.* New York: Dell.

Geertz, C. 1973. *The interpretation of cultures.* New York: Basic Books.

Goldrick-Rab, S. 2009. Valuing children. Retrieved June 17, 2009, from *Brainstorm: Lives of the mind* [*Chronicle review* blog] Website: http://chronicle.com/review/brainstorm/article/?id=1432&utm_source=at&utm_medium=en.

Goodman, E. 2008, August 8. How equality's adding up, *Raleigh News & Observer*, p. 9A.

Gruner, L. 2009. Mothering at mid-career: Whose responsibility? Retrieved August 12, 2009, from Mama Ph.D. [*Inside Higher Ed* blog] Website: http://www.insidehighered.com/blogs/mama_phd/mothering_at_mid_career_whose_responsibility#Comments.

Hays, S. 1996. *The cultural contradictions of motherhood.* New Haven, CT: Yale University Press.

Hochschild, A. (with Machung, A.). 2003. *The second shift: Working parents and the revolution at home* (Rev. Ed.). New York: Viking/Penguin.

Jackson, L. 2008. Reflections on obstacles and opportunities: Suggestions for improving the retention of female faculty. *Women's Studies in Communication* 31, 226–32.

Kirby, E. L. and Krone, K. J. 2002. "The policy exists but you can't really use it": Communication and structuration of work-family policies. *Journal of Applied Communication Research* 30, 50–77.

Kramer, M. 2008. The year of the newborns: A department chair's reflections. *Women's Studies in Communication* 31, 196–202.

Litwin, A. H. and O'Brien Hallstein, L. 2007. Shadows and silences: How women's positioning and unspoken friendship rules in organizational settings cultivate difficulties among some women at work. *Women's Studies in Communication* 30, 111–42.

Nelson, B. 2005. *1001 ways to reward employees.* New York: Workman.

O'Brien Hallstein, L. 2008. Silences and choice: The legacies of white second wave feminism in the new professoriate. *Women's Studies in Communication* 31, 143–50.

Rosen, R. 2007, March 12. The care crisis. *Nation.* Retrieved May 11, 2007 from http://www.thenation.com/doc/20070312/rosen.

Strauss, A. L. and Corbin, J. M. 1998. *Basics of qualitative research: Techniques and procedures for developing grounded theory* (2nd ed.). Thousand Oaks, CA: Sage.

Tracey, S. 2008. Care as a common good. *Women's Studies in Communication* 31, 167–74.

Vavrus, M. D. 2007. Opting out moms in the news. *Feminist Media Studies* 7, 47–63.

Wood, J. T. 1992. Telling our stories: Narratives as a basis for theorizing sexual harassment. *Journal of Applied Communication Research* 20, 349–62.

Wood, J. T. 2004. Monsters and victims: Male felons' accounts of intimate partner violence. *Journal of Social & Personal Relationships* 21, 555–76.

## NOTE

1. We use the term "working parents" to refer to parents who participate in the paid labor force. Our usage does not imply that parents who are not in the paid labor force are not working.

11

# CUTTING THE MEETING SHORT

## Conflicting Narrative Choices in One Woman's Maternity Leave

*Lori West Peterson*[1]

Maternity leave—more than just time away from paid work—is a life experience literally pregnant with divergent meanings and comprised of both choice and constraint. Martin (1990) deconstructed a male CEO's speech about a female employee's birth experience and maternity leave—and exposed the gender suppression and control inherent in a male's discourse about a woman's experience. Similarly, in their textual deconstruction of an organizational maternity leave policy, Peterson and Albrecht (1999) firmly situated maternity leave as a gendered site worthy of scholarly inquiry and critique. Yet, two decades after Martin's seminal article a vacuity of research still surrounds this complex issue and most studies focus on "rationales for certain leave lengths, ways of enhancing women's satisfaction with their leaves, and with company policies and other results that can influence general policy use and revision" (Meisenbach, Remke, Buzzanell, and Liu, 2008, p. 4).

In fact, few studies explore the *actual lived experience* of women who have taken time off work to give birth and then returned to the workplace (for examples, see Meisenbach et. al. 2008; Buzzanell and Lu 2005; Lui and Buzzanell, 2004; and Buzzanell, 2003); and only one of the extant studies offers a truly *in-depth* analysis of an actual lived maternity leave experience by exploring the nuances of one disabled woman's account (i.e., Buzzanell, 2003). The present study: (1) responds to Buzzanell's (2003) call for inquiry into how maternity leave is constructed differently for women of diverse race/ethnicities by exploring the evocative lived maternity leave experience of Patricia, a Black, professional, single mother,[2] and (2) engages the concept of *choice* in terms of the *choice of narrative strategy* with which Patricia (re)constructs her story.

The sociopolitical context of maternity leave has remained stagnant for the past several decades. Following the Pregnancy Discrimination Act of 1978, which allowed for the familiar six-to-eight week (unpaid or paid) leave no innovative legislation regarding maternity leave was introduced until 1993. The Family and Medical Leave Act (FMLA) of 1993 "was supposed to be the beginning of a new movement to reshape the workplace to reflect the needs of working families" (Mencimer, 2008, p. 1). Unfortunately, hopes of advancements in maternity leave policies that the FMLA appeared to presuppose have fallen exceedingly short of public expectation; and maternity leave policy—which is left up to individual states and/or organizations to supplement—remains a struggle between "rights granted and privileges withheld," even as the current administration battles to initiate universal healthcare reform (Peterson and Albrecht, 1999, p. 170).

Therefore, the cultural context of maternity leave policy as a highly politicized, gendered site overarches this study as I explore the ways in which culture is embodied in, and subsequently the tensions of *choice* are exposed in, discourse about maternity leave experience. I explore the concept of choice in this study through an examination of the *discursive choices* Patricia uses to narrate her maternity leave story—choices that reflect the language our culture provides for talking about maternity and maternity leave—choices that reveal the complexity of such issues as selfhood, gender, and identity(ies) surrounding this female-centered experience.

## LITERATURE REVIEW

### Maternity Leave

Feminist research on maternity leave has been sparse compared to the exponential growth of working mothers in the past several decades. Martin (1990) and Peterson and Albrecht (1999) were among the first scholars to study maternity leave through a feminist, deconstructionist lens. Yet, even these studies each only examined one particular text. Peterson and Albrecht (1999) specifically called for future research to explore *women's narratives* of maternity leave experience in order to reveal additional biases embedded within this multilayered experience. Accordingly, recent research has focused on women's talk about arranging maternity leaves using pentadic analysis to reveal that women's discourse usually favors organizational motives (Meisenbach et al., 2008). Other studies offer a feminist, poststructuralist analysis of fifteen women's discursive constructions of their maternity leave, revealing gendered organizing practices (Buzzanell and Lui, 2005), and a feminist ethics critique of fifteen women's maternity leave narratives (Lui and Buzzanell, 2004). Finally, Buzzanell (2003) studied one disabled woman's narrative from a feminist standpoint lens.

Although these studies clearly secure maternity leave as a prolific site of feminist inquiry, all but one (i.e., Buzzanell, 2003) rely on thematic analysis *across* several narratives as a means of exposing micro- and macrogendered organizing behaviors. The present study responds to the call for "further explorations of maternity leaves in women's own words and terms" as a means of uncovering "*additional* understandings of maternity leave and the ways that diverse women experience these leaves" (Buzzanell, 2003, p. 62, emphasis added). Furthermore, I employ a feminist standpoint approach to maternity leave research initiated by Buzzanell (2003) whereby "complicated and richly nuanced understandings of maternity leave tensions" are possible by exploring both the commonality of this experience as well as the difference of individual women's experiences based on social location (p. 54). As such, I engage this study as a researcher *who has achieved a standpoint* on maternity leave—through personal experience and critical reflection—and seeks to celebrate women's struggles in constructing identities and critical reflection through my research. I assert that through in-depth examination of one woman's story about her maternity leave experience, wherein she must develop a narrative strategy to struggle with discursive choices/constraints, the tensions between difference/commonality, personal experience/culture are illuminated.

## Discursive Disjunctions

Sociologist Susan Chase (1995) describes a *discursive disjunction* as a narrative struggle to talk about "different discursive realms . . . conflicting vocabularies for articulating experience . . . different ways of talking about oneself" (p. 11). For example, in her study of female school superintendents, Chase found that these women struggled to articulate their contradictory experiences about professional work and inequality because these two experiences belong to two different discursive realms in American culture.[3] Whereas talk about professional work is a *settled* discursive realm that women speak about with relative ease and unself-consciousness, talk about inequality is an *unsettled*, highly ideological discursive realm that women speak about with awkwardness and self-consciousness.

Similarly, in my interview with Patricia Newman, a thirty-seven-year-old African American budget analyst,[4] the discursive disjunction between *empowerment* in professional and reproductive and relational choices and *subjection* in choices surrounding gender discrimination after returning to work following her maternity leave causes her to narratively struggle. Clearly, maternity leave appears to be like a fault line running through both settled and unsettled cultural terrain. Researchers have explored this terrain in terms of the unique cultural location of maternity leave "at the intersection of procreation and the market" (Peterson and Albrecht, 1999, p. 170) and have illumined how maternity leave cultivates a cultural environment of "gender conflict, uncertainty about workflow stability and key personnel's ongoing workplace participation, and concern about how leaves may affect career prospects" (Meisenbach et al., 2008, p. 4). Hence, women must somehow articulate their way through this knotty terrain—by developing a narrative strategy—when discussing the inherent contradictions embodied in their maternity leave experiences.

## Narrative Strategies

Chase (1995) asserts that the "concept of narrative strategy should help us to understand narratives about contradictory identities . . . or experiences that cross the boundaries of settled and unsettled discursive realms" and offers several examples of such experiences including the birth of a child (p. 34). Consequently, in this study, a narrative strategy refers to the particular way(s) in which a woman approaches (through talk) the disjunctions among the various discursive realms of her maternity leave experience. For example, Chase (1995) uses "the term *narrative strategy* to capture that particular, meaningful juxtaposition in each case, to identify a woman's specific orientation or approach to the disjunction between the discursive realms of professional work and inequality" (p. 24). Thus, a focus on Patricia's particular narrative strategy—that is, how she makes use of available discourse(s) about her maternity leave experience—presupposes a shift from focusing on generalized themes *across* several narratives. Instead, I adopt a method of focusing "on patterns in both content and form *within* each woman's interview—patterns in her use of various settled and unsettled discourses" (Chase, 1995, p. 24, emphasis added). This study is thus grounded in the rich theoretical and methodological traditions of narrative analysis, ethnomethodology, and phenomenology—all of which highlight the fact that "culture is manifest in the actual, particular practices of everyday life; and . . . talk is a form of social action worthy of study" (Chase, 1995, p. 25).

## METHOD

### Rationale

As stated, this study is grounded within the traditions of interpretive studies. Specifically, I rely on interactive interviewing and narrative analysis of a single case—a case I regard as a *universal singular* whereby Patricia's single story reflects larger cultural (i.e., universal) themes surrounding maternity and maternity leave (Denzin, 1989).[5] Through studying one woman's story, I "attempt to uncover this complex interrelationship between the universal and the singular, between private troubles and public issues" (Denzin, 1989, p. 19). I concur with other interpretivist scholars that the best way to analyze the complexities of the relationship between culture and individual experience is through a focus on the embodiment of that relationship in actual practice (e.g., Chase, 1995; Denzin, 1989). To accomplish this methodological goal, the use of *thick description*, or, "accounts which attempt to capture the meanings and experiences of interacting individuals in problematic situations," is essential (Denzin, 1989, pp. 20–21). Hence, a single-case approach is ideal for this purpose.[6]

As with other interpretivist scholars, I argue that each individual case is unique and thus examining the "specific configurations of meaning that operate within a single case" reveals how narration makes self-understanding possible (Denzin, 1989, p. 20). Yet, concurrently, "a life story is never wholly idiosyncratic; its particularity must be culturally intelligible" (Chase, 1995, p. 7). Thus, through a close examination of Patricia's story, I seek to understand the dynamic interplay between culture and experience. Moreover, I seek to understand how my role, as interviewer, affects this interplay; how every retelling of a story is a cocreation between interviewee and interviewer, and how this cocreation can help both parties achieve the critical reflection necessary to develop a standpoint through "conscious reflection on and political understandings of their experiences and oppressions" (O'Brien Hallstein, 2000, p. 12). Finally, as a narrative researcher, I contend that focusing "on narration is itself a way of empowering those whose words we interpret" (Chase, 1995, p. 62). The following questions guide this study:

- What specific narrative strategy does Patricia choose as she struggles with the discursive disjunctions surrounding her maternity and maternity leave?

- How do Patricia's *particular* narrative strategies speak to the more *universal* cultural choices/constraints surrounding maternity and maternity leave?

### Procedures

My interview protocol consisted of simply collecting basic demographic information and proceeding to ask "What is it about your pregnancy, maternity leave, and return to the workplace that made you interested in sharing your story with me?" This initial question yielded rich, thick description of Patricia's maternity leave experiences which I voice-recorded and had transcribed.[7] The following narrative focuses on several nearly contiguous excerpts from my interview with Patricia Newman.

## RESULTS

### Patricia Newman: Surrendering to Delayed Justice and Embracing Maternity

***Emphasizing Drive and Determination in Professional Work*** Patricia Newman, a senior budget analyst for a city government agency in a large metropolitan area, introduced herself to me in 1996 as a "workaholic" and a "determined, crazy type of person."[8] I began the interview with Patricia—who had taken a three-month maternity leave after the birth of her daughter in 1993—with my principal question: "what is it about your experience, being pregnant at work and taking a maternity leave and returning that you feel is significant," to which she responded:

> PN: I think the return to work was very significant [p]. (LP: Okay . . . [p]). So much to the point where I had considered trying to go the legal route [p]. (LP: Oh [p]). I was not knowledgeable on what my true rights were and whether it was something I could win.

Sensing this experience was the focal point of Patricia's desire to tell her story, I backed her up in order to get some basic information about her job:

> LP: Well, let's start at the beginning, then. Can you just walk me through a day in your job . . . what is it that you do?

PN: Well, prior to leaving for maternity leave, I was in a new role, I was acting deputy for that particular boss. In that, I had responsibilities, supervision of about 20 people, direct supervision of about five to six people that reported directly to me, and I was the acting director whenever my director was not available. So, I had a very awful lot of responsibility while pregnant, which was extremely stressful, very demanding, but somehow or another, we made it through there.

Patricia continued on, shaping her job description into a story about her drive and determination and others' high regard for her competence:

PN: [My director], she told me . . . that she would be resigning prior to my return from maternity leave, and she had asked me, well, she asked twice would I consider being acting director upon my return, and I told her no . . . especially with a new baby. . . . I was very flattered, but chose not to.

The way that my basic question about her job prompted Patricia to narrate a story about her professional competence, ability to take on responsibility, and continue in this high-stress environment while pregnant (while earning accolades and promotion opportunities from her director), exemplifies the settled discursive realm of professional work. As previous research documents, women do *not* have to search for words to describe their work histories—indeed, they often speak easily and at length about their professional accomplishments (Chase, 1995). Terms such as "workaholic," "determined," and "aggressive" were peppered throughout Patricia's story; and, she obviously felt comfortable constructing herself as a strong, independent, successful woman.

***Highlighting Autonomy in Difficult Personal Choices.*** Patricia also spoke at length, and with seeming ease, about her decision to go through with her unexpected pregnancy despite having broken the engagement with the baby's father:

LP: So, um, so how did your employees and coworkers respond to your pregnancy? When did you, did you let everyone know at one time?
PN: I didn't let everyone know at the same time [p] . . . but I started showing very, very early, and I'm a single mother, and what made my situation that much more difficult is that the father of my child also worked in the office. (LP: Oh! Okay [p]). So, it made things even more complicated. I had been engaged to him, we had broken off, and here came Krystal. (LP: Oh . . . ).

So, it was not the most . . . um, it was kind of a difficult situation, because I had to deal with whether I wanted to get married and dealing with the fact that I was a single parent and dealing with the fact that I had a very . . .

important responsibility in the office. . . . Um, at the very beginning there was some . . . confusion, I'll say. I debated over whether to get married, and he was pushing me to do that. And then when I decided that it wasn't worth . . . I did not want to get married just because I was pregnant. The relationship had not worked between us and I did not want to take my child through the confusion, heartache, whatever, of a strained marriage. So, I had to make that decision.

Here, Patricia describes herself as consciously *debating over* and *dealing with* complicated and difficult issues surrounding her pregnancy and marital status. She labels herself twice as "a single mother" and "a single parent," revealing she had constructed this identity into existence before the actual birth. Patricia's final statement "So, I had to make that decision" seals her self-determined, active, volitional presentation-of-self who is competent in making choices about an unplanned pregnancy and who refused being coerced into an unwanted marriage. Clearly, Patricia presents herself as an empowered woman by making use of the discursive resources of choice and equality initiated by second wave feminism.

Yet, that Patricia was choosing—with relative ease—from discourse about single parenthood and a complicated workplace romance in 1993, does not indicate these issues are settled discursive realms. Indeed, as her narrative later reveals, a colleague's negative comment about her having a child "out of wedlock" exposes these issues as nonetheless contentious, ideological (i.e., *un*settled) terrain. Hence, Patricia's use of second wave feminist discourse represents her struggle as an empowered woman within cultural norms of mothering and gender roles.[9]

***Shifting from Autonomy to Passivity in Maternity Choices*** Patricia's presentation of self as determined, autonomous, and headstrong is also evident in her account of handling her stressful job while pregnant:

PN: I had a whole lot of issues that I had to deal with, but some way or another, I was able to have a very positive pregnancy, and a very healthy baby. Even though I wondered, you know...my doctor was very upset with me because sometimes I would have very long days, I'd be up on my feet and he threatened to send me home so I could get rest, because toward the end there, I was having stress-related reactions.
LP: Oh. How long did you work up until—?
PN: I worked, my director, as a matter of fact, said go home, and she said, I was going to work up until the last week or so, the last two weeks before I was due, but she sent me home two weeks prior to that, before that. (LP: Wow.). You don't have any sense, you need some time to just get yourself together

and be prepared for it, so she sent me home almost a month before I had the baby.

Yet, there is a discursive shift in this story. Here, Patricia introduces her doctor who "was very upset with me" and "threatens" to send her home; then, she concedes that her director "sent" her home two weeks prior to her actual planned leave date. Although Patricia admits to having stress-related issues, she explicitly describes her pregnancy as a "very positive experience." Therefore, her story about passive compliance with her doctor's and director's recommendations supports research that finds women often defer to other individuals as primary (co)agents of their maternity leave experiences—thus becoming passive participants themselves (Meisenbach et al., 2008).

By the end of her narrative about working during her pregnancy, Patricia makes a conspicuous shift to the second person ("you don't have any sense"; "you need time to just get yourself together"), tacitly arguing that her story about being a self-determined, professional woman cannot be integrated with her story about being a subject who is now "threatened" and "sent home"—in order to get some "sense" and get it "together." Indeed, Patricia's use of the second person distances herself, as subject/agent, in her own maternity leave story and parallels findings that "women often understand themselves as removed from decisions about their own bodies and leaves" because such decisions are placed in the hands of presumably more competent others (Meisenbach et al., 2008, p. 12; Peterson and Albrecht, 1999).[10]

***Reinforcing the Disjunction between Public and Private Realms*** Patricia's use of pronoun switching, from first person to the distancing "you," also structures the following story about how she arranged her maternity leave. This narrative structure reinforces the discursive disjunction between the public realm of professional work and the private realm of pregnancy, maternity leave, and motherhood:

PN: I had quite a bit of leave, and in this particular office where you work, work is your life, basically, so I had accumulated enough comp time, enough annual leave and enough sick leave to stay out three months.
LP: Oh. Was there any kind of mandatory maternity leave? Do you get six weeks through the company, or— (PN: No.). There's nothing like that?
PN: There's nothing. You just have to accumulate your leave, and if you don't have sufficient leave, then you have to take leave without pay. (LP: Wow.) So, it's fortunate that I had accumulated leave.

> LP: So, you had three months with pay. (PN: Right). So, did that help, I mean, did you feel like that was long enough, or do you wish—
> PN: I would have loved to have stayed, you know, six months or a year, but you know, three months, I felt that I was fortunate, because so many people don't have that.

Organizational maternity leave policy exists "amid the mixed attitudinal, behavior climate that may lead to practiced gender bias . . . revealing the essential tension, contradiction, and struggle" (Peterson and Albrecht, 1999, p. 169). Consequently, maternity leave policy is an ideological, unsettled discursive realm.

As Patricia wrestles with the discursive disjunction in her story about arranging her leave, she again vacillates between first and second person. The part of her story she tells in the first person has to do with how much leave she has accumulated and how "fortunate" she felt to have earned this leave. Despite her admittance that she would have loved to have stayed home with her newborn longer, she describes herself as "fortunate" twice in this story (in recognition that less-fortunate women have no such time accumulated for maternity leave). Indeed, Patricia's first-person language co-opts the dominant discourse of managerialism whereby workers are "subjects who generally acknowledge control and predictability as necessary conditions, and fail to fully recognize power inequities" (Buzzanell and Liu, 2005, p. 14); and, paralleling findings of other studies, she uses very matter-of-fact language to explain that her actions were consistent with company policy (Buzzanell and Lui, 2005).[11]

However, when Patricia shifts into second person (e.g., "and in this particular office where you work, work is your life, basically . . ."), she struggles with the disjunction between the discursive realms of public and private spheres. This shift thus supports the idea that "female employees may experience difficulty making their lives fit the expectations and assumptions associated with separate spheres if they must position themselves . . . within two mutually exclusive domains" (Peterson and Albrecht, 1999, p. 179). As Patricia discusses the notion of leaving work (the public domain) to have a baby (the private domain), she cannot simultaneously narrate her self-determined, workaholic, organizational identity in the first person and must shift into the distancing, second-person. Hence, Patricia's discourse embodies scholars' findings that pregnant women in the workplace are caught between "the difference between their lives and ideal worker images with masculine performance evaluation systems" (Meisenbach et al., 2008, p. 12).

***Psychologizing Gender Discrimination*** Still, Patricia's most passionate story is revealed in her talk about the incredible injustice she experienced upon returning to work following her three month maternity leave and finding she had a newly instated male director:

> PN: So, she [Patricia's former director] did carry out her plans while I was on maternity leave, she did resign, and the gentleman that acted in her stead was a gentleman that I had been supervised by when I was an analyst . . . and I, we never really were able to quite fit well as far as personalities were concerned.
> LP: Tell me about him. Why? What was he like?
> PN: I think there was a level of competition between the two of us. There was a level of insecurity between, I felt he felt insecure about me or threatened, I'm not really certain . . . and I think that I was a very strong, intelligent, aggressive woman, and I just don't think that my personality set well with him . . . when this director that resigned came in, she had, she saw me and saw potential in me and had helped me climb up the ladder where I was his equal, okay, at one point he had been my supervisor, I was his equal. . . . And then when she left, then it was like he had to get even. Because I was so close to her, I think that I was his major target.

In this account, Patricia again presents herself as a competitive, determined professional—characteristics generally associated with masculinity. She does not yet concede, in this section of her story, that the rift between her and her new director is gender discrimination, and instead, describes it, using psychological discourse, as a personality-clash. Still, her struggle to articulate the rift with her director represents a burgeoning critical reflection on this clash and thus provides evidence that the context of interactive interviewing may empower women to develop standpoints through active, conscious dialogue that can "uncover submerged power dynamics and hegemonic assumptions" (Litwin and O'Brien Hallstein, 2007, p. 116).

In addition, Patricia's presentation-of-self corresponds to what Wood (2009) describes as the "iron maiden" stereotype of a female professional.[12] Accordingly, given examples of gender discrimination based on such stereotypes, it is not surprising that Patricia discovered she had been denied a promised promotion while she was still on maternity leave:

> PN: When I found out that he [the new director] was in the role, even though I did not hear from him personally, I tried to be professional and so I scheduled a meeting to go in and talk to him. . . . It was horrible . . . he proceeded to let me know that I had been denied my promotion, that I would not be in the role over, what we call a [major division] which was a deputy position, I would

> no longer be in that role. The person that I left acting when I was on maternity leave would continue . . . that I would no longer have my parking space . . . the new director had reassigned the parking space over to this gentleman, so I no longer had a parking space and that I would no longer have my office. (LP: Wow.)—he would make up some type of position for me to act as a special assistant or something to that effect in his office. And I asked him to clarify what it was, and . . . he wasn't really sure. . . . So, needless to say, I left there, that meeting very upset. [p] (LP: Uh Huh)
> PN: I followed up with a letter to recoup what had been stated, and sent it to him so that I had the facts correct. Well, that angered him, so he sent a certified letter stating that he did not understand why I . . . was not comfortable with our meeting. He thought that we had a good meeting, and he, as the new director, he could make changes as he saw fit.

All of this turmoil took place while Patricia was still on maternity leave—a time that should have been spent enjoying her new role as mother. Instead, this collision of public and private life leaves Patricia discursively struggling as she attempts to articulate a story wherein her entire professional identity is being dismantled while she cares for her newborn. Moreover, to add insult to injury, her *perception* is called into question by this new director who claims they "had a good meeting" thus, reinforcing stereotypes of women as being illogical, emotional, and lacking judgment. Finally, her baby, Krystal, is completely left out of her story. This parallels Peterson and Albrecht's (1999) finding whereby a maternity leave policy was completely devoid of any reference to a baby—leaving no way of integrating talk about mothering into organizational discourse.

Patricia continued her story about returning to the workplace and finding herself in charge of a division with which she had no familiarity:

> PN: And, I'm still over that division. (LP: Wow). So, this gentleman has not been the best thing in my life.
> LP: No. No. Okay, so you came back to work, you have no parking space and no office.
> PN: No parking space. The office, he had not asked the gentleman to leave yet, and this gentleman is the one that I left in charge, so how's that?

***Generalizing the Personal in Gender Discrimination*** At this point in her story, Patricia asks *me* a question as if to solicit my interpretation of her experience. Thus far, she has not ventured into the unsettled discursive realm of inequality (the realm of gender discrimination). So, her question prompts me to respond with a direct question:

> LP: Tell me, you know, as I hear you talk and I'm not trying to lead you in this direction or anything, but, is this significant at all that your former director was a female and that . . . your new director is male . . . and then that the person you left in charge who is now, you know, taking your parking space and your office, is also male. Is there any significance in that for you?
> PN: I think that, I think that there's major significance, because even beyond that, all seniors are now male, well, they were. . . . So, it just seems very strange that an organization that did have a lot of female participation at all levels now was adjusted such that women were not in important or critical roles.

The lengthiness of my question—and the way Patricia chose to respond—indicate an unsettledness and self-consciousness that Chase (1995) acknowledges is typical when discussing inequality. At first Patricia admits that "there's major significance" that her career is being seriously jeopardized by a male director; but, then, she conspicuously switches her talk about her own *personal* story of gender discrimination into a generalized reflection on the overall deficit of women in high-ranking positions in her agency. This response is indicative of *disrupted talk*—a linguistic pattern frequently elicited during interviews venturing into unsettled discursive realms—whereby interactants stumble, stammer, make metastatements, and/or a demonstrate the dysfluency of having to "choose a language" (Chase, 1995). That Patricia chose the language of generalized abstraction to reflect on what she understands as a glass-ceiling effect in her agency—over the language of personal gender discrimination—allows her to distance herself from her own subjection.

Patricia's distancing strategy about gender prompted me to venture into another unsettled discursive realm, *race*:

> LP: Hm. And did race play a part in that, also? Were they primarily white males in the critical roles or there are—
> PN: No, there are Black Americans, so I don't think it was race, I think it was just preference.

The abruptness of Patricia's response indicates her unwillingness to discuss potential racial discrimination. However, Patricia's unwillingness may have more to do with the fact that I was a young, white, university professor than with her inability to integrate discourse about racial discrimination into her maternity leave account. Obviously, this discrepancy did not exist in terms of sex—we were both female and had experienced maternity and maternity leave—thus a certain bond of trust and similarity was present when discussing gender inequality that was absent within the discursive context of race. Moreover, feminist standpoint theory suggests that members of oppressed groups may have a clearer vision about their oppression.[13] So, Patricia may simply be right: racial discrimination was not occurring, or, she may have chosen not to address this issue with me.

Of perhaps more importance is that Patricia does not name *gender discrimination* in her response, but opts for a seemingly benign term, "preference," as the root of her professional conflict; and, as she continued her story of returning to the workplace, the subjection in terms of gender discrimination becomes palpable in her words as she explains:

> PN: It has been most devastating to go back to work and have your world turned totally upside down. You feel like you're being accused of doing something wrong, and you simply went out to have a child, you know? (LP: Uh huh). I had considered trying to go the legal route. I was not knowledgeable on what my true rights were and whether it was something I could win.

Again, Patricia distances herself from the most painful part of her story by narrating the devastating events in the second person. When she narrates in first person, her self-determined, volitional identity is now reconstructed into someone who appears hesitant and admits she was "not knowledgeable" about legal rights. Clearly, her narrative now exemplifies how "acknowledging subjection interrupts her conception of self as actively choosing the course of her life" (Chase, 1995, p. 118); and it embodies what much feminist research documents as "the coexistence of power and subjection in women's lives" (Chase, 1995, p. 5).

Patricia's reference to feeling as if she had been accused of wrongdoing—when she simply took time off to have a baby—prompted me to ask:

> LP: Was the baby a significant part of this? What if you had left to, I don't know, take a trip . . . or nurse a sick parent. . . . Do you think it was just, was the maternity portion of it significant, or would this have happened anyway?
> PN: I think that—I have a dual answer. I think the fact that I was gone helped him to do whatever he wanted to do. I think that he may have tried to do something similar but would have had a more difficult time had I been there. I also know that he made comments about my being pregnant and having a child "out of wedlock."
> LP: What kind of comments?
> PN: Something derogatory . . . basically, it was not appropriate for me to have done such, especially in my role, you know. So, he wasn't the smartest person in things that he said and did, and that's why I said I had considered the legal route.

Here, in Patricia's "dual answer" she affirms that, indeed, her maternity was the focus of derogatory comments from her director—who she now refers to as not the smartest person instead of "this gentleman"—comments so inflammatory that she considered pressing legal charges.

As Patricia's discourse reveals her gradual recognition that she was, indeed, subjected to gender discrimination, she explicates her choice not to pursue legal action:

> PN: I had just basically documented all that occurred, and had contacted an attorney, did talk with an attorney, and then I was concerned about being seen, you know, [p] in the level that I am, it's kind of sticky when you go and you are trying to sue the administration, because you get, you're thought of as a troublemaker. . . . I had been given initial advice to just kind of wait, wait it out.
> LP: Advice from, an attorney or—
> PN: Well, the attorney had said, you know, I could wait and see how things changed.
>
> I had also gone to the EEOC (LP: Uh huh) and I had gone to labor relations specialists, and they were all saying, okay . . . you could fight, there's a possibility that you could win, but . . . it might be hard to prove that it was related to maternity.

That Patricia actively sought the advice of an attorney and Equal Employment Opportunity Commission (EEOC) representatives is indicative of her continued desire to present herself as determined and choice-making.

However, in her sense-making of why she eventually chose not to pursue legal action, she again co-opts managerialist discourse. This story is perhaps most poignant in its illustration of how managerialism serves to silence dissent and resistance to subjection; and, it should serve as a rallying cry for an informed workplace where managerialism, as a dominant discourse, is challenged, making room for more discursive choices in an increasingly diverse workforce of women sharing a common experience of maternity and maternity leave.

Subsequently, Patricia ends her narrative describing how—because she took the advice to "wait," and to not be perceived as a "troublemaker" within her organization—she feels delayed justice is being achieved:

> PN: He [her director] is on vacation. He will come back. I'm on vacation, he's on vacation, when I return, he will be elsewhere. So, there is justice. It's been almost three years though. (LP: Yeah. Yeah.) But there is justice. When the new regime came into the office, we're doing major revamping, and we had new authorities that govern our office staff. . . . He [her director] has technical

knowledge and expertise . . . however, his management skills were not the kind that anyone could utilize.
LP: And how did that make you feel?
PN: It made me feel like I wasn't totally inept, you know, or wasn't crazy, that I was onto something. (LP: Uh huh). [p] . . . So, I don't know. I think it's time for me to move to another job. I think that's what the bottom line is.
LP: You mean a completely different job in a different company?
PN: Yeah . . . I think one of my problems is that I'm a workaholic and I think that my daughter was a blessing in that she's made me realize that there's more to life than a job.

Although Patricia's conclusion reveals her belief that delayed justice is occurring, she presents herself in a much different light at the end of her story than at its onset. Here, Patricia is passive and waited "almost three years" for any semblance of justice—justice in which she played no active role. This shift from active to passive voice emphasizes her struggle to make sense of herself as a post–second wave success "story" while recognizing how mothering has impacted her "freedom to choose." Hence, as Patricia finally highlights her identity as mother she actively redefines her identity as workaholic professional. Indeed, as she reconstructs her identity, Patricia now describes being a workaholic as a "problem" whereas, at the onset of her narrative, she spoke favorably about her professional drive and accomplishments. Thus, by unraveling her professional identity, Patricia embraces her identity as *mother* and describes Krystal as a "blessing" who enables her to choose a richer path of life than work.

## DISCUSSION

Patricia's narrative provides unique insight into maternity and maternity leave from the perspective of a professional, African American, single mother; and, the narrative strategy she chose to employ illuminates larger issues regarding the language our culture provides women with to talk about this experience. Patricia's specific narrative strategy of *surrendering to delayed justice and embracing maternity* is manifested in the content and form of her story. Initially, Patricia empowers herself through discourse about her professional drive and determination and narrates her work experience with no mention of subjection—reinforcing the disjunction between the discursive realms of professional work and inequality observed by other scholars (Chase, 1995). She draws upon the equality discourse of second wave feminisms to explain choices she made when confronting an unplanned pregnancy and unwanted marriage—depicting herself as a post–second wave success story.

Yet, a discursive shift occurs when Patricia narrates her pregnancy and maternity leave experience. As Patricia tells this part of her story, her subjection is tacitly—but progressively—revealed as she no longer constructs herself as the volitional agent introduced in her opening story and begins shifting pronouns as a means of distancing herself from conflicting identities and painful experiences. Finally, the end of Patricia's narrative reveals her surrendering due justice regarding gender discrimination and embracing motherhood—reinforcing the disjunction between public and private realms.

Subsequently, Patricia's story raises the question: What does her narrative strategy accomplish and what does it reveal about *choice* in relation to maternity and maternity leave? First, this narrative strategy enables Patricia to confront, reveal, and reshape multiple identities while *choosing* to let go of previous constructions of herself to embrace mothering. Yet, her choices are not completely volitional nor are they made without struggle. Indeed, Patricia's narrative strategy exposes her intense conflict of shifting identities from an empowered, professional woman to a *mother*—and how the norms of motherhood remain disjointed with ideal worker norms. Moreover, this discursive disjunction (between ideal worker versus ideal mother discursive realms) that Patricia wrestled with in 1996, has pursued women into the twenty-first century, as Edelman (2002) laments:

> How does it happen, I wondered both then and now, that even today, in this post–second wave, post-superwoman . . . society we're supposed to live in . . . it's still the mother . . . who cuts the meeting short when the school nurse calls. (p. 174)

This surrendering of professional identity—this "*cutting the meeting short*"—is palpable in Patricia's narrative strategy. Indeed, it is a metaphor for the choice that maternity has imposed upon her professional identity.

Clearly, Patricia's singular story embodies both the universal successes of second wave politics of choice as well as the ongoing struggle to address additional issues in relation to choice surrounding maternity and maternity leave. Specifically, while second wave feminists fought to get women like Patricia *into* the meeting in the first place, Patricia's narrative reveals that large-scale institutional changes are still necessary in order that women who choose maternity also have the choice to *remain* in the meeting. Currently, the choice to remain in the meeting is often fraught with fear of never finding "a way to balance work and family life without constantly compromising one, the other, or both" (Edelman, 2002, pp. 178–79). This fear, as Patricia's narrative so powerfully illustrates, often precipitates a colliding, conflicting, and unraveling of identities—and demands that women make choices among these identities that are not really "choices" at all.

The final layer of *choice* in this study pertains to the choices that I, as an interviewer, made when facilitating this (re)construction with Patricia. I argue that through interactive interviewing into unsettled discursive realms critical reflection may be achieved. Indeed, the "mediation, dialogue, and struggle" required to achieve a standpoint—in attempts to recognize both commonality and difference in women's lived experience—parallels the interpretive interactionist's goals of uncovering the "complex relationship between the universal and the singular" (Denzin, 1989, p. 19; Litwin and O'Brien Hallstein, 2007, p. 117). Litwin and O'Brien Hallstein (2007) explain that feminist standpoint scholars "have noted that the work has yet to be done to develop a specifically feminist standpoint methodology" (p. 116); and, thus standpoint scholars currently embrace multiple methods. Yet, they also assert that a conversational-style interview format especially assists interviewees in achieving transformation and gaining new insights. Interactive interviewing into unsettled discursive realms may intensify this transformation process for both interviewee *and* interviewer and thus translates into a feminist standpoint method as it provides a vehicle for achieving critical reflection by exploring and uncovering submerged power dynamics surrounding maternity and maternity leave and hegemonic assumptions embedded in relationships and institutions such as the disjunction between ideal worker norms and ideal mother norms.[14]

Finally, employing this method of standpoint adds a new dimension to a very "old" feminist idea: *consciousness-raising* for both interviewee and interviewer. Hence, future studies might employ interactive interviewing to further explore how African American (and other marginalized) women construct narrative strategies to tell their maternity leave stories and possibly develop a Black feminist standpoint theory of maternity leave. As scholars identify additional narrative strategies, alternative—*activist*—strategies can be proffered that supplant those perpetuating the status quo. Meanwhile, as we enter the second decade of the new millennium working mothers are still cutting the meeting short; and, maternity leave remains a gendered site replete with contradictions, conflicts, and tenuous choices.

## REFERENCES

Buzzanell, P. M. 2003. A feminist standpoint analysis of maternity and maternity leave for women with disabilities. *Women and Language* 26, 53–64.

Buzzanell, P. M. and Liu, M. 2005. Struggling with maternity leave policies and practices: A poststructuralist feminist analysis of gendered organizing. *Journal of Applied Communication Research* 33, 1–25.

Chase, S. E. 1995. *Ambiguous empowerment: The work narratives of women school superintendents.* Cambridge: University of Massachusetts.

Denzin, N. K. 1989. *Interpretive interactionism.* Newbury Park, CA: Sage.

Edelman, H. 2002. How it was supposed to be. How it was. In C. Hanauer (Ed.) *The bitch in the house*. New York: Perennial, pp. 171–80.

Georgaca, E. and Avdi, E. 2009. Evaluating the talking cure: The contribution of narrative, discourse, and conversation analysis to psychotherapy assessments. *Qualitative Research in Psychology* 6, 233–47.

Litwin, A. H. and O'Brien Hallstein, D. L. 2007. Shadows and silences: How women's positioning and unspoken friendship rules in organizational settings cultivate difficulties among some women at work. *Women's Studies in Communication* 30, 111–42.

Liu, M. and Buzzanell, P. M. 2004. Negotiating maternity leave expectations: Perceived tensions between ethics of justice and care. *Journal of Business Communication* 41, 323–49.

Martin, J. 1990. Deconstructing organizational taboos: The suppression of gender conflict in organizations. *Organizational Science* 1, 339–59.

Meisenbach, R. J., Remke, R. V., Buzzanell, P. M., and Liu, M. (2008). "They allowed": Pentadic mapping of women's maternity leave discourse as organizational rhetoric. *Communication Monographs* 75, 1–24.

Mencimer, S. 2008, June. What family leave? *Mother Jones*, 6, retrieved from http://motherjones.com/polities/2008/06/what-family-leave.

O'Brien Hallstein, D. L. 2000. Where standpoint stands now: An introduction and commentary. *Women's Studies in Communication* 23, 1–15.

Peterson, L. W. and Albrecht, T. 1999. Where gender/power/politics collide: Deconstructing organizational maternity leave policy. *Journal of Management Inquiry* 8, 168–81.

Wood, J. T. 2009. *Gendered Lives: Communication, Gender, and Culture*. (8th edition). Boston: Wadsworth.

## NOTES

1. I would like to thank Lynn O'Brien Hallstein and Sara Hayden for their invaluable support of this chapter in its various stages of gestation.

2. Because Patricia identified herself as a Black American, I introduce her in her own terms to respect her self-presentation. Throughout the chapter, I use the terms "Black" and "African American" interchangeably.

3. Chase (1995) defines a *discursive realm* as the "set of discourses—the network of meanings or ideas—that are culturally available for talking" (p. 17) about lived experience.

4. All names are pseudonyms and identifying information about specific job/place of employment is omitted.

5. An example of maternity leave as a "universal singular" is the fact that all working women must decide when to announce their pregnancy. Although each *individual* woman may choose a different time (e.g., first or second trimester) and means (e.g., in person to a supervisor, formally through an H.R. Department, etc.), *all women are operating within larger cultural and discursive constraints* specific to announcing a pregnancy.

6. Single case study research is prevalent in psychological literature—especially in the subfields of narrative and discourse analytic psychology—whereby single cases are explored and assessment of the client's problem is shifted from "the intra/interpersonal domain to the wider sociocultural domain of available meaning systems" (Georgaca and Avdi, 2009, p. 236).

7. This interview is part of a data set of twenty interviews conducted between 1996 and present. I asked that participants had taken a maternity leave within the past three years (for recall purposes). The average interview lasted one to two hours.

8. Because the sociopolitical context of maternity leave has remained stagnant for the past several decades, women's stories of their experiences in 1996 do not differ substantively from recent interviews I've conducted. Hence, Patricia's story is as relevant today as it was when she told it to me.

9. 1993 is significant because it was a year after then–Vice President Dan Quayle gave his infamous speech demonizing Candice Bergen's TV persona for "choosing" single parenthood. Quayle's statement—along with the colleague's "out of wedlock" remark—epitomizes the ideological nature of the discursive realm of single-parenthood-by-choice at the time.

10. Notably, Patricia's shift to letting "experts" tell her how she should act as a mother confirms one of the core tenets of intensive mothering that tells women that they should and must rely on experts to teach them how to mother, as several chapters in this book reveal.

11. However, Buzzanell and Lui (2005) warn not to view such discursive constructions as simple complicity with policy, that doing so would "conceal the complex hegemonic processes that embody attempts to fix meanings . . . and their simultaneous enactments of resistance" (p. 14).

12. Wood (2009) describes the "Iron Maiden" stereotype as: "a female professional who is independent, directive, competitive, and sometimes tough" and offers examples of women who have been denied promotions and/or fired for being stereotyped as such (p. 235).

13. I wish to thank Lynn O'Brien Hallstein and Sara Hayden for this insight.

14. See Litwin and O'Brien Hallstein (2007, p. 117) for an explication of critical reflection.

12

# TOTAL MOTHERHOOD AND HAVING IT ALL

## Reproduction, Maternity, and Discourses of Choice among Female Police Officers

*Jaime E. Bochantin and Renee L. Cowan*

> There are a lot of choices that go hand in hand with being a female cop. One really important decision to make is whether or not to have children. It is my opinion that the cons usually outweigh the pros of having a kid in this line of work. We put our lives on the line daily, why subject a kid to that? It seems irresponsible to me. (Susan)

Susan's comment reveals complex issues and tensions associated with reproduction and choice for women in law enforcement positions. Female police officers work in a male-dominated, masculine occupation where life-threatening choices have to be made every day.[1] While all police officers inevitably make choices throughout the duration of their career (e.g., "What kind of weapon should I carry?", "What shift do I want to work?"), female police officers have unique choices associated with motherhood and reproduction that must be made during and beyond the course of their reproductive lives. For instance, potential mothers might ask themselves if getting pregnant is responsible given the life-threatening nature of the job.[2] There are also choices to make regarding whether or not to accept "light duty" while pregnant, which is something many police departments tend to prefer, but could possibly jeopardize a woman's career. With these ideas in mind, this chapter explores female police officers' perceptions of pregnancy, choice, and the repercussions and trajectories of those choices. Specifically, it explores three tensions concerning motherhood—(1) Supportive-unsupportive workplaces; (2) Work-family; and (3) Mothering is valued-devalued. The chapter also reveals two dominant discourses female police officers draw on when making decisions concerning pregnancy and motherhood.

## DIALECTICAL THEORY, ORGANIZATIONAL TENSION, AND FEMALE POLICE OFFICERS

Police departments are male-dominated masculine workplaces; female police officers often disrupt this environment and face tensions or unique stress that male colleagues may not (Bochantin and Cowan, 2008). Dialectical theory helps us understand how female police officers experience these tensions especially as they pertain to pregnancy and choice. Dialectical theory developed as an alternative view on relationship maintenance and focused on the "dynamic interplay of opposing tendencies as they are enacted in interaction" (Baxter and Montgomery, 1996, p. 171). The theory concerns tensions (a clash of ideas or principles) and contradictions (times when one idea is in direct opposition to another) in relationships (Baxter and Montgomery, 1996; Stohl and Cheney, 2001). Dialectical theory argues that the ways people make sense of their environment is influenced by contradictory pushes and pulls in that environment (Tracy, 2004).

Dialectical theory has recently been used to understand communication in organizations (Martin, 2004; Putnam and Bochantin, 2009; Seo, Putnam, and Bartunek, 2004; Stohl and Cheney, 2001; Tracy, 2004). Organizational communication scholars contend organizational tensions and contradictions are inherent in the experience of twenty-first-century organizational life (Ashcraft and Pacanowsky, 1996; Stohl and Cheney, 2001). This research demonstrates how contemporary organizational members, especially women, deal with a range of tensions associated with their particular jobs, organizations, and personal lives. Female police officers' experiences in the workplace are a site of organizational tension, thus dialectical theory is an appropriate lens through which to examine those experiences, especially with regard to pregnancy and reproduction.

Scant research exists regarding the tensions female police officers face with regard to pregnancy and motherhood. However, research regarding female police officers' experiences in the workplace has revealed many practices that could shape female police officers' choices regarding reproduction and pregnancy. Research suggests that although women have been in law enforcement positions since the 1960s, they are still subjected to disempowering practices. Some law enforcement agencies still adhere to a male bias in their hiring practices (IACP, 1998). And, when women do make the cut, they are often discriminated against with regard to promotion and can be blocked from management positions (Horne, 2006; National Center for Women and Policing, 2002). Additionally, women in law enforcement positions are still the subject of outdated stereotypes. Women are seen by their male counterparts as being less rational and logical, more emotional, unlikely to do the job well, and incapable of taking charge or managing violent crisis situations (LeBeuf and Mclean, 1997; Price, 1996). And, like many western organizations, law enforcement agencies tend to privilege the life patterns of men. Only recently have law enforcement agencies in the United States begun to address some of the issues that female police officers may face such as pregnancy and the desire to become a mother (Campbell and Hernandez, 2006; Kruger, 2006; Risher, 2006; Schutz, 2003; Whetstone, 2001).

The practices of not promoting female police officers to management positions, adhering to outdated stereotypes, and privileging the life patterns of men could be causing female police officers considerable tension and influencing their reproductive choices. Because of this, we wanted to better understand what workplace tensions female police officers voiced regarding reproduction.

## METHOD

A sample of fifteen female police officers from four different police departments (two suburban departments located in a midwestern state and two rural departments located in a southern state) were recruited to participate in this study. Participants were recruited through the first author's personal contacts in the midwestern state and participants were recruited in the southern state by initially contacting local police departments (within ten miles from both authors' homes) via facsimile. After receiving the facsimile, departments that were interested in the study contacted us and provided a list of names and contact information for female police officers who were willing to participate. We contacted these women personally and set up a day/time to interview them. After each woman (n = 12) was interviewed, she was asked if she knew of other female police officers who would be willing to participate. This network sampling technique yielded an additional three informants for a total of fifteen ($N$ = 15). The sampling technique yielded female employees from all levels of policing and at many levels of authority: six patrol officers, three sergeants, four detectives, one lieutenant and one commander. In addition to rank, length of service varied widely among informants, ranging from 1.5 to 25 years. Martial status also varied; six were married, one was widowed, two were divorced, and the remaining six were single. Five out of the fifteen women had children.

Open-ended, semistructured, in-depth interviews (Lindloff and Taylor, 2002) were conducted with all participants. The participants were asked questions to get at their experiences as female police officers. These questions fell into three main categories: policing history, experiences with femininity/femaleness, and work/life balance. The interviews ranged from forty-five minutes to two hours. Interviews were conducted until saturation was achieved.

Initially, we analyzed the data using a grounded theory approach in order to identify themes or recurring patterns in the transcripts (Charmaz, 2000). While gaining a preliminary understanding of the data, it became clear to each author that issues of contradiction and tension were inherent in the experiences of female police officers. We then went back into the transcripts and coded the data using dialectics as a tool for analysis by identifying opposing tensions. In order to establish the dialectics the participants experienced, we took note of all tensions and oppositions that occurred in the transcripts. In order to get at what constituted a dialectic, we paid close attention to the language used to describe situations. We looked for recurring themes that dealt with seemingly oppositional tensions. Three dialectics emerged from our analysis—(1) Supportive-Unsupportive workplaces; (2) Work-Family; and (3) Mothering is valued-devalued.

## STRUGGLING WITH CHOICES ON PREGNANCY AND MOTHERHOOD: FEMALE POLICE OFFICERS SPEAK

### Supportive-Unsupportive Workplaces

The female police officers voiced the idea that police departments act in both supportive and unsupportive ways simultaneously with regard to pregnancy and motherhood. Experiencing organizations as both supportive and unsupportive is a common tension voiced by contemporary employees and research is replete with illustrations of this tension (Ashcraft and Pacanowsky, 1996; Martin, 2004; Putnam and Bochantin, 2009; Wood and Conrad, 1983). Although this tension is commonplace in workplaces, individuals in various professions can experience this tension differently. Our participants experienced the dialectic of supportive-unsupportive through their discussions of workplace norms and "light duty."

***Workplace Norms*** Workplace norms are routine ways of acting and interacting in organizations (Beebe, Beebe, and Ivy, 2004). The female police officers in this study voiced two common workplace norms pertaining to the supportive-unsupportive dialectic; norms regarding uniforms and the norm of being pushed out of the profession due to pregnancy.

With regard to uniforms, a majority of the women made reference to the uniforms as both an example of how their departments could simultaneously be supportive and unsupportive. These female police officers felt police uniforms themselves were an indicator of the lack of departmental support because they are designed for men's bodies. Although many women can wear these uniforms, they are not designed for the average female body (breasts, wider hips, etc.). The women voiced another norm with regard to uniforms which involved a pregnant officer. Because there are no maternity police uniforms, when a pregnant officer can no longer fit into her uniform, she is prohibited from patrolling the streets and is forced to take light duty (if available) or unpaid leave. However, at the same time, a few of the women mentioned that their departments had the potential to be more supportive in these circumstances if they allowed uniforms that were slightly altered to accommodate a pregnant officer's changing body. Erica's situation is a good example of how police departments can be supportive of pregnant officers. Erica knew that she would be taken off patrol when she could no longer fit into her uniform, so she decided to make her own "maternity uniform" with the help of her tailor. She had an extra piece of fabric sewn into the stomach area to accommodate her expanding belly. She was not forced to take early leave or light duty and she wore the uniform until two weeks before her due date. Because of this uniform and little resistance from her boss, Erica was able to make her own choices regarding her job and her pregnancy. Erica's is an example of how police officers can resist workplace norms, which can result in empowerment.

Another common workplace norm mentioned by the female police officers was the norm of being pushed out of the profession after making the choice to become pregnant. This norm was demonstrated in two ways; not knowing what to do with police officers once they became pregnant and not allowing them to perform certain duties. Our participants told us that once a police officer announced her pregnancy, departments often did not know how to handle the situation. This seemed particularly true in departments that had not experienced a police officer becoming pregnant. Janice and

Sheryl were both the first women to become pregnant in their departments. Janice relates her experience after announcing her pregnancy,

> I was the first woman in the department to become pregnant. I was only one month pregnant and they sent me home because they didn't know what to do with me. They wouldn't give me light duty because they didn't consider it an injury, so I just had to wait at home until they figured out what to do. They told me at one point that they weren't going to hold my job . . . people were saying that I should have known before I got the job.

This example illustrates a practice of what seems to be punishment for becoming pregnant by sending the pregnant officer home. This action, similar to scolding a child for wrongdoing, may deter other women from choosing to become pregnant, thus constraining female police officers' choices with regard to pregnancy.

This idea of punishing pregnancy is further described by the women in terms of "not being allowed" to perform certain job responsibilities because of the physical appearance of being pregnant. For example, Mandy described her job as a Public Information Officer. This job required her to spend a lot of time on camera. She was the "face" of the department and had always been good at her job. However, after she got pregnant, she explained that her boss "was always looking for someone else to do the job, just in case she decided to leave the force to be a stay-at-home mom." She ended up not being "allowed" on camera. Although her boss never explicitly said it was because she had gotten pregnant, she felt this was the reason. Mandy felt "punished" when her boss refused to allow her to appear in the department picture because she was unable to fit into her uniform. Although Mandy loved her job and had no intention of leaving, she felt she was continually punished for becoming pregnant.

Interestingly, it was usually only the newer mothers (those with children under the age of five) who faced this issue of unsupportive workplace norms and less respect from their departments. This could be because being pregnant and even being a new mother, still carrying around extra baby weight and enlarged breasts, is a constant visual reminder to others that brings the private life into the public domain. This can have serious consequences for workplaces because one of the most important goals of contemporary organizations, including police departments, is to desexualize labor (Burrell, Buzzanell, & Mc Millan, 1992). Mothers of older children, then, are exempt from such scrutiny and public reminders of their femaleness and sexuality since they no longer physically reveal the private (i.e., no more swollen breasts and extra baby weight).

Although our female participants' perceptions pointed to workplace norms as unsupportive in some ways, while being supportive in other ways, policies associated with the Family Medical Leave Act (FMLA)[3] or the Pregnancy Discrimination Act (PDA)[4] could communicate further support for pregnant workers and counter the unsupportive nature of some workplace norms. The FMLA requires employers to grant up to twelve weeks of unpaid leave each year to eligible workers who have serious health issues, who need to care for a new child, or who need to care for a spouse, child, or parent with serious medical concerns (Willborn, Schwab, Burton and Lestor, 2007). These policies have the potential to make a workplace more supportive, however many of our participants indicated that oftentimes the policies are not used appropriately. Moreover, many of these policies are not desirable for pregnant police officers and force them into a double-bind situation where they are "damned if they do" and "damned if they don't." For instance, if employees are not aware or do not fully understand the provisions of the FMLA policy, the employer can dictate how the policy will be used. Janice explains,

> Since I was the first to get pregnant, I had no idea how sick time was mandated. They said that I had to come back 10 days after having the baby or they would give away my job! No way a doctor would clear me in 10 days not to mention that my job is protected by law for 12 weeks! I found out how wrong my department was from a friend of mine in another village. When I told my boss he had to give me 12 weeks, he said "Oops! Didn't know that, never had a pregnant lady here before!"

As this example suggests, police departments have the potential to be supportive through mandates like the FMLA, however most of our participants' experiences did not reflect a positive experience with their departments' handling of these mandates. Common issues with the FMLA included women not being eligible because they have not been employed long enough or they did not work enough hours (Willborn et al., 2007). Moreover, even those who were eligible often could not afford to take FMLA leave because it is unpaid; and finally, the twelve-week limit is not enough to cover both a serious pregnancy-related issue and time to recover from childbirth (Kruger, 2006). Thus, based on the FMLA, an employer can say to a pregnant woman that she must either perform all her job duties, despite medical advice to the contrary, or take unpaid leave that she cannot afford. The result is a constrained choice in which all available options have negative consequences.

In addition to the FMLA, the federal PDA prohibits discrimination based on pregnancy, childbirth, or related medical conditions (U.S. Equal Employment Opportunity Commission [EEOC], 2008). Pregnant women who are able to work must be permitted to work under the same conditions as other employees; and when they are not able to work for medical reasons, they must be accorded the same rights, leave privileges, and other benefits as workers who are disabled from working (Willborn et al., 2007). Although the PDA does not require employers to offer maternity benefits to make it easier for pregnant women to work and/or to return to work, research has shown that it is beneficial to law enforcement agencies to accommodate pregnant women (Kruger, 2006). Though not many, there are some law enforcement agencies that provide adequate maternity leave, light duty assignments, continuation of benefits, and seniority credits while on leave (Kruger, 2006). While the PDA is laudable, it does not solve all problems for pregnant police officers. One criticism regarding the use of the PDA in law enforcement agencies is that because it requires, that "employers treat pregnant women as well, or as poorly, as it treats other temporarily disabled employees" (EEOC, 2008), it continues to equate pregnancy with an illness in police departments. It is evidenced from this discussion that with regard to workplace norms, police departments usually act in unsupportive ways toward mothers. The FMLA and the PDA were instituted in an effort to change this, however, as Janice's previous comment demonstrates, the results have been mixed.

***Light Duty*** The women we interviewed voiced a tension between perceiving light duty as something helpful departments could do to support their pregnant officers and as something that could hurt their reputation/career. Broadly defined, light duty is characterized as being transferred to a "less arduous position for the duration of an employee's illness which may include being transferred to lower job classifications or lower salary levels" (Whetstone, 2001). For our participants, the notion of light duty was framed as being both supportive and unsupportive simultaneously.

Mandy, Janice, Erica, and Cassie were all police officers at the time they became pregnant and all mentioned that as soon as they announced their pregnancy, their department automatically assigned them to light duty until they had their children, regardless of whether the women themselves wanted to leave their current positions. However, one female police officer voiced the idea that light duty could be supportive in that the alternative (using sick time or taking leave without pay) was typically worse for a pregnant officer. Joyce explained, "With this new Chief, however, there is no light duty. If you don't have any sick leave then you are up a creek, which is the biggest problem right now. This one girl used all her sick leave and so she is off without pay." Clearly Joyce felt that light duty would have been more supportive and a positive outcome for her fellow officer's situation. Some of the officers who were forced into light duty mentioned receiving the same pay, but their duties and responsibilities were decreased when they revealed their pregnancies. This was seen as being both supportive (because they did not have to endure a reduction in pay) and unsupportive (because they still wanted to do their jobs and did not want others in the department to think they were lazy or trying to take the easy way out) at the same time. Furthermore, a few of the participants, including Erica and Jennifer, felt that light duty was equated with "weak police work" which caused their male colleagues to think they were no longer able to pull their own weight. Linda echoed these sentiments,

> When I look at our pregnant police officers begging the chief for light duty, I think to myself, "Come on! Toughen up and stop requesting special treatment because you decided to reproduce!" Being a police officer is not about sitting behind a desk; it's about getting out there and nabbing the bad guy.

It is clear there was considerable tension associated with light duty whether the officer chose the situation or was forced into taking it. Complicating this issue was the introduction of new legislation on how light duty policies should be applied to pregnant officers. Janice mentioned new legislation that required police chiefs to transfer pregnant women to "less strenuous and/or less hazardous positions" upon the announcement of their pregnancies, regardless of whether the women felt they were ready for the change. This legislation obviously limits the choices of pregnant women, as they are not given the opportunity to decide when they are ready to be put on light duty. To some, this new legislation may seem like progress (i.e., departments are trying to be more supportive of their pregnant officers by taking measures to protect both the mother and the baby). To others, this legislation limits freedoms and masks the fact that subordinates do not truly possess power within the organization.

## Work-Family

The relationship between work and family has become a salient area of concern in today's organizations (Clarke, 2000; Greenhaus and Buetell, 1985; Kirby, Golden, Medved, Jorgenson, and Buzzanell, 2003). This dialectic is revealed by our participants through discussions of having to choose between being an ideal worker or being an ideal mother and it was framed through the notion of risk.

***Choosing between Ideal Worker and Ideal Mother Status*** Our participants expressed considerable tension associated with feeling like they had to choose between their careers and their families. It was evident that many of these women wanted both, but did not know how to achieve this as Susan revealed in her discussion about a colleague's involvement in a perilous situation at work,

> All she could think about was her son and what being left motherless would do to him. But on the other hand, you want to be a superstar employee who saves the day! But what about being a mother? Where does that fit in with a career filled with crime, danger, and fear? She wants to be both a good worker and a good mother. She was faced with the tension of not knowing how to do both.

Susan's comment demonstrates that her coworker knows she cannot perform as an ideal worker and an ideal mother simultaneously. When female police officers want to "have it all" they find themselves faced with trying to achieve an almost unattainable goal, resulting in a forced choice between the two roles. As Janice revealed, "You have to pretty much deny the fact that you are a mother in order to do this job well."

When female police officers choose work over family the "ideal worker" norm gets perpetuated. Williams (2000) argues the ideal worker norm is characterized by the traditional life patterns of men and requires "ideal" workers to work at least forty hours a week all year round and be at the organization's beck and call. The ideal worker norm seems privileged in law enforcement and the typical police officer schedule is not always the most conducive to family life. Working long, odd hours makes caring for children and a significant other hard at times. Jennifer explains,

> I don't want to be a bad mother, but I fear that I am because of doing shift work. Since I work the 3 to 11 shift I never get to put my daughter to sleep at night nor take her to soccer practice. Thank God she has a wonderful father to do that stuff with her, but I still can't help but feel like I am missing out and that she may resent me for it.

Jennifer's comments, which were echoed by Cassie and Mandy, reveal the struggle that ensues when a mother wants to "have it all" but is unable to achieve it all. Although these women want to be both ideal workers and ideal mothers, they felt they had to make a choice between the two roles.

More often than not, the officers spoke of "choosing" their mothering roles over their policing roles. Cassie recalls leaving a detective job she really loved with irregular hours after a year of trying to make it work, "I transferred to this division when my son was about a year old just because of the schedule." And Janice commented that sacrificing at work was almost a necessity if she wanted to be a good mother, "It is really hard, I am stretching myself really thin to be the best wife, the best mother. . . . I know I am not the best employee, however, my life is more important." Hence, choosing to be an ideal mother over an ideal worker takes precedence for some women in law enforcement.

It is important to note here that the women's police departments themselves further aggravate the tension associated with this choice. If an officer/mother needs to adjust her schedule or switch shifts, management usually has no part in accommodating this and it becomes her responsibility to find someone to cover the shift, which was revealed through our discussions with Janice, Jackie, and Susan. The result is the individual employee, not the organization, becomes responsible for all issues concerning how the relationship between work and family is handled. If this relationship is not handled well, the police officer is to blame, removing any accountability from the police departments. This echoes Hoffman and Cowan's (2008) findings, which suggest organizations predominantly adhere to an ideology of work/life balance that contends it is an individual's responsibility to obtain a balance between work and life with limited help from the organization. It is obvious that these women's "choices" pertaining to the dialectic of work and family are severely constrained by their departments and the ideal mother and worker norms (Crittenden, 2001; Williams, 2000).

***Risk*** In addition to struggling between the roles of ideal worker and ideal mother, our participants also had to struggle with the tension of wanting to do their jobs (which can be risky) and dealing with a consuming fear of getting hurt or killed on the job. The officers mentioned that female police officers who are also mothers had to constantly make choices regarding what was more important—their careers or their families. Those who felt family was more important mentioned fear at the thought of leaving their children without a mother. The most revealing example of this was in a story Kelly told about a fellow female police officer who was responsible for making the fatal shot that killed a man. When the officers involved were put through the standard debriefing, the officer who made the shot was asked what was going through her mind as she fired. She responded by saying, "I was face-to-face with the fact that I may leave my baby an orphan. I had no choice. . . . I can't leave my child motherless." And Kelly commented, "When I came back to work after having the baby I had a really hard time with it. I kept asking my husband, 'how can I do this? I am a mother. What kind of mother am I that I have to worry about dying every night?'" Here Kelly frames her choice to return to work as risky and irresponsible.

Others talked about being so dedicated to their jobs that they were willing to engage in risky behaviors even while pregnant. For example, Jackie notes that she was eight months pregnant and still doing heavy patrol work. She told the story of being involved in a foot chase with a young man who had stolen something from a retail store. To catch the assailant, she threw her pregnant belly on top of him. She talked about "bragging" about the capture and used it to demonstrate she was still "one of the guys" even though she was pregnant. Jackie clearly felt her actions illustrated her dedication and commitment to her job regardless of her pregnancy. Although Jackie's story was rare, it points to a privileging of the ideal worker over the ideal mother.

## Mothering Is Valued-Devalued

As discussed above, when our participants voiced a tension between work and family, they also pointed to the skills associated with being a mother as simultaneously valued and devalued by the organization. When women began to enter organizations in professional roles in larger numbers, they were often seen as the token "mother" in the workplace (Kanter, 1977). This role assumes women are good listeners who offer empathy and support, are easy to talk to and sympathetic (Kanter, 1977). Although this has begun to change in contemporary organizations, our participants voiced a tension regarding the simultaneous valuing and devaluing of skills associated with "mothering" on the job.

Specifically, the women voiced a tension with regard to being expected to enact more motherly roles on the job, such as being supportive and nurturing while dealing with children and domestic abuse situations, while at the same time feeling devalued for wanting to be a supportive and present mother to their own children. Cassie, a patrol officer who transferred to become a D.A.R.E officer (which is a position that educates school-aged children about the dangers of drugs and alcohol), commented, "When the position opened up, my boss came up to me and said 'Guess what!' He thought that since I was a woman I would be best at talking to children." At first, she was reluctant to take the job because she saw D.A.R.E officers as engaged in "weak police work"; at the same time, she felt like she should take it because of the daytime schedule. After she took the job, she told us that she did not like it because it was very different to work with children, however, her male colleagues and boss kept telling her how good she was at being a D.A.R.E officer so she decided to stick with it. Similarly, Linda described how she was praised by her department after talking a six-year-old boy out of running away from home. She explained that using empathy, compassion and patience helped her relate to the boy. These examples suggest that organizations commend female police officers for their excellent use of communication skills and for being able to relate to children. However, while female police officers are lauded for their ability to serve as "mothers" to the community, maternal attributes and behaviors are not privileged when it comes to female police officers' own children.

While many female police officers are encouraged to tap into their maternal skills for the benefit of the job and community, most of the mothers who participated in this study pointed to a devaluing of the role of mother when it came to their own families. As Janice describes, "Once I had my first child they [the police department] didn't respect me anymore because they figured I would end up leaving the force to be a stay-at-home mom." This example is just one of several that reveals the tension these women faced after becoming pregnant and entering motherhood. This double-edged sword complicates a female police officer's choice to become a mother and even led some of the women we spoke with to choose not to have children. As Susan commented, "Recently I made the conscious choice to not ever become a parent after I saw the ways in which the mothers are exploited on the job. I don't want to be a community service officer . . . that's where all the moms go. . . . I have bigger goals."

As described by our participants, police departments simultaneously value and devalue mothering skills and tend to encourage the exploitation of these skills while on the job while at the same time they discourage the women from actually starting families of their own. This tension closely mirrors the devaluing of mothering in the larger society. Author Ann Crittenden (2001) argues that society does not view mothers' work as being highly skilled or as a contribution to the economy. She says that motherhood is the only job that you have to pay to do. Her argument centers around the notion that mothers are responsible for producing "human capital," which are the skills, abilities, and creative entrepreneurship of people (Crittenden, 2001). Society tends to ignore the huge contribution mothers make toward the economy, whether directly or indirectly. Although Crittenden makes a financial argument for the value of mothering in U.S. society, it is clear mothering is devalued on many levels. The female police officers in this study pointed to a considerable tension regarding the value of motherhood in their departments. On the one hand, mothering skills are exploited by supervisors, claiming a value in utilizing them while on the job, yet on the other hand, departments simultaneously devalue these same skills when it comes to female police officers' own families.

## PERPETUATING THE DISCOURSE OF "TOTAL MOTHERHOOD" AND "HAVING IT ALL"

The preceding discussion illuminates the intricacies and tensions associated with reproductive choice in a highly masculinized and life-threatening career as expressed by female police officers. The dialectics of supportive-unsupportive workplaces, work-family, and mothering as valued-devalued point to two major discourses that structure how the female police officers understood and talked about the tensions they were experiencing—the discourse of total motherhood and the discourse of having it all. Fairhurst and Putnam (2004) refer to discourse as "general and enduring systems of thought" (p. 7). These larger societal discourses influence our lives in various covert and overt ways and impact our choices and decisions. The following section situates these discourses, reveals how they are reified and perpetuated, and discusses the implications for female police officers who draw on them.

### The Discourse of Total Motherhood

Based on the dialectics we uncovered, it is clear the female police officers' experiences and choices were influenced by the contemporary discourse of total motherhood. According to Wolf (2007), total motherhood suggests that mothers should prioritize their children and their children's needs above all else, reflecting a total subordination of the woman to the role of mother. Similarly, sociologist Sharon Hays (1996) asserts that the dominant motherhood ideology in the United States is that of *intensive mothering*, which furthers this notion of womanhood and motherhood being treated as synonymous identities and categories. This type of discourse suggests that mothers are not really individuals but rather they serve as "vectors of risk" for their babies (Wolf, 2007). It is the fetus, not the mother, who is at the center of a discourse that focuses on regulating maternal behavior (both before and after the birth of the child) in order to minimize risk (Wolf, 2007). Because of this attention to risk, total motherhood implies that the right choice is always the one that is the best for the child. The women we interviewed echoed the idea that participating in some policing activities was irresponsible and risky for children during and even after pregnancy. The female police officers seemed to draw on this discourse when they talked about the tension they often experience between work and family as well as mothering being valued-devalued.

Furthermore, the women we interviewed often dealt with the tension of work-family by prioritizing their families over their work lives, especially if they had young children. While the women we spoke to felt like they were making the conscious and responsible choice to do whatever it took to be a good parent, by making such choices, they were simultaneously perpetuating the idea that a woman's first and most important priority is motherhood. Interestingly, we found that there seemed to be a shift that occurred for the women who have children from once being "ideal employees" to instead focusing their attention on family. Many of the women we spoke to referred to their lives before becoming mothers as filled with dedication and commitment to their work. However, once they became pregnant and had kids, this changed. Career aspirations and advancement no longer seemed as important as being good mothers. As a result, their discussions reflect a discourse of total motherhood with some female police officers forsaking their careers for what they saw as best for their children.

The total motherhood discourse is also revealed through the dialectic of mothering being valued-devalued at work. Police departments have exploited women's "maternal" skills while on the job, encouraging female police officers to "mother" the community, which reflects the police department's buy-in to the discourse of total motherhood. At same time, female police officers are often discouraged from starting families of their own or privileging their home over their work lives. Hence, the discourse of total motherhood is reflected through female police officers being tokenized as "mothers" by police departments but only as it pertains to their jobs.

## The Discourse of Having It All

In conjunction with the discourse of total motherhood, our dialectics revealed the contemporary discourse of wanting to have it all, or more specifically, as the work-family dialectic uncovered, the desire to be an ideal worker *and* ideal mother. The women from our study found it was nearly impossible to enact these roles simultaneously. As mentioned, the ideal worker norm in the United States is characterized by the traditional life patterns of men, which require working at least forty hours a week all year round and being at an organization's beck and call (Williams, 2000). In contrast, an ideal mother, or an *intensive mother* (Hays, 1996) is epitomized as being continually available to provide emotional and instrumental support for her children. Although a common discourse in Western society is that women can have it all or be completely dedicated to their jobs *and* their families, this oftentimes is not a reality. Society tends to offer poor choices for women, especially those who want both careers and families (Williams, 2000; Wolf, 2007).

Furthermore, women are often encouraged to embrace the false hope of being able to juggle both a career and a family simultaneously and equally.

There are even blogs dedicated to this topic such as www.thenewhavingitall.com and www.dilemoms.blogspot.com. These blogs are prescriptive in that they offer tips and quick fixes for how to achieve a perfect balance in one's life. As such, websites like these reinforce the idea that balance is both desirable and attainable for all women, which, as our study revealed, is often not the case. Since the notion of having it all permeates our society, it is no wonder so many women draw on this discourse to understand and make sense of their experiences. The female police officers we spoke to were no exception; they seemed to want to have it all but found themselves coming up short in one area or the other. The discourse of having it all was revealed through the dialectics of supportive-unsupportive workplaces and work-family.

Many of our participants discussed the implications of light duty and whether it was an unsupportive or supportive policy. Since many of our participants drew on the idea of wanting to have both a career and a family, they found the practice of automatically being assigned to light duty as being punitive and unsupportive while also causing their colleagues to devalue and discredit their abilities to do the job. Being forced to take light duty did not adequately allow them to "have it all" since many framed light duty as not really being a police officer. As a result, many of our participants felt that light duty was an excuse to push them out of the profession and did not afford them the ability to be both the best employee and the best mother.

Similarly, the discourse of "having it all" was revealed through the tension between work and family for our participants. This dialectic revealed the struggle between wanting to "have it all" but not knowing how. Although they want to be both ideal workers and ideal mothers, our participants felt that in the end they had to make a choice between the two roles. The result is that women in law enforcement really cannot truly have it all and, in the end, many of them choose to be ideal parents rather than ideal employees, despite their desire to want to be both.

## A PARADOXICAL SITUATION: IMPLICATIONS AND CONCLUSIONS

The two discourses of total motherhood and having it all were continually drawn upon and influenced the choices of our participants. The women were clearly drawing on discourses that told them they should not engage in risky behaviors and that they should put their children above all else while at the same time they should be able to have it all (be an ideal worker and ideal mother). Too often society and the women's police departments directed our participants into situations where they felt they had to choose between total motherhood and total police work. Upon further reflection, it becomes clear that drawing on both the discourses to make sense of and understand their experiences sets up a paradox that is stifling and certainly affects these women's choices.

Paradoxes, as described earlier, are typically seen as situations wherein while pursuing one goal, another competing goal enters the situation and works to undermine the first goal (Martin, 2004; Putnam, 1986; Stohl and Cheney, 2001). The discourse of total motherhood says that a mother must subjugate her entire world to the needs of her children, subordinating all else in favor of the child's well-being (Wolf, 2007). By contrast, the discourse of having it all informs women that they can achieve a perfect balance of being an ideal mother and a stellar employee (Williams, 2000). The goal of each discourse negates the other, yet the women we spoke to draw from both discourses simultaneously and structure their worlds as if achieving both is ideal.

As a result, the women we spoke with were in situations where they could not win. This paradox seemed to cause many of the female police officers considerable tension and some were even contemplating leaving law enforcement. The goal of future research should be to identify discourses within society that might be more accessible and less paradoxical for female police officers to draw upon to help them restructure and make less constraining sense of their situation. Furthermore, structural changes need to be enacted. Policies such as the FMLA and the PDA were implemented to protect people in situations like those faced by our participants, however, many police departments do not properly interpret the legislation and as a result, pregnant female police officers are treated unfairly. Perhaps better training on what these laws entail could help to ensure equality in the workplace. In addition, the PDA should not be written as if it equates pregnancy as a disability or illness. As evidenced by at least a few of our participants, pregnancy is far from a disability; rather, it is a natural part of many women's lives yet it seems as if women are being punished for this natural event. The changes we are advocating need to begin with society reevaluating how reproduction and motherhood are thought of in our culture.

Although female police officers can feel trapped in a double-bind situation regarding pregnancy and reproduction, the future experiences and choices of women in policing still remain undetermined. Will they experience the same negativity that current female police officers face with regard to motherhood, or can change be initiated? Will it be possible for women to become both ideal workers and ideal mothers simultaneously? Is that choice even desirable? Our participants' perceptions and experiences call into question the notion that women with choice "get what they want" when it comes to pregnancy and motherhood. We saw these women struggling with choices they felt would inevitably have negative consequences for either their families or their careers. Their accounts demonstrate that choices are shaped and influenced by a myriad of factors including policies and practices as well as larger societal discourses. The discourses that the police officers are drawing on are constant and pervasive within society and not unique to the policing profession. They point to the idea that reproductive choice in contemporary society is much more varied and complex than first meets the eye.

## REFERENCES

Ashcraft, K., and Pacanowsky. 1996. "A woman's worst enemy": Reflections on a narrative of organizational life and female identity. *Journal of Applied Communication Research* 24, 217–39.

Baxter, L. A., and Montgomery, B. M. 1996. *Relating: Dialogues and dialectics*. New York: Guilford.

Beebe, S. A., Beebe, S. J., and Ivey, D. K. 2004. *Communication: Principles for a lifetime* (2nd ed.). Boston: Pearson.

Bochantin, J., and Cowan, R. L. 2008. On being "One of the Guys": How female police officers manage tensions and contradictions in their work and their lives. *Ohio Communication Journal* 46, 145–70.

Burrell, N. A., Buzzanell, P. M., & McMillan, J. J. 1992, November. Feminine tensions in conflict situations as revealed by metaphoric analyses. *Management Communication Quarterly* 6, 115–49.

Campbell, D., and Hernandez, R. 2006, September. IACP diversity coordinating panel, *Police Chief* 73.

Charmaz, K. 2000. Grounded theory: Objectivist and constructionist methods. In N. K. Denzin & Y. S. Lincoln (eds.), *Handbook of Qualitative Research*, 2nd ed. (pp. 509–35). Thousand Oaks, CA: Sage.

Clark, S. 2000. Work/family border theory: A new theory of work/family balance. *Human Relations* 53, 747–70.

Crittenden, A. 2001. *The price of motherhood: Why the most important job in the world is still the least valued*. New York: Henry Holt.

Equal Employment Opportunity Commission. 2008. Facts about pregnancy discrimination. Retrieved from http://www.eeoc.gov/facts/fs-preg.html.

Fairhurst, G. T., and Putnam, L. 2004. Organizations as discursive constructions. *Communication Theory* 14, 5–26.

Greenhaus, J. H., & Beutell, N. J. 1985. Sources of conflict between work and family roles. *Academy of Management Review* 10, 76–88.

Hays, S. 1996. *The Cultural Contradictions of Motherhood*. New Haven, CT: Yale University Press.

Hoffman, M. F., & Cowan, R. L. 2008. The meaning of work/life: A corporate ideology of work/life balance. *Communication Quarterly* 56, 227–46.

Horne, P. 2006. Policewomen: Their first century and new era. *Police Chief* 73, 1–10.

International Association of Chiefs of Police (IACP). 1998. The future of women in policing: Mandates for Action. Retrieved from http://www.theiacp.org/documents/index.cfm?fuseaction=document&document_type_id.

Kanter, R. M. 1977. *Work and family in the United States: A critical review and agenda for research and policy*. New York: Russell Sage.

Kirby, E., Golden, A., Medved, C., Jorgenson, J., & Buzzanell, P. 2003. An organizational communication challenge to the discourse of work and family research: From problematics to empowerment. In P. J. Kalbfleishch (ed.), *Communication Yearbook* 27 (pp. 1–43). Mahway, NJ: Lawrence Erlbaum.

Kruger, K. 2006, July. Pregnancy policy: Law and philosophy. *Police Chief* 73.

LeBeuf, M., and McLean, J. 1997. *Women in policing in Canada*. Ottawa: Canada Police College.

Lindlof, T. & Taylor, B. 2002. *Qualitative communication research methods*. 2nd ed. Thousand Oaks, CA: Sage.

Martin, D. 2004. Humor in middle management: Women negotiating the paradoxes of organizational life. *Journal of Applied Communication Research* 32, 147–70.

National Center for Women and Policing. 2002. *Men, women, and the police excessive force: A content of civil liability cases, sustained allegations, and citizen complaints*. Retrieved from http://www.womenandpolicing.org/publications.asp.

Price, B. 1996. *Female police offices in the United States. Policing in Central and Eastern Europe: Comparing Firsthand Knowledge with Experience from the West*. Slovenia: College of Police and Security Services.

Putnam, L. L. 1986. Contradictions and paradoxes in organizations. In L. Thayer (Ed.), *Organization-communication: Emerging perspectives I* (pp. 151–67). Norwood, NJ: Ablex.

Putnam, L., and Bochantin, J. 2009. Gendered Bodies: Negotiating Normalcy and Support. *Negotiations and Conflict Management Research* 2, 57–73.

Risher, J. 2006, August. Supervisory law basics for new chiefs and other supervisors. *Police Chief* 73.

Schutz, D. M. 2003. Women police chiefs: A statistical profile. *Police Quarterly* 6, 330–45.

Seo, M., Putnam, L. L., and Bartunek, J. M. 2004. Dualities and tensions of planned organizational change. In M. S. Poole (ed.) *Handbook of Organizational Change* (pp. 73–107). New York: Oxford University Press.

Stohl, C., and Cheney, G. 2001. Participatory practices/paradoxical practices: Communication and the dilemmas of organizational democracy. *Management Communication Quarterly* 14, 349–407.

Tracy, S. 2004. Dialectic, contradiction, or double bind? Analyzing and theorizing employee reactions to organizational tension. *Journal of Applied Communication Research* 32, 119–46.

Whetstone, T. S. 2001. Copping out: Why police officers decline to participate in the Sergeant's promotional process. *American Journal of Criminal Justice* 25, 147–59.

Willborn, S., Schwab, S., Burton, J., and Lester, G. 2007. "FMLA." *Employment law: Case and materials* (p. 434) Danvers, MA: LexisNexus.

Williams, J. 2000. *Unbending gender: Why family and work conflict and what to do about it.* New York: Oxford University Press.

Wolf, J. 2007. Is breast really best? Risk and total motherhood in the National Breast Feeding Awareness campaign. *Journal of Health Politics, Policy and Law* 32, 595–636.

Wood, J. T., and Conrad, C. 1983. Paradox in the experiences of professional women. *Western Journal of Speech Communication* 47, 305–22.

## NOTES

1. According to the 2008 National Law Enforcement Memorial Fund, approximately 140 police officers are killed each year while in the line of duty. That translates to a police officer being killed almost every forty-eight hours. Traffic accidents account for approximately 40 percent of deaths, while gun shot fatalities account for almost 25 percent. Ten percent of all fatalities in 2008 were female police officers, which was the highest percentage in history. Moreover, 80 percent of fatalities occur in major urban settings versus 20 percent in rural areas.

2. Although the focus of this study is on mothers, we questioned whether potential fathers might have similar experiences. Since men do not have the bodily changes/implications that go along with pregnancy, there is not the same physical risk to the unborn baby as for a female. Furthermore, because it is more culturally acceptable for men to work in dangerous professions and fulfill their role of "breadwinner" in the household division of labor, they probably do not contemplate the risk as much as females until perhaps after they have started a family or after an incident on the job. Future research should consider this.

3. The FMLA applies to organizations that have fifty or more employees. To be eligible for this benefit, an employ must have worked for the organization for a minimum of one year and have worked at least 1,250 hours during the twelve-month period.

4. The PDA is contained within Title VII of the Civil Rights Act of 1964 (42 U.S.C. § 2000e(k)).

# Section III

# Ongoing Choices

13

# PURPOSEFULLY CHILDLESS GOOD WOMEN

*Sara Hayden*[1]

In both North America and Europe, the number of women who define themselves as childless by choice[2] is on the rise (Delaney, 2007; Shorto, 2008, U.S. Census, 2008), yet in spite of this growing demographic, there remains a tendency to conflate the concept "woman" with "mother" (Burkett, 2000, Hayden, in press). This tendency is evidenced in the words of politicians who frame children's health, education, and other child-focused policies as "women's issues" (Pelosi, 2007; Vanden Heuvel, 2007; White House, p. 1). It can be found in the pages of women's magazines where readers are provided with a variety of parenting tips and other information designed to help navigate the waters of contemporary maternity (e.g., see www.womansday.com). Even feminist organizations sometimes conflate these concepts, couching policies aimed at helping "mothers" as necessary for the well-being of "women" (e.g., see www.iwpr.org).

Susan Douglas and Meredith Michaels (2004) argue that the conflation of "woman" with "mother" is part of the "new momism." Acknowledging that we live in an era of "choice," the new momism nonetheless maintains that "the only truly enlightened choice to make as a woman, the one that proves, first, that you are a 'real' woman, and second, that you are a decent, worthy, one, is to become a 'mom'" (p. 5). The "new momism" not only calls on women to become mothers, it calls on women to become mothers of a specific type. Anne Crittenden (2001) asserts "the very definition of a mother is selfless service to another" (p. 1). Douglas and Michaels echo this claim, maintaining that in the era of the "new momism," being a "good mom" involves "bring[ing] to child rearing a combination of selflessness and professionalism that would involve the cross cloning of Mother Teresa with Donna Shalala" (p. 5).

In contrast to "moms," women who are purposefully childless frequently are defined as *selfish.* Having chosen not to place their energies into raising a child, they are perceived as "unnatural" women, cold and self-absorbed (Safer, 1996, p. 18; also see Lisle, 1999; Morell, 1994). In the forward to *Childless by Choice: A Feminist Anthology*, Irene Reti (1992) addresses this charge head on. Reti maintains that the women whose work appears in the book have "a passionate desire to contribute to the world" (p. 2). As a result, she writes, "in the truest sense of the word the women in this book *are* selfish" (p. 2, emphasis in the original). They have put themselves—their talents, aspirations, and dreams first—thus enabling them to achieve their goals. Reti applauds these women for the courage they display; yet as Jly Lynn Felman (1992) suggests, such courage comes at a cost: "those of us who do not become mothers rarely have the clarity or sufficient ego to resist these negative stereotypes" (p. 80, also see Safer, 1996; Morell, 1994).

Women who are childless by choice thus face a bind. Through their reproductive choices they open up the potential to craft identities rooted in their individual talents and actions. In doing so, however, they simultaneously abdicate a key attribute of femininity, making it difficult to claim the mantle "good woman." In this chapter, I explore how a group of women have negotiated this bind. Based on interviews with twenty-four women who define themselves as childless by choice, I explore how these childless women navigate assumptions about femininity, selfishness, and selflessness as they craft their identities. In my explorations I follow poststructural theorists including Michel Foucault (1990) and Judith Butler (1990, 1997) who argue that identity is neither static nor essential but instead is performative. In other words, identity is not something that we *are*, it is entailed in what we *do*. This is not to suggest that we are the lone architects of our identities. To the contrary, our individual performances draw from already extant discursive fields; our actions are always reiterative, citing our own and others' past performances. Yet our behaviors are not wholly determined, either. There are ways that we can resist and/or recast the assumptions entailed in the discourses we cite (Butler, 1990, 1997; Weedon, 2004).

The citation of extant discourses was clearly evident in the words of the women with whom I spoke; moreover, their responses reflected both the cultural conflation of "good womanhood" with selfless maternity and the negative attributes associated with purposeful childlessness. As Felman

(1992) predicts, several of my interviewees referenced the negative attributes associated with nonmaternity without contest, reinforcing the harm such judgments confer. Others, however, challenged the negative stereotypes that accompanied their actions, expanding the potential for enacting "good womanhood" in contemporary culture.

## METHOD

The category "childless woman by choice" is fluid. For some women it may reflect a conscious decision not to have children; for others, it may be a label they adopt after finding that they were never in the right relationship and/or financial or emotional place to have a child. Women may assume the label at one point in their lives and later choose to become mothers; similarly, a woman may define herself as "childless by choice" in spite of the fact that she has step- or foster-children. Previous studies have imposed boundaries on this category by including only women who are of a certain age, married, and/or heterosexual, and with no legal maternal relationship to children (Morell, 1994; Park, 2005). Because I am interested in understanding the process through which women themselves craft identities as childless by choice, I did not impose these boundaries and instead opened my study to any woman who so defined herself.

To recruit volunteers, I posted fliers and sent email requests for participants to colleagues, family members, and friends. I interviewed women until I achieved the point of saturation (Strauss and Corbin, 1998). My interviewees were Caucasian women between thirty-one and fifty-four years of age.[3] The majority defined themselves as heterosexual, twelve of the twenty-four were married, and an additional five were in long-term relationships. Although the vast majority of the women had not engaged in any form of parenting, two of the twenty-four women self-identified as both "childless by choice" and as "stepmothers." Prior studies suggest that on average, childless women are better educated, less religious, and more liberal than their maternal peers (Park, 2005). These characteristics held true for the majority of my participants.

Interviews took place face-to-face, through email, and over the phone. Face-to-face interviews were conducted at a place of the participants' choosing—a coffee shop, my office, or the participant's home. At the start of each interview participants were asked to sign an Institutional Research Board (IRB) form and to complete a short demographic survey. The interviews were semistructured, providing for a level of consistency across the conversations while also allowing flexibility to explore issues of importance to the participants. Following is a sample of some of the questions asked:

- Is your status as a childfree/childless woman the result of a conscious choice, a consequence of other choices, or something in-between?
- Have you ever felt pressured to have children?
- Have you ever been asked to explain your choice not to have children?
- Are there advantages/disadvantages to being childless/childfree that you've experienced?

All interviews excluding those conducted over email were audiotaped and transcribed by the author. Interviews lasted an average of twenty-five minutes yielding 132 pages of single-spaced text. Themes were developed using grounded theory (Strauss and Corbin, 1998).

## RESULTS AND INTERPRETATIONS

### Confronting the Charge of Selfishness

> In contemporary culture women who are not mothers are often portrayed by the media or in the movies as damaged or deviant. . . . Such attitudes can make us feel that we are "just not *nice enough*," as a childless wife admitted to me."
>
> —Lisle, 1999, p. 107 (emphasis in the original)

Like the childless wife referenced by Lisle, the majority of the women with whom I spoke indicated that their decisions not to become mothers caused them to feel different from other women—often out-of-place, abnormal, and deficient. Christina[4] observed "Our culture is built up around the nuclear family, where the mother, the father, and the kids is the ideal, and if you're not part of that dream, then you're left out. . . . You know, it just feels that I'm outside the pale, like I don't compute." Cassidy similarly reflected that "much of our culture is predicated on the notion of the traditional family," and as a result, she claimed, "I've often been made to feel odd or lacking."

Several women recalled specific instances in which their childlessness led others to judge them negatively, and as suggested above, one of the most common and hurtful judgments directed against these women was that they were "selfish." Rose, for example, recalled a coworker who gave her "the absolute third degree on why I don't have a child":

> And I said, "Well, for one I'm not married." "Well, but don't you still really just want to have a child? "No" (laughing). "Well, what if you meet the man of your dreams, wouldn't you want to have his child?" "No!" "Well don't you think you're *selfish*?" And that's always a fun one. "Don't you think you're being awfully *selfish*?" (emphasis hers)

Likewise, Eleanor recounted instances when she told people that her life was fulfilling as it was. "People normally think this is a selfish sort of attitude on my part," she said. "Some women my age told me clearly that they thought I was a heartless monster."

My interviewees' responses to the charge of selfishness were mixed. As mentioned, some accepted the charge, reinforcing the negative judgment as they explained their actions. For example, when I asked her to talk about her choice not to have children, Wendy sighed and replied "it could be something that I could add to my life but I feel like, that I may not be, I don't know, that maybe I'm too self-centered, you know?" Molly, who as a younger women was a professional dancer, discussed her own and her peers' nonmaternity in similar terms:

> I spent a lot of time in Europe but you didn't see a lot of moms, you know, people doing the dancing and then taking care of their babies. I mean it was really sort of a single, ambitious, a lot of single ambitious people. We were just kind of, you know, we were very selfish, self-absorbed. . . . You know I feel very selfish and, you know, like not continuing the family stuff.

As a professional dancer, Molly contributed to the world through her unique talents and abilities. However, Molly's decision to prioritize her art was paired with a choice not to have children, and when reflecting on her past she did not focus on *what she had contributed through dance* but instead framed her behaviors in terms of *what she did not do*. Reflecting the cultural norm that good womanhood is marked by selfless maternity, Molly defined her behaviors as self-absorbed.

Now in her forties, Molly remains conflicted about her past life and prior decisions, telling me "I have a lot of shame, I think, living the lifestyle that I've lived, very self-oriented, you know, I'm still not comfortable with it. I have shame around that." Over the past several years, one of the ways Molly allayed her shame was by assuming the role of stepmother to her partner's three daughters. The title, she told me, made her feel like she was "more mainstream" and a "little bit more at service." In particular, she indicated that she enjoyed the small, daily activities that her relationship with her partner's children entailed, such as picking up one daughter from swim team: "I was really into it because suddenly I had a regular errand to do . . . it felt more valid to, swim team felt really comfortable to me because I, *I really had to be there*. And it was really mainstream. All the other mothers were doing it and I was doing it too" (emphasis hers). Thus not only did Molly reiterate the definition of childless women as selfish through her discussion of her past, she augmented that definition through a comparison to her more recent enactment of stepmotherhood. Like the "other mothers" she was being "of service," a frame that reinforces the cultural assumption that good women are mothers whose behaviors are directed toward others' well-being.[5]

Following Althusser, Butler (1990, 1997) argues that we are interpolated as subjects of a certain kind. We are named, and the names we are called to enact reflect already extant value judgments and behavioral norms. The power of interpellation is profound, so much so that we often answer the interpolative call even if doing so contributes to our oppression and perpetuates our pain. Butler (1997) writes:

> There is no way to protect against that primary vulnerability and susceptibility to the call of recognition that solicits existence, to that primary dependency on a language we never made in order to acquire a tentative ontological status. Thus we sometimes cling to the terms that pain us because, at a minimum, they offer us some form of social and discursive existence. (p. 26)

Yet as powerful as interpellation may be, being called to assume a subject position of a certain type does not *necessitate* that we will accept the *form* of that call. Indeed, it is the citational nature of discourse that creates the potential for resistance. As Sine Nørholm Just (2006) maintains: "the very fact that it is necessary for norms to be reiterated or cited by individuals in order for them to maintain their efficacy indicates that we are never completely determined by them" (p. 116).

Referring to childless women as selfish is an act of interpellation that harms those who, like Wendy and Molly, answer the call without contest. As I discuss next, however, theirs was not the only response. Other women with whom I spoke made efforts to resist the negative assumptions entailed in dominant definitions of purposeful childlessness, engaging a variety of strategies to craft identities as "good women" who chose not to have and/or raise children. The implications of their efforts were mixed, reflecting the complex and subtle processes through which language both liberates and constrains.

## Reversing the Dominant Discourse of Maternity

> Given that selfishness is a term inextricably bound up in the childfree debate, it's odd that those who don't want children often feel more responsible for the world we'll leave behind us than those who do.
>
> —Defago, 2005, p. 95

In *The History of Sexuality: An Introduction*, Michel Foucault (1990) argues that discourses can be simultaneously liberating and oppressive. He maintains "we must make allowance for the complex and unstable process whereby discourse can be both an instrument and an effect of power, but also a hindrance, a stumbling block, a resistance, and a starting point for an opposing strategy (pp. 100–1). Several of my interviewees employed this discursive flexibility in order to defy the charge of selfishness, appropriating the positively valued terms they are denied to frame their own actions while simultaneously raising questions about others' behaviors. Heather, for example, told me that in response to her parents' queries, she periodically reminds them that she does not plan to have children. "Sometimes I have a feeling that they probably think I'm being selfish, but I don't think I'm being selfish," she said. "You know, I think it's more selfish to, you know, give into those societal whims and to try and find some sort of fulfillment with that. There are a lot of environmental reasons for not having children. I kind of buy into those a little bit myself." Like Heather, Anna argued:

> If you choose to be childfree, somehow it's a selfish decision. And I don't get that at all. I see it as the opposite. To me it's more selfish to have a brood of children and put more pressure on a planet that's already kind of to the max as far as resources are concerned.

Thus rather than accepting the selfish label, in the statements above, Heather and Anna *reversed the charge*, arguing that their actions were driven by concern for the planet. At the same time, they suggested that those mothers who gave into "societal whims" or who failed to consider the environmental impact of their behaviors are the ones who behave selfishly.

Heather and Anna were not alone in their efforts to reverse the charge of selfishness. Mary similarly suggested that her decision was made carefully and deliberately as opposed to "those parents" who gave into "outside pressure." Mary defined herself as someone who "really thought, sat and thought about what would be best for them as well as their, it sounds weird, but as well as for their children":

> Like, if you didn't think you were, it's such a huge commitment, if you didn't think you were the right person for it, then you made the right choice for that child to not have that child.

In this particularly interesting reversal, Mary not only suggests that her decision not to have children was based in other-oriented concerns, she suggests that her *potential children* were the *source* of those concerns. Cassidy made a similar point, telling me that she and her partner

> earn modest incomes and live frugally, and would have been pressed to afford a child. We live in a city with poor public schools and could not have afforded private tuition. We've also had some difficult financial periods, and could never have asked children to sacrifice as we've had to at times.

Thus whether focusing on environmental or financial concerns, the women cited above challenged the notion that their actions were self-centered, instead suggesting that their behaviors were designed to avoid harm to the planet or to their potential children. Unlike Wendy and Molly, then, these women were able to protect themselves from the pain that accompanies internalizing a negatively valued subject position. Indeed, by framing their decisions in other-oriented terms, they assumed attributes that are linked to dominant constructions of "good womanhood."

Reversing charges may provide relief for those employing the strategy; nonetheless, as several scholars have argued, it is a strategy with limitations. Karlyn Kohrs Campbell (1999) maintains that reversals do not provide new roles, "just versions of the old ones. They do not provide new identities" (p. 141). Catherine Pelissier Kingfisher (1996) makes a similar point in a study of mothers living on welfare. Kingfisher observes that the women with whom she spoke consistently resisted definitions of self as *welfare* mothers—women lacking in self-sufficiency, responsibility, and individual drive—and instead embraced definitions as welfare *mothers*—women who were responsible for the well-being of their children (p. 536). Kingfisher acknowledges that this act of reversal enabled the women to resist "imputations of laziness"; however she argues that in doing so, they simultaneously embraced a hegemonic construction of maternity and a work ethic that have functioned as forms of social control. "In using such strategies of resistance," Kingfisher writes, "the women in effect reproduce the dominant discourses of motherhood and work, both of which are constitutive of an oppressive social order" (p. 538).

Like the welfare mothers discussed by Kingfisher, when they insisted that they were not *selfish* and instead cast their actions as *other-oriented*, Heather, Anna, Mary, and Cassidy each suggested that their behaviors were in line with dominant discourses of "good womanhood." Importantly, though, the "good womanhood" they invoked is part of a social order that shunts women into meeting others' needs and desires at the expense of their own. Moreover, in discussing their actions, Heather, Anna, and Mary implicitly cast aspersions on *mothers*, implying that unlike themselves, some women with children have not considered carefully the implications of their actions. As such, they reinforce a binary construction whereby women are judged either "good" or "bad" as a result of their reproductive choices, participating in what might be understood as a "new" version of the so-called mommy wars wherein women are pitted against other women (Dunteman, 2006). On its own, then, reversing charges may be useful for assuaging one's own pain and guilt in the face of negative value judgments; however, in the process it serves to enact yet another oppressive construction of the "good woman."

## Echoes of the Second Wave

### *The Demand for Choice*

> Why become pregnant? Why have a child? We as women are talking about having versus not having children. Some of us feel strongly that there are no good reasons for having children. Some feel it's self-indulgent for us to have our own children but all right to adopt children who need homes. And some believe that giving birth to and rearing our own children can be a creative, even revolutionary act.
>
> —The Boston Women's Health Course Collective, 1971, p. 74

Above I have argued that the discursive construction that links "good womanhood" to "selfless maternity" holds a central position in contemporary culture. However, it is far from the only discursive construction surrounding maternity. As Chris Weedon (2004) observes, "discursive fields, which produce meanings and subjectivities, are not homogenous. They include discourses and discursive practices which may be contradictory and conflicting and which create the space for new forms of knowledge and practice" (p. 19). The writings of white second wave feminists provide a particularly significant source for alternative discourses of maternity for the women I interviewed. Indeed, largely due to feminist efforts and as explored throughout the chapters in this book, at the same time that we live in an era of the "new momism," so too do we live in an era of choice.

The demand for "choice" was first articulated as part of the 1970s abortion debate. Feminists insisted that women had a right to control their reproduction through the use of birth control, and if that was unavailable, unused, or otherwise failed, they had the right to safe and legal abortion. Although it has evolved over the years, the demand for choice remains a potent part of contemporary discourses, challenging the central role of maternity in women's lives (Hayden, 2009).

Importantly, however, while white second wave feminists insisted on reproductive control, they did not necessarily *advocate* childlessness. Indeed, Snitow (1992) argues that second wave feminists "set out to break these narrative taboos—those surrounding the mothers and the non-mothers—but for a variety of reasons we were better able to attend to mothers' voices than to imagine a full life without motherhood" (p. 5). Thus the quotation from the Boston Women's Health Course Collection that initiates this section is an early, direct, but *rare* second wave challenge to the inevitability of motherhood. Faced with a backlash against feminisms, by the 1980s, contemplations of nonmaternity were seldom voiced in feminist texts (Snitow, pp. 9–10).

Yet of course, childlessness is one potential outcome of the demand for choice, and although feminists may have shied away from discussing this outcome, some of my interviewees intimated that at least in part, their decisions to forego maternity grew out of second wave feminist discourses. For example, Barbara told me that she was "happy to see that people's choices in general seem to be becoming more accepted." She continued:

> I don't feel like there's much pressure on me, or the next generation, particularly of women, to you know, produce kids, or to be married, or any of that, to be even heterosexual. I think we're moving in the right direction in terms of . . . the idea that a woman stops and thinks, "do I want children?" as opposed to when my mother [was of childbearing age].

Barbara reflected on this generational shift in discourse, noting that while her mother believed that having children was "just the thing to do . . . at least for myself, I didn't feel that I had to [have children] and it was my choice. And I think most women my age and younger also feel it's their choice, although not always, but by and large." In her early fifties, Barbara came of age when second wave feminism was at its peak. Her appreciation for the fact that she has more reproductive options than her mother as well as her specific repetition of the word "choice" suggest that she has *internalized* and *extended* the feminist discourse that surrounded her.

Rose similarly echoed the discourse of choice when she reflected on the coworker who accused her of being selfish: "I don't like to think of it that way because I don't think it's, it's not a selfish thing to have babies, it's not necessarily a selfish thing not to. It's just a choice. It's a simple choice."

At the core of the demand for choice is the recognition that reproductive freedom is essential to women's autonomy (Rosen, 2000). Echoing this principle and in direct contrast to those women who implicitly question the actions of some mothers, Rose resists *any* effort to judge women's reproductive decisions whatever they may be.

Jill was more direct than either Barbara or Rose, specifically attributing her decision not to have children to feminism:

> I'm extremely glad I grew up at a time when feminism was so strong and positive; I even felt like my choice to become a nun could be an expression of positive feminism.[6] . . . I'm awfully glad to have no children, and I have many friends of my age and younger who have not had them and who do not plan to have any.

Thus as demonstrated in the words of Barbara, Rose, and Jill, although feminist scholars and activists may not have emphasized childlessness as one of the opportunities made possible through reproductive control, others extrapolated from the call for choice to craft a space where nonmaternity was a legitimate option.

***Challenging the Institution of Motherhood*** White second wave feminists not only insisted that women have the right to choose, they also challenged the hegemonic construction of maternity (Rosen, 2000). Adrienne Rich's (1976) *Of Woman Born* is perhaps the most influential early publication that questioned motherhood as constructed in patriarchal societies. When embraced and enacted, Rich argues, the role of mother is often "painful and incomprehensible" (p. xvii), precluding a woman from developing herself:

> Typically under patriarchy, the mother's life is exchanged for the child; her autonomy as a separate being seems fated to conflict with the infant she will bear. The self-denying, self-annihilative role of the Good Mother (lined implicitly with suffering and with the repression of anger) will spell the "death"

> of the woman or girl who once had hopes, expectations, fantasies *for herself*. (p. 161, emphasis in the original)

As others did with the call for choice, several of my interviewees echoed Rich's critique as they reflected on their decisions not to bear or raise children. Sonia, for example, noted that she grew up in a "really traditional household" where motherhood "*was* the role for women" (emphasis hers):

> And just growing up that way and watching my mother, she seemed depressed a lot. And I was the youngest and when I was an adolescent she got a job outside of the home and then she seemed happier and she was much more fun to be around. So when I thought that was going to happen, I found it depressing. . . . And as I got older and matured, I decided definitely I didn't want to do it [become a mother].

Christina offered a similar reflection:

> When I was a little girl I always thought I would have children, but I also looked around and saw how exhausted they made parents, like my mother was always exhausted by us. . . . And then my girlfriends started having kids and they didn't have their own life, their whole life was subordinated to their kids and their marriages too. . . . I didn't want to give up my whole identity like that.

Thus echoing Rich's insights, both Sonia and Christina perceived maternity as a negative role, wholly other-oriented and leading to depression and exhaustion. Stemming from that perception, they chose to forego motherhood in their own lives.

Importantly, Rich is careful to distinguish the *institution* of motherhood from the *potential* entailed in mothering. Whereas Rich argues that the former is profoundly oppressive, she insists that the latter presents significant opportunities for women to express creativity and to experience joy. At the same time, Rich acknowledges that it is difficult for most women to recognize this distinction:

> The twentieth-century, educated young woman, looking perhaps at her mother's life, or trying to create an autonomous self in a society which insists that she is destined primarily for reproduction, has with good reason felt that the choice was an inescapable either/or: motherhood or individuation, motherhood or creativity, motherhood or freedom. (p. 154)

Like the women Rich observed, the women quoted above did not distinguish between motherhood as an institution and motherhood's potential; as such, they were unable to envision a route to a liberated and empowered mothering in their own lives.[7]

***Putting Themselves First*** White second wave feminists' critiques of motherhood were not limited to negative assessments of the maternal role. Rather, along with these critiques came a positive call for greater options for women. In *The Feminine Mystique*, for example, Betty Friedan (1963) both points to the limitations of women's traditional roles and she also insists that women have the right to consider their own wants, needs, and desires; to put themselves first. The women with whom I spoke embraced the opportunities and pleasures that resulted from Friedan's and other second wave feminists' efforts. Indeed, although they had widely varied experiences, attitudes, and opinions, when I asked whether there were advantages associated with purposeful childlessness, each woman answered with a resounding "yes." To a person, they recognized and appreciated their ability to focus on themselves, to meet their individual needs, to follow their dreams and desires.

For example, Jill told me: "I consider not having children the single wisest decision I made for my life. I have had an extraordinary life, traveled the world, studied at elite universities." Rose similarly reflected on "the choices I've been able to make:"

> I've been invited to Europe. Okay. Wrangle around a little bit, get the money and go. Okay. That was pretty easy. Get invited to go to Japan. Okay. I'll go to Japan. Get invited to go and work in Seattle for three months. Okay. I'll go.

Other women focused on how their childless status enabled them to develop their careers. An academic, Elaine talked about periods of time when she worked "very, very long hours." She continued:

> I've gone on research trips that have required me to be away from home anywhere from like one week to eight weeks at a time. I think being without child made those hours and trips, if not made them possible, it certainly made them easier to undertake.

Heather, a university librarian, similarly talked about her childfree status as a boon to her career. She noted that from the time she was a young girl her parents encouraged her to put her professional aspirations first:

> Both my parents, once they realized I wanted to go to school and have a professional career, whatever form it took, they were constantly guiding me into, you know, "Don't get pregnant before you're ready." Or "Don't get pregnant at all," practically.

Heather followed her parents' advice and claims "Now that I'm in the career path that I'm in, I don't have time for a child."

Whereas Jill, Rose, Heather, and Elaine focused on major life events, other women highlighted the small, daily freedoms that childlessness allows. Leslie noted that she can "be spontaneous, I can stay up late and read, I can sleep late. I'm untethered." Sharon pointed out "you get to go work out and not have to worry about coming home and making dinner. You can set your own agenda." Anna told me "if I get up tomorrow morning and decide I want to take the dogs for a two-hour hike, I can do that. I don't have to think about, well, I'll have to arrange to get somebody to get the kids on the bus." Thus whether focusing on major life events or small, daily freedoms, the women discussed above engaged the space created by feminist discourses, considering their own interests, needs, and desires as they made decisions in their lives. Moreover, they made clear that these actions led to profound personal satisfactions.

Of course, the feminist discourse that insists women have the right to put themselves first stands in direct opposition to dominant discourses that link good womanhood to selfless maternity. By prioritizing personal fulfillment, then, these women open themselves up to accusations of selfishness. Yet as Weedon (2004) observes, it is the tensions between contradictory and conflicting discourses which "create the space for new forms of knowledge and practice" (p. 19). As I discuss next, several of my interviewees engaged the tensions between feminist and dominant discourses. By framing their actions as neither wholly self- nor other-oriented, they offered new ways to enact "good womanhood" at the same time that they promoted a different kind of "good society."

## Purposefully Childless Good Women

In her influential article on second wave feminist rhetoric, Campbell (1973) observed the disparate criteria men and women needed to meet in order to be considered successful. "Success for men," she wrote, "is defined as instrumental, productive labor in the outside world whereas 'wives' are confined to 'woman's place'—child care and domestic labor in the home" (p. 77). More than thirty years later, and as discussed throughout this chapter, "good womanhood" continues to be linked to the domestic sphere generally and to selfless maternity specifically. Importantly, however, domesticity is no longer the *only* attribute associated with "good womanhood." As Julia Wood (2008) argues, growing up feminine in the contemporary United States means, in part, being called to become "superwomen." In addition to being good wives and mothers, women are simultaneously expected to achieve public success. The superwoman persona is yet another oppressive role for women, a perversion of feminist arguments and demands (Rosen, 2000). Nonetheless, as evidenced by many of my interviewees, the fact that "good womanhood" is linked at least *in part* to public success provides important discursive material from which purposefully childless women can draw.

For example, Elizabeth, a judge, considered what her life might have been like had she chosen to have a child: " It's hard to imagine, you know . . . I can't imagine it because work has always been such a *huge, huge* part of my life. Having a career, you know, making a contribution to society as a whole" (emphasis hers). Thus for Elizabeth, career precluded bearing or raising children; in fact, her professional life is so central to her identity she cannot even *imagine* having a child. Importantly, however, at the same time that Elizabeth discussed her work as central to her sense of self, she simultaneously called attention to what work enables her to *give*, emphasizing that "having a career" enables her to make "a contribution to society as a whole." In this way, Elizabeth echoes the women who reversed the charge of selfishness by framing their nonmaternity as other-oriented. Like these women, she suggests that although her actions are not focused on her children, they nonetheless serve the greater good. Yet *unlike* the women who framed their reproductive choices *only* in terms of what it enabled them to give, Elizabeth also acknowledges that she is proud of what she does and that she enjoys the status her work confers. "I've always wanted to be my own boss and, you know, run the show," she said, "and for all intents and purposes I do. So, that's great." Moreover, when reflecting on her life in general she told me that the slogan "work real hard, play real hard" captures her approach. "I like that. I think that's a good philosophy for me. I have a great lifestyle. I'm not hampered by having to put a little person's needs above my own." Thus Elizabeth *both* embraces the pleasures and status that come from pursuing her own goals and interests *and* she emphasizes what such pursuits enable her to give to others.

Several of my interviewees referenced their careers in similar terms, suggesting that their work provides pride of accomplishment and a positive sense of self while also enabling them to contribute to others. Moreover, some of my interviewees drew explicit comparisons between their actions and maternal behaviors. Elaine, for example, noted that she chose a "career path that is not particularly conducive to pregnancy and childbirth as well as actually raising a child," yet she compares the contributions she makes through her work to mothers' contributions to their children: "I'm a teacher and I feel like I'm getting my, you know, if there's some kind of need to pass on knowledge or values to another generation, I get plenty of that at work. I don't need to do it in my personal life." Heather also reflected on what her career enables her to give while acknowledging the pleasure she receives from the contributions she makes. After telling me that she didn't "have time for a child" she continued: "You know, I feel that what I'm doing with my career, I feel like I'm touching lots of young people, people's lives, and helping them, and that makes me really happy." Although Heather indicated that she couldn't "really associate this to motherhood or maternal feelings" she suggested that "one way to look at it would be that I'm helping to raise lots of people's kids even though they're like eighteen to twenty-one. The work I do is very satisfying to me in that regard."

It was not only their careers that enabled my interviewees to give to others. Emily, for example, indicated that her flexibility and freedom as a childless woman enabled her to help her siblings, and like others, she indicated that the gift she gave was a source of personal pleasure. When her four nieces and nephews were growing up, she said, she "would take vacations and take care of them while their parents would take a vacation. And I thoroughly enjoyed that." In a like fashion, Joan talked about how childlessness enabled her and her husband to pursue interests including camping, traveling, and entertaining and she reflected on how they were able to share those experiences with their friends' children:

> We like spending time with them. We hope that we can show them a different side of life that maybe their parents don't. We are a little more free-spirited simply because we . . . both have a lot of freedom. We participate in different sports and activities than their parents do. And so, we hope to be able to bring those adventures to our friends' children. And we revel in it. We love their kids.

Thus whether through their leisure activities or their careers, the women discussed above have followed their own interests and desires; however, they insist that by developing themselves, they simultaneously contribute to others. As such these women reject the simplistic assumption that behaviors are either selfless or selfish, drawing a more complicated picture of the motivations that drive their behaviors and the satisfactions they receive as a result. In doing so, they present themselves as purposefully childless good women, people who meet their own needs, interests, and desires while also making significant contributions to the world.

## Caregiving in a Good Society

The women I interviewed not only crafted space through which they could claim the mantle "good women" for themselves, by comparing their actions specifically to maternal behaviors, several of these women participated in the expansion of the framework through which *childrearing* is understood. Again, while these women may not be mothers, several of them nonetheless insisted that they helped to raise children, whether by "passing down knowledge and values" or by exposing children to a broader set of behaviors and activities. As such, they imply that the responsibility for raising children does not lie solely with individual mothers and instead is something we all share.

Indeed, several of my interviewees explicitly addressed this point, insisting that raising children necessarily is a community responsibility. Barbara asserted "it's our duty as a society to support good parenting and children in general" and Ruth, a member of a city council, talked about how she worked to "take children's interests to the forefront, not as a political move but because I *am* interested in kids. . . . I don't want to have kids hanging around and I don't particularly enjoy them to play with, but I really care about them, about their education and welfare, which are totally different things." Elizabeth similarly reflected "you know, when you think about it, as a society we all help to raise children in our own way, whether I allow it as an employer at work and kind of take a little bit of lack of productivity or if I just decide that I'm Aunty Elizabeth and I'm going down to see [my nephew] and I'm going to miss four days of work."

The discursive construction that calls on women to enact selfless maternity grew out of a social system based in separate spheres: the public sphere, where supposedly independent (male) workers earned wealth and acclaim through the application of their individual talents and efforts, and the private sphere, where supposedly dependent (female) caregivers supported and cared for others, their work unseen and unpaid (Tronto, 1994). The past several decades have seen a shift in this social system as women have joined the paid labor force in ever increasing numbers. However, women's entry into the public world of wage labor has not been accompanied by a corresponding shift in how caregiving activities are addressed (Rosen, 2007; Williams, 2000). The care of children—as well as the elderly and the infirm—continues to be based largely in the private sphere and women continue to be expected to provide this care. This, in turn, perpetuates the oppressive institution of motherhood as first identified by Rich (1976).

The childless women discussed above call this system into question. They are women who insist on the right to participate in the public sphere without tending to the private caregiving needs of children in the home; however, they do not neglect the call to care for others in toto. Negotiating the borders of dominant discourses that call on women to serve others as well as feminist discourses that insist women must be allowed to develop themselves, these women pursue their interests and goals while simultaneously recognizing and meeting their responsibilities to the community at large—part of which includes attending to the welfare of the community's children. Tacitly recognizing the lack of public support that contributes to the construction of motherhood as an oppressive institution, these women suggest that "good women" can and should consider their personal interests, needs, and desires, and they suggest that a "good society" is one in which all adults help support and raise children.

Importantly, then, my interviewees' discursive negotiations have implications not only for childless women but for mothers, too. In the discursive constructions articulated by these childless women, mothers are no longer called on to serve as the sole, selfless caretakers of their children. When caring for children is framed as a societal responsibility, others, including childless women, fathers, and childless men, are called on to participate in caregiving activities. This, in turn, opens up time and space for mothers to pursue some of their nonmaternal interests and goals. The move toward greater community responsibility for childcare echoes a practice that has long been a part of African American communities. Referred to as "other mothering" or "community mothering," many contemporary feminist maternal scholars see such practices as crucial strategies of resistance to the "new momism" (Collins, 1991; O'Brien Hallstein, 2010).

Simultaneously, through their discursive negotiations, the childless women I interviewed extend and complicate the call for choice. Not only do they insist that choice must include the opportunity not to mother; they simultaneously resist the neoliberal framing of reproduction and childrearing as wholly personal (Vavrus, 2007). As articulated by several of my interviewees, although reproductive choices are individual, the responsibility for caring for children and other vulnerable members of society must be shared. As constructed by these childless women, then, a good society is one in which all of us—mothers, fathers, and the childless by choice—have opportunities to develop ourselves while also meeting our responsibilities to care for children and the world at large.

## CONCLUSION

In contemporary Western cultures, maternity is considered central to womanhood; as such, women who are childless by choice must struggle to craft their identities. Accused of being "unnatural women," selfish and self-absorbed, the purposefully childless can either accept such accusations or they can fight back. In this chapter, I have examined how twenty-four childless women have met this challenge. Their responses varied widely, reflecting the complex and nuanced processes through which we *all* struggle to enact identities in the context of oppressive social systems and through discursive constructions that both liberate and constrain.

As Felman (1992) suggests, the negative discourses surrounding childless woman have a powerful hold on those of us who have assumed this subject position. It is not surprising, then, that some of the women with whom I spoke internalized and reinforced the negative attributes associated with purposeful childlessness. Others, however, resisted such judgments. Whether by reversing charges, by referencing alternative discourses, or by negotiating the borders between dominant and alternative discourses, these women illustrate the multiple, creative, and often subtle means through which we can resist and challenge oppressive discourses. Like the strategies themselves, the implications of these acts of resistance were multiple. Some strategies provided relief for those employing them while simultaneously reinforcing parts of the oppressive social order they were struggling against. Other strategies had greater potential to provide broader liberation. Seen as a whole, the efforts of these childless women offer important lessons to us all as we pursue our personal goals and desires while also meeting our responsibilities to our planet and to one another.

## REFERENCES

Boston Women's Health Course Collective. 1971. *Our bodies, ourselves*. Boston: New England Free Press.

Burkett, E. 2000. *The baby boon: How family-friendly America cheats the childless*. New York: Free Press.

Butler, J. 1990. *Gender trouble: Feminism and the subversion of identity*. New York: Routledge.

Butler, J. 1997. *Excitable speech: A politics of the performative*. New York: Routledge.

Campbell, K. K. 1973. The rhetoric of women's liberation: An oxymoron. *Quarterly Journal of Speech* 59, 74–86.

Campbell, K. K. 1999. "The rhetoric of women's liberation: An oxymoron" revisited. *Communication Studies* 50, 138–42.

Collins, P. H. 1991. *Black feminist thought: Knowledge, consciousness, and the politics of empowerment*. New York: Routledge.

Crittenden, A. 2001. *The price of motherhood: Why the most important job in the world is still the least valued.* New York: Henry Holt.

Defago, N. 2005. *Childfree and loving it!* London: Fusion Press.

Delaney, J. 2007, October 18–24. Global shrinking birth rates reaching crisis levels in some countries. *Epoch Times*, A4.

Douglas, S. J. and Michaels, M. W. 2004. *The mommy myth: The idealization of motherhood and how it has undermined women.* New York: Free Press.

Dunteman, D. 2006, October. Women vs. women. *Sacramento*, 184–95.

Felman, J. L. 1992. Meditation for my sisters: On choosing not to have children. In I. Reti *Childless by choice: A feminist anthology*. Santa Cruz, CA: Her Books.

Foucault, M. 1990. *The history of sexuality: An introduction*. New York: Vintage Books.

Friedan, B. 1963. *The feminine mystique*. New York: Dell.

Hayden, S. (in press). Lessons from *The Baby Boon*: "Family-friendly" policies and the ethics of justice and care. *Women's Studies in Communication*.

Hayden, S. 2009. Revitalizing the debate between "life" and "choice": The 2004 March for Women's Lives. *Communication and Critical/Cultural Studies* 6, 111–31.

hooks, B. 1984. *Feminist theory: From margin to center*. Boston: South End Press.

Just, S. N. 2006. Embattled agencies—How mass mediated comparisons of Lynndie England and Jessica Lynch affect the identity positions available to female soldiers in the U.S. army. *Scandinavian Journal of Management* 22, 99–119.

Kingfisher, C. P. 1996. Women on welfare: Conversational sites of acquiescence and dissent. *Discourse & Society* 7, 531–57.

Lisle, L. 1996. *Without child: Challenging the stigma of childlessness*. New York: Ballantine.

Morell, C. M. 1994. *Unwomanly conduct: The challenges of intentional childlessness*. New York: Routledge.

O'Brien Hallstein, L. D. 2010. *Contemporary white feminisms and maternity*. New York: Palgrave Macmillan.

Park, K. 2005. Choosing childlessness: Weber's typology of action and motives of the voluntarily childless. *Sociological Inquiry* 75, 372–402.

Pelosi, N. 2007, May 11. As a mother. *Huffington Post*. Retrieved from www.huffingtonpost.com/rep-nancy-pelosi/as-a-mother_b_48254.html.

Reti, I. 1992. Introduction. In I. Reti *Childless by choice: A feminist anthology*. Santa Cruz, CA: Her Books.

Rich, A. 1976. *Of woman born: Motherhood as experience and institution*. New York: Bantam.

Rosen, R. 2000. *The world split open: How the modern women's movement changed America*. New York: Penguin.
Rosen, R. 2007, March 12. The Care Crisis. *Nation*. Retrieved from http://www.thenation.com/doc/20070312/rosen.
Safer, J. 1996. *Beyond motherhood: Choosing a life without children*. New York: Pocket Books.
Shorto, R. 2008, June 29. No babies? *New York Times Magazine*. Retrieved from http://www.nytimes.com/2008/06/29/magazine/29Birth-t.html.
Snitow, A. 1992. Motherhood: Reclaiming the demon texts. In I. Reti *Childless by choice: A feminist anthology*. Santa Cruz, CA: Her Books.
Strauss, A. and Corbin, J. 1998. *Basics of qualitative research*. Thousand Oaks, CA: Sage.
Tronto, J. C. 1994. *Moral boundaries: A political argument for an ethic of care*. New York: Routledge.
U.S. Census Bureau. August 2008. *Fertility of American women: 2006*. Washington, DC: U.S. Department of Commerce.
Vanden Heuvel, K. 2007, January 7. Pelosi—mother, grandmother, speaker. *Nation*. Retrieved from http://www.thenation.com/blogs/edcut/155266/.
Vavrus, M. D. 2007. Opting out moms in the news. *Feminist Media Studies* 7, 47–63.
Weedon, C. 2004. *Culture and identity: Narratives of difference and belonging*. Berkshire, GBR: McGraw-Hill Education.
White House. The agenda—Women. Retrieved January 28, 2009 from http://www.whitehouse.gov/agenda/women/.
Williams, J. 2000. *Unbending gender: Why family and work conflict and what to do about it*. New York: Oxford University Press.
Wood, J. T. 2008. *Gendered lives: Communication, gender, and culture* (8th ed.). Belmont, CA: Wadsworth.

## NOTES

1. Many thanks to the twenty-four women whose stories make up the data for this chapter.

2. The question of what to call women who have chosen to forego motherhood is a difficult one. Some activists for people without children prefer "childfree" to "childless," arguing that the latter term implies a loss or lack. Others resist the term "childfree" as too glib (Lisle, 1999; Safer, 1996). In this chapter, I seek to respect the preferences of my interviewees, using the woman's term of choice when possible and using the term "childless" when discussing women without children generally.

3. The racial homogeneity of my interviewees reflects the communities of women to which I had access and does not imply that childlessness is primarily a

choice made only or even primarily by white women. To the contrary, according to the U.S. Census, approximately 16 percent of black women, 18 percent of Asian women, and 14 percent of Hispanic women between the ages of forty and forty-four were childless in 2006. This compares to approximately 22 percent of white women of the same age (U.S. Census Bureau, 2008). Feminist scholars have argued decisively that women of different races experience mothering in unique ways. In particular, white feminists have critiqued the institution of motherhood as oppressive, and as I argue later in the chapter, some of my interviewees refer to the idea of oppressive motherhood when they discuss their decisions to remain childless. African American feminists, on the other hand, have argued that motherhood has not traditionally been an obstacle to African-American women's freedom (hooks, 1984). As such, my discussions in this chapter likely do not have parallels in the lives of African American women and additional research that explores the specific experiences of women of different racial backgrounds is warranted.

4. Names have been changed for the sake of anonymity.

5. The phrase "other mothers" is Molly's and is not meant to invoke the concept of "Other-mothering" which Patricia Hill Collins (1991) argues is common in the African American community.

6. Jill later came to see the church as "woman-oppressing" and left the monastic life.

7. See O'Brien Hallstein, 2010, for a discussion of the significance of Rich's argument for second wave feminists' conceptions of motherhood.

**14**

# WHAT MEN SAY ABOUT WOMEN

## Fathers Contemplate Work-Family Choices and Motherhood

*Patrice M. Buzzanell, Suzy D'Enbeau, and John Duckworth*[1]

Although media accounts discuss the rise of single-mother pregnancies as well as childrearing by gay, lesbian, and bisexual couples, the majority of births and adoptions within the United States occur within traditional heterosexual households that involve couples who are legally married at the time of or soon after birth or adoption (Jones, 2009; Ventura, 2009). Within these households, researchers have documented mothers' accounts of births and caregiving, but few have explored the ways fathers talk about and make sense of their own and their partners' decisions about reproduction, family leave issues, childcare, and work-life balance (for exceptions, see Duckworth and Buzzanell, 2009; Golden, 2000, 2001, 2002, 2007; Golden, Kirby, and Jorgenson, 2006; Petroski and Edley, 2006; Miller, 2008). In our analysis of men's interviews about fatherhood, masculinity, and work-family balance, we critique the discourses of choice to uncover a different and productive entry point into discussions about gendered divisions of labor.

## LITERATURE REVIEW

The decision to have a child seems to upend previous couple discussions about maintaining egalitarian relationships (Gornick and Meyers, 2008). This decision is associated with the single most important time in couples' lives and is the trigger event for couples', especially women's, reconsideration of career interests and/or ways to manage work. Diverse groups of women may attend to somewhat different parts of discourses surrounding workplace pregnancy, maternity leave, return to paid labor, and childcare arrangements. Their responses relate to particular life experiences. These experiences involve: their own health or that of their infants, their need or desire to bring in income, their perceived loss of collegial companionship, their insistence that they have the "best of all worlds" by being working mothers, and/or their concerns, guilt, or sorrow about leaving their infants (Buzzanell and Ellingson, 2005; Buzzanell, Meisenbach, Remke, Bowers, Liu, and Conn, 2005; Buzzanell, Waymer, Tagle, and Liu, 2007). As a result, we acknowledge that there are profound disparities among women's, and men's, abilities to enact work-family desires (e.g., Buzzanell, 2003; Buzzanell and Liu, 2005; Johansson and Klinth, 2008; Wilkinson, Magora, Garcia, and Khurana, 2009).

Men, too, discuss life changes with children's arrival. Most men do take, or say that they would prefer to take, paternity leaves (Waller, 2009; see also Johansson and Klinth, 2008) and enact involved fatherhood (Wilkinson et al., 2009). They express regret about leaving infants to return to paid work; they may consider or become stay-at-home fathers (Waller, 2009). Yet, most men still do not perform the same measures that women do. Instead, when people make decisions about whether and how both parties should contribute to caregiving, women often alter their career and family balance.

Women's change is expressed as a joint decision based on economic issues and reassessments (Wall and Arnold, 2007). Their partners may earn more than they do. Sometimes, financial calculations indicate that it costs more for her to work full-time than to stay home or to lower her employment hours (i.e., her income does not cover childcare, transportation, and other expenses). Other women stay in the labor force but find that they want to lower their work commitment (Waldman, 2009). Besides economic reasoning, their rationales may be influenced by dominant parenting discourses that insist that one parent stay home full-time (Maher and Saugeres, 2007). These discourses reinforce dichotomous parental roles to maintain the gendered status quo (Foster, 2005).

Couched as a joint decision, the positive effects of women's work outside of the home typically are not considered. Mothers experience greater perceived well-being and health by engaging in paid labor, especially if they are career-oriented, do not have very young children at home, and work in managerial or professional positions (Arber, Gilbert, and Dale, 2008;

Pietromonaco, Manis, and Markus, 1987). Long-term consequences for labor force reentry and retirement funds may not be calculated into decisions (Hewett and Luce, 2006)—consequences that Gornick and Meyers (2008) refer to as the "mommy tax" (p. 317). Moreover, couples' relational structures and dynamics may not be discussed. For men with stay-at-home wives and children, the payoff is career advancement (Correll, Benard, and Paik, 2007). There is no comparable beneficial structure for women. Ironically, despite talk about desires for more family time, fathers typically work longer hours per week than their childless counterparts (Gornick and Meyers, 2008).

Because of these inequitable gender discrepancies between how paid work, housework, and childcare are distributed throughout many households, feminists have explored familial caregiving and unpaid work issues (e.g., Folbre, 2008; Medved, 2007, 2009; Vavrus, 2002). We, too, write from feminist spaces in the pursuit of gender justice as we examine men's discourses in terms of choice in familial caregiving. Choice regarding reproductive rights, motherhood, and work has long been associated with second wave feminism (Nicholson, 1990). However, O'Brien Hallstein (2008) points out that a focus on discourses of choice may have prevented some women from adequate exposure to discourses that prepare them to mother. Moreover, the ways in which men perceive and talk about their own and their partners' choices remain understudied.

Choices are influenced by diverse life aspects including relationships with others. Choices differ from decisions insofar as decisions are event driven and may preclude feelings of free will and agency. Choices presume some agency, albeit constrained and contested. Boudreau (2009) defines *contested human agency* as "actively challenged, coerced, controlled, or actually changed and even destroyed in contention with other individuals or groups as they confront a variety of geographies, ecologies, actors, and social structures" (p. 133). Choice assumes that one does not fall within habitual patterns dependent on norms of human conduct but exercises mindfulness. We ask: *where and how do men perceive choices in their own and their partners' decisions about maternity*?

## METHOD

The data for this chapter were derived from in-depth interviews with eighteen fathers, conducted by the third author, John, for his master's thesis. Interview protocol questions addressed issues pertaining to choice, parenting, and work-life balance. We utilized interview data because individuals uncover their personal stories, including individual turning points or milestones regarding relational and work aspects of their lives, through this data gathering and sense-making technique (Riessman, 2002, 2008). We individually then collectively reviewed all eighteen interviews in an iterative fashion, taking notes on how fathers talk about choice-making processes, such as having children, paid employment, and the distribution of household tasks. We looked for specific cases in which choice factored prominently and differently in the men's discourses. We selected five cases that enabled us to explore the depth and range of non-choice as taken-for-granted or assumed behaviors and choice as agentic action. The remaining thirteen interviews were consistent with the selected cases insofar as they exhibited aspects similar to those found in one or more of five cases but they did not do so with as much clarity or explanation by participants.

## RESULTS

We present five mini-cases of five men from different occupations, socioeconomic statuses, race/ethnicities, and life stages who discuss choices in their partners' lives. All are married or in committed relationships but two are no longer in relationships with their child's mother. These five cases are identified by the men's pseudonyms, themes, and actual discourse. They are arranged thematically from: unexamined choice in taken-for-granted gender relations (Andrew), partial awareness and choice about *when* to have children but not about caregiving arrangements (Dan), and choice both dictated by gender, class, and fatherhood ideologies and by the challenges that having children represent (Joshua); to constrained choices (Graham) and choices reflecting and resisting divergent and sometimes unconventional gender priorities (Bob). We begin with Andrew and tell the story of each man's perceived work-life choices. We draw together our insights about choice in our discussion.

### Andrew: The Politics of Choice vs. the Reality of Choice ("You Can't Have It All")

Andrew is a Caucasian, forty-five-year-old father of one pre-teen and two teenagers who describes the family as upper class. With an MBA from Harvard, Andrew works full-time as an executive vice president for a financial firm. His wife currently works part-time as an editor of educational textbooks, and the family practices Orthodox Judaism. When asked about the decision to have children, Andrew explains:

> I think we always felt that we wanted to have children, so I don't know that it was much of a conscious decision to do it or not do it. I mean I think we wanted to be younger parents, and we accomplished that. . . . We were too young. We were twenty-seven when Michael was born. So I mean we were just . . . ragingly stupid.

Andrew reflectively adds that the couple was "ragingly stupid" about raising children but they never questioned whether or not they would have children. Throughout his interview, Andrew never felt the need to justify this choice. In fact, he does not appear to construct the decision to have children as a choice; it was taken for granted.

Although the couple did not consider whether to have children, they did undertake significant choices concerning work and caregiving. Andrew notes what he describes as a disconnect between the politics and the realities of choice. He laments the mythic, political version of choice that was presented to women in the 1980s, "Like every *Cosmo* cover was like 'How to have it all,' right? How to have the great job and the great love and the great this. . . . You can't have it all." Indeed, according to Andrew, families today cannot have it all. To Andrew, the reality of women's choice to work and have a family is nonexistent. Andrew compares his home life following the birth of their children when his wife did not work to his current situation in which his wife works part-time:

> When my wife wasn't working, she was the backstop, right? 'Cause when I came home, she had all this energy to listen to me. But now she's in the workforce. So when she comes home, if she had a bad day and I had a bad day, we're both scrambling for attention, we've got three kids that need attention, and you've got to rise above that fray. It's all about balance. It's the biggest . . . challenge.

According to Andrew, now that his wife has returned to work, there is no one whose primary responsibility it is to take care of him, the family, and the house. Because he perceives much "scrambling" to get things done, he says that women cannot "have it all."

Andrew does not consider that he could take more responsibility for the household. When asked about how they divvy up household work, Andrew says, "I'll be honest. I think she probably does. . . . It's probably like 80 or 90 percent. . . . I think people fall into roles. . . . We've sort of . . . for twenty years we've divvied up a certain way. I guess that's maybe a mature way to say it." Andrew explains that even though his wife now works, she still does the majority of the housework because those are the roles that they carved out early in their relationship, when she stayed at home with their children. His rationale is consistent with research indicating that men currently do more housework than men of the past, but that women's participation in household tasks has not decreased (Hook, 2006).

Andrew is self-reflective as he thinks through his responses. Indeed, he often appears to be actively crafting and justifying the way in which paid employment decision-making processes played out in their family: "Lots of people have kids and have nannies and work the same seventy hours. So I mean, you have to make a decision. Are you going to live that life or are you going to live a different life? . . . De facto, you're going to have to make that decision."

In this example, Andrew does not indicate *who* makes the decision (about a specific situation) and whether there is an untethered choice, but he does provide explicit advice to John for his future marital and fathering relationships. He offers his thoughts and feelings about, for instance, families who employ nannies. *That* life, according to Andrew and borne out by research, is one in which parents work long hours, employ outside caregiving help, and have little time to spend with families because work-issues bleed into family time (Ilies, Schwind, Wagner, Johnson, DeRue, and Ilgen, 2007). Yet, Andrew suggests that their decisions were made as a team, an implication confirmed by the interviewer, John, "So obviously as a team, you decided she was going to stay at home and you were going to continue to be the breadwinner?" To which Andrew replied, "Yes. We decided that." Andrew does not question the "team" decision for his wife to be the primary caregiver (the family is Orthodox Jewish which may influence gendered caregiving patterns; see Shai, 2002). Later, he explains that with marriage, "you can't just make decisions based on you." And with the birth of a child, "There's a third person now involved in the decision-making." Although the child may not voice preferences, in Andrew's view, the child still operates as a stakeholder in family decisions.

> Andrew speculates about how his wife would respond to John's questions: If you ask my wife, which would be interesting, her perception I'm sure would be that it's more work and less family. My perception is it's been a little more even but probably tilted more toward work. I mean, I am the primary breadwinner.

Andrew frequently engages in self-reflective thinking processes throughout the interview. He may feel comfortable engaging in these activities because the interviewer is male. As he crafts his stories, he enacts identity negotiation and construction strategies that require shifting, reframing, and adapting to relationships, contexts, and experiences (see Brown, 2008). He adds, "As we're talking here, it's clear to me, just by the way I've answered the questions, that my main drive has sort of been work first and family second."

The question remains, will this self-reflective and critical thinking lead to changed behaviors? Because Andrew relies on discursive divides between the politics and realities of choice, it seems unlikely. He rationalizes choice-making processes through appeals to the status quo, the idea that children come first (for his wife at least), and gendered assumptions that position men as breadwinners and women as caregivers.

### Dan: The Pursuit of Gender Equality ("What We Had to Do Was Realize What Really Needs to Be Done, What Can We Let Slide")

Dan is a thirty-seven-year-old, married, upper-middle-class Caucasian legal consultant with two children. His wife, Laura, currently works part-time as a pharmacist. Dan talks about their decision to have children:

> Laura was definitely the person who was more pushy than I was. I think we had been thinking about it and talking about it a lot and she was ready probably a little bit earlier than I was. And I just needed a little more time just to make sure because I was still working a lot, I wanted to see how my job was going, where we were living, and all that. And I think I finally came to the realization that it was an important thing [for] us. We both wanted to do it and if we waited too long, we wouldn't be able to enjoy it.

Dan perceives that his wife was ready before he was to have children but they both agreed that they wanted to be young parents. Again, the choice of whether or not to have children is not considered; the choice was *when* to have children. There is also little to no discussion of how their work lives would change with the birth of their child.

Later, Dan explains the decision for his wife to leave her full-time job doing risk management in health care to become a part-time pharmacist after the birth of their second child because "obviously, kids have to come first":

> She was working full-time and we had Nick, who is our first child, and we were just finding that full-time was a little bit too much—just for both of us in

> terms of getting everything done. So, Laura switched jobs to a part-time job as a pharmacist. . . . We just thought that was easier. . . . Because the kids are in daycare on Mondays, Wednesdays, and Fridays. . . . Every other Monday she is off. So this gave her kind of a day to just get everything organized and some time. . . . So it gave us both a little more flexibility.

Dan explains that children come first, a popular parenting mantra that has typically been enforced on mothers' childrearing practices (O'Brien Hallstein, 2008). Given that he expresses this mantra, it is interesting to explore how work-family balance, the division of household tasks, and paid work choices play out in his life. Dan comments on the stress of household management when both he and his wife worked full-time. At first he says that his wife was given an extra day to get things organized but then he qualifies that statement by saying that this arrangement gave them *both* more flexibility. Because Dan's job required more travel and because his wife's part-time job paid the same as her full-time job, the decision was to have his wife work part-time:

> We'd be always stressed at her job rushing to get through things and then picking the kids up, then get them home, then get them dinner and everything or I would be rushing to get home ahead of her to get dinner ready. We were always both just running like crazy trying to basically support the kids in daycare, which didn't make any sense to us because the money wasn't that much of a differential. We looked at it and said what's the better way for both of us to have a little more free time, have a little more time with the kids, and not always be stressed about where we are or where we have to get to at a certain time.

Dan and his wife actively worked to make their lives "simpler" and to stop struggling to be "perfect" parents. Eventually, they made strategic choices together ("Okay, we got to talk about this because we're both not doing too good"):

> We both were worried too much about making things perfect, and instead, what we had to do was realize what really needs to be done, what can we let slide, how can we work this. . . . Both of us would feel guilty taking any kind of break and so we basically both were getting up at five in the morning and going all the way until 10 at night without any breaks and that was just really difficult. And obviously not a smart way to do things so we both found a way. . . . What things we can do to give each other breaks.

Although the couple employs a maid (Dan says, "We were doing well financially—we could afford it. So it was definitely a very easy decision for both of us to put most of that work off on someone else"), Dan explains that he and his wife try to split the rest of the housework evenly, although his wife frequently worries that Dan is taking on too much, "Laura is always pushing me to not feel like I have to do everything when I come home. It's not a good thing to try and do too much." Later, John remarks that "it sounds like you two are really partners," to which Dan replies, "we try" and elaborates:

> When you have a certain amount of time to do things you kind of have to work that way. And that's always kind of been the way our relationship is. We're very comfortable talking to each other about how we feel and about what is not working for us.

To Dan, the couple actively works toward an equal partnership. They communicate frequently about things like household tasks and taking care of the children's needs. And yet, Dan does not mention a possible choice of him switching careers, working fewer hours, and becoming the primary caregiver for the children. Although his wife was able to work part-time for the same amount of money, he does not describe this situation as the reason the couple chose to have her work fewer hours. We are left wondering if this situation is really equal and what his wife's story might be.

### Joshua: Masculinity, Obligation, and Choice ("Being a Man, Being Responsible for Your Kids and Not Being a Deadbeat Dad, Trying to Be a Good Father")

Joshua is a twenty-six-year-old, African American, middle-class, single father. He works full-time as a janitor, has one son, and is expecting a baby with his girlfriend, Yolanda. His son lives with his mother, Kisha, and Joshua gets to see him every week. When asked about the decision to have his first child, Joshua explains: "I was a senior in high school, she [Kisha] was a junior. I was about to graduate and she had a year left. We, you know, we just really was into each other. It was an unplanned pregnancy." Yolanda's pregnancy was unexpected although the couple had discussed having children: "she just got pregnant on the shot. . . . I mean, we was planning on it down the road, but it's unplanned because it happened kind of quick." In both of these situations, Joshua did not describe the timing of his children's birth as his choice.

Joshua did make other choices. He reflects on his decision to go to college four hours away from Kisha and wonders if this is one reason their relationship fell apart:

> I could have went to college here in the city, but I chose to go away to school because [of] less distractions. . . . You know, maybe family matters, anything . . . we had communication with each other and, you know, I guess she eventually felt bitter about it because I chose that route instead of just staying here in the city and going to school here. . . . If I would have stayed here, things could have worked out much better between me and her.

In this passage, Joshua explains his choice to go to school out of town. He had a football scholarship and had been told that he had the talent to go far in a sports career. However, Kisha expressed displeasure in his decision and apparently did not feel as though her preferences influenced his choice. Eventually, Joshua decided to return home.

Joshua also refers to masculinity pressures in terms of appropriate gendered roles for men and women. Joshua enjoys the fact that he does not feel a lot of workplace pressure in his job as a janitor because he feels there is enough pressure as the "man":

> But I mainly enjoy the fact that, you know, I don't have a lot of pressure, because I feel I got enough pressure now, things on my shoulders that I make myself, being the man, being responsible, trying to take care of and hold down my fort, myself.

Although his choice to attend school disrupted his ability to provide for his son, he maintains that men are still primarily responsible for breadwinning, or at least he did not try to mask that he felt that pressure. Indeed, Joshua eventually dropped out of school because, "I had to do what I had to do, being a man, being responsible for your kids and not being a deadbeat dad, trying to be a good father." Later, Joshua explains the pressure he feels to financially provide for his current girlfriend and his son:

> She [Yolanda] like to get her hair and nails done, which I told her, when I got with her and met her that that's something I'll do for her because I like to see that done on my girl as well. But sometimes, you know, I might not be able to give her the extra . . . it's not really that much, but all the little extra money counts because everything is taxed so much right now. . . . And like with my son, he might . . . like he want . . . sometimes he want . . . he got a PlayStation 2. He be . . . he wants tons of games. Sometimes he got to wait on that game.

> I can't get it right then and there, you got to wait for me to be able to have enough money, maybe next pay period, and I'll give it.

Joshua's discourse begs the question, what is the role of masculinity in paternal caregiving discourses? In their review of popular parenting articles, Wall and Arnold (2007) found that "the masculinity of involved fathers needs emphasis . . . that masculinity must be affirmed is a nod to the fact that warm, loving, and involved parenting and primary caregiving is still considered feminine" (p. 521). Waller (2009) suggests that following separation from the mother, some fathers increased their caregiving practices in response to changing circumstances in the mother's life (e.g., job loss). These fathers were "motivated to rise to this challenge" (p. 167). In these instances, paternal caregiving was framed as a challenge that must be conquered or overcome. Similarly, Joshua frames his paternal caregiving as a series of challenges and choices.

### Graham: Constrained Choice ("I Think It Should Be 50–50.")

Graham is a forty-nine-year-old, upper-middle-class Caucasian who works in financial services. He is remarried and shares joint custody of his adopted daughter with his ex-wife. When asked about the decision to adopt, Graham explains,

> We had . . . been married eighteen years. This is probably fourteen or fifteen years ago, but we had . . . or I should say, my ex-wife had several false starts . . . bad pregnancies or just didn't take. And we decided that we didn't want to pursue modern science's approach to that. We knew that there were orphanages in China that were full of little girls because of their one child rule.

When John asked about conversations regarding different choices that the couple had in terms of paid work and work-family balance, Graham adds,

> I guess it was spoken about some, but it was more sort of understood. I was working full-time as I am now. She was not working full-time. She was working part-time doing largely volunteer work. And we thought we would have and we did hire someone to help us at times when neither one of us could be with our daughter. So that was . . . it was not . . . at the time it wasn't particularly contentious. I do remember some contentious things later on in terms of scheduling, but I think that was more related to our marriage kind of coming to an end rather than specific difficulties. Juggling one child is a lot easier than juggling two or three children. It was never particularly difficult.

Graham explains that the decision for him to continue working full-time after the adoption was "understood" because his wife did not engage in paid work at the time. He does not indicate if the couple's decision included discussions about his wife eventually returning to paid work. Later, Graham reveals that his wife may have resented him:

> When I was married to Matti's mother, she . . . the resentment that she had for my uprooting her from her first job clearly never left and there were times when she resented, I think, my not being there at the end of the day when she felt I should be there at the end of the day when she was with our daughter. So juggling my schedule and her schedule—making those two work together.

Graham and his first wife eventually divorced which has created many frustrating situations that, according to Graham, have constrained his available caregiving choices:

> And the thing that to me is more, this is not easy to talk about because it makes me angry, but the most galling thing to me about it is my ex-wife was someone who's [a] very strong believer in women's rights. And I am, too. And I come from a long . . . my mother who is 88 is as radical a feminist as I know. And to me, when the shoe was on the other foot, to not have it be equitable . . . it still makes me so angry I could spit. And I know what the bias of the court is. The bias of the court is toward the mother.

Graham even invokes feminist equality arguments to point out what he perceives to be his wife's gendered advantage in terms of child custody. He adds,

> Matti is with us 50 percent of the time when school is out and she's with us about 40 percent of the time during school. I think that's not equitable. I think it should be 50–50. And for me to pursue 50–50 would require my taking my ex-wife and my daughter to court.

Graham does not like the option of getting his ex-wife and daughter involved in what could become a heated custody dispute. Thus, he perceives his ability to engage in good parenting to be constrained by larger contextual issues and situational factors.

### Bob: Resistance to Gendered Parenting Roles ("I Find It a Lot of Fun. I Believe She Finds It a Chore.")

Bob is a thirty-seven-year-old Caucasian assistant professor who hesitates to call his family upper-middle-class although their combined income places them at "the top 10 percent of households in the country" (Bob adds, "We're struggling to make ends meet with two kids and childcare"). Bob's wife works full-time as a clerk for a federal judge. He explains the different choice-making strategies in which he and his wife engaged that pertain to paid work. Bob selected employment that he perceived to be family-friendly in anticipation of having children. In contrast, he describes his wife's choice as one that prioritized financial security. When the couple had children, his wife made the transition to a job that was more accommodating to family:

> I specifically chose a career in teaching well before we had the kids, knowing that it would be a family-friendly job. She chose the law because it provided economic security at a time when she didn't know if she'd ever get married. . . . Decided she wanted to downshift that, went to a different firm where she did have time, met me and now has shifted into government work, which is even less demanding, in part because she wants to be with the kids.

Bob strategically chose a career that would allow him flexibility in terms of time and location. He notes that his wife was unsure if she would marry which is why she chose a job that would afford her financial security. In framing his wife's employment choice as one that privileged financial security, Bob fails to address other possible rationales such as work enjoyment, ambition, or independence. However, he perceived that, "She worked at a big firm, worked all these hours, hated it," although he did not provide her own wording to support his claim.

According to Bob, his wife is not a "super mom" so he works to keep her as happy as he can in an attempt to persuade her to have another child:

> I want to keep her happy enough so she might want to have a third child, too, which is a lot of pressure. . . . I'm always trying what I think is my hardest to help her out or to, you know, give her the downtime she wants, give her the . . . you know. If she wants something, well, I try not to worry too much about spending. If she needs something, you know, go get it because I want to keep you happy because I don't want this raising children thing to be painful . . . she'll admit, "I'm not a super mom." Other mothers are way in there and it's the dad who's like, "Oh God, I can't deal with this." For whatever reason . . . it's not a gender thing . . . I find it a lot of fun. I believe she finds it a chore.

Bob disputes gendered assumptions that dictate mothers' love and fathers' fear of childrearing. He finds his situation different, but does not view it as ironic, contradictory, or as a rejection of traditional gendered norms ("it's not a gender thing"). However, Bob does indicate that this situation causes him a lot of pressure and stress. As Bob explains,

> she has a much harder time dealing with the kids and the chaos than I do. To me, it goes in one ear, out the other. For her, you know, she wants to keep the floors clean, she wants to eat at a regular time, she wants the kids to eat what's put in front of them. . . . I think she's frustrated, perhaps, by my lack of discipline. Not discipline like when they do something bad, but . . . she wants more structure. She wants the world to be more ordered and more regular and I just recognize that kids are just not going to conform to that level.

In this example, Bob describes the parenting dilemmas of divergent priorities. Bob's wife earns more so the family and Bob's employment is oriented around her schedule. He seems resentful at times and irritated that she still wants the house to be perfect (e.g., toys must be put away immediately, laundry done and folded daily).

Bob's talk reveals the different stresses, priorities, and subsequent choice-making processes after childbirth:

> So our big decisions are kind of these, you know, can . . . what can we afford in a house and this creates a lot of stress for my wife. You know, she has a vision for what a house ought to look like and knows that we can't quite afford that . . . I don't need a big house. I don't need to live in the most exclusive suburb. So we're really wrestling with . . . and a lot of couples do this when they're married and this is very much a part of marriage. You wrestle with lifestyle expectations. What is your vision for life, what your life ought to be like?"

Bob's talk reveals points of frustration and struggle as he and his wife navigate a variety of parenting, lifestyle, and work choices. Bob is the one with the flexible schedule, an enjoyment of parenting, and the desire to have another child. Bob also expresses satisfaction with their living situation. However, he notes that life is not harmonious. His wife makes more money, seems to find parenting a "chore," and worries about their living situation. Bob does not equate his frustration with what appears to be the couple's disruption of dominant gendered parenting roles.

## DISCUSSION

We pull together the dominant themes of each case to draw out the assumptions underlying fathers' talk about choice, caregiving, maternity, and work-life balance. First, each father believes that he is doing the "right thing" by his partner and children, given the circumstances and situations each father faces. Although the specific choices may differ, these fathers rarely hesitate as they rationalize their decision-making processes. They recognize the points in which they perceive agency and in which they believe their agency is constrained and might be contested by the interviewer (John) and others.

Second, many fathers do not question the choices they have made about caregiving and work. They do, however, acknowledge that their wives and girlfriends may have different narrative versions and may feel resentments (as they sometimes do, too). When their actions conform to normative identities and life stories, these men do not elaborate. These fathers simply state what they needed to do or did. In other words, fathers do not feel compelled to explain the choice to have children because it is considered to be a normal life phase. They do not feel compelled to explain how and why they made the decision unless their experience diverges from the norm (e.g., they are really old or young; they had an unplanned pregnancy). Thus the choice to have children, and other choices that are consistent with popular narratives, are unremarkable unless considered deviant.

However, these choices and the accompanying decisions to act (or not) in particular circumstances are still embedded within sociopolitical-economic contexts (Buzzanell, Dohrman, & D'Enbeau [forthcoming]). Indeed, although some fathers express disillusionment with the notion that women can "have it all," others may not want to appear unsupportive in what they perceive to be today's postfeminist era. Therefore, fathers, especially upper-class fathers, do justify their position as primary breadwinner and head of the household, their wife's role as primary caregiver, and their wife's reduced working hours. Fathers frame these decisions based on appeals to economy, logic, equality, and popular "family first" discourses. In a postfeminist era in which gender equality has presumably been attained, these fathers must carefully articulate how they and their partners went about determining paid and housework arrangements. The only father who does not comment on this is Joshua, possibly because the option to have a partner stay home is inconceivable given finances and extended family commitments. For Joshua, the lack of choice is largely classed.

Third, these interviews expose issues of social control, that is, direct and indirect ways in which individuals attempt to control others' behaviors through persuasion. Yet, one partner may perceive some decisions as supportive (e.g., the decision to have one partner stay home so that she has more time to get the house organized) while another may find the same decisions manipulative (e.g., feelings of resentment if one partner routinely comes home late from work). Moreover, appeals to economy are logical; it makes sense to have the partner who earns less be the primary caregiver. In other cases, if couples decide early in their relationship, explicitly or implicitly, how to split household tasks, it might make sense to maintain that status quo. Thus paid and household work and caregiving arrangements are sustained via social controls that appear logical and rational.

Last, these fathers are more focused on the personal struggles pertaining to choice and caregiving than on structural issues. The recognition of structural issues could lead to organizational and policy change. Indeed, choice not only operates within family systems but also is embedded within health, legal, organizational, and other structures and discourses. For instance, Graham felt that his choices were constrained by a threatening legal system that could effectively grant him equal child visitation. Furthermore, the quality of choice has meaning in the balancing of different needs to act autonomously and communally, in the interest of the individual and of the family. Quality of choice is dependent on resources or perceived and actual material conditions that are raced and classed. For example, contemporary societal mandates for fathers' daily involvement in their children's lives are raced and classed (Glauber, 2008; Wilkinson et al., 2009). If men have difficulty maintaining at least an adequate lifestyle for their families on a fairly continuous basis—even with the employment of partners and other family members—then choice regarding participation in leisure, family time, and other activities would be curtailed. The bases on which men are evaluated as good fathers would differ.

Discourse and materialities about choice are not simply about who does what to effect certain decisions, fit within normative expectations about family and work, and redistribute chores. Instead, we have shown that much of the unfinished second wave and much needed third wave feminist work is to enlarge the discursive space surrounding choice. This space, then, would encourage men and women to realize that there is choice and agency in situations currently perceived as taken-for-granted through gender normative lenses. Moreover, the fathers in our study did not regard reproduction and parenthood to be choices but they did indicate that the consequences had varying implications for them and many for their female partners.

Despite our analyses about choice, we have unanswered questions. These questions relate, in part, to limitations of our dataset. However, they also reflect a lack of theorizing about choice. We note that we have delved into gendered and marital ideological controls about caregiving. However, there are situational constraints that might mitigate or open up opportunities for choice. These include autonomy in occupations (Graham and Bob) and gendered work in Jewish Orthodox rituals (Andrew). Thus, discussions about choice regarding maternity, caregiving, and other work-family issues are incomplete without greater contextualization.

Furthermore, although we presume that having John interview other men would create conditions whereby male participants would more freely disclose their thoughts and feelings about decisions, we do not know the extent to which men framed their answers to be socially acceptable. We also do not know the extent to which John-as-interviewer was implicated in participants' stories. Interviewers sometimes simply record interviews/stories or they can help interviewees construct their stories. These are important differences (Mischler, 1986). At times, it appears that the interviewer interjects labels (e.g., "team") that contribute to the crafting of these fathers' stories, Moreover, according to Goffman (1959, 1974), people frame things in ways so that they will be regarded positively. These interview data, then, become opportunities and tools of identity negotiation (Gubrium and Holstein, 2000; Nelson, 2001; Somers, 1994).

Finally, we do not know if fathers ever feel selfish when talking about work-family decisions. Some talk about feelings of obligation, but we wonder at what points they ignore these feelings and how they rationalize these decisions. Researchers report mother guilt about events such as returning to work after having children. But do fathers ever feel selfish or guilty if they don't engage in caregiving equitably? When necessary, the fathers in our study rationalize decisions that appear to advance gender inequalities. We do not know if they engage in rationalization to appease anticipated political and feminist objections or because they feel uneasy about caregiving distributions.

In closing, we navigate between choice and decisions without clear resolution. Our suspended thinking has to do, in part, with the fact that these fathers rarely acknowledged choice for themselves and suggested differences in what their partners might say about choice. Furthermore, we envision choice to be constrained, contested, and enabled by different societal discourses, the material and social constructions in everyday life, and the partial or full penetration of individual sociopolitical-economic-cultural locations (see Willis, 1977). Rarely, if ever, do the fathers voice full awareness of their lived conditions or acknowledge choice. Instead, they discuss routine life events in a taken-for-granted fashion without elaborations and justifications. Indeed, most of their decisions have fallen within boundaries of acceptable gendered, marital, fatherhood, and classed norms, thus requiring little explanation. Only when these fathers had to justify their decisions to others, including John as interviewer, did situated choice processes come into play (e.g., Joshua's deferred dream of a college education and better paying job to be present for his son; Bob's choice of a family-friendly academic job is striking contrast to his wife's decision to go into law for financial reasons). In the end, we may know less about choice than about the habitual ways in which men justify paternal and broader work-life patterns for themselves and their female partners.

## REFERENCES


Arber, S., Gilbert, G., and Dale, A. 2008. Paid employment and women's health: A benefit or a source of role strain? *Sociology of Health & Illness* 7, 375–400.

Boudreau, T. E. 2009. Human agonistes: Interdisciplinary inquiry into ontological agency and human conflict. In D. Sandole, S. Byrne, I. Sandole-Staroste, and J. Senehi (eds.), *Handbook of conflict analysis and resolution* (pp. 131–43). New York: Routledge.

Brown, T. 2008. Desire and drive in researcher subjectivity: The broken mirror of Lacan. *Qualitative Inquiry* 14, 402–23.

Buzzanell, P. M. 2003. A feminist standpoint analysis of maternity and maternity leave for women with disabilities. *Women & Language* 26(2), 53–65.

Buzzanell, P. M., Dohrman, R., and D'Enbeau, S. (forthcoming). Problematizing political economy differences and their respective work-life policy constructions. In D. K. Mumby (ed.), *Organizing difference: Research, pedagogy, and practice*. Thousand Oaks, CA: Sage.

Buzzanell, P. M., and Ellingson, L. 2005. Contesting narratives of workplace maternity. In L. M. Harter, P. Japp, and C. Beck (eds.), *Narratives, health, and healing: Communication theory, research, and practice* (pp. 277–94). Hillsdale, NJ: Erlbaum.

Buzzanell, P. M., and Liu, M. 2005. Struggling with maternity leave policies and practices: A poststructuralist feminist analysis of gendered organizing. *Journal of Applied Communication Research* 33, 1–25.

Buzzanell, P. M., Meisenbach, R., Remke, R., Bowers, V., Liu, M., and Conn, C. 2005. The good *working* mother: Managerial women's sensemaking and feelings about work-family issues. *Communication Studies* 56, 261–85.

Buzzanell, P. M., Waymer, D., Tagle, M. P., and Liu, M. 2007. Different transitions into working motherhood: Discourses of Asian, Hispanic, and African American women. *Journal of Family Communication* 7, 195–220.

Cheney, G., Zorn, T., Planalp, S., and Lair, D. 2008. Meaningful work and personal/social well-being: Organizational communication engages the meanings of work. In C. Beck (ed.), *Communication yearbook 32* (pp. 136–85). New York: Routledge.

Correll, S. J., Benard, S., and Paik, I. 2007. Getting a job: Is there a motherhood penalty? *American Journal of Sociology* 112, 1297–338.

Duckworth, J., and Buzzanell, P. M. 2009. Constructing work-life balance and fatherhood: Men's framing of the meanings of *both* work *and* family. *Communication Studies* 60, 558–73.

Folbre, N. 2008. Reforming care. *Politics & Society* 36, 373–87.

Foster, E. 2005. Desiring dialectical discourse: A feminist ponders the transition to motherhood. *Women's Studies in Communication* 28, 57–83.

Glauber, R. 2008. Race and gender in families and at work: The fatherhood wage premium. *Gender and Society* 22, 8–30.

Goffman, E. 1959. *The presentation of self in everyday life*. New York: Anchor Books.

Goffman, E. 1974. *Frame analysis: An essay on the organization of experience*. London: Harper and Row.

Golden, A. 2000. What we talk about when we talk about work and family: A discourse analysis of parental accounts. *Electronic Journal of Communication/La Revue Electronique de Communication* 10. Retrieved from http://www.cios.org/www/ejc/v10n3400.htm.

Golden, A. 2001. Modernity and the communicative management of multiple role-identities: The case of the worker-parent. *Journal of Family Communication* 1, 233–64.

Golden, A. 2002. Speaking of work and family: Spousal collaboration on defining role-identities and developing shared meanings. *Southern Communication Journal* 67, 122–41.

Golden, A. 2007. Fathers' frames for childrearing: Evidence toward a "masculine concept of caregiving." *Journal of Family Communication* 7, 265–85.

Golden, A., Kirby, E., and Jorgenson, J. 2006. Work-life research from both sides now: An integrative perspective for organizational and family communication. In C. Beck (ed.), *Communication yearbook 30* (pp. 143–95). New York: Routledge.

Gornick, J. C., and Myers, M. K. 2008. Creating gender egalitarian societies: An agenda for reform. *Politics & Society* 36, 313–49.

Gubrium, J., and Holstein, J. 2000. *The self we live by: Narrative identity in a postmodern world*. New York: Oxford Books.

Hewlett, S. A., and Luce, C. B. 2006. Extreme jobs: The dangerous allure of the 70-hour workweek. *Harvard Business Review* 84(12), 49–58.

Hook, J. L. 2006. Care in context: Men's unpaid work in 20 countries, 1965–2003. *American Sociological Review* 71, 639–60.

Ilies, R., Schwind, K. M., Wagner, D. T., Johnson, M. D., DeRue, D. S., and Ilgen, D. R. 2007. When can employees have a family life? The effects of daily workload

and affect on work-family conflict and social behaviors at home. *Journal of Applied Psychology* 92, 1368–79.
Johansson, T., and Klinth, R. 2008. Caring fathers: The ideology of gender equality and masculine positions. *Men and Masculinities* 11, 42–62.
Jones, J. 2009. *Who adopts? Characteristics of women and men who have adopted children.* NCHS data brief, 12. Hyattsville, MD: National Center for Health Statistics.
Maher, J., and Saugeres, L. 2007. To be or not to be a mother?: Women negotiating cultural representations of mothering. *Journal of Sociology* 53, 5–21.
Medved, C. E. 2007. Investigating family labor in communication studies: Threading across historical and contemporary discourses. *Journal of Family Communication* 7, 225–43.
Medved, C. E. 2009. Crossing and transforming occupational and household gendered divisions of labor: Reviewing literatures and deconstructing differences. In C. Beck (Ed.), *Communication yearbook 33* (pp. 300–41). New York: Routledge.
Miller, K. I. 2008. My father and his father: An analysis of World War II correspondence. *Journal of Family Communication* 8, 148–65.
Mishler, E. G. 1986. *Research interviewing: Context and narrative.* Cambridge, MA: Harvard University Press.
Nelson, H. L. 2001. *Damaged identities, narrative repair.* Ithaca, NY: Cornell University Press.
Nicholson, L. (ed.). 1990. *The second wave: A reader in feminist theory.* New York: Routledge.
O'Brien Hallstein, D. L. 2008. Silences and choice: The legacies of white second wave feminism in the new professoriate. *Women Studies in Communication* 31, 143–50.
Petroski, D., and Edley, P. 2006. Stay-at-home fathers: Masculinity, family, work, and gender stereotypes. *Electronic Journal of Communication* 16(3 and 4). Retrieved from http://www.cios.org/www/ejc/v16n3400.htm.
Pietromonaco, P., Manis, J., and Markus, H. 1987. The relationship of employment to self-perception and well-being in women: A cognitive analysis. *Sex Roles* 17, 467–77.
Riessman, C. K. 2002. Analysis of personal narratives. In J. F. Gubrium and J. A. Holstein (eds.), *Handbook of interview research* (pp. 695–710). Thousand Oaks, CA: Sage.
Riessman, C. K. 2008. *Narrative methods for the human sciences.* Thousand Oaks, CA: Sage.
Shai, D. 2002. Working women/cloistered men: A family development approach to marriage arrangements among ultra-Orthodox Jews. *Journal of Comparative Family Studies* 33, 97–115.
Somers, M. R. 1994. The narrative constitution of identity: A relational and network approach. *Theory and Society* 23, 605–49.

Vavrus, M. D. 2002. Domesticating patriarchy: Hegemonic masculinity and television's "Mr. Mom." *Critical Studies in Media Communication* 19, 352–75.

Ventura, S. J. 2009. *Changing patterns of nonmarital childbearing in the United States*. NCHS data brief, no. 18. Hyattsville, MD: National Center for Health Statistics.

Waldman, A. 2009. *Bad mother: A chronicle of maternal crimes, minor calamities, and occasional moments of grace*. New York: Doubleday.

Wall, G., and Arnold, S. 2007. How involved is involved fathering? An exploration of the contemporary culture of fatherhood. *Gender & Society* 21, 508–27.

Waller, M. R. 2009. Family man in the other America: New opportunities, motivations, and supports for paternal caregiving. *Annals of the American Academy of Political and Social Science* 624, 156–76.

Wilkinson, D., Magora, A., Garcia, M., and Khurana, A. 2009. Fathering at the margins of society: Reflections from young, minority, and crime-involved fathers. *Journal of Family Issues* 30, 945–67.

Willis, P. 1977. Learning to labor: How working class kids get working class jobs. New York: Columbia University Press.

## NOTE

1. This chapter is based on interview data collected by John Duckworth for his MA thesis, *The discourse and practice of fatherhood: Identity negotiations of masculinities, caregiving, and work-family issues*, completed Purdue University, in 2006, under the direction of the first author. John earned the 2007 Outstanding Thesis Award from the Organization for the Study of Communication, Language and Gender for this work.

15

# OUTLAW MOTHERS RAISING GENTLE-MEN

## Choosing to Disrupt Hegemonic Tensions between Masculinity and Feminism

*Cindy Griffin and Kirsten J. Broadfoot*

> If gendering is a process by which individuals are made to make cultural sense, it is important to see that this sense-making process is not necessarily grounded exclusively in the talk or behavior of the individuals being "gendered." Rather such talk or behavior is contextualized within wider social discourses that make it intelligible or unintelligible, appropriate or inappropriate.
>
> —Ehrlich, 2002, p. 745

Following Adrienne Rich's (1986) call for "conspirators, outlaws from the institution of motherhood" (p. 194), in *Mother Outlaws*, many mothers describe their attempts to raise their sons far from maddening masculine norms, re-creating, and creating, new norms for their children in order to "create a new man—sensitive, expressive, nonviolent, respectful and loving of women" (O'Reilly, 2004; Thomas, 2001, p. 128). Outlaw mothering, mothering that disrupts hegemonic notions of masculinity and femininity, or mothering that brings into focus the tensions between "good" and "bad" mothering (Rich, 1986), is no easy task given the ways in which institutions in society exert a greater influence on gendered roles than the home. Rich suggests that rather than situating the two practices in opposition, *bad mothering* actually has the potential to be *good mothering* because it goes against patriarchal norms for parenting, and thus, occupies an "outlaw" status (O'Reilly, 2006). The women in Thomas's (2001) and O'Reilly's (2004) studies of feminist mothers take up Rich's call, and report the struggle to move "bad mothering" into the category of "good mothering," as most intense around the "expectations of the school system, peer group pressures, the mass media . . . the influence of their son's father and other adult role models" (Thomas, 2001, p. 129).

As studies suggest, building good relationships with our sons significantly increases their resilience and decreases their desire to act out (usually performed in a response to a closing of venues for appropriate emotional expression) (Dooley and Fedele, 2001). The mother-son relationship can be a sanctuary in which boys learn how to connect, express their emotions, and grow into adulthood (Dooley and Fedele, 2001). But how do mothers create sanctuaries of respite and learning of alternative masculinities for their boys? The tensions are obviously great: mothers must reject, reframe, and re-create historical, societal, and familial pressures and codes as they navigate away from what often feel like unnecessary and unnecessarily limiting norms for their sons. Simultaneously, they must also embrace aspects of masculinity that will allow their sons to exist, survive, and even thrive in the worlds they, as boys and men, occupy. Clearly, not all of masculinity is to be discarded, but what aspects are to be kept, and in what moments and situations? How do we nurture our sons' outward energy, their boisterous moments of passion, and their incredible zest for life, independence, and adventure, while also nurturing their inward moments of contemplation, their hearts, and their gentle observations, actions, and natures?

In this chapter, we explore aspects of our own mother-son relationships in an attempt to close what we see as a theoretical gap between hybridizing masculinity, feminism, and maternal choices. What exists in this gap, we suggest, are obvious and not so obvious tensions, which must be consciously and continually communicatively negotiated in order to understand and clarify what is meant by, and what happens when one makes a "choice." To begin to fill this theoretical gap, we examine the active choices we have made as feminist scholars and mothers in negotiating hegemonic and subordinate masculinities for, through, and around our sons and the reflexive consequences of such choices. We follow the approach taken by many of those writing within the "outlaw mothering" literature and, using our own narratives of mothering, we explore tensions between feminist commitments, alternative forms of masculinity, and the autonomous choices of our sons, as we negotiate the pressures of hegemonic masculinity that surround our lives. With O'Reilly (2006), we suggest that outlaw mothering, with its antisexist and activist components, functions as a counternarrative to larger political, institutional, and cultural structures. What our counternarratives speak to, we think, are the tensions inherent in the choices mothers must and do make as they negotiate the tricky terrain of masculinity and feminism.

To give our narratives a theoretical foundation, though, we begin this chapter with a discussion of gender work, which is the creation and negotiation of gendered identities over time. We argue that masculinity is a hybrid identity, an identity that evolves and shifts over time and place. This hybridity opens a space for outlaw mothers to do a disruptive kind of gender work; one that allows for, and honors, the existence of gentle male identities. We argue that, even while this disruptive work frees our sons from hegemonic constraints, it is accompanied by informative, but no less disruptive, tensions in our own lives. In order to explore and explicate some of these tensions, we share several of our own stories as mothers attempting to dislodge hegemonic masculinities from our son's lives, and speculate on those tensions and what they might tell us as communication scholars about choice, the reproduction of masculinity, the production of hybridity, and for us, gentle men.

## GENDER WORK: A BOY'S (HYBRID) LIFE

Gender roles in general, and masculinity in particular, are incredibly complex cultural constructions, constantly in flux and, therefore, constantly amenable to change (Prendergast, 2002). Gender *work* is an active process of creating and re-creating gender over time, with particular tasks becoming salient at particular moments in our lives, enabling us to respond (or not) interactively and communicatively to the changing dynamics of powerful gender relations in our world (Kaufman, 1994). Developing masculine and feminine identities is a social process, grounded in interaction within family relationships, in which femininity, as represented by maternal figures, and masculinity, as represented by paternal figures, embody and encourage cultural constructions to come to life in the bodies of young children (Kaufman, 1994). However, according to Cornwall and Lindisfarne (1994), familiar oppositions of "male-female," "masculine-feminine" obscure a social reality that is far more complex than these binaries suggest. *Masculinity* as a cultural construction and expression is composed of "multiple masculinities," and "an enacted performance is a diverse, mobile, even unstable construction" (Beynon, 2002, p. 2). Moreover, as Cornwall and Lindisfarne (1994) argue, "there is no 'natural' nor necessary connection between men and masculinity" (p. 37). Masculinity is a situated, embodied act, always subject to cultural surveillance, approval, and punishment as any particular audience deems fit. Indeed, there still are clear rules, however unspoken, for what constitutes "masculine" and "feminine."

In U.S. hegemonic culture for example, a boy's evolution, as a boy, often takes the following trajectory: between the ages of three and seven, a boy exists in the world of "superheroes" who teach him to be invincible, independent, strong, and stoic; this is followed by a culture of "bullies, banter, and bravado," which occurs between the ages of eight and thirteen, and is marked by a competitive ethic, a "winning at all costs and exploiting power over others" attitude. He then finds himself in the "locker room culture" during his teenage years, focused on ideas of "physical and sexual dominance and submission" as well as learning to become immune and desensitized to violence; finally, he arrives at young adulthood, and worries about being "too attached," and how to live this life of separation (Dooley and Fedele, 2004, p. 371).

In contrast to this socialization process, is the word, *gentle*, which comes from the Latin *gentilis*, meaning *of the same tribe or clan*, and *that which belongs together by birth* (gentle, n.d.). Although the word contains many connotations (often relating to a high or noble birth), *gentle* can mean "excellent," but most commonly means not violent, not loud or disturbing, nor harsh or stern. Instead, to be *gentle* is to be kind, soft, mild, soothing, easy, tender, compassionate, and even subdued. As a result, *gentleness* is largely associated with feminine traits and rarely associated with "desirable" masculine ones. Superheroes are reluctant to be soft; bullying rarely contains a soothing or tender component; and physical and sexual dominance stands in stark contrast to kindness and compassion.

There is obviously little that is gentle in the socialization of boys into hegemonic masculinity. Indeed, a disconnection from all-things-gentle is crucial to its preservation (Jesser, 1996; Kaufman, 1994). This disconnect ultimately teaches children that to be masculine is "not to be feminine" (Thomas, 2001). Furthermore, the separation of boys from mothers and femininity, while an unwritten social rule, opens the door to both the mother and son interpreting such necessary distance as a withdrawal of affection (Dooley and Fedele, 2001; Thomas, 2001) and a weeding or separating out of "gentle" behaviors and traits in boys.

Even though, as Dooley and Fedele (2001) assert, the mother-son connection is cautioned against, ridiculed, prohibited, and maligned, in case we produce "mama's boys" and "cry babies," and mothers are increasingly aware of the "expectations placed on them to conform to and replicate" oppressive structures (Green, 2004, p. 33), many mothers resist this separation and withdrawal of connection. These outlaw mothers are rewriting the rules for "good mothers" and "healthy sons" (Forcey, 1987). Despite the fact that society does not reward the engagement of feminine responsibilities by men, and hegemonic U.S. masculinity is grounded in a particular value system—strength, independence, dominance, aggression, forcefulness and unemotional behavior—there are frequent transgressions of this value system as performers of masculinity (and motherhood) bend, twist, and improvise alternative forms of masculinity in situ (O'Reilly, 2004; Jesser, 1996). Many mothers, feminist and not, have found ways to move their boys away from "boy culture."

However, such transgressions can earn young boys and men the adjective "unmasculine," particularly when and if they express emotions (Jesser, 1996), which, although human, are defined as inconsistent with masculine forms and performances of power (Kaufman, 1994). In "boy culture," boys "must lose their *relational voice*, the voice that reflects authentic feelings and affiliative needs" (Dooley and Fedele, 2004, pp. 361–63). Yet, the loss of this relational voice can cause an immense amount of pain for grown men as these "unmet, unknown and unexpected emotions and needs do not disappear but rather spill into our lives at work, on the road, in a bar, or at home. The very emotions and feelings we have tried to suppress gain a strange hold on us" (Kaufman, 1994, p. 149).

It is no secret that hegemonic masculinity is established through these negotiations of power and consent. As Beynon (2002) argues, the history of masculinity is one of constant interaction between dominant and subordinate forms of masculinity, transforming and impacting on each other in the process. To "be a man," in sum, is to be a man in "particular places at a specific time" (Beynon, 2002, p. 16). The processes of becoming masculine and feminine are forms of acculturation, variable across cultural contexts and interpreted and experienced in culturally specific ways. These processes and their gendered products are not culturally bounded, however. Cultured performances and conceptualizations of masculinity and femininity are open to being borrowed by and from diverse others, indeed, these configurations conflate "with local ideas to produce new configurations" (Cornwall and Lindisfarne, 1994, p. 12). The results are "hybridized" forms of masculinity and femininity, experienced and performed in diverse ways across diverse contexts, and often infused with contradictions (Beynon, 2002; Galasinski, 2004; Morgan, 1992). Thus, masculinity can also be considered a "bricolage," the result of cultural borrowings and "mash ups" of diverse performances over time. The concepts of husbandry and the gentleman help demonstrate such bricolage/hybridity, and the tensions created for mothers raising sons against the grain.

The word "husband" etymologically derives from the Old English *husbandra* (to be bonded to home) and the Old Norse word *bua* (to dwell) (Kimbrell, 1995). Originally, the term "husband" traditionally incorporated a masculinity deeply related to family, home, community, and soil (Kimbrell, 1995). As Mannis contends, "the essence of husbandry is a sense of masculine obligation—generating and maintaining stable relationships to one's immediate family and to the earth itself. At its heart, husbandry reflects a bonding to both family and nature through a clear appreciation of the responsibility inherent in the role of provider, caretaker and steward" (1991, p. 70). Yet, as Mannis (1991) continues, as men were increasingly "wrenched from their families and the earth upon which they worked, they . . . lost their appreciation for what it meant to live the role of the steward of the land and caretaker of our resources. Over the generations there has been considerable erosion in the sustaining role of husband" ( p. 71).

A second form of hybridization, and its manifestations, is evident in the term "gentleman." Originating in the twelfth century, a "gentleman" was a man of noble or gentle birth—a man with chivalrous qualities, propriety, and correct behavior (Merriam Webster, 2009; Javitch, 2002). "Gentleman" morphed quickly, however, and by the sixteenth century, it encompassed the idea of civilized men as *Courtiers* who not only served the Prince in Court but, in doing so, became "another person" by putting on "different mask[s]" as different occasions demanded them (Burke, 1995, p. 31). The performance of masculinity, in short, moved from husbandry and caretaking to a pretence and mask in just a few hundred years (Galasinski, 2002).

By the late seventeenth century, Locke (1693/1996) argued for a masculinity that, through proper education, involved "four things, virtue, wisdom, breeding and learning" (p. 102). This newly "mashed-up" prescription remained relatively constant for white, European males for quite some time. However, in his study of the creation of modern man through magazines and consumer culture, Prendergast (2000) outlines yet another shift in dominant forms of masculinity that occurred between 1900 and 1950. As the new century dawned, the ideal Victorian man "was a property owning man of character who believed in honesty, integrity, self-restraint, and duty to God, country and family; as such he upheld the social and economic order of which he was an integral part" (Prendergast, 2000, p. 10). A shifting economic structure, however, propelled changes in social structures with the American nation struggling to manage immigration, increasing urban populations and political reform (Prendergast, 2002; Stearns, 1994). These shifts undermined the ideal Victorian property-owning man as the now ideal modern gentleman: masculinity now emphasized "personality, sexuality, self-realization and a fascination with appearance" (Prendergast, 2002, p. 13; Roetzel, 1999).

Clearly, Victorian ideals linger in this construction and performance of modern masculinity, and Miner (2004) argues, even today, the gentleman must adopt many of the qualities of the chivalrous knight or warrior, and "defend those weaker," possess a love of country, and display "bravery in the face of the enemy" (p. 25). But, as Dooley and Fedele (2001) contend, although most "every mother of a son hopes to prepare him for life's 'battles,'" she also hopes to preserve "his emotional/relational side" (p. 185). Thus, as our hybrid male negotiates the world of superheroes, he must also learn to negotiate the world of dependence and vulnerability. As he "bullies and banters," he must also begin to learn compassion and to resist peer pressure. Beyond the numbing violence of his teenage years, he can come to understand the multidimensionality of relationships and importance of mutual dialogue, empathy, and respect for others. And, as he enters young adulthood, his hybridized masculinity might reveal itself as responsive and gentle, even capable of generating and maintaining emotionally complex and stable relationships (Dooley and Fedele, 2001).

Obviously, the tensions and contradictions in all of these stages take innumerable shapes and forms. A mother's choices reveal her own personal and political tensions, as well as the tensions impressed (or forced) upon her from the "outside" world. There are the tensions present in her decisions to honor her son's wishes, in the decisions to go against them, and as she attempts to understand the consequences of either choice; there also are the tensions present in her efforts to make those choices seem intelligible (when they feel unintelligible) and appropriate (when she is told they are not), as she and her son work to negotiate and understand hybridity and its implications for gentle male identities.

In order to tease out and explore some of these tensions, we turned our attention to our own processes of mothering. Like other mother outlaws, we went "inside" so to speak, and chose to tell a few of our own stories raising our sons. We offer our stories, or counternarratives, as small case studies, and as examples of what mothers might face as they negotiate "good" and "bad" mothering practices and selves in their attempts to raise hybrid and gentle men. We identify and explore some of the tensions we faced and the active choices we made in order to begin to understand our resistance to hegemonic and hybrid forces as well as our decisions to "pass" on an outlaw moment. What we discover is that "choice," of course, is almost always entrenched in complexities and consequences.

## TWO OUTLAWS, THREE HYBRIDS: TALES OF HOPE, HEGEMONY, AND AUTONOMY

Our sons exist at both ends of this process and so we begin our narratives with Kirsti, as her two boys are young and currently demanding her daily presence and attention. We follow with Cindy, as her son now is living on his own, and less in need of that immediate, daily, mothering. Our goal here is to illustrate many of the tensions that reside in "choice" as it is actively practiced and to suggest that communication scholars, in reporting and reflecting on conscious and self-reflexive choice must consider *whose* choice is being acknowledged and honored, *what* choice is being made, and what consequences might ensue.

### Kirsti's Choices

I wouldn't call myself a feminist. By that I mean, I am not trained in feminist thought. Do I hold feminist commitments though? Perhaps, if that means that I value diverse ways of being and performing, wish to keep dialogues open around alternatives and recognize the ways in which society organizes to value particular forms of being over others. As a mother raising multicultural sons in a cultural context different from my own, I struggle on a daily basis. I struggle with my politics and how they engage or not with my milieu. I struggle with my commitment to raise honorable, strong, passionate, compassionate, artistic, free-thinking men in the face of peer and school pressures which would prefer physically aggressive, individualistic, emotionally reticent, conformist, athletic men. I struggle also with the future consequences of my current actions in mothering my sons. What follows is a series of vignettes from an outlaw life with gentle boys and our toils and troubles therein.

***"Mama, you're a sweet babe," Théo, age 4*** "Dude." I can't remember exactly when that omnipresent word of contemporary popular culture entered my house. I do remember, however, discussions between my husband, two pre-K sons, and I over whether Mama could be a dude because she was a girl. As we informed our sons that you don't usually call women "dudes," my very perceptive five-year-old asked his father what you did call them. "Babes" says my husband, son of a French feminist mother, chuckling. I cringe beside him. "Mama's a *babe*," giggles my four-year-old, not quite realizing what he is saying.

A month later, after an exhausting emergency international trip, I arrive home late one night and go in to kiss my boys. My sleepy four-year-old,

Théo, rolls over and gets me in a headlock. "Mama, I missed you. You're a sweet babe," he mumbles sleepily to me. I sigh, wondering about the future conversations we will have to have around his use of that term.

Now as a poststructuralist, I believe language constitutes social reality. Do I want to be called a "babe"? No. Do I think that's an appropriate term for a woman regardless of age? No. Do I wish my husband had corrected my son? Yes. But so should have I. I should also have not left it to my husband—aside from my belief that my sons are learning what it is to be masculine from him, they are learning it from me. So, why didn't I correct them then? Eventually, I will have to. But in the moment, unaware as he was of what "babe" means culturally, I knew my son was using it as an endearment, a way of expressing his deep attachment to his favorite person and I wasn't quite ready to sever that just yet.

## Zak's Pink Pussycat Boots

About a year ago, in Target with my then four-year-old son, Zakary, we shopped for new rain boots. We examined all boots on offer: Camouflage. *Yuck. I really don't encourage military-style clothing.* Ladybugs, might work. *It's important to care for all living creatures.* Frogs. My boys are half French, *I wonder about the cultural consequences of dressing them in frog boots (it's a cultural joke, perhaps)* and then there were the pink pussycat ones. *No way, I thought. No way, can this already tall four-year-old gentle human being wear pink pussycat rain boots to school? He'll be humiliated!* Of course, those are the ones Zak wanted. I take a breath. I calm myself. I say, "Are you sure, Zak?" He says, "Yes, Mama, I love cats." *Alright then.* Instinctively bracing myself for what I feel will be an inevitable conversation around gender and clothing, we head for the cashier. My face remains impassive but I am aware I am hurrying the interaction and our time there. I pray no one comments on Zak's choices. Sure enough, another mother approaches with her son of the same age. The boy sees Zak's boots. He says, "Look Mom, that boy's wearing girls' boots." I look at Zak. He's oblivious. I glare at the child and then I try to breathe again as we rush out of the store.

The next day, we go to school, Zak resplendent in his pink pussycat boots. He walks in and meets Mr. Patrick, a tall, slim, yogi with dreadlocks who teaches at his school and with whom Zak shares a deep love of basketball. "Those are some cool boots Zak," he says, glancing at my face. I smile, I think. "Right on, dude," says Mr. Patrick. He slaps Zak on the back, and Zak skips by as another mother and her son enter the school. She whispers in my ear, "Pablo loves those boots—you wait, the kids will be brawling over them by the end of the day. He also likes the pink tank tops with sparkly sequins, what can you do when over three-quarters of the store is filled with girls clothing and the boys get camouflage?" What can one do, indeed?

I want to hold choices open for my son. I want him to feel free and confident to choose what he wants and not give a damn what others think. I want him to be strong enough in spirit to hold onto the masculine and feminine parts of himself. But I don't want him to suffer for his independent choices, and it's the recognition of inevitable suffering that I experience in this situation. As his mother, I know full well the hegemonic gendered expectations others hold of him. I see his height. I hear people comment on how great he will be at football. I hear people praise his stoicism. And so does he. I am profoundly glad that my son has men in his midst who perform diverse forms of masculinity for him, however, because their courage emboldens me to continue to honor his choices and his autonomy in his life. As frustrated as I am with the gendered choices my son and I face, I relish our chances to push on some boundaries of dominant masculinity together because in some ways, it is because of my son's physicality that he will be enabled to perform masculinity in an alternative way should he choose to. In that moment, he will begin to navigate the choices I now navigate as his feminist mother.

***Zak's Long Neck Mama*** I am in the garden, trying to encourage some reluctant tomatoes to at least try and stand up properly. Zak has been watching part of *The Land Before Time* on YouTube. He comes to see me. "Mama, they killed the long neck Mama" he whispers. "Who killed the long neck Mama?" I ask, somewhat confused. "The T-Rex" he replies. I watch his eyes fill with tears, then he hangs his head as my already stoic five-year-old tries to calm himself. Anxious to ease his pain, I say, "It's OK Zak, it's not real. It's just a story." *I kick myself. What am I saying? Nice work silencing his feelings. What kind of mother am I?* I regroup. I say, "ah yes, I remember. That's the part when the T-Rex comes to get the baby long neck, right?" Zak nods quietly. "And . . . the Mama fights him off, right? Cos she's protecting her baby." Zak nods again. "She fights very hard; that's what Mamas do," I say as I take off my gardening gloves. "Do you want to help me in the garden?" I ask, hoping we can continue our conversation in a more nonthreatening way as I sense we're not really out of the woods yet. He nods and we set to work with the weeds. "That's a sad part of the movie, the little long neck is left without his Mama," I add. Zak gulps and begins to cry. "It's very sad when somebody dies," I say. Zak asks, "were you sad when your Dada died, Mama?" "I am still sad," I say. "I miss my Dada very much." "I love you Mama," says Zak. "I love you too, *mon grand*," I say.

Because I am committed to raising passionate and compassionate men, I am committed to helping them experience themselves emotionally. Their expressions of affection, sadness, jealousy, rage, honesty, happiness are all of utmost importance to me, but, I don't always do a good job of allowing them that range of expression, mainly because I fear their pain. The consequences of their pain for myself. So I make a choice to walk into Zak's obvious suffering, to help him begin to explore with me, in a nonthreatening way, some of the darker sides of our human existence. This is, of course, my agenda, and yet, the fact that Zak chooses to share his distress is also important, and so my agenda, my choices and his, begin to intertwine in our conversation together. I push away my own fear which silences him and, in so doing, I once more encourage him to expand the ways he does masculinity. He, of course, as always, expands the ways in which I mother!

***"You hurt my feelings!" Théo*** So says my four-year-old son, glaring across the table at his older brother after yet another struggle over random toys and their possession. My oldest son is baffled. He cannot respond. I am also astounded. *We don't use those words in my house. This is a foreign phrase to us. I am perplexed. How to respond?* Which feelings are we discussing? Is it really the feelings or the self that is hurt? None of these questions my four-year-old can answer, repeating as he is something he has heard and knowing its power, deployed against his brother. The effect is immediate silence. Paralysis.

Later that evening, I recount this story to my husband. "Do you say such things in French?" I ask, knowing that in my ten years of knowing him, while I have witnessed the performance of much emotion, I do not recall the utterance of said phrase. "No!" he says. "No. Never." Hmm. Later, on a trip to New Zealand, I ask my sister and brothers, telling them the story. They all chuckle, saying, "if that was here in NZ, we would say 'who give a $%^& about your feelings, harden your %$^ up!'" More importantly, they confirmed, you just wouldn't say that in NZ, no matter what gender. Concluding that this indeed, must be a cultured phrase, and perhaps somewhat of an attempt at communicating emotion by my son in a respectable and respected way, I tuck it away in my mind. Within one to two weeks, this phrase is uttered once more by Théo, battling with me over his wishes for dinner. He asks for something else. I respond in the negative. He counters with "Mama, you hurt my feelings!" But this time, I up the ante. I say, "you know what hurts my feelings, Théo? It hurts my feelings when I cook this dinner for you and you refuse to eat it. It hurts my feelings when I ask you for help and you pretend not to listen. These things hurt my feelings." My son sits stunned. This was a little more than he anticipated.

Théo's choice of phrase was so unfamiliar to us, I was at a loss. But I was stunned more by what it accomplished communicatively, and I struggled profoundly with its consequences. Without a cultural equivalent, I had another struggle on my hands. What was this (what I had framed as) pseudo emotional expression communicating about his cultural identity? Was my son doing "American boy" and how did I feel about that? In my response to him the second time, I made a choice. I chose not to accept what I considered to be an act of silencing. In my efforts to counter his expression of bounded emotionality, I tried to communicate my own emotions. Did my choice impact him at all? I don't know. He has never said those words again. Now I ask him very specifically about how he feels in a conscious effort to discuss his emotions honestly. I make a choice, based on a feminist agenda, yes, but also based on cultured communicative practices central to his multicultural identity, an identity that I wish him to continue. I share this story with Cindy later on. She recounts a similar use of the phrase by her own son, much older. And her shocked silence. Hmm, we wonder. What is going on here?

## Cindy's Choices

My son is a white, middle-class, able-bodied male. All signs point to his heterosexuality, although I purposively kept the conversations and options free and open as he matured and evolved. Because he is an "adult child" (he is twenty-two years of age), and old enough to reflect on his experiences as my son, I decided to ask him to help me with this project. Rather than tell the stories as I remember them, I opted to ask him what stories he might tell, or how he remembered my own stories, and to include them here. I chose this approach because the role of "feminist mother" has always been filled with tension—it has been both natural and awkward for me throughout his twenty-two years in my life—and, I hoped his voice would help illustrate some of that tension.

When he was young, I could find few other women who were personally and politically committed to feminism in the ways I was. Outside my home, I often felt like I was going it alone and going against the grain. I kept a low profile. Inside my home, I felt much more "out" but that doesn't mean the choices and decisions were always fluid or seamless. As the years unfolded, I "collected" a never-ending series of stories that reflected our choices to raise him as a different sort of male, a gentle male. But I wanted to know what he remembered and what my decisions might mean for him. So, I mustered my courage, and I asked.

***The Other Kids Were Jealous*** On the phone with my son, who works summers in Alaska, I ask: "What is it like to have a feminist for a mom?" I did not expect his answer: "Normal," he offered in a completely neutral way. Feeling certain my feminism must have caused some harm (most other people were sure it would), I took a different tack: "Growing up, do you recall anything unusual because of the ways your father and I parented?" His answer: "Nope, it seemed normal to me." Because my own choices as a feminist mother had been challenged endlessly by those outside my close family and friends, I tried yet another approach—I wanted to be sure he wasn't telling me only what he thought I might want to hear: "Do you recall things growing up that marked you as different or stand out because of the way we parented?" A pause, then:

> Nothing really comes to mind. I knew I was a little different, and maybe others were jealous, but that's about all. I knew I was being raised differently, my mother was a feminist and my father was a liberal, and that was just fine with me. I mean, I knew my mother was a feminist, and when I was small, I didn't really know what a feminist was, except that you were teaching me different things and that was fine, it's just who you were. And when I got older and learned what a feminist was, it seemed perfectly natural. And, later, people would ask me what my mom did, and I'd say "she teaches feminist theory" and they'd say "that's really interesting"—I was never made fun of or laughed at. It was just normal.

My son's amazingly casual attitude stands in stark contrast to many of my own tense experiences as a feminist mother. That others might be "jealous" never occurred to me as I've reflected on the choices I (and his father) made raising him. I felt a constant tension as I negotiated feminism, masculinity, femininity, and raising a son. Because other people had critiqued my choices when they did not match closely with hegemonic masculine standards, I thought he might have felt some of the tension. In his response, however, I learn how normal and even envious-to-others my choices seemed to him. This stands in direct opposition to the consternation and dismay displayed by others toward his father and me. Our son's hyphenated last name, for example, often met with a "how could you do such a thing to your child?" question. His father's commitment to being as involved in the daily mechanics of raising him as was I, usually prompted concern for a lack of responsibility and the question, "when is Mike going to get a real job and support his family?" And, the feminism that was as important to our understanding of ourselves and the world prompted one teacher to ask my child, with concern, "what's it like to have a feminist for a mother?" as though we might be causing some major defect in this poor, unsuspecting young male.

As choices and tensions go, I learn that in honoring my own feminism and approach to motherhood, I seem to have done him little harm. Through his lack of tension, I learn that, although notions of the importance of hegemonic masculinity were constantly pressed (forced) upon me as he grew, his less-than-mainstream identity seemed quite appropriate and even special to him.

***Would You Call That Gentle?*** In the same phone conversation, I ask my son, "What about now, as a young man. Do you see yourself as different?" There is a pause, then his reply: "Ummm, not really, maybe a little bit—I'm not quite as hot headed, not so ready to go down—I think it's just who I am and doesn't have anything to do with how I was raised. I don't like confrontation. I mean, I'll get into it if I have to, but I don't get angry much—it takes a lot to get me angry. I think I'm more passive. People say 'Joe, oh, he's such a nice guy.'" I ask, "Would you call that gentle?" Again, an easy reply, "Yes, definitely. I am a gentle man and have no problem with that." I ask for his definition of gentleman. He thinks for a moment, then shares: "Someone who respects women, treats women fairly. Treats them how we expect to be treated." He is quiet and thinks some more. Then, "It's also someone who opens the door for her, helps her with her coat, and blah blah blah. I pay for dates at first, it's just something I think I should do. It's respecting women. I see this as respecting women, that's the way I was raised." I ask him if he would be ok if the woman picked him up and paid for things, and he shares "oh, yea, I've had that happen a lot. I'm ok with that." We talk a bit more and then he concludes: "It's not that they can't take care of themselves, it's just how I am, it's not meant to make them feel like they can't take care of themselves, it's a way to be respectful."

In his thoughtful response, my son reveals his bricolage and feminist-informed version of chivalry and of male power—he's sharing with me his story of respect and care for others. Although he identifies this as "just how I am, not how I was raised," I recall choices I agonized over that likely influenced this gentle young man. For example, when, at two, he desperately wanted a pair of shiny, red patent-leather, Mary-Jane style shoes, clearly situated in the "girl" section of shoe store, I said "no" (the consequence of red Mary-Jane's on my male child in 1989 midwest United States were too severe) but looked for years for a red tennis-shoe to substitute (I never found them). When, at four, he said, "Mom, the other kids say that I can't have a Barbie, do you think Santa will bring one?" Barbie arrived on the twenty-fifth, but not without my honest assessment that, were Joe a girl, I might not have caved so easily (I later shared my dilemma, and choice to honor his wishes, with him).

In seventh grade, he came home with a bruise on his cheek—the result of a male teacher pushing his head down on the desk (to teach him to behave). Although my enraged-feminist mother response urged me to, I did not call the principal immediately to seek retribution and call out male violence. Instead, we negotiated as a family what might be the best way to allow Joe to reclaim his voice and dignity, and to also approach the teacher in gentle, but firm, ways. When bullied in eighth grade, I listened for weeks as he worked out the response (verbal rather than physical), which was far more brilliant and successful than any I'd been able to offer. In high school, we daily processed the oppressive ideologies he swam through: why there were no women on the list of "most famous" scientists or artists; why debating an issue was not the only (nor best) option; why "abstinence only" was the only presentation allowed in school; what parts of the history of Thanksgiving remained untold, and on and on. And, upon his first romantic heartbreak, I watched as enormous tears streamed down his cheeks, tried to explain "why life was so hard," and "how big a heart can be." I listened to him express his desire not to hurt her back, and openly told him how much I respected the care he took with both her, and his, feelings.

Throughout his childhood, his father and I supported, negotiated, and struggled over when to step in and when to step back. We listened and chose communication over avoidance, however uncomfortable. We redefined, pointed out inconsistencies, tried to explain why, exposed contradictions, and sorted through options. At times, the tension between the three of us was high. Often, that tension came when we were negotiating whose choice or choices to honor and the consequences of that choice or choices. Even today, the tension appears—which choice, why that choice, what consequences, and so on.

***It Doesn't Cause Too Much Trouble*** As our conversation closes, I ask my son another question: How will you raise your sons? "I'll raise sons the same way I was. Teach them to be like me (he laughs). Pretty laid back, nonchalant, go with the flow. Seeing what happens, not following the pack. And, they'll have a feminist grandmother" he says, and I hear his smile. "What about if you have girls, I ask." "It'll be the same." I have one final question for him, before we hang up: "So it's possible to be both gentle and male?" "Oh, it doesn't cause too much trouble," he replies, "it's how my friends and I are."

**Kirsti and Cindy**

The presence of these male children in our lives keeps us honest—consistently requiring that we be clear about what our feminism means and how it works communicatively and materially in the world. Daily, we navigate the tensions between feminism, masculinity, and femininity. Hourly, we negotiate the tension-filled choices that lie in the ways feminism values our own selves, our sons, their fathers, the different ways we experience the world, and the different ways the world responds to us. A moment of choice brings a series of consequences, and it is to these conscious and purposive choices and their consequences we now turn.

## OF CHOICE AND CONSEQUENCE

When we decided to write this chapter, we also decided to complicate the concepts of "choice," "maternity," and "reproduction." We wanted to demonstrate that in the context of mothering hybrid masculinities and gentleness, "choice" is fleeting, contentious, contextualized . . . an ongoing process of choice-making and taking up for continued negotiation. "Choice," far from being infused with freedom to act as is commonly implied, is tension riddled, contradictory or inconsistent at times, reflective of the needs of the interaction in a particular time and space, as we have experienced it. At any moment of "choice," there must be full and careful consideration of the multiplicity of individuals involved in that interaction, and the nature of their involvement, both present and future. Such reflections cause us to wonder if it is "choice" we are actually experiencing.

Indeed, if you examine the synonyms of choice—options, alternatives, preferences, selections, and elections, is "choice" the correct word to describe these decision points of outlaw mothering? Outlaw mothering involves a conscious and conscientious decision to do "otherwise" in full recognition of the array of options available. It is an exercise in judgment (active choice, as we have described it earlier), and purposive. We are hardly "free" in these moments. Aware, yes; but this awareness forces us to recognize the bounded nature of what actions might be taken (honoring Zak's emotions, for example) and what consequences might follow (Joe's easy acceptance of a gentle identity) in the simultaneous processes of honoring particular, as well as hybrid, ways of being.

These forms of conversation recover and reinforce the fluidity of the gendering and sense-making processes that construct and reconstruct identities in the hopes of discovering and supporting new forms of masculinities that might reduce masculine power, reduce masculine pain associated with the alienation of their feminine dimensions of humanity, and reduce the pressure on boys to climb into the straight-jacket of masculinity (Ehrlich, 2002). Such conscious, purposive, sometimes resistant, self-reflexive acts when shared with our sons (such as Cindy's story of Joe's Barbie) can also assist them in openly and safely exploring, expressing, and negotiating their own outlaw identities as a space opens for hybridity and gentleness. Our "bad" mothering, as Rich might say, in terms of our unwillingness to keep quiet with regard to the absolutes of gender socialization, might be called "good" mothering at these times. But our active decisions at times to follow gender norms and roles ("good" mothering according to patriarchy), speak to the difficulty of enacting outlaw practices at every moment of our boys' lives as we fully recognize the power of dominant masculinity and the need for our sons to navigate that world. We hope that our narratives reflect how seriously we are committed to the dislodging of hegemonic masculinity but also the consequences of our transgressions of masculine hegemony (Coltrane, 1994; Gutterman, 1994; Kaufman, 1994),

As outlaw mothers, our counternarratives expose the tensions we constantly and actively negotiate as we hold onto the importance of fluid masculine identities, of masculine emotionality, and of gentle forms of masculinity. Our narratives suggest that as we communicatively backtrack, reflect on, revisit, and often redo a moment or decision, we begin to identify the conditions under which particular forms of masculinity and femininity become validated, salient, and even honorable in everyday life at every step along the journey of gender work. The communicative processes Kirsti engages with her two sons who have not yet attained "the age of reason," reflect some of the practices Cindy engaged as Joe was growing up, in a different time, with perhaps different forms of masculinity available for constructing his life as a young man. They may also construct a communicative outcome similar to Joe's identity as a "gentle man," but it won't be without cultural struggle. Our narratives suggest that there are internal and external forces that weigh in on those processes of choices as, and long after, we make them. Yet, within the struggle, in the moments of communicative revision and hybridizing masculinity as we search for alternative frames for our sons, we are reminded of our feminist commitments and empowered by the same. After all, while our stories speak most obviously to our work as mothers, studies (and our own personal lives) have shown that the involvement of fathers with young children has significant consequences for gender equality also as they subvert microstructures of gender inequality (Coltrane, 1994). Societies in which men are highly involved with their children exhibit at the least, reductions in, at the most, eliminations of, hypermasculine displays, competitive posturing and all male enclaves (Coltrane, 1994). Our vision therefore, as outlaw mothers making what seems to be an endless series of "choices" about raising our sons, is to not only give voice to our acts, but to honor and give voice to the gender work of their gentle fathers, and our sons, as future gentle men.

## REFERENCES


Beynon, J. 2002. *Masculinities and culture*. Buckingham, UK: Open University Press.

Burke, P. 1995. *The fortunes of the* Courtier*: The European reception of Castiglione's* Cortegaino. University Park: Pennsylvania State University Press.

Coltrane, S. 1994. Theorizing masculinities in contemporary social science. In Harry Brod and Michael Kaufman (eds.), *Theorizing masculinities* (pp. 39–60). Thousand Oaks, CA: Sage.

Cornwall, A., and Lindisfarne, N. 1994. *Dislocating masculinity: Comparative ethnographies*. London: Routledge.

Dooley, C., and Fedele, N. 2001. Raising relational boys. In A. O'Reilly (ed.), *Mothers and sons: Feminism, masculinity and the struggle to raise our sons* (pp. 185–216). London: Routledge.

Dooley, C., and Fedele, N. 2004. Raising relational boys. In A. O'Reilly (ed.), *Mother outlaws: Theories and practices of empowered mothering* (pp. 357–85). Toronto: Women's Press.

Ehrlich, S. 2002. Legal institutions, nonspeaking recipiency and participants' orientations. *Discourse and Society* 13 (731–47).

Forcey, L. R. 1987. *Mothers of sons: Toward an understanding of responsibility*. New York: Praeger.

Galasinski, D. 2004. *Men and the language of emotions*. New York: Palgrave Macmillan.

Gentle. (n.d.) In *Merriam-Webster's online dictionary*. Retrieved from http://www.merriam-webster.com/dictionary/gentle.

Gentleman. (n.d.) In *Merriam-Webster's online dictionary*. Retrieved from http://www.merriam-webster.com/dictionary/gentleman.

Green, F. J. 2004. Feminist mothers: Successfully negotiating the tension between motherhood as "institution" and "experience." In Andrea O'Reilly (Ed). *Mother outlaws: Theories and practices of empowered mothering* (pp. 31–42). Toronto: Women's Press.

Gutterman D. S. 1994. Postmodernism and the interrogation of masculinity. In Harry Brod and Michael Kaufman (eds.), *Theorizing masculinities* (pp. 219–38). Thousand Oaks, CA: Sage Publications.

Javitch, D. (ed.). 2002. *The book of the courtier: An authoritative text/criticism*. New York: W. W. Norton & Company.

Jesser, C. J. 1996. *Fierce and tender men: Sociological aspects of the men's movement*. Westport, CT: Praeger.

Kaufman, M. 1994. Men, feminism and men's contradictory experiences of power. In Harry Brod and Michael Kaufman (eds.), *Theorizing masculinities* (pp. 142–63). Thousand Oaks, CA: Sage Publications.

Kimbrell, A. 1995. *The masculine mystique: The politics of masculinity*. New York: Ballantine Books.

Locke, J. 1693/1996. *Some thoughts concerning education*. R. W. Grant and N. Tarcov (eds.), Indianapolis, IN: Hackett Publishing.

Mannis, R. F. May–June, 1991. Husbandry, reawakening a lost masculine ethic. *Utne Reader*, 70–71.

Miner, B. 2004. *The complete gentleman: Modern man's guide to chivalry*. Dallas, TX: Spence.

Morgan, D. H. J. 1992. *Discovering men*. London: Routledge.

O'Reilly, A. 2004. *Mother outlaws: Theories and practices of empowered mothering*. Toronto: Women's Press.

O'Reilly, A. 2006. Between the baby and the bathwater: Some thoughts on a mother-centered theory and practice of feminist mothering. *Journal of the Association for Research on Mothering* 8, 323–31.

Prendergast, T. 2000. *Creating the modern man: American magazines and consumer culture 1900–1950*. Columbia: University of Missouri Press.

Rich, A. 1986. *Of woman born: Motherhood as experience and institution*. New York: W. W. Norton.

Roetzel, B. 1999. *Gentleman: A timeless fashion*. Cologne, Germany: Konemann Verlagsgesellschaft mbH.

Stearns, P. N. 1994. *American cool: Constructing a twentieth century emotional style*. New York: New York University Press.

Thomas, A. M. 2001. Swimming against the tide: Feminists' accounts of mothering sons. In A. O'Reilly (ed.), *Mothers and sons: Feminism, masculinity and the struggle to raise our sons* (pp. 121–40). London: Routledge.

# INDEX

# ABOUT THE AUTHORS

**Jaime Bochantin** is a doctoral candidate in the Department of Communication at Texas A&M University and a lecturer at DePaul University. She completed her BA and MA at DePaul University in Chicago. Her research focuses on organizational communication with a focus on work-life, gender, and aging in the workplace. Her dissertation focuses on the relationship between work and family for public safety employees (i.e., police officers and fire fighters) and their families. She graduates in August 2010 and then begins a new job as an assistant professor in the Department of Communication at Western Illinois University in the Fall of 2010.

**Jennifer Emerling Bone** holds a Ph.D. in communication and rhetoric from the University of Colorado at Boulder. She is the basic course director for the communication studies department at Colorado State University, and an affiliate faculty member for the Women's Programs and Studies Office. Jennifer's research examines how storytelling and narratives function to construct social and political arguments. Currently, Jennifer is examining the use of narratives in the United States Birth Control Movement. She also teaches courses in public speaking, gender and communication, theories of persuasion, public address, and rhetorical criticism.

**Kirsten Broadfoot** (Ph.D., University of Colorado at Boulder) is an assistant professor at Colorado State University. Kristen's scholarly work is founded in dialogic approaches to organizational and cultural communication and the discursive construction of work, knowledge, technology, and self for, and by organizations and individuals. Her research centers on issues diversity, care, and innovation and the construction of creative, carefull and culturally sensitive organizations. Using ethnographic methods and critical discourse analysis, Kirsten's current work draws on postcolonial forms of organizing and communicative practice, good work and communication, and she is especially dedicated to communication in clinical contexts. Kirsten is the cofounder of COMMUNEcation, an online international community and conference of scholars involved in the study and critique of global organizing practices.

**Jennifer J. Bute** (Ph.D., University of Illinois at Urbana-Champaign) is an assistant professor in the School of Communication Studies at Ohio University. She studies communication about health in interpersonal relationships and public discourse about women's health. She is particularly interested in issues related to privacy, social support, and gender. She teaches graduate and undergraduate courses in health, interpersonal, and gender communication. Her work has appeared in numerous edited books and journals, including *Health Communication*, *Human Communication Research*, *Communication Studies*, *Review of Communication*, *Qualitative Health Research*, and *Social Science and Medicine*.

**Patrice M. Buzzanell** is professor and the W. Charles and Ann Redding Faculty Fellow in the Department of Communication at Purdue University. Her research centers on leadership, work-life issues, and careers, particularly gendered careers and those associated with science, technology, engineering, and math (STEM). Buzzanell has edited *Rethinking Organizational and Managerial Communication from Feminist Perspectives* (2000), *Gender in Applied Communication Contexts* (2004, with H. Sterk and L. Turner), and *Distinctive Qualities in Communication Research* (2010, with D. Carbaugh). Author of 100 books, articles, and chapters, she also has edited *Management Communication Quarterly* and has held key leadership positions in communication associations. A former research board member for the National Communication Association (NCA) and president of the Organization for the Study of Communication, Language and Gender (OSCLG), she is currently immediate past president of the International Communication Association (ICA) and current president of the Council of Communication Associations (CCA).

**Renee L. Cowan** (Ph.D., Texas A&M University, 2009) is an assistant professor in the Department of Communication at the University of Texas at San Antonio. Her research focuses on organizational communication with a focus on contemporary work/life balance issues and workplace bullying. Her recent research centers on employee requests for work/life accommodation and the rules and resources that govern the negotiation of work/life issues in organizations.

**Summer Cunningham** is a full-time single mother and full-time doctoral student in communication at the University of South Florida. She has conducted research and written on a variety of topics including gender, sexuality, feminism, organizing, swing dancing, and single-motherhood. She is often assisted in the field, at conferences, and occasionally in the classroom by her son, Benjamin.

**Suzy D'Enbeau** (Ph.D., Purdue University) is an assistant professor in the Department of Communication Studies at University of Kansas. Suzy studies work-life issues, popular culture, and feminist organizing processes, particularly, the branding of feminism in a neoliberal economy. Her work has appeared in *Feminist Media Studies* and *Qualitative Inquiry*. She has also coauthored book chapters that explore intersections of class, parenting, and work.

**Bonnie J. Dow** is associate professor and Chair of Communication Studies and associate professor of Women's and Gender Studies at Vanderbilt University. She is the author of *Prime-Time Feminism: Television, Media Culture, and the Women's Movement since 1970* (University of Pennsylvania Press, 1996), and the coeditor (with Julia T. Wood) of the *Sage Handbook of Gender and Communication* (2006). She is also a coeditor of *The Aunt Lute Anthology of U.S. Women Writers, Volume One: 17th–19th Centuries* (Aunt Lute Books, 2004). Dow's research interests include the rhetoric and representation of the first and second waves of feminism in the United States and her current book project is tentatively titled *Framing Feminism: Television News, Women's Liberation, and 1970.*

**John Duckworth** (MA, Purdue University) is a financial advisor in Chicago and a new father.

**Karen A. Foss** (Ph.D., University of Iowa) is Regents Professor and professor of communication and journalism at the University of New Mexico. Her research includes feminist perspectives on communication, social change, and contemporary rhetoric. She is the coauthor of *Women Speak: The Eloquence of Women's Lives*, *Inviting Transformation: Presentational Speaking for a Changing World*, *Feminist Rhetorical Theories*, *Contemporary Perspectives on Rhetoric*, and *Theories of Human Communication*; she is also coeditor of the *Encyclopedia of Communication Theory*. Karen teaches courses in gender and communication, rhetorical theory and criticism, and history and philosophy of communication. Karen has been named Scholar of the Year, Presidential Teaching Fellow, and Gender Scholar of the Year; she was also awarded the Francine Merritt Award, given by the National Communication Association, for contributions to the lives of women in communication. She served as a Senior Specialist Fulbright scholar at the University of Southern Denmark in 2006.

**Elissa Foster** (Ph.D., University of South Florida) is a medical educator in the Department of Family Medicine at Lehigh Valley Health Network, where she supports graduate medical education through research and faculty development activities. Her principle areas of research are health communication and interpersonal relationships specializing in end-of-life communication and ethnographic methods. Her book *Communicating at the End of Life* (Erlbaum, 2007) won the 2009 Distinguished Scholarly Book Award from the Applied Communication Division of NCA. She has also published book chapters and peer-reviewed articles on a variety of topics including marital conflict, motherhood, and spirituality in health care; her research can be found in *Qualitative Inquiry*, *Journal of Ageing and Identity*, *Journal of Cancer Integrative Medicine*, *Women's Studies in Communication*, and the *Southern Communication Journal*. She was the 2007 recipient of the Janice Hocker Rushing Early Career Research Award from the Southern States Communication Association.

**Cindy L. Griffin** is a professor in the Department of Communication Studies, and the Faculty Chair of Women's Studies, at Colorado State University. Her research interests include feminist communication theory, intersectionality, civility, and invitational rhetoric. She is the author of *Invitation to Public Speaking Handbook* (2011) and *Invitation to Public Speaking* (2009), coauthor of *Feminist Rhetorical Theories: Readings* (2004) and *Feminist Rhetorical Theories* (1999) (with Karen Foss and Sonja Foss), and has published articles and book chapters that engage feminism with rhetorical and communication theories. She served as editor of the journal *Women's Studies in Communication* from 2006 to 2010. Her current research projects involve developing the theory of invitational rhetoric, particularly as it relates to civility and epistemology, and a coedited book with Karma Chavez, *Standing in the Intersection: Feminist Voices, Feminist Practices in Communication Studies*.

**D. Lynn O'Brien Hallstein** (Ph.D., Ohio State University) is an assistant professor of rhetoric in the College of General Studies at Boston University. Her current research focuses on contemporary maternity, feminist theory, and women's studies in communication. She has been published in *Quarterly Journal of Speech*, the *Western Journal of Communication, Women's Studies in Communication, Text and Performance Studies, Critical/Cultural Studies, National Women's Studies Journal*, and *Women's Studies*. Her book, *White Feminists and Contemporary Maternity: Purging Matrophobia* was published in March 2010, and she is the coeditor with Andrea O'Reilly for an edited collection titled, *Being and Thinking as an Academic Mothering: Theory and Narrative*, Demeter Press, January 2011.

**Lynn M. Harter** (Ph.D., University of Nebraska) is the Steven and Barbara Schoonover Professor in the School of Communication Studies at Ohio University. Her scholarship uses narrative and feminist theory to explore organizing processes, health, and healing. She is senior editor of *Health Communication* and has published over fifty articles and book chapters. She lives in Athens, Ohio, with her husband, Scott, and daughter, Emma Grace.

**Sara Hayden** (Ph.D., University of Minnesota) is professor of communication studies at the University of Montana. Her research focuses on the rhetoric of women's health, sexuality, and maternity and has been published in journals including the *Quarterly Journal of Speech, Communication and Critical/Cultural Studies, Journal of Applied Communication, Women's Studies in Communication, Communication Studies*, and the *Western Journal of Communication*. She has received honors for her published work including the Western States Communication Association's B. Aubrey Fisher Outstanding Journal Article Award (1998) and the Faculty Prize for Outstanding Research or Creative Activities in the Study of Women or Gender awarded by the Women's Studies Program at the University of Montana (1998, 2000, 2002, 2004). She served as editor of *Women's Studies in Communication* 2004–2007. She was the recipient of the 2008 University of Montana Distinguished Teaching Award.

**Erika L. Kirby** (Ph.D., University of Nebraska–Lincoln) is a professor and chair of communication studies at Creighton University. A teacher-scholar of organizational communication, her teaching/research interests emphasize how differing social identities (especially gender) assimilate into ↔ collide with organizations. Broadly speaking, she is interested in the everyday intersections of working and personal life, and has published widely in that area. She coedited *Gender Actualized: Cases in Communicatively Constructing Realities* with Chad McBride and has published in outlets such as *Communication Monographs*, *Journal of Applied Communication Research*, *Management Communication Quarterly*, and *Communication Yearbook*. She is President of the Organization for the Study of Communication, Language, and Gender and Vice-Chair of the Organizational Communication Division of the National Communication Association. She has trained/consulted for multiple constituencies within Creighton University as well as in organizations outside of academe. She lives in Omaha, Nebraska, with her partner Bob, daughters Meredith and Samantha, and cat Otis.

**Charlotte H. Kroløkke** (Ph.D., University of Minnesota) is associate professor of cultural studies, Institute of Culture, literature, and media, at the University of Southern Denmark, Denmark. Her research includes feminist perspectives on communication with a particular interest in new reproductive technologies, new visualization technologies, new media, and consumer theory. She is coauthor of *Gender Communication Theories and Analyses: From Silence to Performance* (published in 2006 by Sage), has published articles on the branding and marketing of Danish sperm (*Journal of Consumer Culture*, 2009) and written on the topic of 3D ultrasound sonography and the performance of parenting during the ultrasound session. Charlotte teaches courses in Gender and Communication, Gender Studies Theories and Methodologies, and Consumer Culture Theories. Charlotte has been named Teacher of the Year (University of Southern Denmark, 2007) and been the recipient of grants from the Danish Research Council on Culture and Communication (2004, 2006, 2008).

**Tracy Marafiote** (Ph.D., University of Utah) is an assistant professor at the State University of New York at Fredonia. Motivated to bridge her environmental activism and academic work, Professor Marafiote's scholarly interests lie broadly with the discursive/cultural constructions of identity and difference, and the environment. Working from the perspectives of cultural studies, critical intercultural, and environmental communication, her work examines the intersections of gender, race, class, and nature. Her current research focuses on the impact of cultural forces and identities on the environment, intercultural relations, and social change. She has published in such outlets as the *Handbook of Critical Intercultural Communication*, *Environmental Communication: A Journal of Nature and Culture*, and the *Environmental Communication Yearbook*. Dr. Marafiote lives in Western New York with her wonderful partner, Jamie, and their beautiful son, Elias.

**Elizabeth Meyers-Bass** has been an adjunct instructor in the Communication Studies Department at Colorado State University for the past six years. Courses she teaches include public argumentation, group communication, political communication, and public speaking. She and her husband live in Fort Collins with their three children: an artsy, independent five-year-old and energetic, mischievous three-year-old twins. Elizabeth plans to return to school for her Ph.D. once the twins enter school.

**Natalie Fixmer-Oraiz** (MA, UNC–Chapel Hill) is a doctoral fellow at University of North Carolina–Chapel Hill whose research centers on contraceptive technologies, cultural (re)production, rhetorical theory, and feminism. In her dissertation, she is exploring the discursive terrain in which reproductive politics unfolds, particularly surrounding technological innovation and emergency.

**Catherine Helen Palczewski**, Ph.D., is a professor of communication studies and affiliate faculty in women's and gender studies at the University of Northern Iowa, where she also served as debate coach for fifteen years. She teaches courses in the rhetoric of social protest, argumentation, gender, and political communication. She is coauthor, with Victoria Pruin DeFrancisco, of *Communicating Gender Diversity* and has published her scholarship in *Argumentation and Advocacy*, the *Quarterly Journal of Speech*, *Women and Language*, *NWSA Journal*, and the *Southern Communication Journal*.

**Amy R. Pearson** (MA, University of Montana) is a doctoral student in the Hugh Downs School of Human Communication at Arizona State University. Her primary research interests include organizational theory, resistance, and gendered communication. Her work has been published in *Qualitative Inquiry*. She works as a Park Ranger in Glacier National Park during the summertime.

**Lori West Peterson** (Ph.D., University of South Florida) is associate professor of communication at St. Edward's University in Austin, Texas. Dr. Peterson regularly teaches classes in interpersonal communication, family communication, mothers and daughters, and gender communication. Her research interest in maternity leave is inextricably intertwined with her own lived experience as an academic and mother of three.

**Jennifer A. Sandoval** is a Ph.D. candidate in culture and communication at the University of New Mexico. She holds a Master's in dispute resolution from Pepperdine University School of Law. Her research interests include the body as a rhetorical space and its intersection with culture, gender, and public policy. Jennifer is a member of several ongoing research teams that focus on community-based participatory projects in New Mexico. She is currently focused on exploring international fertility tourism from a feminist and postcolonial framework. Jennifer teaches courses in intercultural communication, interpersonal communication, and conflict and communication.

**Marie Thompson** is a woman in the midst of an extraordinary journey, who considers herself thoroughly blessed with the friendship and mentoring of strong, brilliant women, good friends, and three adult children who spent their entire lives teaching her how to be a human being.

**Julia T. Wood** (Ph.D., Pennsylvania State University) is the Lineberger Professor of Humanities and the Caroline H. and Thomas S. Royster Professor of Graduate Education at the University of North Carolina at Chapel Hill. During her career, she has authored seventeen books and edited ten others. In addition, she has published more than eighty articles and book chapters and has presented over 100 papers at professional conferences. She has received twelve awards for teaching at undergraduate and graduate levels and thirteen awards for her research. Her most recent research focuses on intimate partner violence. She lives with her partner, Robert Cox, and their dog, Cassidy, in Chapel Hill, North Carolina.

Breinigsville, PA USA
08 February 2011

255144BV00001B/3/P

9 780739 138908